WHEN CARE WORK GOES GLOBAL

Gender in a Global/Local World

Series Editors: Jane Parpart, Pauline Gardiner Barber and Marianne H. Marchand

Gender in a Global/Local World critically explores the uneven and often contradictory ways in which global processes and local identities come together. Much has been and is being written about globalization and responses to it but rarely from a critical, historical, gendered perspective. Yet, these processes are profoundly gendered albeit in different ways in particular contexts and times. The changes in social, cultural, economic and political institutions and practices alter the conditions under which women and men make and remake their lives. New spaces have been created – economic, political, social – and previously silent voices are being heard. North-South dichotomies are being undermined as increasing numbers of people and communities are exposed to international processes through migration, travel, and communication, even as marginalization and poverty intensify for many in all parts of the world. The series features monographs and collections which explore the tensions in a "global/local world," and includes contributions from all disciplines in recognition that no single approach can capture these complex processes.

Previous titles are listed at the back of the book

When Care Work Goes Global

Locating the Social Relations of Domestic Work

Edited by

MARY ROMERO
Arizona State University, USA

VALERIE PRESTON
York University, Canada

WENONA GILES
York University, Canada

Routledge
Taylor & Francis Group
LONDON AND NEW YORK

First published 2014 by Ashgate Publishing

2 Park Square, Milton Park, Abingdon, Oxfordshire OX14 4RN
52 Vanderbilt Avenue, New York, NY 10017

Routledge is an imprint of the Taylor & Francis Group, an informa business

First issued in paperback 2020

British Library Cataloguing in Publication Data
A catalogue record for this book is available from the British Library

The Library of Congress has cataloged the printed edition as follows:
Romero, Mary.
When care work goes global : locating the social relations of domestic work / by Mary Romero, Valerie Preston, and Wenona Giles.
pages cm.—(Gender in a global/local world)
Includes bibliographical references and index.
ISBN 978-1-4094-3924-0 (hardback)
1. Women household employees—Social conditions. 2. Women foreign workers—Government policy 3. Women's rights. I. Title.
HD6072.R5966 2014
331.4'8164—dc23

2014006166

ISBN 978-1-4094-3924-0 (hbk)
ISBN 978-0-367-60047-1 (pbk)

Contents

List of Tables

Notes on Contributors

Bridget Anderson is Deputy Director and Senior Research Fellow at the Centre on Migration, Policy and Society (COMPAS) at the University of Oxford. She has a particular interest in immigration and low waged labour markets (particularly domestic workers and au pairs), trafficking, immigration enforcement, citizenship and the politics of immigration controls. Publications include *Doing the Dirty Work: The Global Politics of Domestic Labour*, winner of the Philip Abrams memorial prize, and *Us and Them? The Dangerous Politics of Immigration Control* (Oxford: OUP). Her most recent book is *Migration and Care Labour: Theory, Policy and Politics*, edited with Isabel Shutes.

Catherine Bryan is a PhD Candidate in Social Anthropology at Dalhousie University in Halifax, Canada. She has a BA (Honours) in Women's Studies from the University of Winnipeg and a Master's in Social Work from McGill University. Her most recent work includes 'Multiplying Mothers: Migration and the Work of Mothering in Canada and the Philippines', published in Demeter Press' *Mothering in the Age of Neoliberalism* (2014), and an upcoming article in *Refuge: Canada's Journal on Refugees*, co-authored with Myriam Denov, entitled 'Social Navigation and the Resettlement Experiences of Separated Children in Canada'. Her research interests include migration, transnationalism, political economy, and social reproduction. Broadly stated, her dissertation focuses on the multi-sited origins of a small, but growing, Philippine community on the Canadian Prairies.

Pauline Gardiner Barber is a Professor and Chair of the Department of Sociology and Social Anthropology at Dalhousie University, Halifax, Canada. Working from a theoretical perspective in critical historical political economy, her long-term research considers the effects of globalization and neoliberal restructuring on communities and livelihoods. Her Philippine research on migration and development raises questions about how migration is reshaping class and gender relations in Philippine communities and how trends in global migration relate to the changing configurations of global capitalism. Recent co-edited volumes include *Migration in the 21st Century; Political Economy and Ethnography*, 2012, with Winnie Lem (Routledge); *Confronting Capital*, 2012, with Winnie Lem and Belinda Leach (Routledge); and *Class, Contention and a World in Motion*, 2010, 2013 with Winnie Lem (Berghahn). She is a co-editor of the Ashgate Series *Gender in a Global/Local World.*

Marguerite Cognet is a Professor of Sociology at the University of Paris Denis Diderot (Paris VII). She is a specialist in the sociology of ethnic relations and racism. She carried out several studies in France and Canada on these questions in connection with health care. She has recently published several articles on the subject: 'Nursing practices. Ways of seeing things and manners to make in the Canadian health services' in the review *Migrations Santé*, 'Health of the migrants in France: the effect of ethnic and gender discriminations' in the *Revue Européenne des Migrations Internationales* and 'The conflict: a dynamic element of the interethnic clinical situations' in an issue of the journal *Anthropologie & Sociétés* dedicated to the ethnography of hospitals.

Cynthia J. Cranford is an Associate Professor in the Sociology Department at the University of Toronto, Mississauga. Her work probes the intersection of economic restructuring, migration, gender and labour organizing. She is a co-author of *Self-Employed Workers Organize* (McGill-Queens University Press) and has published on cleaning and caring labour and precarious employment more broadly in several book chapters and journals including *Gender & Society*, *Gender, Work and Organizations*, *Relations Industrielles*, *Work, Employment and Society*, and *Social Problems*. She is currently doing field work on gender, migration and personal care work in multiple North American cities.

Conely de Leon is a Doctoral Candidate in Gender, Feminist and Women's Studies at York University, and Graduate Associate at the York Centre for Asian Research. de Leon received her Master's of Arts in Sociology and Equity Studies in Education, and Women and Gender Studies at the University of Toronto. She also received her Bachelor of Arts (Honours) in Women's Studies, and English Language and Literature at Queen's University. She recently held a Visiting Research Fellowship at the University of the Philippines' Center for Women's Studies, Diliman. Her research interests include gender and migration, transnational feminist praxis, critical race theory, and the development of Critical Filipino Studies in Canada.

Jennifer N. Fish is Chair of the Department of Women's Studies at Old Dominion University. Her research focuses on women's labour and migration in the informal economy, civil society organizations, and social reconciliation. Over the past 12 years, she has worked with the South African Domestic Service and Allied Workers Union and the International Domestic Workers Network to promote workers' rights. Her book publications include *Domestic Democracy: At Home in South Africa* (Routledge, 2006) and the co-edited collection *Women's Activism in South Africa: Working Across Divides* (University of KwaZulu Natal, 2009). She is a member of the Women in Informal Employment: Globalizing and Organization (WIEGO) research policy institute at Harvard University and the Social Law Project at the University of the Western Cape.

Sylvie Fortin is Associate Professor at the département d'anthropologie, Université de Montréal. Her research interests lie in urban diversity. As a social anthropologist working in the health domain, she looks at social, cultural, ethnic and religious diversity in hospital milieus and clinical encounters. She presents the clinic as a social space permeated by norms and values that echo those of the cosmopolitan localities where her studies are carried out. Migration issues as well as majority–minority relations, identity practices and affiliations are also core interests. Her recent publications concern conflict and recognition in the clinical encounter, bioethics and diversity, the paediatric clinic as a negotiated social space and Muslim migrants and perinatal care. She is co-editor of the journal *Diversité urbaine*.

Judy Fudge joined Kent Law School in the UK as a Professor in September 2013, after stints as a law professor at the University of Victoria and Osgoode Hall Law School. Her research interests are employment and labour law in Canada, the European Union, and at the international level, feminist political economy approaches to the legal regulation of work, and the nexus between migration law and labour law. Currently, she is working on projects relating to migrant workers, unfree labour, gender and labour law, constitutionalizing labour rights in Canada and the European Union, and the legal regulation of precarious and informal work.

Wenona Giles teaches in the Anthropology Department at York University. Most of her research on gender, the politics of migration, militarized violence and humanitarianism has been housed in the Centre for Refugee Studies at York University including the Borderless Higher Education for Refugees (BHER) project in the Dadaab refugee camps, Kenya that she co-leads: http://crs.yorku.ca/bher. She is currently completing a co-authored book on long term refugee situations with Jennifer Hyndman. For a full description of her publications and teaching, please see: http://www.yorku.ca/laps/anth/faculty/wgiles/.

Ray Jureidini is Professor of Sociology and Director of Research on Migration Ethics at the Center for Islamic Legislation and Ethics in Doha, Qatar. His research interests include migration, human and labour rights, human trafficking, gender discrimination, racism and xenophobia. After teaching Sociology in several universities in Australia, he spent six years at the American University of Beirut from 1999 where he began researching and publishing on human rights abuses of migrant domestic workers in Lebanon. At the American University in Cairo from 2005, he became director of the Center for Migration and Refugee Studies in 2008 and conducted a number of research projects on migrant and refugee issues. In 2012, he spent a year as consultant at the Qatar Foundation in Doha that led to reform standards for migrant worker welfare and a report on migrant labour recruitment from Asia to Qatar. He is currently working on a book manuscript: *Domestic Workers in the Middle East: Status Enhancement and Degradation in Arab Households.*

Maja Korac is a sociologist and Reader at the School of Law and Social Sciences, University of East London, UK. Her research is in the area of conflict, gender, migration and integration. Maja's books include *Remaking Home: Reconstructing Life, Place and Identity in Rome and Amsterdam* (Oxford: Berghahn Books, 2009), *Linking Arms: Women and War in Post-Yugoslav States* (Uppsala: Life & Peace Institute, 1998), and *Captives of Their Sex: Social Identity of Young Rural Women between Traditional Culture and Contemporary Values* (Institute for Sociological Research, University of Belgrade, 1991) (published in Serbian). She co-edited *Feminist under Fire: Exchanges across War Zones* (Toronto: Between the Lines, 2003) and *Women in Conflict Zones, Special Issue, Canadian Women's Studies*, 2000, 19:4 (York University Publications).

Deirdre Meintel is Professor of Anthropology at the Université de Montréal. She is cofounder and editor of a journal called *Diversité urbaine* and directs an interdisciplinary research group of the same name. She is also one of the two directors of the Centre de recherches en études ethniques des universités montréalaises, a research centre for the study of ethnic and religious diversity. It includes 51 researchers in the social sciences and humanities from various universities in Montréal and Sherbrooke, Québec. Deirdre Meintel has worked on ethnicity, migration and family, ethnic identity, transnationalism and mixedness. She has done fieldwork in Mexico, the Cape Verde Islands, New England (USA) and Québec. In recent years she has been working on religion and modernity. Since 2006 she has been directing a team study on religious and spiritual currents that have developed in Quebec since the 1960s.

Valerie Preston is Professor in the Department of Geography at York University where she teaches and publishes in the areas of urban and social geography. Dr Preston's research examines immigration and settlement issues in Canada with particular attention to gender and racialized inequalities. With Drs Leah Vosko and Robert Latham, she has co-edited a volume for McGill-Queen's University Press entitled *Liberating Temporariness*.

Mary Romero is Professor in Justice and Social Inquiry, Arizona State University, where she teaches and publishes in the areas of racial justice, women, law and social control and work and gender. She is the author of *Maid in the USA* (Routledge, 1992/2002) and *The Maid's Daughter: Living in and Out of the American Dream* (NYU, July 2011). She has co-edited several books, including *Interdisciplinary and Social Justice: Revisioning Academic Accountability* (SUNY Press, 2010) and *The Blackwell Companion to Social Inequalities* (Blackwell, 2005). She is currently writing a book on anti-immigrant sentiment and its reflection on race relations in the US. Recent articles were published in *Law Journal for Social Justice, International Journal of Sociology of the Family* and *Contemporary Justice Review.*

Susanna Rosenbaum is Assistant Professor of Anthropology in the Department of Interdisciplinary Arts and Sciences at The City College of New York. Her research focuses on Mexican and Central American domestic workers and their (primarily white) middle-class employers in Los Angeles. She is currently completing her manuscript, *Domestic Economies: Women, Work, and the American Dream in L.A.*

Maya Shapiro completed her doctorate in the Department of Anthropology at York University. She has worked as an activist, advocate, researcher, translator and organizer with agricultural workers and caregivers in Ontario and British Columbia, and with undocumented migrants and asylum seekers in Toronto and Tel Aviv. Maya's current teaching and research interests include reproduction, women's health, carework, labour migration, undocumented migration and global cities. She works part-time as a counsellor at a pregnancy assessment and abortion clinic.

Laura Stefanelli is a graduate from the Université de Montréal, Canada and the University of Bologna and is currently project manager for national and European projects for the public/private and non-profit sectors and international cooperation agencies. She has a specialization in gender migration, care work and integration of migrants. She has worked as a consultant for the Delegation of the European Union in Morocco within the Governance and Migration section and NGOs; and as a Research Fellow in numerous universities – Canada: Université de Montréal and McGill University; France: IEP-Bordeaux; Italy: University of Bologna and University of Trento; and Morocco: Centre for Cross Cultural Languages in Rabat.

Preface

When Care Work Goes Global addresses the complexities and transformations of care work in the context of globalization. With the emergence of the so-called Global Division of Labour much has changed in the way work is organized and articulated in the context of broader socio-political changes. Not only have labour markets become increasingly segmented, but the outsourcing of production and services has also affected the way in which work and labour relations are being articulated. Outsourcing in particular has engendered a disconnection between (type of) work and geography. In other words, the previous International Division of Labour, which was characterized by a territorial specialization of work between centre, periphery and semiperiphery, has given way to more complex transnational or global labour relations connected to global value chains. These new arrangements in turn have also created new inequalities, which tend to be superimposed on or reinforce existing ones. Looking at the new Global Division of Labour from a gender perspective reveals some of these inequalities. *When Care Work Goes Global* addresses what is sometimes referred to as the Global Care Chain, an important and often under-represented part of the Global Division of Labour. The contributors discuss how the need for care work has been on the increase globally, not only in the North but also in the Global South. Against the background of increasing numbers of more (middle class) women having joined and continuing to join the workforce and with neoliberal policies shifting the burden of care on nuclear families and women in particular, care work is increasingly outsourced. Migrant women from the Global South are increasingly targeted to fulfil reproductive tasks. The present volume focuses in particular on migrant women and their role in domestic work. The nature of domestic work is distinguished by the intimacies involved in working in the home of the employer and the difficulty of separating the work place from one's private sphere, especially for live-in employees. The different contributions of *When Care Work Goes Global* provide an incisive analysis of the complexities of domestic work, ranging from the working conditions and lives of migrant women to their often problematic relations with their families and children back home, who are at the 'non-receiving end' of the Global Care Chain. It also reinvigorates a series of feminist debates over the nature of social reproductive labour in a world where increasing numbers of women are entering the workplace.

Marianne H. Marchand
Jane L. Parpart
Pauline Gardiner Barber

Acknowledgements

We appreciate the contributions of researchers who wrote chapters and those who participated in the workshop that was the impetus for this book. All of you broadened our knowledge of the women who migrate to do care work around the world. Numerous people deserve thanks for their contributions to the successful completion of this book. At the German Historical Institute, Anke Ortlepp; research assistants at York University, Silvia D'Addario, Kirsten Raodica, Tonia Richards, Mayan Richer, Nele Michels and Mi Hae Ahn; and Laurie Baker helped us complete the manuscript. We are grateful to Dirk Hoerder for his assistance in the early stages of the book, even as he dealt with Christiane Harzig's untimely death. With gratitude, we acknowledge funding from the German Historical Institute, York University, and SSHRC through CERIS – The Ontario Metropolis Centre, for the initial workshop. We are also very thankful to the *International Journal of Comparative Labour Law and Industrial Relations* (IJCLLIR), vol. 28, no. 1, 2012 for permission to publish the chapter by Fudge; to Routledge for a version of the chapter by Gardiner Barber and Bryan previously published in *Migration in the 21st Century: Political Economy & Migration* by Pauline Gardiner Barber and Winnie Lem (eds), 2012; and to Taylor and Francis for permission to publish the chapter by Meintel, Fortin and Cognet previously published in *Gender, Place and Culture: A Journal of Feminist Geography*, vol. 13, no. 5, 2006. As Christiane expected, working across borders has been a rewarding experience and an opportunity to learn more about the varied forms that globalized care work takes and the complex ways that it connects women worldwide.

List of Abbreviations

AFSCME	American Federation of State, County, and Municipal Employees
CCDA	Centre for Conflict and Dispute Arbitration
CCNL	National Collective Labour Contract – Contratto Collettivo Nazionale di Lavoro Colf e Badanti
CEDAW	Committee on the Elimination of All Forms of Discrimination against Women
CGE	Commission on Gender Equality
CLSCs	*Centres locaux de services communautaires*
COMPAS	Centre on Migration, Policy and Society
COSATU	Congress of South African Trade Unions
DPSS	Department of Public Social Services
EEA	European Economic Area
ESRC	Economic and Social Research Council
FADWU	Hong Kong Federation of Domestic Workers
FDM	Foreign Domestic Movement
FILCAMSCGIL	Federazione Italiana Lavoratori Commercio Alberghi Mense e Servizi, Confederazione Generale Italiana
FOSATU	Federation of South African Trade Unions
FWP	Foreign Worker Program
GMAC-UIF	Gender Monitoring and Advocacy Coalition for the Unemployment Insurance Fund
GTA	Greater Toronto Area
HWTC	Home Care Workers' Training Center
IDF	Israeli Defence Forces
IDWN	International Domestic Workers Network
IHSS	In-Home Support Services
ILCs	Independent Living Centers
ILO	International Labour Organization
IUF	International Union of Food, Agricultural, Hotel, Restaurant, Catering, Tobacco and Allied Workers Associations
KAFA	Enough Violence and Exploitation
KM	Kabataang Montreal
KUDHEIHA	Kenya Union of Domestic, Hotel, Educational Institutions, Hospitals, and Allied Workers
LCP	Live-in Caregiver Program

LTCWU	Long Term Care Workers' Union
MPMC	Multicultural Policies and Modes of Citizenship in European Cities
MUA	Mujeres Unidas y Activas
NDWA	National Domestic Workers Alliance
NGO	Non-governmental Organization
OFWs	Overseas Filipino Workers
OSCE	Organization for Security and Co-operation in Europe
OSS	Operatrice Socio Sanitario
PASC	Personal Assistance Services Council
PMSC	*Pilipinong Migrante sa Canada*
PWC-BC	Philippine Women Centre of British Columbia
SADSAWU	South African Domestic Service and Allied Workers Union
SADWU	South African Domestic Workers' Union
SEIU	Service Employees International Union
SEWA	Self Employed Women's Association
SSHRC	Social Sciences and Humanities Research Council
UIF	Unemployment Insurance Fund
UN	United Nations
UNHCR	The Office of the United Nations High Commissioner for Refugees
WIEGO	Women in the Informal Economy: Globalizing and Organizing

Chapter 1

Care Work in a Globalizing World

Mary Romero, Valerie Preston and Wenona Giles

Women who migrate into care work are the single largest female occupational group migrating globally at present (Human Rights Watch 2010: 12). This is an extremely mobile group that moves internationally to care for family and non-family members and continues to draw the attention of scholars across the social sciences. Their impact on receiving as well as sending societies is profound, often changing gendered aspects of migration in both societies, as well as social and economic development in these sites. This book reflects a keen interest to find out more about how sending societies are affected by the out-migration of sizeable numbers of married and single women who care for their families transnationally from a distance, and how reproductive labour changes in the receiving society when it is done by women who are subject to multifaceted othering or racializing processes.

The genesis of this collection lies in social history, as well as the editors' and contributors' enduring interest in the links between international migration and social reproduction. Beginning with a workshop in 2009 that brought together sociologists, historians, anthropologists and geographers to consider the trends and explanations for the contemporary international migration of domestic workers, the book evolved out of ongoing conversations and research among some of the participants in the workshop, as well as others who are working in sites around the world on this issue. We draw on research in Europe, North America, the Middle East, Africa and Asia to examine the contemporary migration of women to take up domestic work.

The project began at the urging of Christiane Harzig, a historian who studied the movement of German peasant women to domestic work in towns and cities across Europe and North America. In the edited collection entitled *Peasant Maids – City Women, From the European Countryside to Urban America*, she and her collaborators investigated how women had experienced the challenges and potentials of migration from rural Europe to North American cities. She insisted that even with all the disruptions and the exploitation that many women experienced as domestic workers, that scholars must also recognize the benefits of migration for many women. The question of who was likely to benefit from this migration and who would suffer persistent social disadvantage was crucial to her analysis of the gender dynamics of historical and contemporary migration.

This book builds on the social-historical foundations established by Christiane Harzig[1] and links them with those of sociology, anthropology and geography. Her untimely death has meant that the current collection necessarily reflects the editors' own views and opinions, however, in all our decisions, we have sought to maintain the originality of Christiane's scholarship that was always open to considering apparently contradictory views.

As our edited volume goes to print, we are witnessing hopeful signs that the working and living conditions for the 52.6 million men and women domestic workers around the world are improving (ILO 2010, ILO 2013a). The 100th Session of the International Labour Conference in June, 2011 adopted the Convention on Domestic Workers. The Convention recognized the 'significant contribution of domestic workers to the global economy' who perform labour that is 'undervalued and invisible, and is mainly carried out by women and girls, many of whom are migrants or members of disadvantaged communities'. It affirmed that these workers have the same fundamental rights as other workers:

- the rights to freedom of association and collective bargaining
- the elimination of all forms of forced labour
- the effective abolition of child labour, and
- the elimination of discrimination in respect of employment and occupation.

This international attention from the ILO underscores the plight of women crossing national borders to care for families in other countries. Locating social relations in contemporary care work shines a spot light on the growing global gap between wealthy and poor countries; the state regulations of specific receiving countries that increasingly restrict the movement and labour choices available to migrant[2] workers; the complexities and inequalities inherent in traditional notions of women's work and the intersections of race, class, ethnicity and citizenship in care work that is delivered globally. There is an increasing need for care work in countries throughout the world and a wide range of work arrangements that exist simultaneously in these global sites. An overview of workers' migration patterns offers a glimpse of the various recruitment processes and the ways that citizenship restrictions influence the decisions made by these working women. Working conditions reflect the devaluation of work perceived as 'women's work', unskilled and outside the legal regulation offered to other workers. The work that migrant domestic workers do under restricted conditions or as undocumented increases

1 Christiane Harzig was instrumental in obtaining funding from the German Historical Society for the workshop that contributed to this collection.

2 Given the diverse immigration and labour policy regimes that affect women migrating into care work, we have labelled all of them as migrants. While we recognize that migrant care workers are known as immigrants in some places, few have access to permanent residence, so we have used the terminology followed by the majority of researchers and policymakers.

their vulnerability. We conclude with a look at the wide range of organizing activity among domestic workers around the world.

This collection recognizes the breadth and diversity of care work, the activities involved in looking after and providing for the various physical, social and emotional needs of others (Oakley 1974 cited in Luxton 2011: 13). Care work allows dependent people to function at a socially determined acceptable level of capability, comfort, and safety, be they children (before they are legal adults), those who are either temporarily or permanently ill or disabled, or elderly (Friedemann-Sanchez and Griffin 2011: 514, Williams and Brennan 2012). It also supports the workplace attachments of able adults, male and female (Luxton 2011). As a form of social reproduction, care work is an essential aspect of every society. This definition of care work includes housework and services provided to individuals such as child care and elder care. While the activities that we have called care work are sometimes labelled domestic work, care work is not necessarily confined to domestic locations. For example, people who are ill may be cared for by paid workers and unpaid friends and families in hospitals and other institutional settings. Indeed, paid elder care in institutional and domestic locations is one of the most rapidly growing forms of care work (Williams and Brennan 2012). We use the term domestic work to refer to housework and services provided within private homes. In this context, domestic service refers to the hiring of workers to undertake domestic work for pay in the home of the employer. Our focus is on the migrant workers recruited to undertake domestic work, often in the homes of their employers and sometimes in other private homes. Often viewed as unskilled workers, the migrant workers examined in the chapters that follow rarely benefit from the policies and programs designed ostensibly to facilitate the migration of increasing numbers of highly skilled care workers such as nurses, teachers, and social workers (Kofman and Raghuram 2006, Yeates 2009).

Debates about domestic work have centred on its location, its status as paid or unpaid work, and its gendered nature. Much domestic work takes place in homes rather than formal workplaces where it is devalued by virtue of its location in a private residence beyond the purview of state regulation (England 2005). Although paid domestic work is a growing phenomenon, much domestic work is still unpaid work that many view as an intrinsically rewarding labour of love that does not require payment (England 2005, Lutz 2011). Several authors have argued that the gendered nature of domestic work which is still done disproportionately by women and has proven remarkably resistant to change also contributes to its devaluation (Lutz 2011, Luxton 2011, ILO 2013a). Many processes contribute to the gendered nature of domestic work specifically and care work generally, however, recent studies offer little evidence of change and have argued that live-in arrangements constitute a re-familialization of domestic work (Michel and Peng 2012), which keeps it in the shadows (Arat-Koc 2006). Careful analysis shows that well paid, professional women who devote less time to domestic work than other working women achieve these time savings by hiring a domestic worker who is almost always another woman (Luxton 2011). Other analysis has called attention to four sets of relations that apply to all forms of care work including domestic work: the migrant worker and those she is hired to care for; the family members she has left behind and who she cares for through remittances; family members traveling with her; and her own welfare (Kofman and Rhaguram 2010).

Recent literature addresses the impact of globalization on care relations from three perspectives (Yeates 2009). Some argue that a new international division of reproductive labour has arisen in tandem with and in support of the new international division of labour (Lan 2006, Lutz 2011). According to this analysis, female migrant workers are recruited from poor countries to do care work in wealthier ones. The impacts of the persistent gender and racial inequalities evident in the devaluation of care work are borne disproportionately by female migrant workers who are viewed as minorities in the societies where they work (Parreñas 2008). Scholars of care regimes suggest that the demand for migrant domestic workers is also fuelled by neo-liberal policies and tendencies that have stimulated a growing demand for care workers in general (Mahon et al. 2012, Michel and Peng 2012). Government funding for paid care work has diminished rendering many of these jobs so poorly paid and insecure that they do not appeal to local workers. Reduced government funding has also increased the demand for privately provided care workers to assist patients and clients in hospitals and other institutional settings. Thus, a second perspective examines how responsibility for care work is also being individualized, so that parents, adult children, households and voluntary organizations are expected to take on more care work (Lutz 2011, Mahon et al. 2012). In response to these tendencies and aided and abetted by the state's migration policies, working women in the wealthy nations of the global North have recruited migrant workers to do the domestic work that would otherwise have fallen to them. The same tendencies, reinforced by a long history of domestic service, have also increased the demand for migrant workers in the global South. Neoliberal governments around the globe have implemented policies that facilitate the recruitment of migrant women to meet the growing demand for domestic workers. Studying transnational families, a third body of research has examined the social relations of care that develop when female migrant care workers care for their families across borders (Parreñas 2005, Baldassar, Baldock and Wilding 2007, Pratt 2012). This collection contributes a global view to our understanding of the new international division of reproductive labour by juxtaposing case studies drawn from the global South and the global North. Addressing the motivations and migration experiences of domestic workers and their conditions of work, the chapters also demonstrate how various care regimes impinge upon the everyday lives of migrant domestic workers and the tensions between women's herculean efforts to maintain transnational families and the regulations that heighten their absence.

The articles in this collection examine the experiences of the women who move around the globe to engage in care work in different locations. Although their legal status varies from one context to another and, over time, we describe them as moving across national borders as migrants. Some, such as those who migrate to Canada as live-in caregivers, may enter legally and eventually obtain permanent residency as immigrants. Others move illicitly across borders and work without permits, for example, in Israel and Italy; still others enter legally as temporary residents who are barred from ever becoming permanent residents, particularly in the Middle East and the Gulf Region. Consequently, receiving countries of globalized care work have had a significant impact upon the limited citizenship rights of workers (Sarvasy and Longo 2004). Individual chapters in this collection recognize the diverse circumstances of women migrating to do domestic work in specific places. Despite their diverse migration histories, all of the women who move for domestic work share the experiences of disruption and upheaval associated with relocation, the trials of caring for others from different cultural and social backgrounds, and the challenges of continuing to provide care for people left behind.

The Global Demand for Care Work

Over the last 100 years, social scientists predicted the demise of domestic service, arguing that household labour would be modernized and disappear with the introduction of household appliances, the commercialization of domestic work and the unwillingness of employers and employees to replicate outdated social relations of mistress and maid who served as 'one of the family' (Coser 1973). In the global South, researchers also expected that the constant turnover of employees from rural areas who sought employment in better neighbourhoods in the city once they had some experience as domestics would lead to the end of domestic service (Chaplin 1967). In Central and South America, this hypothesis, known as 'phasing out', clearly did not happen (Leon 1989). The commercialization of domestic work and the introduction of modern appliances did not reduce the amount of labour required to maintain a household in either the global North or the global South.

In contrast, the prediction that only migrants and racialized groups would continue to do the stigmatized work of serving others has proved prescient. For over 40 years, women have migrated from rural areas to urban areas and across national borders in search of work as nannies, domestic workers and caregivers. The migration has been fuelled by growing economic inequalities within and between countries. The demand for migrant domestic workers in the Middle East and Gulf states was stimulated by the oil boom in 1970 that created wealthy national elites. Young women from poor families in the Middle East frequently worked as domestic workers for wealthy families in exchange for food, lodging and clothing. In Lebanon, Jureidini (2009) found that poor women and girls from local villages were hired to work in Lebanese households along with Kurdish, Syrian, Egyptian and Palestinians. After the civil war of 1975, non-Arab workers, namely Asian and African migrant women, were hired. In the early 1990s, large numbers of Sri Lankan women migrated to Lebanon to work in private households as domestics (Jureidini and Moukarbel 2004). The international division of labour has reproduced a hierarchical care chain based on gender, nationality, class, ethnicity, and race (Onuki 2011). This distinct work force engaged in domestic work continues to be stigmatized (Tronto 2011a) linking 'the narrative of global inequality to the narrative of taking care of my family' (Tronto 2011b: 167).

Economic inequalities between countries are important for understanding recent shifts in the geographical flows of care workers and in their social backgrounds. Unlike previous waves of European women, African slaves or indigenous women who worked as domestics in the United States (Kaztman 1981), Central and South America (Chaney and Garcia Castro 1989), Canada and Australia (Higman 2002) in the 1800s and early 1900s, today's care workers are predominantly from Asia, North Africa, South America and Central America where low wages and limited employment opportunities push many women to migrate. Women migrants are crossing national borders to work in private homes as nannies, caregivers to the elderly and domestic workers in countries around the world, including in Thailand, China, Lebanon, Malaysia, Canada, Italy, Spain, Saudi Arabia, Bahrain and the USA. Current migrants move between countries of the global South as much as they migrate from countries of the global South to destinations in the global North (Lan 2006, Hujo and Piper 2007). Current flows include Bolivian and Paraguayan women migrating to Argentina, Nicaraguan and Salvadoran women migrating to Costa Rica; Peruvian women to Chile (Blofield 2012); Caribbean and Mexican women migrating to the United States (Brown 2011, Hondagneu-Sotelo 2001); Ecuadoran and Colombian women to Spain; Indonesian women migrating to Saudi Arabia and Malaysia; Filipinas migrating to Canada (Stasiulis and Bakan 2005), Italy (Parreñas 2001a), Ireland (MRCI 2012), Malaysia, Kuwait, Saudi Arabia, Qatar and the United Arab Emirates (Vlieger 2011); Moroccan and Tunisian women to France (ILO 2013a); Burmese to Thailand (Panam 2004); women migrating from Indonesia, and Sri Lanka to Saudi Arabia, Kuwait, the United Arab Emirates, Bahrain, Jordan, Lebanon, Singapore, Malaysia, and Hong Kong (Human Rights Watch 2010). Rural to urban migration is also common for domestic workers in South Africa, Ethiopia, Zimbabwe, and Botswana, and, to a lesser degree, in Nigeria and Ghana.

Limited economic opportunities in their own countries encourage well educated women to migrate and work as caregivers – an occupation that does not acknowledge either their educational qualifications or their work experience. This is the case for many women from the Philippines who have more education and work experience than previous generations of domestic workers. They are migrating abroad to obtain higher wages than those available to professionals in the Philippines (Parreñas 2001a). As care work becomes a significant part of the contemporary globalized economy, migrant women workers who often have insecure or temporary status in their countries of work have come to dominate the workforce. Their remittances provide crucial support for families, local communities and national economies in their countries of origin. Scholars have labelled the increasing reliance on women's remittances as the 'feminization of survival' (Sassen 2000).

Care Work in the Global North

Changing trends in women's work, limited public funding for childcare, elderly care and other forms of care work, changing middle-class consumerism, neoliberal policies promoting individual responsibility for care work and increasing inequality between countries are important factors contributing to the significant growth in care work in the global North over the last two decades (Parreñas 2008, Lutz 2011, Mahon et al. 2012). ILO researchers estimate that 'between 1995 and 2010, the number of domestic workers rose from approximately 33.2 million to 52.6 million – an increase of more than 19 million' (2013a: 24). While some household tasks, such as cooking and dry cleaning, have shifted outside the home, changing domestic standards, such as the pressure to prepare home-cooked meals with organic ingredients and the increasing presence of wash and wear clothing that can be laundered at home, have increased household work in many American and European homes. Modern appliances, such as washing machines and vacuum cleaners, alongside new standards of cleanliness and an obsession with germs have resulted in more laundry, scrubbing and general housecleaning. Although the silver is no longer polished on a regular schedule, laundry is done more than once a week, and floors, kitchen counters and bathrooms are constantly cleaned. Several researchers have noted that contemporary parenting strategies, such as child-centred family activities, sports participation requiring transportation and parent involvement and a variety of after school lessons, not only require economic resources but are time consuming activities that are very labour-intensive (Hays 1996, Nelson 2010).

As family life in the global North shifted away from kin care, more work shifted to parents and, more specifically, to mothers. The nuclear family, rather than extended family members who frequently live far away, is responsible for care work and household labour. A general increase in the number of women who are employed outside the home has heightened the need to replace women's unpaid domestic labour with that of paid workers. Since the 1970s, married women's work histories have also changed in Europe and North America. Rather than leaving the workforce after the birth of their first child and returning only after all the children are in school, working mothers have drastically shortened the period that they are absent from the workforce. Unless paid maternity leave is available, many women return to work within a few weeks or months of each child's birth. Young mothers are no longer able to rely on extended family members to assist with childcare because more adult women are employed full-time and kin no longer live nearby. In the United States, publicly-funded child care is dwindling or non-existent and commercial child care is not always affordable. The rigid schedules of many child care providers rarely serve the needs of working parents facing long commutes and irregular work schedules (Hrdy 2002). Growing numbers of elderly are living alone, far from their children and grandchildren, adding to the need for paid labour to help clean, cook and do care work (Baldassar, Wilding and Badcock 2007). At the same time, a strong independent living movement among the disabled has arisen in numerous countries in Europe and North America. Growing numbers of disabled persons reside outside institutions and in independent living arrangements where they require care, often provided by paid attendants (Boris and Klein 2012). The growing demand for care has occurred at the same time as neoliberal social policies have reduced the public provision of care for children, the elderly, and other vulnerable individuals in many countries of the global North. There is more pressure on families and individuals to purchase care by hiring maids, nannies and care attendants (Mahon et al. 2012, Michel and Peng 2012). In these privatized arrangements, few employers can afford to pay more than minimum wage and few if any benefits.

These trends vary slightly among countries of the global North where diverse public policies affect the demand for care workers (Mahon et al. 2012, Williams and Brennan 2012). For example, the availability of paid maternity leave in countries such as Sweden, Norway, and Canada reduces the demand for child care for infants while the absence of paid maternity leave in the United States and Australia has the opposite effect (ILO 2013a). The extensive public provision of elder care in the Nordic countries also contributed to low numbers of paid care workers, however, recent government policies promoting the marketization of care work are reversing past trends (Mahon et al. 2012).

Care Work in the Global South

The history of care work in the countries of the global South is as complex although perhaps not as well documented as in the global North. Colonization, income inequality within and between countries, and national policies concerning definitions of work influence contemporary understandings of the migration of care workers. With a history of colonization in which indigenous women and some men served in the households of European colonizers, domestic service has a long history in South and Central America and the Caribbean. Recently, the number of domestic workers employed in the region has grown rapidly, largely due to the increasing numbers of working women and high levels of income inequality (ILO 2013a). 'Female employment expanded dramatically throughout Latin America in the period from 1940 to 1970, in response to generally improved economic conditions and to sectoral changes favoring women' (Kuznesof 1989: 29). Helen Safa (1977) notes that this period is also marked by increasing class distinctions between employed women throughout Latin America. High levels of income inequality mean that households at the top of the income hierarchy have the resources to hire domestic help and poor women are willing to take these jobs despite difficult working conditions and low wages. Although women still migrate from poor rural areas to urban centres in Mexico and Brazil, many migrant domestic workers now cross national borders, moving to work in Argentina, Costa Rica and Chile.

The oil boom in the 1970s created a demand for professional labour in the Middle East and Gulf region. Skilled professional migrants from Syria, Lebanon,

Jordan, Egypt and Yemen sought jobs in the oil-rich countries. In the 1980s, a drop in oil prices encouraged many of the wives who had migrated to become employed outside the home (Anti-Slavery International 2006). Women in the United Arab Emirates began participating in the work force in the 1970s and their numbers have been increasing ever since, primarily in the federal and local government sector. However, the number of expatriate women is much larger (Sabban 2002). Consumerist lifestyles, an emphasis on the nuclear family, and fewer full-time stay-at-home mothers increased the need for migrant domestic workers (Anderson 1993). In certain regions of the Middle East, hiring a domestic worker is a status symbol of middle-class identity and privilege. Most of the migrant domestic workers in the Middle East and Gulf regions came from South and South-East Asia in the late 1990s and early 2000s. Over a million migrant women from the Philippines are estimated to be working in the Middle East (Anti-Slavery International 2006).

In Africa, as in Central and South America and the Caribbean, domestic service is associated with a long history of colonization. In South Africa, apartheid perpetuated the employment of large numbers of domestic workers by white households (Fish, this volume). Although many migrant workers came from rural areas, large numbers have also migrated from adjacent countries. Apart from Namibia, Lesotho, and Zimbabwe that share South Africa's colonial history, only Ethiopia reports large numbers of women working in private households (ILO 2013a). In other African countries, the numbers of care workers in private households are low and include substantial numbers of men in some countries and workers in rural areas. The International Labour Organization (2013a: 35) suspects undercounting since care work in private homes is not considered in many national labour force surveys in central, western and eastern Africa.

Asia is home to the largest number of care workers, and is simultaneously, the largest source of foreign care workers (ILO 2013a). The Philippines, Sri Lanka and Indonesia are the major sources of foreign care workers in the region, with large numbers moving to work in private homes in Singapore, Hong Kong, Taiwan, and Malaysia, as well as migrating to the Middle East, Europe and North America. The three source countries also employ large numbers of local domestic workers. This is particularly true in the Philippines where local workers are younger, come from poorer and rural areas, and less educated than the Filipinas who migrate abroad for jobs as care workers. In India and China, the two largest countries in the region, the numbers of care workers are difficult to estimate. In the case of India, domestic service has a long history reinforced by its colonial history and income inequality along with growing numbers of working women as in Central and South America and the Caribbean. Much less is known about China where child care was provided collectively until the 1990s.

Migrating to Care Work

The means used by migrant women to obtain employment as care workers is largely determined by the receiving countries' immigration policies and labour regulations. Countries employing foreign care workers establish the paths of entry and working conditions (Parreñas 2008, 2011). However, certain paths of entry may only be available to workers migrating from specific countries or may differ according to the workers' citizenship status. This includes contracts and special visas, as well as being trafficked into care work and thus becoming undocumented. For instance, the United States offers a myriad of visas for care workers, including 'A-3 visas to work for ambassadors, diplomats, consular officers, public ministers, and their families; G-5 visas to work for officers and employees of international organizations or of foreign missions to international organizations and their families; and B-1 visas to accompany U.S. citizens who reside abroad but are visiting the United States or assigned to the United States temporarily for no more than four years, or foreign nations with non-immigrant status in the United States' (Human Rights Watch 2001: 4). In contrast to special visas given primarily to women from the global South, the J-1 visa is increasingly used to bring young and middle-class European women as nannies or au pairs who identify 'educational and cultural exchange' as their primary purpose (Zarembka 2001: 27–28). Similarly, Ireland offers migrant workers different residency statuses, favouring foreign workers from the European Economic Area (EEA) who have more rights and privileges. Workers migrating to Canada under the Live-in Caregivers Program experience state regulation and are given access to permanent residence after working two years. Under this program, workers are required to reside in the home of the employer providing care for children, the elderly or a disabled family member (Arat Koc and INTERCEDE 2001, Pratt 2004). Migrant domestic workers are typically given a two year employment visa in Singapore, Malaysia, Saudi Arabia, Kuwait, Jordon and Lebanon that may be renewed but cannot be converted to permanent residence. The common legal restrictions prohibiting migrants from becoming citizens and obtaining social benefits have created a liminal status that Parreñas (2011) has called 'partial citizenship'. The insecure status imposed on many migrant domestic workers has been the impetus for scholars in political science and philosophy to theorize about democracy and citizenship (Tronto 2013) and the ethics of care (Mahon and Robinson 2011).

In many cases, the recruitment and placement of migrant domestic workers is unregulated, creating opportunities for unscrupulous recruiters who are known to give false information and charge excessive recruitment fees (Lan 2006). For instance, migrants placed in Singapore and Malaysia find themselves owing recruiters the first six to 10 months of their salary for a placement (Human Rights Watch 2010); employers in Lebanon and Bahrain are reported to take the first three months' salary from their migrant domestic worker as compensation. Some domestic workers are never compensated for their work during their time abroad (Anti-Slavery International 2006).

Many countries in the Middle East and Gulf region regulate immigration through a Kafala system of 'sponsorship' programmes, which places the worker under the legal and economic responsibility of the employer (Anti-Slavery International 2006). The Kafala system of sponsorship is a system of structural dependence and is on the Human Rights Watch list for domestic servitude, exploitation and abuse. Numerous countries, such as the United Arab Emirates and Lebanon, rely on employment contracts to standardize working conditions. Other countries, such as Singapore and Saudi Arabia, allow recruiting agencies to draw up contracts, which is an improvement over no regulation but does not replace labour laws that protect workers. For instance, standard contracts in Singapore allow employers and employees to negotiate from one to four days off per month or an option to work for pay instead, however, workers have no right to overtime pay and there are no restrictions on the total number of work hours per day. The optional nature of time off gives the employer more power. Workers often have little bargaining power in negotiations about their work schedules and they fear losing their jobs and being repatriated. Whereas Singapore's contract at least provides an option; the United Arab Emirates contract does not specify any days off. 'As the immigration sponsor, the employer can typically have the domestic worker repatriated at will, provide or withhold consent on whether she can change jobs, and in Saudi Arabia and Kuwait, obstruct her ability to leave the country. In practice, termination of employment often means the worker is obliged to leave the country immediately with no opportunity to seek redress for abuses or settlement of unpaid wages' (Human Rights Watch 2010: 14). Singapore has a strong record for prosecuting employers and recruiters who physically assault migrant domestic workers. However, gaining access to courts that provide assistance in the workers' language and the lengthy legal process remain major barriers to obtaining justice. In the case of migrant domestics in Saudi Arabia, they may also face immediate employer retaliation in the form of accusations of theft, witchcraft and adultery when trying to seek legal restitution (Human Rights Watch 2010).

A few countries have taken an active role in sending women abroad to work as care workers, usually as an effort to repay national debts or as a means of addressing high unemployment rates at home. Working abroad, women employed as care workers send remittances in preferred foreign currencies that contribute significantly to the reduction in national foreign debts of their homelands. The two most widely cited countries recruiting women to work abroad as care workers are the Philippines and Sri Lanka. Both countries established government agencies to handle the recruitment, training and placement of workers. Government policies regulate the time worked outside the country and vary in their attempts to monitor conditions (Cox 2006). 'In Saudi Arabia, the Indonesian, Sri Lankan, and Philippine embassies handle thousands of complaints of unpaid wages, physical or sexual abuse, or poor working conditions each year' (Human Rights Watch 2010: 16). The Philippines' elaborate marketing and advertising of domestic workers has not always been matched by their ability to ensure the safety of Filipinas employed in Saudi Arabia, the Emirates and China (Guevarra 2010, Parreñas 2008b). Several high profile cases over the years have underscored human rights violations and the lack of monitoring by the Philippine government of the working conditions of their citizens abroad. One notorious case is that of Flor Contemplacion who was executed in Singapore for murder (McKay 2011). More recently, the Philippines has taken steps to stop exporting domestic workers to countries with human rights violations against foreign employees (OSCE 2010). Other countries establishing bilateral agreements with receiving countries are Indonesia and Malaysia. The Philippines, Indonesia and Sri Lanka provide emergency shelters for domestics awaiting the outcome of 'complaints of unpaid wages, poor working conditions, or physical abuse' (Human Rights Watch 2010: 15).

Undocumented workers employed as care workers include migrants who have crossed national borders without authorization, overstayed visas, violated contract arrangements by finding another employer or are working without authorization. Limited visas and quotas in numerous countries block women from gaining lawful employment and many turn to the underground economy as nannies, care workers and private household workers. Workers without authorization may experience limited movement within and across borders, which results in long separations of family members. However, as pointed out below, being an authorized worker does not necessary mean higher pay, better working conditions or protection from human rights violations.

Visa and immigration restrictions force many women to leave children and family behind in their countries of origin. The period of separation from their children depends on their ability to afford return visits and the visa requirements of the receiving country, which may mandate a specific number of years of employment before the worker can return home or require workers to return home after a stipulated period of work. Foreign care workers face multiple state restrictions that limit the time they can work abroad, their ability to migrate with children and family members, and that tie them to an employer, thus cutting off the ability to find a better working situation. Undocumented women do not have the ability to move freely across borders without risking their ability to return to work. A few countries have temporary visa programs for migrant care workers who are eligible to apply for permanent residence after working in an employer's home for a specified number of years. Canada also allows the worker's dependent children and spouse to enter as permanent residents when the care worker qualifies for permanent residency. Other countries prohibit children from traveling to live with their working mothers. In sum, the family arrangements of many migrant women are constrained by their citizenship status, nationality, religion, immigration visa regulations, and the absence of adequate labour law coverage.

The demand for care workers, particularly those who work in their employers' residences, is also filled by trafficked women and girls, and less frequently by trafficked boys. Traffickers may be the person who directly recruits the victim as a care worker into their household, or agencies that serve as intermediaries. A report released by the Office of the Special Representative and Co-ordinator for Combating Trafficking in Human Beings states that 'victims of trafficking for domestic servitude are even more difficult to identify and therefore, they rarely receive assistance and redress. The ILO estimates that there are 12.3 million victims of "forced labour worldwide, 2.5 million of them as a result of trafficking"' (OSCE 2010: 10). Invisible to the public gaze, these workers labour in private homes in foreign countries, and lack knowledge of the language, culture and local laws. Many victims have had their passports confiscated to ensure that they cannot escape their employer or the country. In some cases, employers pay high recruitment fees to agencies and then withhold pay from the worker to cover the expense. Expensive fees also contribute to an employer's sense of ownership over the migrant worker. Their possessiveness is confirmed when workers who seek help find themselves returned to the employer from whom they escaped. The lack of consistency in defining care work and its working conditions and the power that employers wield over migrant workers pose major hurdles in efforts to fight domestic servitude in the courts. Human rights advocates confront different understandings of domestic work in various cultural and national contexts. In some situations cooking, gardening, caring for pets and a range of personal services may be incorporated into the work expected of a maid, nanny or care attendant. Working conditions are particularly complex for live-in workers who labour in private residences. Their accommodations, meals, and freedom of movement are often grounds for claiming human rights violations, however, they are difficult to document in the homes of their employers. In their private residences, employers act outside the public eye and exert enormous influence over the worker's access to the law or assistance with leaving an abusive employer. Labour laws and visa systems also contribute to employers' power over migrant domestics.

Working Conditions

While domestic service has survived the transition from feudalism to capitalism, the occupation has evolved in most countries. Fewer households in Europe, North America, Central and South America, the Caribbean, the Middle East, Asia, and Africa employ large staffs. For the most part, the large staff-maintaining aristocracy of conquistadores in Spanish towns across Central and South America and the Caribbean is a lifestyle of the past (Kuznesof 1989). The same is true in much of Asia and Africa where large staffs are found only in the homes of the very wealthy. Evidence of the decline in domestic service is apparent in new housing in Europe and North America, where few houses are built with a separate staircase for the help to move around the house unnoticed. The maid's room next to the kitchen, commonly identified as the domestic's primary work area, is also rare in new housing. Unlike the days of numerous servants in a household that included cooks, butlers, chauffeurs, lady's maid, valet, footman, kitchen maid, housemaid and footman, most domestic workers are now women and find themselves working alone and with a vague and expansive job description. While many employers hire help to clean their house, domestics and caregivers may also be expected to cook or do laundry. Nannies hired to care for babies or pre-school age children and workers employed to care for the elderly and disabled are frequently required to cook, do laundry, clean the house, and go grocery shopping. In general, the household labour that traditionally fell under the category of 'women's work' is shifted to these workers. Similar to the view that certain labour is 'women's work', care work is frequently considered 'natural' for some migrant women and treated as unskilled labour. According to the Organization for Security and Co-operation in Europe:

> Domestic work is a vague notion, especially when trying to define the work itself. It is generally accepted that it comprises a range of tasks and services connected to the daily functioning of the household. However, legally speaking, for countries that regulate domestic work, there are several different definitions, which may or may not include the provision of certain services linked to a person (such as caring for children, the ill and the elderly), to pets or any other services (such as gardeners, drivers, butlers, agricultural work, etc.) (OSCE 2010: 13).

Research in the Middle East and Gulf region suggests that the vague and all-encompassing definition of the tasks and duties required in care work, particularly in private homes, may be true around the world. One report found that workers' duties were extremely broad, including 'cleaning, washing, dusting, taking out rubbish, cleaning windows, helping to prepare meals, taking care of the children, shopping, taking care of the pets, and serving the guests' (Anti-Slavery International 2006: 28).

Along with job titles (e.g. private household worker, nanny, care worker, housekeeper) that may not reflect the work actually done for an employer, the work arrangements and working conditions in the occupation vary. The most common distinction is between workers who live-in and those who live-out. Domestic workers and nannies have tended to live in their employers' home, sometimes with a designated day-off. Visa requirements that render employers legally and economically responsible for migrant domestic workers, such as those in the Middle East and the Gulf region, create additional incentives for employers to hire only live-in workers. In Canada, employers may only recruit live-in caregivers. However the emphasis on live-in care work in the Middle East, the Gulf Region, and Canada contrasts with the tendencies to hire live-out help or day workers in other regions. This is a trend noted in Rio de Janeiro and other parts of Brazil since the 1980s (Pereira de Melo 1989) and found as early as the 1930s in the United States (Nakano Glenn 1986). A growing number of workers employed to clean houses are more likely to work for numerous employers, often going to one or two different homes a day, juggling weekly and biweekly schedules per employer (Mattingly 1999). These day workers or 'live-outs' reside with their own families. Many workers prefer this arrangement because they have a space away from their employers, which makes the distinction between work time and personal time possible and easier to control (OSCE 2010). Even though live-in nannies are still preferred by many families seeking care for young children, more nuclear families with two full time wage earners are opting to hire day workers to either clean once a week or to assist with childcare during the hours that parents are working rather than to incorporate another person into their households (Blofield 2012: 27).

In some countries, such as Germany, Canada and the United States, some care workers are not employed by the family or the individual for whom they care. Rather, caregivers for the elderly or disabled may be hired by a third party such as the state, a state institution, or a nursing home (Lutz 2011, Cranford and Meintel et al., this volume). A recruitment agency may also serve as a third party and send employees under contract across the world to work for a period of time as in the case of Filipina care workers who are hired by transnational agencies in the Philippines to work in Canada (Bakan and Stasiulis 1997, Gardiner Barber 2008). Cleaning agencies that send out teams of workers to clients on a weekly or biweekly basis have also become common in many places such as Great Britain. Some migrants are employed initially by a cleaning agency and later work independently to increase their pay and flexibility. The emergence of co-ops has been another way that migrant women have improved working conditions (Estey 2011). As members of a domestic workers' cooperative, migrant women negotiate directly with employers and present contractual obligations that assure decent work. Once they obtain adequate capital and management expertise, the cooperatives have the ability to offer 100 per cent pay without intermediaries, such as recruitment agencies, and can offer a range of services such as education. These independent worker coops, such as Cooperativa Valenciana de Empleadas de Hogar del Levante in Spain and Se Puede, Amigos and Manos Cariñas in the US, are more likely in regions where domestic service is part of the informal economy and employees and employers come together to negotiate pay and work (ILO 2013b).

Working conditions for care workers vary depending on the nature of the job. Two major occupational health risks frequently cited are the use of toxic chemicals and injuries resulting from lifting and moving clients with limited mobility. In their report, *Home Is Where the Work Is*, Domestic Workers United (2006) identified exposure to the toxic chemicals in most cleaning detergents, caring for people with contagious illnesses, a heavy workload with infrequent breaks, and long hours in dangerous working environments as increasing the prevalence of health hazards and the incidence of mishaps for workers. In a survey of California household workers by Mujeres Unidas y Activas (MUA) and the Day Labour Program Women's Collective of La Raza Centro Legal (2007), 63 per cent of domestics reported hazardous conditions on the job, namely the presence and need to use toxic cleaning chemicals and human contagions, as well as the danger posed by the need to clean 'hard-to- reach' areas and lift heavy objects. These reports are consistent with other research that finds that domestic workers are vulnerable to a wide range of occupational hazards while performing their cleaning work, cooking childcare and caring for the elderly (Alfers 2011, Babin 2006, Smith 2011a). Domestic workers are rarely provided with protective gloves and masks when using harmful cleaning agents, nor given the choice of using non-toxic cleaning items. Care workers for the elderly are not provided lifting equipment or assistance in moving clients, and those who care for children do not always have access to elevators to transport baby carriers – which can be quite heavy – to upper floors.

Domestic workers' rights are violated world-wide when they are offered substandard working conditions, such as limited food, medical care and sleep, as well as long hours and inadequate and unsafe sleeping accommodations. Violations of personal rights include domestic violence, limitations on freedom of movement and expression, and privacy invasion. Various psychological and physical abuses are unregulated and unreported to authorities. These include verbal, physical and sexual abuse. Violation of workers' freedom of movement has been reported among employees employed by foreign diplomats and the staff of international organizations. Freedom of expression is violated when domestic workers are not allowed to communicate with families and friends, when threatened with deportation or with retaliation toward family members in their country of origin. Invasion of one's privacy occurs when workers' phone conversations are monitored, mail is opened, and belongings are searched. Facing the risk of deportation, undocumented workers are most likely to be in the informal job market where they have little power to negotiate with employers. Of all migrant care workers, they are the most likely to experience long hours, low pay and no benefits (Gallotti 2009). Violations of human rights are not only found in the Middle East (Shapiro, this volume), the Gulf Region, and Asia but they are also a problem in the global North. In a report prepared for the UN Human Rights Committee, Human Rights Watch (2001) found that the rights of domestic workers in the US are violated often. Some live-in domestic workers face forced servitude and endure isolation from other workers; they may be prohibited from leaving their employers' homes; lose access to passports that are confiscated by employers, and may be threatened with deportation if they do not carry out the wishes of the employer. Migrant women with limited fluency in the language of the country, few contacts in the community and a general lack of information about available resources, are particularly vulnerable.

Visas and sponsorship programs that tie migrant workers to individual employers create a 'relationship of structural dependence' that has the most potential for abuse (ILO 2013a: 45). Human rights advocates have voiced concern about procedures, guidelines, laws and regulations governing visas and migrant worker programs which may construct circumstances that tolerate and conceal employer abuses, and restrict workers' rights (Human Rights Watch 2001). Violations and abuses include confiscation of personal documents, limited freedom of movement and ability to communicate with others, employer threats of deportation, assault and battery, rape, servitude, torture, and trafficking. Women are reluctant to report abuse because they fear losing their jobs, deportation, or retaliation against their families in their countries of origin. State protection is often weakened by the lack of enforcement, which continues to be a problem (Arat-Koc et al. 2001, Jureidini, this volume).

State Regulation of Care Work

Throughout the world, care workers in private residences have either been left out of labour regulations or have fewer rights than other workers. The major obstacle that they face is their exclusion from national labour legislation and regulations. These labour codes include a right to a minimum wage, a ceiling on the maximum work hours in a week, social security, pension benefits, access to severance pay, vacation, maternity leave unemployment insurance, safety guidelines and protection against discrimination. Most researchers point to the gendered nature of the work done in the home, which frames the occupation as not 'real work' or as a labour of love (England 2005). The old adage, 'one of the family' in reference to domestic workers, also blurs the boundaries of work and labour. Racism and xenophobia contribute to viewing migrants, particularly workers of colour, as less deserving of labour rights than citizens. These women, and sometimes girls, are frequently from marginalized and vulnerable communities in their countries of origin and face discrimination and human rights abuses working in an occupation that is unregulated and conducted behind the employers' closed doors.

The systematic treatment of domestic workers as outside the labour force makes workers dependent on employers for fair treatment, decent wages and safe working conditions. The ILO (2013a) reports that only 10 per cent of all domestic workers or 5.3 million workers worldwide share the same legal protections as other workers, and 29.9 per cent or 15.7 million domestics are completely excluded from labour laws. A common argument is that the terms of employment, such as the length of the working day, the nature of the work, the pay, rest and meal time or 'in-kind payments' of food and lodging are difficult to negotiate and enforce informally. Nevertheless, workers in some countries such as Hong Kong, South Africa and Brazil have the right to a minimum wage, overtime pay, a weekly day of rest, maternity leave, and paid annual leave. Jordon includes domestic workers in its labour laws (Human Rights Watch 2010).Without legal regulation and enforcement mechanisms workers struggle to conserve the conditions stipulated in the original informal agreement, while employers tend to add additional tasks and lengthen the work day without increasing pay and other benefits (Smith 2011b, Romero 2002). Exclusion from labour protection has particularly devastating consequences for an occupation that lacks clear contractual terms of employment. This aspect of domestic work underscores workers' vulnerability.

A case in point is the systematic exclusion of domestic workers from US labour regulations, which is similar in many other countries such as Egypt, Lebanon and Trinidad. The most significant federal statute for salaried and wage workers is the Fair Labour Standards Act (FLSA), also known as the Wages and Hours Bill, passed in 1938. Even though domestic service was an occupation with documented reports of abuse and was the major occupation employing women from 1870 to 1940, these workers were excluded from wage and overtime protection coverage in the FLSA. Racism prevailed and the federal government eliminated migrant and predominantly Black women from labour protections passed under the New Deal[3] (Nakano Glenn 2010). In the United States, wage and overtime protection was not extended to domestic workers until 1974. Even then, Congress excluded wage and over-time protections for those who were providing companionship to individuals unable to care for themselves. The fact of living-in their place of employment has been used against live-in domestic workers to deny them legal protection. While the Department of Labour (DOL) asserts that it is difficult to compute the actual time worked by employees residing in the employers' home, they have no problem with other employees with similar working conditions. Legal scholar, Peggy Smith (2011b: 180–181) argues that live-in conditions should not be used to exclude domestic workers because the DOL has been able to address wage and overtime protection for other live-in employees, such as 'firefighters, resident managers of storage facilities, assistant deputy probation officers, a damtender, residential care assistants, maintenance monitors of power generating plant, apartment resident site managers, house parents of boys' facility, a garage watchman, telephone operators, and park caretakers'.

Domestic workers in the United States also experience another major legal exclusion from coverage under the Occupational Safety and Health Act (signed into law in 1970). While the OSH Act does not specifically exclude domestic workers, the Department of Labour regulation does so by excluding private individuals who hire others for household labour, such as childcare, cooking and cleaning. Concerns about home privacy seem to be a primary motivation in excluding domestic workers. The only workers protected by law are those employed by a third party, which is a very small portion of domestic workers (Smith 2011b).

Another characteristic of domestic service cited by the US government for excluding these workers from most labour laws concerns the exemptions given to small employers. Domestic workers do not fare well under statutes aiming to protect small businesses because they generally work for employers who hire less than 10 employees. The exemption of small-employers is also used to exclude domestic workers from the National Parental leave program (enacted in 1993). 'The Family and Medical Leave Act (FMLA) requires employers to allow eligible workers to take up to twelve weeks of unpaid job-protected leave each year' (Smith 2011b: 186). As numerous scholars have noted (e.g. Brown 2011, Smith 2011b), exemptions for small employers can be used to deny rights under the Civil Rights Act of 1974, which 'provides protection against harassment based on illegal discrimination of race and sex. Title VII applies only to those employers with fifteen or more employees, it excludes from coverage the vast majority of domestic workers employed by households' (Smith 2011b: 176–177).

3 In response to the Great Depression, President Franklin D. Roosevelt and Congress passed a series of domestic economic programs between 1933 and 1936, which are known as the New Deal. The period is significant because historians identify the period as a time that the most progressive labour laws were enacted.

This employer exemption is a serious oversight given the high rates of sexual harassment reported by domestic workers.

The same kind of systematic exclusion from labour laws and rationale can be found in the global South. For instance, Saudi Arabia's Shura Council excluded a provision that mandated rest for domestic workers between 10 pm and 5 am on the basis that it '"contradicted" the needs and traditions of Saudi families' (Human Rights Watch 2010: 20). Women report working an average of 15 hours a day in the UAE (Sabban 2002) and Sri Lankan domestic workers in Lebanon report between 14 and 17 hours a day (Jureidini and Mourkabell 2004). Singapore's Ministry of Manpower argued that specific aspects of domestic work could not be regulated. Among these aspects were hours of work and hours for rest (Human Rights Watch 2010). In her analysis of domestic workers in Latin America, Merike Blofield (2012) points to the different labour codes established for workers when they are employed in a household. For instance, she compares and contrasts the difference in maximum work hours per week between domestic workers and other workers in each South American country's labour codes. In general, the difference ranges between 12 and 64 hours. The work codes of 11 of the 18 countries stipulated a maximum of 48 hours of work per week in 2010. Domestic workers in Argentina, Chile, Nicaragua, and Paraguay face a maximum of 72 hours a week. Honduran and Venezuelan domestic workers' maximum weekly is 84 hours; Panama is 90 hours a week and Guatemala is a maximum of 96 hours. Mexico and Brazil permitted a 16-hour workday in 2010. Many countries give domestic workers little or no rights to severance pay and enforcement of these rights is nonexistent. For example, Paraguay allows domestics to be fired for 'lack of honor or morality'. Venezuela's law is similar but includes 'respect' as another criterion for firing a domestic worker. Maternity leave and family allowances are not given to domestic workers in Argentina, although several countries, such as Brazil and Chile have legislated maternity leave provisions for domestic workers over the last decade.

State regulation through labour laws is not the only area of public policy affecting the lives of migrant care workers. Immigration laws determine the conditions and length of time that migrant women can work in a country. A number of countries in the Middle East have relaxed visa restrictions for migrant workers in the construction and manufacturing sectors, but the changes explicitly exclude migrants who are recruited as domestic workers. In 2009, Kuwait and Bahrain removed the stipulation that had prohibited many migrant workers from changing employers, but they did not extend the right to change employers to migrant domestic workers (Human Rights Watch 2010).

Organizing and Gaining Workers' Rights

Migrant domestic workers have been persistent in organizing nationally and internationally and this has resulted in a slow movement toward state recognition of domestic workers' rights. World-wide domestic workers have been involved in the creation of organizations and trade unions to obtain and protect their rights. Gradually countries are beginning to develop some legislation designed to protect domestic workers. For example:

- the Hong Kong Federation of Domestic Workers (FADWU) was founded in 2010 claims a membership of 300,000 members;
- the Kenya Union of Domestic, Hotel, Educational Institutions, Hospitals, and Allied Workers (KUDHEIHA) is developing new strategies to reach domestic workers;
- the Federazione Italiana Lavoratori Commercio Alberghi Mense e Servizi, Confederazione Generale Italiana (FILCAMSCGIL), a union in the commerce, tourism and services sector, has negotiated a national collective agreement for privately employed domestic workers (WIEGO n.d.);
- Self Employed Women's Association (SEWA), a trade union of informal women workers in India has begun to organize domestic workers;
- Toronto Organization for Domestic Workers' Rights (Intercede), a community outreach programme provides information and support concerning employment, education, and life skills for care workers.

NGOs advocating for domestic workers' rights and encouraging workers to organize is a world-wide phenomenon. Working alongside *Enough Violence and Exploitation*'s (KAFA) campaign to assist migrant workers who are the victims of abuse, the 24/7 Campaign is trying to eliminate stereotypes of Asia and African migrant workers among Lebanese employers. Migrant-based organizations in the US, including Brazilian Immigrant Center in Massachusetts, CASA de Maryland, Coalition for Humane Immigrant Rights of Los Angeles CHIRLA in Los Angeles, and many others in the National Domestic Workers Alliance (NDWA), are campaigning for better wages, benefits, the right to rest breaks, and protection from sexual harassment for domestics. Domestics have gained access to collective bargaining in France, Belgium, and parts of Switzerland (WIEGO n.d.). 'Italy has a comprehensive collective agreement covering domestic workers which unions and employers re-negotiate every four years, with wage levels being revised each year' (Bonner 2010: 16).The Philippines established a *Magna Carta for Household Helpers*. A Domestic Servant Service Policy was introduced in 2012 in Ghana to regulate contracts and working conditions (WIEGO n.d.). The Malaysian Trade Union Congress is trying to improve working conditions for Malaysian domestic workers abroad but is faced with bans against trade unions in Saudi Arabia.

The International Domestic Workers' Network (IDWN), which includes domestic worker organizations from over 50 countries, played a leading role in lobbying the Governing Body of the International Labour Organization to include decent work for domestics on the agenda of the 99th session. The result was the Domestic Worker Convention, ratified by the ILO and recommended for ratification by UN member states in 2011 (ILO 2010). The significance of ILO ratification of the

Domestic Worker Convention and the recommendations concerning Decent Work for Domestic Workers cannot be underestimated. As mentioned at the beginning of the chapter, the ILO sets standards for international labour rights and monitors implementation. Ratification represents a global consensus for developing labour legislation to protect the rights of domestic workers. As of Fall 2014, Uruguay, the Philippines, Mauritius, Bolivia, South Africa, Columbia, Germany, Dominican Republic, Italy, Nicaragua, Paraguay Argentina, Costa Rica and Ecuador[4] governments have ratified the Convention. Labour organizers are lobbying more governments to recognize the rights of domestics and to include migrants in the policy changes. In October 2013, the IDWN held its first Congress and created a new global federation, the International Domestic Workers Federation (IDWF) in Montevideo, Uruguay.

In the chapters that follow, the contributors examine the social relations of global care work as they are negotiated at the workplace, within families, labour organizing and in local and state governments. The research presented here points to new areas of exploration as we move further toward creating decent working conditions for all those engaged in domestic and care work.

The Book

Our book is organized into four parts. The chapters in Part I examine contemporary theorizing about domestic work and migration, and in particular, how social conceptions of domestic work and gender are embedded in migration policies. From different viewpoints, the authors re-evaluate reproductive labour. Household labour has traditionally been seen as unskilled on the one hand, but when commercialized by private companies its cost often matches that of skilled labour. Many of the recent moves towards outsourcing care work affect a complex social system developed in order for the wife/mother to do work in the home without remuneration. With ever more women entering the skilled labour force we see another wave of outsourcing of household work (child care, cooking, laundry, and cleaning). A new assessment of the macro-economic value of reproductive labour is necessary: is the definition of 'unskilled' still justified (if it ever was)? Are there policy implications that should accompany a re-definition of reproductive labour and its economic value? By addressing these questions, the authors in this part demonstrate the origins of contemporary migration regimes in assumptions that domestic work is unskilled and inherently feminine. Their case studies show that the skill requirements for domestic work are increasing despite static and rigid migration policies that reify domestic work and the migrant women who undertake it. Their findings confirm that the undervaluation of domestic work

4 Costa Rica and Ecuador have only ratified the Convention in their national legislatures and are still engaged in this process as this manuscript goes to press.

in the contemporary international division of social reproduction perpetuates racialized and gendered hierarchies of migrants.

In this first part, ***Gardiner Barber and Bryan*** situate Philippine care worker labour migration in an historical context of regional and global inequalities. Through individual migration histories, their chapter shows the shifting directions and volumes of migration flows and the systemic deskilling and skewed class dynamics that confound even the best prepared migrants' journeys. By exposing the incredible diversity of migrants' education and expertise, the chapter highlights the systemic inequalities that define contemporary global migration and the constraints on migrant agency. ***Korac*** argues that processes of adjustment to the economic circumstances and socio-cultural codes of receiving societies are shaped by gender, ethnicity, age and class. She examines how relationships of power influence the strategies and coping mechanisms of women in exile who have fled violence and socio-political turmoil. Her research focuses on the settlement and integration of women who fled war-torn Yugoslavia and settled in Rome, particularly their resistance to the victimisation and stigmatisation caused by settlement policies and assistance programs set up to 'manage their needs'. Again in Italy, ***Stefanelli*** has studied how migrant domestic and care workers have replaced local women domestic workers. Paid domestic work has become a structural and stable part of the gendered division of the reproductive labour in advanced welfare states, such as Italy. ***Anderson*** describes immigration controls in Europe as having a kind of 'magical' quality insofar as they are more or less visible depending on the national politics of the moment. She regards state immigration controls as embedded in specific histories and social circumstances. ***Jureidini*'s** chapter documents the dangers of domestic service in Lebanon and Egypt, where there are no legal protections for migrant domestic workers. His research highlights the challenges confronted by domestic workers in countries where instability and militarized crises are a daily reality.

In Part II the contributors address the impact of the increasingly important migration of married women domestic workers. Awareness of their wage earning potential abroad leads women to migrate, often to improve their families' economic circumstances. With each woman's departure, gender relations in the family and the household of origin shift. Often another (less fortunate) woman is hired to do the housework and child care or the tasks are delegated to female relatives of the migrating woman. The concept of transnational motherhood captures many of the challenges involved when women try to maintain family relationships from a distance and substitute the labour of relatives or paid workers for their own labour. Here, the authors extend our understanding of the social relations of care in two directions, exploring their impacts on the children of domestic workers and their employers. Investigating how migrant women's involvement in domestic work affects the circumstances of their children confirms once again its adverse impacts (Parreñas 2005, Pratt 2012). In the short run, children reunited with their mothers after long separations struggle in a new context and in the long run, their mothers' involvement in domestic work impedes the social mobility of adult children.

Hiring migrant women to do domestic work challenges their female employers' normative expectations about family roles, particularly those of mothers. The findings from these three case studies raise important questions about the costs and benefits accruing to workers, their families, and their employers from the current international division of social reproduction. ***Romero*** argues that individual child care solutions that involve hiring nannies and care workers transfer the hidden costs of paid reproductive labour to the families of the workers. In the absence of a nationally funded and regulated child care program, employers are unwilling to pay a living wage and benefits to care workers. In the context of current cultural expectations that women will engage in intensive child-centred, emotionally demanding and expensive mothering the physical and taxing part of child care is transferred to migrant care workers while employers upgrade their own status to mother-managers. Interviews conducted with the adult children of domestics and nannies demonstrate that private child care arrangements reproduce inequality between families and the globalized unequal distribution of reproductive labour. According to ***Rosenbaum***, the American Dream is only sustainable through the physical labour of those on the outside, i.e., migrant care workers, who support the lifestyles of those on the inside, middle class American-born men and women. The boundaries between insider and outsider are constructed by denying entry to particular ethnic, racial, religious, or national groups, particularly in middle-class homes. Hiring a migrant care worker disrupts the construction of the middle-class home as a refuge from and counterbalance to the amoral world of politics and markets. The presence of a Spanish-speaking, migrant woman forces middle-class employers to see the social inequalities that underpin their lifestyles and casts doubt on the widely-held belief that success is fully earned by individual effort. ***De Leon*** analyses the post-reunification period, that is, the period following the immediate years of family reunification as it is experienced by Pinay[5] mothers who migrated to Canada under the former Foreign Domestic Movement (FDM) and their adult daughters. Drawing on in-depth, one-on-one interviews, the analysis highlights the ways in which the post-reunification process is marked by a need to rebuild broken relationships and to repair the violence inflicted upon Pinay migrant domestic workers and their families. The chapter investigates possibilities of 'post-reunification reconciliation' through various forms of Pinay activism.

In Part III we turn to authors who address the emotional labour and personal intimacy associated with domestic work that challenges the power of the state to protect migrant workers from exploitation. State policies that regulate the relationships between the employers and women seeking work (e.g. Hong Kong, Macao, Canada, Lebanon, Gulf States, etc.) have the potential to offer some protection against the most brutal forms of exploitation. However, the nature of care work which often involves close personal relations between employee and employer complicates efforts to regulate this labour. The chapters explore the unique qualities of care work and their impacts on the valuation of care

5 Colloquial term for Filipina woman.

work by migrant women. The findings from case studies of Canada and Israel underscore the complexities inherent in the current international division of social reproduction. While many migrant workers feel exploited and vulnerable as a result of the failure to regulate care work (Pratt 2004), these case studies show that some migrant workers, particularly those engaged in elder care, feel valued and appreciated. For them, the oppression inherent in the current international division of social reproduction is related mainly to migration policies, rather than the nature of domestic work itself. The findings raise questions about where advocates and activists should concentrate their efforts. Should they seek regulation of domestic work conditions, revamped migration policies, or some combination of the two?

Meintel, Fortin and Cognet investigate care workers' attachment to their work by exploring the contradiction between the oppression of home care workers and their reported satisfaction with their work. Drawing on recent theories about the gift, they use a case study of migrant home care workers in Quebec to show that the emotional aspects of care work are seen as a gift that is inherently rewarding to care workers. ***Shapiro*** examines the temporary labour migration of South and Southeast Asian women to Israel where their care for the elderly is a class-making process in which employers and employees use personal relationships to both challenge and reinforce their social and economic positioning vis-à-vis the nation state and the global labour market. This ethnographic case study focuses on eldercare as a unique labour niche that carries specific limitations and possibilities. Migrant eldercare workers in Israel constitute an 'intimate class' of migrant workers whose deep emotional engagement with their employers who are Israeli citizens sets them apart from other migrant workers (such as agricultural and construction workers), and indeed other marginalized Others within Israeli society.

In Part IV, the authors take up the vexed questions of how to regulate the care work of migrant women and protect them in the face of an international division of social reproduction shaped by neoliberal policies and imperatives. The effective regulation of domestic work to ensure the rights of migrant workers in private residences and formal workplaces is a troubling issue around the world (ILO 2010). Hidden from public view in private homes and constrained by their limited knowledge of the local context and its languages, many migrant workers suffer a litany of challenges. Recognizing that the migration of domestic workers is likely to continue and represents an important avenue for economic improvement for many women, contributors in this part explore innovative strategies for enhancing and ensuring the rights of individual migrant workers. They range from community unionism to international agreements, buttressed by an on-going commitment to protect vulnerable workers by redistributing power and resources. By emphasizing the agency of migrant women employed as domestic workers, the chapters reveal avenues for promoting progressive change in the international division of social reproduction. Analysing the employment of personal assistance services (PAS) in the private and public sectors of Los Angeles, ***Cranford*** documents the conditions under which care workers can obtain flexible employment that is also secure and adequately paid. In the public sector, innovative legislation combines with creative community unionism to provide more secure employment, higher pay and better benefits to public workers, while a lack of regulation and unionization heightens job insecurity for private workers. Temporary status combined with women's persistent subordination in many labour markets mean that many of the women who leave the South to work in the North end up in unstable jobs marked by low wages, meagre benefits, and poor working conditions. ***Fudge*** argues that global redistribution is needed to achieve gender equality. Policies should allow women in the North and the South to choose the balance between employment and domestic life that is best for each of them. Fifteen years after South Africa's installation of a public democracy, domestic labour remains the largest sector of employment for women of colour. In her chapter, ***Fish*** discusses the complexities of care labour in South Africa through a case study of South Africa's leadership in the international domestic workers rights network. The analysis illustrates the emergence of a movement to resist the globalization of care work through the collective mobilization of women workers across geographic settings.

By drawing on diverse examples concerning the international migration of care workers around the globe, the chapters add valuable theoretical and empirical information about the changing nature of domestic work and the diverse experiences of migrant workers within the shifting landscapes of global restructuring. The comparisons that arise from the chapters of this book are a direct legacy of Christian Harzig's own research. She was convinced that comparing and contrasting the experiences of women migrating to take up domestic work in different national contexts would provide unexpected and important insights into the gendered nature of migration. And this is certainly the case for the substantive contributions to this eclectic and international collection.

PART I
Situating the International Movement of Domestic and Care Workers: Social Reproduction and Globalization

Chapter 2

'Value plus plus': Housewifization and History in Philippine Care Migration[1]

Pauline Gardiner Barber and Catherine Bryan

Philippine care labour migration is situated within an historical context of regional and global inequalities fuelled through the indelible expansion of capitalist modes of organization and accumulation. Interconnected, these facets of capitalism continuously alter social reproduction in order to stimulate capital growth. In this way, while capitalism represents a powerful mode of cultural and social organization, it is both adaptive and transitory. This is particularly true where women are concerned. For example, in many contexts we see an historical confluence of social and economic processes which redefined and repositioned women's labour in the household, a process Maria Mies (1986) captured in an earlier period of ambitious feminist theorizing with the concept of 'housewifization'.[2] The processes characterized in this earlier, pre-postmodern phase of feminist scholarship are now seen to have partially given way to the feminization of labour, the new international division of labour, and the feminization of labour migration itself (Piper 2007). International care labour migration emerges as a means of maximizing capital accumulation for both employers and states. It can be understood as an outcome of capitalism's insatiable drive for profit. It can also be used as a lens through which to understand capitalism – and increasingly neoliberal capitalism – as casting and recasting social identity.

In an era of neoliberal capitalism, care labour migration becomes a central feature of the dispersal and reorganization of social reproduction of labour globally. At once it affirms and alters what Mies and other feminist and Marxist scholars described as 'the sexual division of labour', as it emerged under prototypical capitalism; gender is partially recast to meet the emerging demands

1 A longer version of this chapter is included in *Migration in the 21st Century: Political Ethnography and Ethnography*, edited by Barber and Lem (forthcoming). It is used here with permission from Routledge. We thank the press.

2 Mies contends that women became the optimal labour force because their redefinition as housewives cheapened their labour. As housewives situated within the domestic sphere and subject to the authority of state sanctioned male kin, their labour is 'unfree' relative to men's. These processes were particularly acute for women in the colonies where there was 'increasing convergence between the sexual and international division of labour' (1986: 116).

of capital accumulation, while earlier ideological models are retained. Women are encouraged to migrate for paid employment, yet their paid employment is directly connected to conventional understandings of gender both in terms of the kind of employment they can access and in terms of the reasons why they seek out this employment. When situated in an historical and gendered account of capitalism, care migration represents a global reinitiating of a gendered (and increasingly racialized) process of 'housewifization'. So calibrated, migrant women's labour is not valued for the multiplicity of learned skills it demonstrates, nor its critically important social and economic contributions.

Central to this process is the continual adjustment and readjustment of social reproduction both within the Philippines and the labour markets to which care migrants travel. Hence, our theoretical contribution is to suggest that care labour migration cannot be viewed as epiphenomenal, the by-product or secondary effect of failed capital investment or short-sighted structural adjustments (although it is influenced by both). Nor can it be regarded as simply the individual undertaking of a growing number of women. Rather, care labour migration is central to the processes of contemporary global capitalism, a means of reorganizing social relations and reproduction in multiple sites, sharing some similarities in the organization of social reproduction and gender divisions of labour, and connected through the transnational social networks of migrants and migration industries. From this vantage point, care migration can also be seen as a strategy to redress the drawbacks of unfettered accumulation under neoliberal capitalism and its antecedents. Since the value accorded social reproduction is continually undermined, care labour and those who produce it for wages see their work 'cheapened', if not degraded. This occurs through a combination of the stigmatization associated with the nature of the work itself and the gendered cultural performances associated with particular kinds of migrants and migration flows.

The title for this chapter most obviously references value drawn from social reproduction labour. But '*value plus plus*' also plays on a Filipino idiom for signalling the taxes added to the price of goods and services at the point of purchase. Hence our title emphasizes the unforgiving market logic whereby Filipinos, as exemplary global care migrants, obtain tertiary level education to be competitive in select labour markets. They do so encouraged by the state, unscrupulous recruiters, assorted migration industries who promise more and better opportunities will result from their products, and because normative practices change through migrants' word of mouth stories. And so it becomes self-fulfilling that care migrants set a higher bar by seeking levels of post-secondary training, even when this is known to be politically problematic amongst migrant advocacy groups. Employers benefit from but do not credit the additional levels of skill in the wage calculations; in effect they receive *value plus plus* from their employees. Thus our analysis probes the social complexity and value distortion underlying contemporary processes of deskilling in care migration.

Later in the chapter, examples of individual migration histories, historical and contemporary, drawn from Barber's 16 years of Philippine-based ethnographic fieldwork illustrate the social complexity of care migration, both in terms of the shifting directions and volumes of migration flows, and in terms of the systemic deskilling and skewed class dynamics that confound even the best staged migrants' journey.[3] However, in order to better contextualize the ethnographic context, we first draw upon Mies' concept of 'housewifization' to sketch the sexual division of labour and address the historical tension between productive and reproductive work under global capitalism.

This first section highlights the ephemeral yet immutable character of capitalism. It establishes the conceptual and theoretical context informing the migration histories presented in the second section. In concluding, we bring together the theory and migrants' stories, highlighting the complexity of care labour migration in relation to shifting patterns of gender and reproductive labour. Overall we contribute to the ongoing conversations about the how and why of gendered systemic inequalities defining contemporary global migration but we do so with full attention to the complexities of migrant agency. As the third top source country for global migrants in 2010, the Philippines provides an important case to address these questions.

Housewifization, Care as a Commodity, and Fictions of Social Reproduction

Historically under capitalism, European women (and their colonized counterparts) emerge as housewives, as carers, as non-productive entities or as labour reservists, not because they are these things, but because they have been constituted as such (Lutz 2004, Macintosh 1981, Stolcke 1981, Wichterich 2000, Yeates 2005a); their reproductive labour, unlike the productive labour of men, construed as natural rather than human, ancillary at best, and immaterial at worst (Mies 1986). This enduring ideological sleight of hand deprives reproductive labour of economic consideration while prioritizing capital accumulation over human needs. The disjunction between reproduction and production has both intensified and abated under neoliberalism as national regimes reconfigured by decentralization and privatization refuse or become unable to address social and human needs (Li 2009). Following neoliberal rationalization, a gap in care provisioning necessitates that women, whose paid labour is undervalued and whose domestic labour is regarded as infinitely flexible, take up this social intervention. Just how this occurs varies by class and context as different women respond to correlated, yet diverse neoliberal outcomes. This has direct implications for the understanding and expression

3 Pauline Gardiner Barber gratefully acknowledges the Social Sciences and Humanities Research Council of Canada for two standard research grants. The first project 'Beyond Victims and Heroines' (1999) focused on the transnational circuits of Philippine care migration to Hong Kong. The second project was a collaboration with Belinda Leach; 'Performed Subordination: Global Migration and New Economic Subjectivities' (2006). We compared class streamed migration from the Philippines and Trinidad into Canada.

of gender in myriad social and cultural contexts, as women meet their social reproductive responsibilities in new ways (Sarvasy and Longo 2004, Yeates 2005a, Barber 2008a). Some women commit all their energies to social reproductive tasks, others work a double-day, and for others still it means employing and managing a domestic care labourer. Domestic care labour represents a convergence of women's undervalued productive and unvalued reproductive roles. The value of their labour is simultaneously informed by the logic of the labour market and the emotional and relational underpinnings of care provision. This becomes all the more relevant where migrant care labour is concerned. Here, employers are able to access the benefits of domestic labour, as well as those of migrant labour (Chin 1998).

Care labour migration is rooted in a global political economy characterized by intensive capital accumulation and increasingly diametric class structures. In addition to redressing limited state funded social services, the availability of feminized migrant care labour represents one of the ways in which capital accumulation is facilitated by and for the benefit of both individual employers and the state. Even where the state provides some protection to workers, through work permits and regularized status, the ambiguities of paid care are frequently – if not deliberately – exploited by individual employers. Here, surplus value, both monetary and emotional, is extracted. At the same time, the receiving-state maximizes 'indirect surplus value', or the surplus value accumulated through taxes and managed by the state. Migrant care labour serves to supplement the 'indirect surplus value' available to states. Here, the conflict of 'who gets what when' (Wolf 1982) is mediated through the private provision of care, and 'indirect surplus value' is invested into industry, rather than social reproductive services. This surplus is further augmented by the status of care labour migrants in receiving-countries; unable to access state supports, they (unlike local-born workers) generate direct and indirect surplus without costing the state anything. In light of the hegemonic status achieved by neoliberal doctrine and discourse, such an arrangement, satisfactory to some but not all, remains largely unproblematized. Again, the rhetoric of balance and osmosis between two equal partners is salient; while 'the [domestic] worker who moves across continents may seem the logical result of capitalism's individual subject, the juridical person, torn from all social contexts, selling her labour power in the global market place' (Anderson 2000: 108), she is, in fact, herself a commodity. She does not just complete tasks, she fulfils a role.

For most sending-states, the anticipated outcome of care labour migration, and labour migration more generally, has not materialized. Instead, as is the case in the Philippines, development objectives have been delayed rather than hastened (Chin 1998). In spite of this, labour migration has been established as a long-term rather than short-term solution to the consequences of structural adjustment, liberalization, and stabilization programmes (Barber 2008b). This has occurred in part because labour migration meets the objectives of both international capital (the continuous flow of cheap, pliable labour) (Wichterich 2000) and sending-states that rely on remittances as a source of foreign capital. Meeting these objectives necessitates the vigorous promotion of labour migration by sending-states. As the Philippine case demonstrates, this includes the mobilization of those segments of national populations regarded as most likely to remit income and, as Kunz (2008) has shown for Mexico, the reconceptualization of that segment as particularly well-suited to migration. In light of the caring roles culturally assigned to women, mothers and daughters emerge as ideal candidates. Gender, then, becomes central in the discourses surrounding care labour migration and women's migration more generally. Individual migrants are re-socialized according to the needs of capital as embodied in the actions and objectives of states and employers. In essence, they are subjected to a global process of housewifization and the cultural and social meanings embedded within it.

Framed by discourses of familial obligation, remittance-sending is increasingly regarded as an extension of women's responsibility towards their families. As Kunz maintains, the conflation of care, migration, and remittances directly 'contribute[s] to the reproduction of social expectations of women's roles and behaviours in the remittance process, and the social pressure that goes with it' (Kunz 2008: 1404). Such social pressures are evident in state recruitment strategies that link labour migration to national identity and loyalty, a trend that has been particularly marked in the Philippines.[4] They are also manifested in local and inter-personal dynamics (Fouron and Glick Schiller 2001), and experienced directly by individual women as livelihood opportunities are considered and embarked upon (Chin 1998, Gamburd 2000, Wichterich 2000). It is to these women that we now turn in our example of the Philippines.

Philippine Care Migration Histories

Migration has a lengthy and complex history both within the Philippines and beyond its shores. Found in over 190 countries, Filipinos work in varied labour markets but primarily in gendered in-demand slots in service work, including care. In 2009 there were 1,236,013 Filipinos deployed overseas, an increase of 15 per cent over the previous year. The top six occupational categories posted by the Philippine Overseas Employment Administration for new hires in 2009 were: i) household service workers; ii) nurses; iii) waiters, bartenders and related workers; iv) charworkers, cleaners and related workers; v) wiremen electrical – the only male dominated category; and vi) caregivers and caretakers.

Much of the literature on Philippine migrants has focused on women as caregivers who are sometimes nurses working in deskilled employment

4 For example, in February 2011, the website for the Philippine Overseas Employment Administration shows an image of past president Corazon Aquino against a backdrop of its Manila office at the EDSA intersection. The caption reads 'POEA and EDSA where heroes converge'. EDSA is the infamous site of the large mass rally in 1986 that provoked the resignation of then president Marcos, reviled for his abuse of power.

(Pratt 2004, Stasiulis and Bakan 2005). But in certain migration flows, such as to the US, Philippine nurses are also recruited to work as nurses (Choy 2003). Indeed responding to this, the Philippines deliberately produces an oversupply of nurses for the global market place. Given the promise of work abroad for nurses and caregivers, many potential migrants commence but do not complete nursing education and board examinations. This has led to a pernicious cycle of deskilling whereby employers favour care workers with some medical training so women contemplating care migration feel compelled to get some. High failure rates for Philippine nursing board exams – as high as 57 per cent in 2007 – in part reflect the entanglement of migrant ambition and state deficiencies in regulating migration related industries, including educational institutions. Thus the cycle of preparation for migration and the indebtedness that typically accompanies it now includes money spent on educational qualifications that have become the new norm. This pattern was apparent in the late 1990s but it has intensified through the early years of the twenty-first century. While both women and men work in nursing and care provision, these occupations are feminized as is the overall migration flow out of the Philippines. This pattern first emerged in the mid-1980s when Middle-eastern markets for male labour became less reliable.

But there are historical precursors within the Philippines itself both for state sponsored labour export and contemporary care migration. Barber's research in the Visayas during the 1990s identified four types of care work which can be seen to set the stage domestically for care migration. Each set of relationships holds class, gender, and age specific properties that are translated across the various forms of care work described and reflected in the subjectivities associated with the normalization of care migration in daily life. The examples also illuminate the fine calibrations of production and social reproduction: the gender and class distinctions between labour providers and those benefiting from such labour.

First, in the most clear-cut example of historical class divisions, in the sugar producing regions of Negros, people recalled how workers on haciendas had capitalized upon the labour of daughters who worked in household servitude for their landlords. This was one means of response to the interminable burden of the sugar labourer's debt cycle; interminable because the relationship was quasi-feudal. Hacienda workers were 'born' into the work, with whole families participating in the production cycle during the busiest seasons. They were typically landless, dependent on landlords for daily necessities and without access to resources for subsistence farming or other means of supplemental but essential cash income. Indebtedness to one's landlord was fundamental to the class relationship, yet was sometimes smoothed over by kindly patronage and generous social provision on the part of property owners. In some cases, workers were able to grow modest agricultural crops on hacienda lands, a practice that became contested as a basis for land claims in the post-Marcos period (after 1986). Even in the 1990s, some schools were hacienda based and different haciendas had different reputations for their treatment of resident workers' families. Still indebtedness was pervasive, and women's and girls' social reproduction labour, in addition to their field labour, was subject to the command of male kin, patriarchs and patrons alike.

In the second example, still practiced during the 1990s, children (boys and girls) as young as 10 years old from poor rural households were sent to 'board' with households in nearby towns. No money changed hands. Rather, in return for food, clothing, and school supplies, the children were expected to serve the households as 'helpers'. These young helpers performed such daily tasks as sweeping inside and outside the residence, running errands to the local market visited daily, and caring for livestock, particularly pigs which are labour intensive, but also goats, chickens, and occasionally one or two cattle. More often than not, the helper's labour was all the more intense because the households where they took up residence were not well-off so the chores associated with sustaining those households were time-consuming and diverse, sometimes without benefit of electrical appliances or a reliable supply of potable water to the household. Any emotional bond forged between the child helpers and their 'patrons' was mostly incidental to the functionality of the arrangement. Parents were relieved from the responsibility of feeding and educating the child; patrons received labour at a relatively low cost. The potential for exploitation was great. However, there was usually some social connection between the two households which, potentially at least, curbed abuse, or at least so it seemed. In one example, an 11-year-old boy lived with an older couple in a modest two-bedroom dwelling. The boy was a distant relative and had moved to the town because, it was explained, the school in his mountain village kept unpredictable hours as a result of the teacher's long commute. The boy slept on a portable cot in the couple's kitchen. When not at school, he was summoned by the clapping of hands and sometimes scolded for being lazy. But he was also given special foods and fruits, and required to attend school. Although not entirely free to seek the companionship of other children his own age, he was curious rather than timid and showed no signs of distress or ill health. His chores were not so different from those assigned to others in his age range, although daughters were preferred household assistants and child minders with sons attending to livestock and errands. Always, child labour was described as a familial obligation, with more responsibility assigned to daughters than sons. These cultural prescriptions for gendered labour echoed adult divisions, with women's labour expended over more tasks for considerably more hours of the day than men's (see Barber 1995). Resignation on the part of girls and women to the cultural scripting of gendered tasks, with their variable class dimensions, was pervasive. But women also recognized the challenges associated with managing their household economies and men acknowledged women's role as 'holders of the purse strings'.

The third example of adult 'domestic helpers' is equally long-standing and widespread throughout the country. It lays the foundation for the global export of Philippine care labour which proliferated when migration became feminized during the 1980s (Barber 2008b).

Domestic help, as it is institutionalized within the Philippines, is typically provided by live-in workers and takes two forms. Most households with the capacity to do so utilize some sort of domestic help, typically women's live-in labour but also men's to a lesser degree. For example, middle-class households are likely to employ one or two helpers whose working days are not unlike those of their counterparts abroad. In return they receive wages in addition to the promise of long-term support for themselves and family members should the need arise. Unlike their counterparts abroad and because the Philippine relationship occurs within a decidedly familial cultural idiom (fictionalized as that may be) they are also in a position to negotiate some flexibility relative to hours worked and tasks performed. It is not uncommon for the relationship between helpers and employers to span several generations, adopting a kin-like quality barely discernible to visitors unfamiliar with the household composition. Alternatively, some helper-employer relationships are more 'professionalized'. This was the case of one well-off household we visited in 2010, where two helpers with a nursing education each worked a 12-hour shift to care for an elderly woman whose daughter had migrated to Europe. Their care work was in addition to the labour of a male worker. He served as the gardener and driver, as well as running errands and performing various kinds of heavy work and household maintenance. In this example, the house was well situated and had sufficient rooms to enable separate sleeping quarters for all the household workers. In another example, university students lived with professors and served as household helpers running errands, marketing, cooking, and cleaning in return for free accommodation. Again, these relationships were often established through social networks enabling both the introductions and references necessary to gain credibility for both the labour providers and receivers. Kin-like ties smoothed over the harsh edges of the long hours, the poor wages, and the wealth and social disparities.

In the final example, child care is provided by Philippine *ya yas* (nannies); young women who, because they are paid less than a subsistence wage, are necessarily dependent upon their employer. As with most ethnographic examples of nanny employment, *ya yas* often do various other household tasks. The scenario is a cultural variation on the emotionally fraught outsider/inside relation of caregiving/service work, for example in Hong Kong (Constable 1997), or indeed in Canada (Bakan and Stasiulis 1997, Macklin 1994). There are class variations to the proper conduct of employees in this line of work. Unlike in Canada, where the identity of the nanny is often visibly marked by ethnic and/or cultural difference, many Philippine middle-class employers insist upon marking the insider-outsider roles through comportment. So in public spaces, it becomes apparent just who is kin and who is not from the deferential demeanour of the female worker and the spatial discretion she observes. Always proximate to the family group, whether walking behind or discretely parallel, she waits for the signal, sometimes quite ostentatiously ordered with a slap of the hands, or a brisk command, to assume responsibility for her charges. Sometimes, she wears a uniform signalling publicly that, potentially at least, she is educated as a health-care professional. And our research shows that indeed she may be. Hence the uniform serves as status marker for her employer but it is also a matter of ambivalence, sometimes deeply felt, for the worker herself. She may find the uniform practical and she is definitely proud of her educational accomplishments. At the same time, the situation is potentially humiliating; a condition she is resigned to and accepts, but not so completely she cannot grumble to relatives and friends even as she takes pride in her work. The case bears resemblance to the subjective rendering, nationally, accompanying the placement of Philippine women workers in global care work. In the example just given, the nanny's subordinate status is publicly marked so she contributes to but is herself socially distanced from the class aura of her employers. Patronage may, however, provide benefits in as much as she moves through the city on the periphery of elite consumption. Hence, we see the coming together of the subjective, the material and the symbolic logics of gendered class expression underlying Philippine care worker labour export. These tensions are particularly marked in wealthier urban centres, such as in Makati, Manila's first financial district which hosts high-end retail malls and restaurants. In the provinces, the social markers are less visible but the fundamentals of the relationship remain the same; women provide undervalued and feminized social reproductive labour to replace the labour of their more economically and socially privileged female employers. This class scenario is played out across the global markets of Philippine gendered labour export.

By 2005 when Barber's fieldwork was focused more specifically on the classed aspects of migration, it was becoming much more difficult for middle-class women to recruit working-class women willing to work as *ya yas*. This was as true in Manila as it was in the provinces where there had previously been a rural-to-urban migratory pattern. Increased opportunities for overseas migration were blamed for this labour shortage. Wages for *ya yas* in 2005 varied significantly by geographic and class context and ranged from 1,000 to 10,000 pesos per month, supplemented by room, food, and occasional gifts.[5] In 2005, the legal wage for a maid in Hong Kong was P23,100 (72.18 US) reduced from P25,859 (82.74 US) in 2003 because of a recession. This wage difference, in part, explains the material equation that is calculated every time Philippine women seek employment abroad.

As can be seen from the above examples, women from poor fishing and farming households have long migrated to regional centres for service sector work. Through the lens of one migrant's journey, we will now show in more detail how migration pathways are forged and situated in shifting global economics.[6]

In a coastal area of Negros, because of degraded environmental conditions along the Philippine coastline, households that once subsisted on fishing and

5 The rate of conversion then was approximately 32 pesos to one US dollar

6 Maria Perez's migration journey to Canada is also reported in Barber 2010 but is here considerably revised. It bears retelling because it covers an extensive time period and conveys much that is characteristic of how women stage migration. It also encapsulates some key aspects of migration's class effects for care migrants.

small scale agriculture have increasingly become dependent upon income from remittances. Maria Perez was one of the first women to leave her *barangay* in the late 1970s. She did so leaving behind her infant son in the care of her parents. The boy's father was no longer in the picture. Here is Maria on her decision to leave:

> My relatives were very poor so I decided then that it was my role to help my family … In the 1970s, domestic work was frowned upon. It was a matter of pride. It's a low status job. Now so many do it and it's accepted. I ignored criticism and did what I had to do. What use is pride if people are hungry? Now, when I come home, people ask me for advice and even high school graduates cannot get jobs here [in the Philippines]. To get a job in government you need *compadres*. It's not *what* but *who* you know. But today also, more girls are keen on education and there is a shift in values. The young generation doesn't respect elders' values any more. This is a new thing. It's because of TV. Also some young ones travel overseas for work and they tell their friends about values they see overseas. (Interview with Maria Perez, 1993)

Assuming economic responsibility for the family is one of the facilitating cultural practices for Philippine women's migration. When Maria first left home, her parents assumed responsibility for her son assisted by Maria's siblings who lived in adjacent houses on the same plot of land. Such household clusters are common because both land and finances are in short supply. They are also convenient for co-operative childcare practices now essential to family life in households with family members working abroad. Maria practised transnational parenting (Parreñas 2008b) through letter writing and occasional phone calls made to and from public telephones because land lines were scarce in the 1990s. Since then, cellular technologies have enabled greater contact between migrants and kin but with complicated results (Barber 2008a). Communication often includes talk of economic woes at home, compounding the difficulties of transnational living arrangements. In Maria's case, migration supplemented her extended family's meagre livelihood from artisanal fishing and subsistence agriculture. But, her primary goal was to provide a good education for her son. This was not to be. Not only was he disinterested in post- secondary study, but, she reported, he also became overly invested in material goods and 'girls'. Here again, Maria's circumstances mirror a common pattern indicative of class and consumption dynamics fuelled through migrant remittances. Migrants understand very well that many people anticipate some material benefit from their earnings abroad. Indeed most workers factor this into their homecoming, planning for months in advance by purchasing consumer durables to serve as the customary gifts (*pasa lubong*) given when travellers return. This is in addition to their relentless struggle to tackle migration debt and to save for the various household projects that occasioned the migration in the first instance.

Prior to international migration, Maria first travelled to Manila where she secured a series of low wage retail and factory jobs. Eventually, she took a position abroad as a maid in Hong Kong, her preferred destination. While she suffered bouts of acute 'homesickness', she managed to save for regular remittances, which she recounted with pride. In contrast to the accounts of employer abuse in the literature, Maria claims she did not feel particularly exploited because, she explained, 'in Hong Kong, domestic workers have rights'. In this aspect she was relatively well informed, unlike many workers in Constable's (1997) study. Her resignation to the protracted hours of domestic service in Hong Kong – basically being on-call 24 hours a day, but for the legislated 12 hours off – is best understood through comparison with Philippine wage rates.

After a second two-year contract, followed by the mandatory return to the Philippines, Maria secured a third contract in Hong Kong, this time with a Canadian couple, parents of a one-year-old child. Maria remained with this family as the number of children increased. When the family returned to Canada, they arranged the necessary papers and covered the costs for Maria to travel with them. Maria was conflicted, partly because of geographic distance but described the employment offer as 'too good to refuse'. Under the terms of her visa, after three years of live-in employment, Maria became eligible to apply for permanent residency in Canada. At this time, she commenced night classes to gain a practical nursing certificate. With this qualification she sought employment in a facility providing care for the aged. This is one of the care related occupations where Filipinos predominate in Canada and in many other countries, most often through a career trajectory not unlike Maria's. However, in recent years, the care workers are more likely to have higher levels of relevant tertiary education than Maria did (Barber 2008b). Indeed, the burgeoning institutional care industry's reliance upon Filipinos is tied to a set of cultural stereotypes that similarly captures attention from employers and workers (Bakan and Stasiulius 1997). In a common pattern of staged familial migration, when Maria launched her Canadian career as a permanent resident, she secured employment for her sister with her initial Canadian employers.

Maria's story of resilience, strategizing, and ongoing mobility is not uncommon. With very few exceptions, the approximately 60 women interviewed by Barber described their work abroad, even with all its hardships, as an essential component of survival in their household's livelihood. For a few, however, it was a means to accomplish personal projects unrelated to the needs of kin. Most described their work abroad with pride even though indebtedness and sometimes, sheer bad luck, may have left them no farther ahead economically. For this reason, despite their initial desire for one or two contract cycles, many women engage in protracted circular migration.

Maria's story also reflects transnational ambivalence in as much as her attention remains divided between people and places in the two countries of her citizenship. In 1993, as a Canadian citizen, she mused about retiring in the Philippines. During 2002, she again travelled to the Philippines to research property options for a retirement home. The 'dream' of return is shared by many in the Philippine diaspora. It is also a debate that carries over to the next generation when the children of emigrants question their relationship to Filipino identity. Ignacio's (2005) study of internet dialogues amongst the children of immigrants to the US also affirms the ideal of the Philippine homecoming as an important feature of life in diaspora families. Yet, given the degree that 'homecoming' depends upon Philippine economic stability and this, in turn, is linked to migration and its de-territorialized gendered labour markets, this seems improbable.

Conclusion: Social Reproduction and Care Labour Migration under Neoliberalism

While neoliberalism is a global force 'shaping all aspects of human life according to market criteria of efficiency and rationality' (Bakker 2007: 553), as we have seen, its processes and outcomes are experienced differently dependent upon social location, nationality, and gender. Women, then, are affected by neoliberal discourses and policies in a variety of ways, and as such the effects of these discourses and policies are redressed in a variety of ways. In relation to care labour migration we can identify, at minimum, three groups of women who contend with neoliberalism in related, yet divergent ways: those who employ care labourers, those who migrate as care labourers, and those who remain in their country-of-origin, caring for the children of those who left and engaging in a variety of other survival strategies. These three groups are connected in their social reproductive efforts (Hochschild 2000, Mattingly 2001). That said, their diverse positions within global hierarchies inform the strategies they employ in mediating the challenges of neoliberalism. In essence, as different women assume different aspects of social reproductive work globally, neoliberal capitalism initiates a new process of housewifization. The sexual division of labour is confirmed yet divided; it remains obscured and its ideological underpinning retains saliency.

While some individuals, by virtue of their social locations and positions within global hierarchies, are unable to migrate, others, by virtue of theirs, do not need or wish to. Nonetheless, their lives are shaped by migration, and they belong (knowingly or not) to vast linkages of individuals, families, communities, and states. These linkages, defined by Hochschild as 'global care chains' express 'an invisible human ecology of care, one kind of care depending on another and so on' (Hochschild 2000: 131). They are embedded in transnational social relations established under capitalism and neoliberalism. They embody the global reorganization of social reproductive tasks, a current manifestation of capital's ability to cast and recast social relations and subjectivities. In all of this, the woman in the middle, the care labour migrant, is pivotal. She is, in essence, the transnational link. Through her, migration becomes a central component of the social reproductive strategies of different groups of women (migrants and non-migrants alike); those who depend on her to provide direct care through labour, as well as those who depend on her to provide indirect care through remittances.

In this way, an extended group of non-migrants are integrated in and connected to transnational social fields.

While the care chain concept is a useful analytic tool, highlighting the international division of social reproductive tasks, it fails to address issues of simultaneity, it ignores broader issues of transnationality, particularly in relation to networks, and it neglects the gendered political economy in which social reproductive tasks are rearranged and dispersed. With this in mind, it seems useful to broaden the concept, moving beyond the linear transference of private care responsibilities between women globally, to a more nuanced and situated understanding of the redistribution or dispersal of care labour and social reproduction under neoliberal capitalism.

If we view the global care chain as a dispersed network of social reproductive tasks and objectives, myriad spatial scales emerge (Pessar and Mahler: 2003): the households in the sending- and receiving-countries, the communities of the women involved, and the sending- and receiving-states. Conventional notions of femaleness are upheld as female employers actively seek out other women to perform gendered work, as migrants are propelled into this gendered work and away from other types of employment, and as migrants rely on female family members or other women to care for their own children. These notions are reinforced at different scales: at the level of the state through migration policies, in communities in both the sending and receiving states, through layered transnational relations between family and friends, and the dynamics between labourers and employers. The links between migrants and non-migrants, those who remain in the country of origin, are particularly vital.

Migrants are connected to non-migrant kin in the Philippines in multiple ways. These connections are facilitated by the relative ease of international travel, the increasingly important role of migration in both sending- and receiving-contexts, and the perpetual evolution of communication technology (Levitt 1998). In particular, as we have mentioned, the availability of technology such as cell phones, email, and instant messaging means that the transfer of social reproduction does not occur in a linear fashion, but rather that it filters and shifts through transnational spaces as care labour migrants engage in the daily activities and routines of both their employer's household and their own in the Philippines.

The possibility of international communication adds to the complexity of the lives of migrant care labourers. Technologies such as cell phones and instant messaging results in the 'stretching of intimacy' and the establishment of 'an absent presence' over the distances that physically separate migrant women from the children and kin (Parreñas 2008b, Barber 2008a). In this context, care for children and kin in the country of origin is not entirely displaced onto other family members or paid labour. Rather, the migrant woman, responding to obligations to provide support that is both financial and emotional, remains available to children and kin via these technologies. And while more regular contact may relieve stress and guilt, it may also produce anxiety when face-to-face intervention is impossible (Barber 2008a). In addition to this anxiety, migrant women are forced to carry the social reproductive tasks of two households; doing physical work in the employer's house, while managing and supervising her own (Parreñas 2005a). The result is transnational 'double duty'. Despite their productive reproductive labour, cultural and gendered scripts in the country of origin necessitate that migrant women – when possible – attend to the social reproductive needs of their own children and kin. In this way, filtered through migration and communication technology, social reproductive labour is reorganized and rearranged, spatially, emotionally, and so on.

The global care chain represents, then, a transnational site where 'gender is imagined and lived across multiple social and spatial scales. The disciplining force and seeming immutability of any given gender regime is reinforced through repetitions in the ways in which gender is embedded and re-enacted between and among these scales' (Pessar and Mahler 2003: 818–819). Here, migrant care labourers often depart from a system of gender stratification to enter another one in the receiving country (Parreñas 2008b). Where gender hierarchy is less visible, for example in advanced capitalist states where there are high levels of female labour market integration, the propensity to hire female care labour migrants elucidates gender hierarchy, while simultaneously obscuring it. This follows from the 'social location' of migrant care labourers in the receiving-county, and the intersection of gender, class, ethnicity, and nationality.

'Social location' refers to a person's positions within interconnected power hierarchies. These are created and sustained through historical, political, economic, kinship-based, and other socially stratifying factors. An individual's social location confers upon them, in particular times and locales, certain advantages or disadvantages. 'Social location' is not merely dependent upon nationality; rather, it includes complex hierarchies of class, ethnicity, sexuality, and gender. These variants operate at multiple scales; they make up a person's identity, shaping, informing, and positioning people, their points of views, their activities, and their relations. Social location shifts within the context of the global dispersal of social reproduction. Rather than a static outcome of migration, these shifts are ongoing; they are both physical, reflected in the act of relocation, and conceptual, related to how people understand themselves and how they present themselves. Here, issues of class and ethnicity are particularly salient. Care labour migrants may engage in a variety of actions and behaviours that can be understood as performances of class subordination and complicity (Barber 2008a). These performances, in some instances, are premised on cultural stereotypes pertaining to particular ethnic groups. These stereotypes are harnessed by migrants, employers, and sending- and receiving-states alike (Chin 1998, Gamburd 2000, Barber 2008a).

Care labour emerges not only as a set of social reproductive tasks (cooking, cleaning, caring), but as gendered performances of subordination 'that [are] produced knowingly, in order to accomplish not just employment but a position with the most desirable employer under the circumstances. This can be read as a classed performance of what we might also call an *economic subjectivity* responsive to new gendered geographies of class and power in commodified domestic labour'

(Barber 2008a: 30). Such performed subordination includes compliance with gender scripts, minimizing assertiveness, and downplaying aspects of identity that might suggest class advantages, constraint of body language, and the depiction of a subordinated self that draws on cultural perspectives of Filipinos as subservient (Barber 2008a).

Responding to the spatial scales of household and receiving-states, and the social and relational scales of employer-employee dynamics and corresponding stereotypes, social location in the country of origin is deliberately recast in the receiving-country. Social location is not, then, a condition or an outcome, but a process, a negotiation, and a performance. While this conceptualization appears to prioritize the migrant's agency, her ability to act as a free, rational agent, this agency is relational, predicated upon multiple social and spatial scales, the meanings assigned to particular facets of identity (for example, gender and ethnicity), the value assigned to care labour, and class hierarchy. In this way, the reorganization of social reproductive tasks globally is not just a matter of care transference. Rather it is a matter of pliable relations, conditional agency, and structural constraints. In the current era, such constraints have been characterized as neoliberalism. Here, we situate them within the history of 'housewifization' under capitalism.

Chapter 3

Refugee Women Doing Paid Domestic Work in Rome: Disempowering Structures of Settlement and the Question of Agency

Maja Korac

Introduction

Literature on migration, globalization and domestic work reveals that women migrants take on paid domestic work as their main survival strategy in the receiving society (Anderson 2000, 2001, Cole et al. 2006, Lutz 2008a). Moreover, in the context of forced migration, as my research and other studies demonstrate, women working in domestic services are often main providers for their families (e.g. Lutz 2008a, Harzig 2006, Korac 2009).

Inequalities between rich and poor regions, as many authors argue, exploit (by the mechanisms of capitalism) the vulnerabilities of people migrating from poor(er) countries, placing them in low status jobs, such as paid domestic work. Migrant (women) domestic workers leave their places of origin and migrate to countries and economies of the world where they can earn more and sustain their families left behind. In this sense, as Morokvasic points out, these women leave home because they want their homes to be sustained and not because they wish to start and establish a new home somewhere else (Morokvasic 1994 cited in Lutz 2008a: 3). This type of orientation to place is underpinned by transnational households and family lives, characterized by limited integration into the host society, often leading to the construction of the notion of 'perpetual foreigner' among migrant women doing paid domestic work (Parreñas 2008a). Although they play a vital role in the economy of the developed world, they are very often subjected to exploitation, ill-treatment and deprived of basic rights (Anderson 2001, Parreñas 2001a). The perilous situation of migrant women doing paid domestic work is structurally determined by legal, economic, social and political conditions of their settlement.

Unlike many migrant women, refugee women who flee violence and socio-political turmoil leave their places of origin in search of safety and of a place to establish a new home. Their options, choices and opportunities are severely constrained by disempowering and imposing structures underpinning forcible displacement. Like the overwhelming majority of migrant women, women refugees find work in the domestic service sector of receiving societies, adding one more layer of oppressive structure to their already precarious situations.

Yet, if we examine specific refugee populations and contexts of their settlement, and look more closely at who are the actual women (and men) who flee violence and socio-political turmoil, what are their aims, and short and longer-term goals, we may be able to look beyond these macro, meso and micro structures of exploitation embedded in and linked to paid domestic work, as well as forcible displacement. This can enable us to understand not only how broader scale structures shape settlement experiences and affect the construction of agency, but also, how women's agency in specific contexts and relations of power can transcend exploitative conditions and relationships to fulfil their individual aims, goals and needs.

In this chapter I examine two disempowering contexts, underpinned by imposing repressive and exploitative structures. Instead of analysing how refugee women are being pushed around within these structurally imposing systems or how they are victimized by exploitation and/or violence, I explore their agency by examining the micro level structures of their day-to-day lives. I want to emphasize how exile and settlement experiences, intersecting with women's socially constructed roles and identities, may become processes through which they 'resist' as they gradually 'recuperate' power (Butler 1997) over their lives by creating or opening themselves up to new opportunities.

More specifically, I want to explore the role and meaning of paid domestic work in the lives of women refugees by examining multiple and intersecting factors that shape their settlement goals, aims, survival strategies and experiences in exile. I focus on gendered experiences of settlement of women who fled war-torn Yugoslavia and found refuge in Rome.[1] I argue that their orientation to place, their aim to gain control over and reconstruct their lives in the receiving society is central to the perceived and actual role of paid domestic work in their settlement. Their place-making efforts to establish a new home in Italy intersect with their class, as well as ethnic/racial background; they are also underpinned by the character of their legal status in the receiving society. These intersections are central to the organization of their experiences of settlement and shape their notions of loss and gain, disempowerment and empowerment in exile.

Doing Paid Domestic Work in Exile: Disempowering Structures and the Question of Agency

Women's agency is central to developing strategies of survival and betterment. This agency is evident in their willingness to renegotiate their gender and other intersecting identities in order to adapt to their new circumstances in exile, thereby

1 This article reflects upon some aspects of my research on settlement of refugees in Italy, and the Netherlands (Korac 2009).

creating new opportunities for themselves. Often these 'opportunities', initially at least, mean underemployment and loss of social status. Despite these setbacks, they actively resist exploitation, marginalization and stigmatization. Their resistance is not only about surviving exploitation and victimization associated with displacement and paid domestic work. It is also often about transforming these experiences into an opportunity, into a functional part of their future, more meaningful life in exile.

Refugees create opportunities within the limitations of their predicament. This process is influenced by the intersection of micro and macro factors. Individual and group social positioning and local dynamics intersect with structural and global dynamics in different ways in specific contexts. This process is critically shaped by refugees themselves through their actions and motivated by their goals and aspirations. These are negotiated at different levels and scales of organization, and through networks of relations with various actors, including governmental and other institutions. Agency is hence 'embodied in social relations' (Long 2001: 15).

Settlement and the process of incorporation in the new society is a 'goal oriented' process entailing major obstacles that have to be negotiated before newcomers can attain a level of societal participation that is in harmony with their integration goals (Valtonen 1998: 57). However, the prime determinant of subjective wellbeing of refugees during this process, as Valtonen's research reveals, is not the degree of discrepancy between goals and actual conditions of settlement (Valtonen 1998). Rather, their subjective wellbeing is determined by 'the extent to which agency can be exercised in the resettlement situation' (Valtonen 1998: 57).

Researchers are increasingly emphasizing the importance of agency for studying the experiences of people fleeing their places of origin and their forced dislocation (e.g. Essed et al. 2004, Korac 2003, 2005, 2009, Turton 2003). The notion of refugees and other migrants as social actors who have the 'capacity to process social experience and devise ways of coping with life, even under the most extreme forms of coercion' (Long 1992: 22) has been introduced into the field of (forced) migration with the application of Giddens' concept of structuration (e.g. Richmond 1993). Giddens (1984: 173) pointed out that social structures not only constrain behaviour and peoples' social lives, but also enable their actions. While he argued that the constitution of social structures cannot be understood without allowing for human agency, he viewed agency as embedded within institutional structures and processes (Giddens 1984: 11). This should not imply however that an actor 'follows a pre-given ideological script' (Dissanayake 1996: 8, cited in Long 2001: 15). Social actors and their agency are guided by both reflexivity and motivation. Turner (1988), among others, argued that a theoretical interpretation of social action must go beyond cognition and consciousness to include perceptions of security, trust, group inclusion, intersubjective understanding, and symbolic, as well as material gratification, as important factors shaping agency.

As social actors, refugees are continuously creating 'room for manoeuvre' (Long 2001) in the context of severely limited options and choices associated with forcible dislocation. They are actively engaged in confronting liminality characterized by uncertainty and improvised existence based upon ad hoc short-term strategies at best, or day-to-day survival at worst. The liminal character of refugee existence is a consequence of the separation that is inherent in forced movements and therefore is part and parcel of the very nature of the experiences of forced migrants. It is also produced and reinforced by a variety of policy 'solutions' to the refugee 'problem', which keep people fleeing their countries of origin into situations of prolonged insecurity that affect their legal status and social rights.

While liminal existence is indeed a severely disempowering experience, it is also a condition that refugees actively confront in a variety of ways in their search for and creation of solutions to their predicament. This does not imply that refugees always have clear views on how their perceptions of reality are formed, and thus, that their strategies and actions are based on rational decisions and/or options. As Long (2001) points out, choices, strategies, and behaviour of social actors, as individuals or groups, are shaped by 'larger frames of meaning and action' (14) formed through the links between the 'small' worlds of actors, and larger-scale 'global' phenomena and structures. In uncovering the complexity of factors involved it is crucial, he argues, to contextualize actors' strategies through a systematic ethnographic understanding of the lived experiences of the variously located social actors (Long 2001: 14–15). Without this type of contextualization, the notion of refugee agency is as abstract as is the notion of victimhood.

The Context: Paid Domestic Work in Italy and the Women in My Study

Paid domestic work in Italy is increasingly becoming the occupation of migrants, and migrant women in particular (Cole et al. 2006). They started arriving in the 1960s, from Cape Verde, Somalia and Ethiopia, and were then followed by women from the Philippines who dominated the sector until the 2000s, when the number of migrant women arriving from Eastern Europe increased sharply (Colombo 2007). In Rome, however, Filipinos are still the largest migrant group in the city (Parreñas 2008a). Despite this significant increase in the number of (women) migrants doing paid domestic work, it is important to point out that migrant women (and men) in Italy are overwhelmingly employed as live-in housekeepers, childminders or those caring for the elderly, while Italian domestic workers still dominate part-time work in this sector (Colombo 2007, Scrinzi 2008).

Unlike local, Italian women, immigrant women do not necessarily come from the poorest strata of society and they usually have above average education (Harzig 2006). Indeed, these are the characteristics of the European situation in general, as Lutz (2008a) documents. In fact, as she points out, a section of them are from a middle-class background, some migrating after they obtained higher education and sometimes after years of professional experience (2008: 3). Consequently, a number of these women have an equal and at times an even higher level of education than their employers, as Colombo (2007: 217) documents. She further points out that the status of their jobs in their countries of origin, although not the income, also often equals, and at times even exceeds the professions of people they work for in the destination countries (Columbo 2007). These women move alone, often leaving behind partners or a family with (young) children.

Many of the women I met in Rome fit this class and educational profile. The majority also fled their places of origin alone and did not have any family networks in Italy. They were, however, overwhelmingly single and without children. Very importantly, as I emphasized earlier, they fled their homes primarily in search of safety and a place to establish a new home. Consequently, their settlement goals importantly shape their orientation to place, the development of coping strategies and ideas of connecting and belonging.

Upon their arrival in Italy and Rome people fleeing conflict(s) in Yugoslavia were granted temporary permits to stay, renewable on a yearly basis, based on a special Government decree. Because their stay was classified as temporary they did not qualify for permanent resident status, initially at least, which would eventually give them the opportunity to qualify for Italian citizenship. This type of status is indeed problematic, because it implies a continuous threat of expulsion and hence creates insecurity and causes anxiety among people who hold such a permit. Moreover, those granted temporary humanitarian status do not have the right to family reunification, which only adds to their precarious situation. In this sense, there is no doubt that not allowing people fleeing war-torn Yugoslavia to claim asylum under the Geneva Convention caused serious problems for them (Vincenzi 2000, Sigona 2005).

Nonetheless, in considering the situation of people granted humanitarian status in Italy based on special government decrees, it is also important to acknowledge that although temporary (i.e. renewable on a yearly basis), this status is usually granted without any lengthy determination procedure associated with the Convention asylum claims. More importantly it includes the immediate right to work and study. These rights were critically important for the people fleeing the Yugoslav conflict(s), regardless of the fact that having the right to work was not a straightforward way to their empowerment (Korac 2009).

Indeed, for many, becoming self-sufficient came at a high cost, because they were forced to enter a niche of the labour market from which it is very hard to move up the economic and social ladder. Rada's words echo the accounts of a number of people I met in Rome. She was 32 years old when I met her, working as a sales person in a retail shop, she said:

> It was a struggle in the beginning [in 1993, when she arrived] and it is the same struggle now – to have a place to sleep, to have something to eat. There's no security here, I work an awful lot and it's a vicious circle from which there's no way out. I'm okay for them [the receiving society] and that holds while I am relatively young, while I'm free [single], while I am able to give. God forbid that I should fall ill or that I should have some serious problem. I can't even imagine what would happen then … I don't see that any of us has settled down so that she/he can say that she/he's satisfied.

The cost for those who had to interrupt their schooling to flee was a delay or abandonment of their education in the face of the immediate need to find any kind of work. Cica, who came to Italy in 1992, was a student in Rome when I met her. She recalled how she struggled to continue her education, interrupted by the war and the subsequent flight:

> I couldn't bear my life here anymore. It boiled down to 10–12 hours of hard and senseless work that could only secure basic living. We [she and her partner, also a refugee] couldn't even dream of continuing our studies and planning for the future … All they [the Italian government] did was to give us permission to stay and work, but we had to do everything else ourselves … But when my partner and I could finally afford to continue our studies everything changed. I'd regained my hope for the future.

The opportunity to study, for those who were able to afford it, was perceived as a way forward, a further step towards a common goal: to bring normality and meaning into their lives. Although it marked the beginning of a new stage in their lives, combining university education and working to earn a living was a challenging experience. Many women continued to work in the domestic sector, as part-time, hourly paid housekeepers and cleaners while studying.

Despite these difficulties, working reportedly made these people 'feel better', as one of them put it, 'regardless of what kind of jobs' they had. That is what helped them 'keep their wits' about them and what kept them 'sane' after their arrival in Italy (Korac 2003: 408). Organized programmes of reception and integration associated with Refugee Convention status in the Scandinavian countries or in the Netherlands or Germany, for example, were often seen as disabling individual initiative, therefore, undermining self-esteem, or as limiting basic rights, such as the right to free movement or the right to work. Hence, these conditions were often considered detrimental to the wellbeing of people 'managed' by such programmes, because they became inward looking, preoccupied by their past and socially isolated (Korac 2009).

The gravity of this type of temporary humanitarian permit to stay also meant that the vast majority received no assistance to settle in the country. As a result, the overwhelming majority encountered profound problems in achieving a minimal (financial) security, because very few actually received even minimal support in finding shelter and work. Consequently, employment became a matter of extreme urgency because it literally meant physical survival. Still, the advantage of their situation was that they could work, formally at least, in almost any sector of the job market; also they were not undocumented, as are many other migrant women (and men).

Creation of Livelihoods: Patterns of Employment and Access to Paid Domestic Work

In their initial struggle for physical survival some faced more difficulties than others; the elderly or those with (small) children, for example, were particularly affected by the lack of any initial support upon their arrival (Korac 2009). Also, finding jobs and accommodation on arrival was a gendered process, often favouring women. On arrival, a general pattern of looking for and finding jobs emerged. Most of the younger, unmarried women would find work within a matter of days as live-in housekeepers or nannies. Older, married women were employed as 'live-out' or 'part-time' domestics and lived with their own families, often becoming the sole providers for their families. Despite the hardship this caused for many, and for a prolonged period of time, the accounts of women (and men) I met in Rome were interwoven with feelings of self-respect for being active in finding solutions and for being self-sufficient. The fact that they did not rely on aid made them aware that this situation has potential benefits for their day-to-day interactions with Italians, and the way they were perceived.

Milka's account echoes the experiences and views of the many people I met. She was 45 years old when I met her and her family in Rome, where she was employed as a live-out housekeeper. The family had financial difficulties for years, as her husband was not able to find any steady work for a very long time. Even so, Milka said:

> There was nothing here, no assistance or any kind of support for us, and I'm glad about that. Everywhere they look at foreigners as people on whom the taxpayers' money is being spent. I think that's one of the major issues in most EU countries today, and it's less so in Italy. We've earned [she and her husband] whatever we have here. If I'd gone to Caritas[2] to ask for something, I'm sure my [Italian] neighbours would be looking at me in a different way. This way, they respect me.

The importance of maintaining self-respect was paramount among the people I met. So much so that even when some form of assistance was available, in the form of provision of free meals at Caritas, for example, the refugees tended to avoid relying on it. Although the people I met in Rome confessed to being on poor diets for months, and some even for years upon their arrival, and hence in dire need of food, they emphasized the importance of dignity as the critical factor that kept them going. As they were allowed to work and, therefore, were permitted some level of choice as to whether or not to rely on aid, almost all of them opted for independence, often regardless of the hardships involved.

2 Caritas is a prominent church organization operating in Italy and worldwide. Caritas, as other church organizations in Italy, provides support for the destitute, including refugees and other immigrants.

Thus, in terms of finding jobs, women were much better off than their male compatriots. This was due to the situation in the labour market in Rome that offers opportunities in domestic services,[3] but it was also related to the kinds of social networks the women from the region had in the city.

During the 1970s and 1980s, a number of young women, predominantly from Dalmatia, Croatia, and Herzegovina, the south-eastern part of Bosnia-Herzegovina, came to Rome for six months or a year to work as live-in housekeepers. They earned a little, learned the language, and returned home. Before their flight many of the women I met in Rome had direct or indirect contacts with women from the region who worked as domestics. Vesna explained one of the many ways in which these initial contacts and networks were established:

> During the war [in Croatia], my parents used to go to a nearby shelter regularly, at the time when our neighbourhood was heavily shelled. In the shelter, they met a middle-aged woman who happened to know a woman, Helena, who was a live-in domestic in Rome in the late 1980s. That is how I got to know of her and later got in contact with her. She helped me find my first job here. I was among the first to arrive here, I helped many other women who came later.

Contacts like this were instrumental in gaining vital information about how to search for work in domestic service. After the first refugee women found work, they served as a source of information and contact for those who arrived later.

The Croatian Catholic Church in Rome was also helpful in assisting women who arrived with the influx of refugees in the 90s, and this was irrespective of their ethnicity or religion. The role of the Catholic Church in Italy in supporting immigrant women in finding jobs in domestic services is well documented in the literature (e.g. Reyneri 1998, Scrinzi 2008). In explaining the central position of the Church in the organization of the domestic sector, Scrinzi points to the role of a 'Catholic Network' of missions, parishes and religious organizations based on voluntary work that underpins the role of the Church in this sector (2008: 37). In her analysis, she notes that this support has been historically provided to women migrating from Catholic countries in the 60s (Scrinzi 2008: 36). Among other motives, the presence of these women was seen as a way of developing and reinforcing the moral and religious values of families of their employers (Scrinzi 2008: 37). Because of this role in the domestic sector, Italian families in need of domestic help, childcare and/or elderly care, usually contact the Church and its organizations in search of reliable help.

3 For more information on the character of the labour-market in Italy in the 1990s, and the opportunities immigrants have in domestic services see Reyneri (1998).

Exploitation, Isolation and Beyond: The Experience and Meaning of Paid Domestic Work in Rome

A live-in housekeeper's job not only secured a modest salary for women, but also accommodation, food and an environment to learn Italian. In some cases, women were actively encouraged by their employers to take Italian language courses and arrangements were made enabling them to do so. In a context of settlement with no government provision, these were extremely important aspects of employment, regardless of how undervalued and difficult the actual work was. Indeed, this is one of the main reasons that live-in domestic work is predominantly done by immigrants, not only those who are also refugees (e.g. Colombo 2007).

The women in my research described their work as live-in housekeepers as a 'difficult period'. But as Emira recalled the experience of her first six months in Rome, working as a live-in housekeeper was not difficult because employers 'behaved badly', but because she was doing a job she 'never did before' and had 'always (been) protected in her family' from such labour since she was from a middleclass background.

Live-in domestic work was referred to as an 'exhausting job'. Living with one's employers, usually implies being 'on duty' all day, except for one day a week. They reported being so tired at the end of a working day that they did not have energy to watch television in the evening, which most of them had in their rooms, or to read newspapers, let alone a book. Since they knew little 'concerning money matters', they soon realized that what they were paid 'was actually very little'. Wages in the domestic work sector are low, indeed, and even more so for live-in work in Italian families (Scrinzi 2008). The wage system is unequal and racialized, favouring women of a particular national/ethnic/racial background, with Filipina women among the highest earners in the sector (Pojmann 2006).

While their narratives reference live-in housekeeping jobs as exhausting, difficult, and low paid, they did not perceive their situation, at the time or in retrospect, as more exploitative than other jobs available to the refugees from war-torn Yugoslavia. Compared to their male compatriots, who found work in manual and low-paying jobs such as building, painting or gardening, and who often worked hard and long hours for a fraction of a wage or no pay at all, the women's jobs were difficult and low paid, but they were paid regularly. Men said they had difficulty finding 'a trustworthy boss'. This situation made the lives of many men miserable, because the vast majority had no means to sustain themselves. Their difficulties with finding jobs quickly were compounded by not being able to locate affordable accommodation. Nevertheless, the women employed as live-in domestic workers, experienced a 'prison-like' existence resulting from the lack of control over their time and feelings of isolation from the outside world. Most of the women I met in Rome knew none or very few people in the city and could not afford the time to search for contacts. The Church played an important role in helping refugees establish their first social contacts and was a focal point for many women in my study, as it was for many people who fled the Yugoslav conflict(s) and arrived in Rome. These initial contacts helped develop networks in the city and beyond. For example, Emira explained, 'with the help of a nun of the Croatian Catholic Church' with whom she had 'initial contact through a family friend' from her hometown, she found out 'about the places where the folks from our country [Yugoslavia] gathered. That was the church of Santo Geronimo [St Hieronymus] in front of which people of all ethnic origins [from the Yugoslav successor states] would get together. There, I met many people I'd known before but wasn't even aware that they had got here as well'.

The role that public urban spaces play in assisting migrant women doing domestic work has already been documented (Harzig 2006). Women in my study were refugees whose arrival in Rome was spontaneous, rather than facilitated by chain migration; thus, they had hardly any social contacts in the city or the country. For them, the existence of these public spaces and gathering places was paramount to ending their initial isolation. Over time, as their networks developed and closer ties were formed with compatriots, as well as other immigrants and locals (Korac 2009), their gathering places became integrated into the public social space of the dominant society. This has not been the experience of other (visible) immigrant and refugee groups in Rome or Italy, particularly women doing paid domestic work who experience both occupational and spatial segregation in Italian society due to racism (Parreñas 2008a, 2001a).

As employers often have a sense of entitlement over employee's time and labour, especially in the context of live-in work, it is not surprising that the literature on women and domestic work, sometimes refers to this type of work as 'modern day slavery' or 'contracted slavery' (e.g. Ehrenreich and Hochschild 2002). While there is no doubt that domestic work involves structural inequality and that workers experience exploitation, subordination, and victimization, my research found that refugee women approached their work in domestic service as an important stepping stone to a better future. In pursuit of long-term goals, they inserted their agency to make the system work for them. From this perspective, the live-in phase of their life in Rome, may be viewed as a 'refuge' or 'shelter job' (to borrow the terms from Cole et al. 2006 and Colombo 2007), that which was helpful in their initial adjustment and functional settlement in the country.

Vesna's experience makes this point as she detailed the pattern of work and life during the women's first year in Rome:

> The way for us women was first to get a job as a live-in housekeeper. You stay in a family until you've saved enough money which enables you to look for a new job. It took me ten months and when I'd set enough money aside I left the family. When you leave the family you worked for as a live-in housekeeper you find a flat and your jobs are either in a café or cleaning people's houses.

Change of employment usually occurred after six months or a year, when they had enough money to find their own accommodation and look for another job, usually in cafés or retail shops. A majority of foreign workers in Italy share this employment pattern (Colombo 2007). Research shows that the longer women are in the country, the less likely they are to be working as live-in domestic workers, suggesting that this type of work is a step in a working and migratory career of a woman, rather than her destiny (Columbo 2007: 221).

After several years in the city, most of the younger, single women were able, determined and resourceful enough to create opportunities to continue their education interrupted by war and flight or to retrain and find work in their new professions. For example, Vesna fled Croatia and arrived in Rome in 1992, and by the time I met her in 1999, she was 33 years old and working as an IT specialist in a small firm.

These women described their initial loss of social status as a difficult but invaluable learning experience and part of a crucial period during which they learned Italian and gained first-hand experience about the 'Italian way of life' and culture. They described this early phase as a critical period for learning about themselves, their strengths, abilities and potential as women. Thus, their early exile experience, although difficult, enabled the women to gain self-respect and they came to see themselves as *survivors* rather than victims.

I Do My Work Highly Professionally: Negotiating Low Social Status

A percentage of immigrant women do not succeed in moving out of live-in arrangements or out of domestic service (Colombo 2007: 221). Studies have found that migrant women experience occupational segregation because they lack a diploma or specific skills, and experience racialized practices and racism in destination countries (Lutz 2008b, Parreñas 2008a, 2001a). Likewise, there were women in my study who were not able to alter their situation. Older (over 40-years-of-age) married women were not able to move out of the domestic service sector, although they were well-educated and often had considerable experience in their professions. For them, the loss of social-status was negotiated at two intersecting levels. At one level, they drew boundaries between their work and personal identity by defining what they do as a profession. At another level, they negotiated the low status and stigmatization associated with domestic work in the realm of their care-taking and care-giving roles as mothers and wives. These latter roles remained the core of their identities, regardless of their education and profession. Lepa, who fled Croatia and arrived in Rome with her family, was one of these women. Her words illustrate this type of negotiation:

> I do my work here [as a housekeeper] highly professionally. I respect it because it enables my family and me to live. That is paramount. Since we fled, I was ready to do almost any kind of work to support my family.

Lutz (2008b: 51–57) has also found that professionalization of domestic work is often a strategy of normalization among immigrant women doing this type of work. She argues that this profession-like construction is, however, precarious. Balancing distance and closeness with one's employer is one of the central problems of paid domestic work, which makes it difficult for women to keep up with their strategy of professionalization (Lutz 2008b). However the personalized character of work may result in unintended friendships between employer and worker and such relationships are vulnerable and can be destroyed through conflicts.

Elements of closeness and friendships established in the context of paid domestic work are indeed vulnerable to unequal relationships of power. Anderson (2001) observes that often power is practiced through the manipulation of kindness, switching from the expression of a relationship as familial and friendly, to one that is work related at the convenience of the employer. Not surprisingly, not all women in my study had or indeed wanted friendly or close relationships with people they worked for, because their priority was to maintain a professional-like attitude in the work they did. However, at the same time, the contacts and support received from Italian families they worked for and networks of their friends and relatives was critical to their integration.

The Importance of Contacts with Italian Families for 'Getting By', 'Getting On With' and 'Getting Ahead' with Life in Rome

The lack of organized assistance and provision, mentioned earlier, prompted women (and men) I met in Rome to engage in intensive networking within and between groups of compatriots to form an alternative *self-reception system* to address their most basic needs (Korac 2009). In addition to co-ethnic and cross-ethnic networks, the process included intensive, informal and spontaneous networking between people. Their contacts with Italian families, their employers and networks of friends, were central to further facilitating their *functional* adjustment through language training, diploma recognition, additional skill and job training. Women's networks that included Italians helped many men to *get by* too, by helping them find first jobs or accommodation.

As bridging links with Italian, co-ethnic, and cross-ethnic groups were established early on, these contacts helped refugees to *get by*, *get on with*, and *get ahead* by providing vital information, contacts, and enhancing the use of the considerable human capital they had brought to the receiving society. Working for 'a family of a former Italian ambassador', for example, meant that the family had 'all the right contacts', as Spomenka described in her interview. She and her husband who were both medical doctors were able to obtain information about diploma recognition, and gradually return to their professions.

Although not all the women I met developed supportive or friendly relationships with their employers, this type of work provided many of them with valuable initial contacts with Italians. In many cases these hierarchical, non-supportive ties gradually developed into supportive ones. Wellman (1981: 181) suggests that non-egalitarian and non-reciprocal social ties can be significant because non-supportive ties often provide access to other, potentially supportive relationships. For many women in this study, the contacts with Italian families for whom they worked developed into closer relationships not only with their employers, but also with their relatives and friends.

Contacts with Italian employer families were also central to the process of *getting inside* and getting a feeling 'of place'. These types of bridging links and networks not only channel information and provide access to resources, but also *interpret* information and articulate meaning. In this sense they serve as a *dictionary* to local urban settings, as well as the wider society and culture. For women who were in Rome to establish a new home these contacts were invaluable sources of information and support.

Two-way communication between the women in my study and citizens of Rome occurred because of the efforts of these women and their strategies to achieve such communication. This type of communication was possible because there were many locals (Italians) who were willing to engage with individual people and to approach them as 'a stranger in need'. Openness and engagement characterizing these contacts go beyond stereotypes, biases and labels constructed about specific groups defined by their ethnicity, culture or type of migration. The establishment of these contacts was facilitated by demographic and other characteristics of the women in my study making them a 'tolerable' if not a 'desirable' Other.

Concluding Remarks

In this chapter I have explored the role of paid domestic work in the lives of refugee women who came to settle in Rome. I was particularly interested in examining how in a specific policy context paid domestic work might play a critical role in the process of adjustment and settlement of these women. Not only does the work offer a modest wage and other material advantages (e.g. food and shelter), but it often provides more subtle but not less important forms of support in settlement. The personalized character of contacts between employers and employees is indeed one of the main sources of tension for those doing paid domestic work, as many researchers have noted. However, the very same contacts are often central to how these women re-activate their human capital and move on with their lives because they provide access to information, enhance the development of contacts and links with local people and the dominant society, and offer more tailor-made forms of support. These latter forms of support are paramount for tackling problems of (in) equality and inclusion in receiving societies and are missing from organized forms of assistance and provision for refugees and other newcomers.

It is important to examine and challenge the imposing social structures that underpin displacement and domestic work. Such endeavours provide important information about their scope, character and wider social consequences, as well as contribute to improving legal and other conditions for refugee women in receiving societies. It is equally important, however, to explore the women's agency in specific contexts. This can provide an understanding of how refugee women navigate through these systems, how they experience them, what meaning they attach to these experiences, and how they negotiate elements of loss and gain associated with processes of displacement and emplacement. This can help us develop a more nuanced understanding and analysis of empowerment and disempowerment.

Chapter 4
Care Workers and Welfare: Foreign Migrant Women in Italy[1]

Laura Stefanelli

Introduction

Over the last 30 years in Southern Europe, and in Italy in particular, foreign domestic migrant care workers have been replacing Italian internal migrants. The domestic workers' issue has evolved from one of class to one of ethnicity and nationality and become a structural and stable part of the gendered division of reproductive labour in many European welfare states. If welfare states are defined as 'institutions designed to ensure the commodification of labour thereby freeing workers from the discipline of the labour market' (Jenson and Sineau 2001: 6), then these welfare states have succeeded in freeing their male and female workers by purchasing the labour of migrant women to fill the traditional feminine role in domestic space.

In this chapter, my analysis of domestic work focusses on the nexus of care, gender and migration regimes (Lutz 2008a) to explain the living and working conditions of domestic workers in Italy and to examine how recent social, economic and political transformations have contributed to the expansion of care performed by women migrants. Selecting Italy as a case study among the Southern European countries allows me to demonstrate the interrelationship of the labour market, social welfare and the (im)migration model of entry. I argue that working in the care sector is a first step toward a higher paying occupation for many migrant women. I use an ethnographic approach to identify the reasons for migration and to understand the 'care chains'[2] that are established in leaving one's country.

Since the 1970s, and especially since the late 1990s, migration has become increasingly feminized. As well, in Italy, women's labour force participation has

1 I would like to thank Dominique Caouette and Deena White for their invaluable comments on this chapter, which is part of a thesis conducted at the University of Montreal; and the editors of this volume for the remarks and review of this chapter. I express my gratitude to Matthias, Carlo and Lorenzo for their inspiration, joy of life and for providing an example of how to care for an aunt from afar.

2 Hochschild (2000: 141) defines a 'global care chain' as 'a series of personal links between people across the globe based on the paid or unpaid work of caring', where each care worker depends for care work on another.

increased, the population is aging, and the lack of welfare social services for dependent persons has created a crisis (Caponio 2008, Castagnone et al. 2007, de Filippo and Pugliese 2000, Degiuli 2007, Ferrera 1996). In this chapter, I argue that women immigrate for domestic and care work using either legal or illegal entry because it provides the first opportunity to be incorporated into the labour market and a chance for a work permit and a legal status. These contemporary flows of migrant women may lead to the emergence of a 'service caste' (Anderson 2000) in the host societies.

The supply and demand for low skilled jobs is affected by several characteristics of contemporary Southern Europe, including the newness of in-migration, the heterogeneity of immigration flows, the international division of reproductive labour, the structure of local labour markets and the processes by which migrants are inserted into them, the informal economy, the migratory projects of migrants, the inequalities of gendered relations and the enforcement of state immigration control policies through quotas (Lutz 2008a, Nakano Glenn 1992, Ribas Mateos 2000, Colombo and Sciortino 2004, Colombo 2007, Parreñas 2008b). These characteristics reinforce gendered and ethnicized labour market niches, particularly for unskilled workers.

The phenomenon of female caregivers, who care for non-dependent adults, has not changed, but the social characteristics of women who migrate for this work are different. Today, migrant women who do care work may still move for family reunion, or may leave kin and children behind. However, many women have more education from their countries of origin than in the past (Glick Schiller et al. 1999, Pessar and Mahler 2003, Hondagneu-Sotelo 2001, Russell and Zontini 2000, Ehrenreich and Hochschild 2003, Korac in this volume).

Economics alone does not determine care workers' migration to another country. Pull and push factors are not pertinent for understanding the complex and dynamic phenomenon of care and domestic work. Other issues need to be taken into account, such as women's agency in determining their migratory projects and objectives. Recognizing the significance of women's agency draws attention to women's empowerment and the experiences of their families in the countries of origin.[3] The agent-centred perspective adopted in this study addresses the issue of why women 'opt' to work as domestic workers/caregivers. This agent-centred approach goes beyond the passive victimization of women presented in certain feminist literature that tends to speak for women and considers them trapped by the unequal distribution of resources and 'global economic forces' (Sassen 1998, 2000). These approaches argue that migrant women are solely economic actors in need of money. However, migrant women also take risks (e.g. by leaving a violent husband or a militarized country) and act on their own volition in leaving their homeland. This chapter considers the decision to migrate

3 Postcolonial scholars are committed to '[M]ake visible agentic capacities of formerly non-agentic non-subjects and underline their ability to resist/subvert Western hegemony' (Bilge 2010: 18). See Collins (1990) and Bilge (2008: 100–133, 2010: 9–28).

from an individual point of view without '[O]ver-romanticiz[ing] ... those who might be seizing such opportunities to escape poverty, [abuse], violence or to see the world', (Anderson 2006: 8).

I locate this research in two bodies of literature. Recognizing that political, social, and economic structures influence individual decision-making, I draw upon the literature concerning the Southern European welfare state and immigration model (Caponio 2008, Castagnone et al. 2007, de Filippo and Pugliese 2000, Degiuli 2007, Ferrera 1996). As well, transnationalism brings gender back into immigration studies by examining women's work in the domestic and care sector as part of the 'international transfer of reproductive work among women' (Parreñas 2000: 577).

The Southern Immigration System and the Labour Market

Each year, countries such as Italy and Spain formulate immigration policy through quotas that accommodate demands for cheap labour in the catering, tourism, building services, care and domestic service industry. The underground economy is already well-rooted within Southern Europe and has been strengthened by the quota system which facilitates the movement of undeclared workers from the underground economy into the official sectors of the Italian economy, as I explain below. The entry of migrant workers consolidates ethnic niches in the labour market where migrant workers are hired as 'inexpensive and flexible labour in marginal areas of employment', (Chell 2000: 105). This process has nurtured the growing segmentation and fragmentation of the Italian labour market. New migrants often accept poor working conditions, and women especially, end up as live-in caregivers and domestic workers.

The 'domestic help' phenomenon is related to important changes in the southern welfare system, typically sustained by conservative familial practices. Purchasing foreign labour force involves a de-familialization of welfare services, a form of externalization of domestic tasks achieved by the employment of migrant women.[4] Rather than the state taking responsibility for aiding families in the social reproduction of everyday life, market-based strategies have led to an international division of care work that places the burden of care work on migrant women workers. The term 'social reproduction' is used by feminist scholars to refer to the set of activities and relationships involved in maintaining people both on a daily and intergenerational basis: '[R]eproductive labour includes activities such as purchasing household goods, preparing and serving food, laundering and repairing

4 De-familialization as per Esping-Andersen (1990) is a key concept in understanding the central role of households in the new post-industrial economy. The de-familialization process refers to policies that lessen an individual's reliance on the family and maximize the individual's command of economic resources independent of familial and conjugal obligations (Esping-Andersen 1999).

clothing, maintaining furnishing and appliances, socializing children, providing care and emotional support for adults and maintaining kin and community ties' (Nakano Glenn 1992: 1).

Transnational Care Work

The 'globalization of care' (Parreñas 2008b) that is exemplified by the global migration of women to fill the demand for care work raises questions concerning gender relations, the status of local and migrant women in the labour market and the construction of gender in migrant women's labour. Nonetheless, the progressive tertiarization of care work employment, the high cost of maintaining a welfare state and insufficient social services for dependents result in a market-based[5] recruitment of migrant workers to fill the 'care deficit'. To meet the need for care work, migrant women feed, nurture and care, in other words, they carry out the work of reproduction, outside their own homes. Paradoxically, this arrangement reaffirms the notion that women's domesticity belongs in the home. Migrant women do this work in informal and formal labour markets, as documented and undocumented workers, in the private and public spheres.

Migration to domestic work may represent a significant movement of ethnic minority women, constituting a *transnational transfer* of reproductive labour from origin to destination countries. The segmented and ethno-stratified market for low-skill and care jobs contributes to wage inequalities, power differences, ethno-cultural preferences, subordination, 'occupational stigma' (Ozyegin and Hondagneu-Sotelo 2008) and social marginalization, which involves the invisibilization of women, both in the work sphere and in the socio-economic sphere. Most domestic workers are employed without a regular labour contract. In Southern Europe, this emerging 'service caste' is characterized by preferences for migrant workers from Central and South America in Spain, Portugal and Italy, and from Eastern European in Italy and Greece.

As my research demonstrates, the 'international transfer of caretaking' (Parreñas 2000, 2008, Lutz 2008a) has consequences in both the destination societies and in the countries of origin. In the latter, the departure of adult females results in better social and economic conditions for their families left at home, whereby a care chain to care for dependents is established. According to the literature on remittances, regular money transfers are important economic resources for families left behind and contribute significantly to the GDP of many sending countries. Families back home have the possibility of accessing higher education for their children, building larger homes and upgrading social and well-being levels. However, the tasks of looking after children, the sick or elderly relatives seems to be passed on to other mainly *female* family members (grandmothers, aunts, adult daughters) or by hiring women who may need to migrate internally

5 Market-based strategies and bargaining are used to buy migrants' work for households (Williams and Gavanas 2008).

within the country of origin to perform this care work.[6] In a few cases, men also take on the responsibility of caring.

Located 'in the middle', between two countries, migrant women working as caregivers/domestic workers are agents of 'Transnational Welfare' (Piperno, Tognetti and Bordogna 2012). This new form of producing well-being is framed simultaneously by social, cultural, and economic factors in both countries. Transnational migration recognizes more than one *modus vivendi* in the migration project and goes beyond identifying the predominant form as unidirectional and consisting of a one-time change in residence from one country to another. Rather, transnational migration suggests another way of thinking about migration, which involves migrants encompassing a number of different residences or geographical spaces (Pries 1999). This is particularly true for the growing movement of women into domestic work, a migration project which is neither one-time nor unidirectional. Transnational welfare workers maintain multiple homes, defined not by nation-states or geography, but by social relations with siblings and other family members located in different places. This contemporary form of migration can be considered a 'third way' that may need to be added alongside the classical forms of assimilation or pluralism experienced in continental Europe (Glick-Schiller et al. 1999, Nakano Glenn 1992, Pessar and Mahler 2003, Pries 1999). Migrant women develop forms of 'reterritorialized homes' through their social relations, development work and social positioning, which enable well-being in their households at home and abroad. These women contribute to socio-economic well-being and growth in the destination country as well as back home, redefining the nature and the scope of welfare. Transnational welfare is here understood as a conceptual vehicle that requires the articulation of space, time, and well-being, beyond the national boundaries of nation-states. It requires a conceptual re-engagement with women's multiple tasks that are accomplished simultaneously, such as development of the home community, well-being, personal empowerment, family responsibility, keeping home and providing care.

The chapter is divided into three main parts: the first tackles the Italian case study, outlining Italian legislation about immigration, the field of research, the methodology and the interviews. The second part analyses the interviews, examining the social consequences of the migration; the support networks; women as active subjects; patterns of employment; and lastly the future plans of women migrants. The third part proposes a mobility model for the migration of workers in the domestic/care work sector.

6 Parreñas argues: '[In] the [global] international transfer of reproductive labour, women do not subvert but instead pass on their reproductive labour responsibilities to women less privileged. Consequently, the burden of reproductive labour poses challenges to, instead of supporting, solidarity between women' (2008b: 17).

Case Study: Italy

The choice of Italy as case study is justified for two reasons. On the one hand, Italy combines the 'mercantile logic' of a quota system, the (in)effectiveness of the Southern welfare state model, and the flexibility of a labour market, with a high proportion of undocumented immigrants working in an underground economy (Ferrera 1996). The quota system reserves special entry slots for seasonal workers, as well as care and domestic assistants, as was the case for the ad hoc legalizations for non-EU domestic and care assistants in 2009, 2010 and more recently in October 2012.[7] This ad hoc legalization concerns a precise category of workers, whose employers' families bear the costs of their legalization. If this migratory system dies away, Italian households requiring live-in workers and the Italian welfare state reliant on the ethnicization of care work will be seriously compromised (Colombo 2009). On the other hand, Italy is an example of a 'recent immigration country' in Southern Europe that receives large, heterogeneous, and rapid flows of (im)migration. As a result, the large availability of foreign caregivers reinforces the Italian welfare system for assistance and care of elderly people.

Institutionalizing care work in Italy also has two aspects: i) as a public and local responsibility and ii) as a private and familial burden. On the one hand, in some cases, support for care work consists of 'cash for care' transfers, which subsidize daily living expenses and pay for essential medications for the elderly. In other cases, the cash for care payments are used to supplement the minimal incomes of the elderly, rather than to pay caregivers. Some who receive the bonus cash for care payment, use it to pay 'off the book' caregivers or helpers. On the other hand, personalized family-based care is endorsed as opposed to commercialized, hospitalized, institution-based care. Welfare states are increasingly pushing care work out of hospitals and institutions and handing it back to families. The 'family is expected to substitute for welfare measures and services' (Trifiletti 2009: 2), and particularly, the women within these families. In the last 15 years, Italy has turned the responsibility for social assistance over to the regions[8] and has quickly (but unevenly) developed social policies at the local level to help families in caring tasks in general. Increasingly, Italian families are reluctant or unable to institutionalize elderly or dependent people, either for moral or economic reasons. In this new framework, care work relies on the employment of migrant women as a systemic solution for the publically provided care deficit. To provide individualized care for

7 At least three factors have contributed to an 'unsuccessful' ad hoc legalization. First, incorrect estimates by the Home Office about the number of workers holding a legal residence permit, but employed without regular contracts; and the number of illegal workers. Second, the costs of regularization were high and burdensome for many families. Third, the effects of the last European expansion to include Romania and Bulgaria in 2007 affected the status of new European citizens of those countries who were employed in the domestic sector.

8 For more details on Bill nr. 328/200 see Italian Parliament 2000.

their elders, families hire foreign live-in eldercare assistants who will provide care in a more familiar environment, in which it is believed that elderly people are more comfortable. The cost of employing migrant workers is relatively low – wages vary greatly, from 1200 Euro per month for a live-in worker with a residence permit to 750–450 Euro per month for a live-in worker who has just entered the country illegally.[9] Thus the institutionalization of elderly or disabled people in hospitals or care homes is, if possible, postponed or avoided.

Italian Legislation

Italian immigration legislation has always been porous, since the first attempt of Law 39/1990 (The Martelli Law), the main concern of which has been to define the migrant as an asylum seeker or refugee; establish control through quotas that specify the number of migrants allowed to enter the country; and provide frequent amnesties, whereby irregular immigrants are regularized. The main endeavour of regulating immigration was established by Law 40/1998 (the Turco-Napolitano Law). Law 40/1998 – created by the centre-left coalition when it was in power from 1996 to 2001 – allowed a generous part of the quota to be allocated for immigrants[10] to enter and 'seek work', guaranteed by a sponsor (a person who could be foreign, or an organization) who undertook to support the immigrant for a year, until he or she was employed or repatriated. Each Italian region, province and city is assigned a specific quota in each category of labour. If some slots are not used – a rare occurrence – the Welfare and Labour Ministry (*Ministero del Lavoro e del Welfare*) may redistribute them.[11] The new centre-right government, elected in 2001, modified the way of subdividing the overall slots by regions, provinces and cities and increased the number of seasonal slots.

A significant attempt to establish a domestic workers' employment profile occurred after the last mass amnesty in 2002[12] (Law 189/2002 art. 33, the Bossi-Fini Law), which was the largest amnesty of foreign migrants ever seen

9 For more details consult (National Collective Labour Contract – Contratto Collettivo Nazionale di Lavoro Colf e Badanti [CCNL] 2013). It has been effective since 1 July 2013.

10 The slots are available for specific national groups, who have contracted bilateral agreement and/or partnership between their country of departure and Italy. As for example 1,000 out of 80,000 slots are reserved for Libyan citizens in accordance with the partnership between Libya and Italy signed on the 30th of August 2008. For details on Law no. 2699 see Ministero del Lavoro, della Salute e delle Politiche Sociali 2010 and Ministero del Lavoro e delle Politiche Sociali (Circolare 19 aprile 2010, n. 14) 2010.

11 To give an example, at the end of December 2008, the Work Department re-allocated 8,436 slots of the quotas from the previous year. The unused slots represented 5 per cent of the total number of immigrants to be admitted and were distributed to domestic and care workers.

12 There has not been another amnesty in Italy since 2002. In 2005, the last amnesty occurred in EU, specifically in Spain. After that, the European Parliament branded amnesty as an 'immigration tool of managing the income and outcome of flows'.

in Europe, attracting 700,000 applicants (Reyneri 2004). Following the 2002 amnesty, legislation aimed at establishing stronger restrictions on the legal entry of economic immigrants by introducing more restrictive quotas than those established by Law 40/1998. The number of long-term permits – theoretically attainable after four years of staying in Italy – was curtailed. As well, the definition of domestic work in relation to the earlier vague and unclear definition that had been in effect was improved and strengthened.[13] This definition became part of the framework of the National Collective Labour Contract (CCNL) The first legal definition for a care worker was introduced within the finance bill in 2005 (Law 30 December 2004, no. 311 'Finance Bill for the year 2005').[14] On the 1st of March 2007, the new National Collective Labour Contract for domestic work defined care workers as 'home care assistants'. In June 2010, the International Labour Organization (ILO) approved the international convention on decent work and rights for domestic workers, entitled '*Domestic workers across the world: global and regional statistics and the extent of legal protection*'. The Italian government ratified it on the 22nd of January 2013 as the first country to have signed the ILO Convention[15] (ILO 2013a) According to the ILO Italy is ranked as the third-largest European country to employ foreign domestic workers (429,500), after Spain and France, with 747,000 and 589,900 workers, respectively.

The Research Field Site

Turin and Bolzano exemplify the large Italian metropolitan cities (Turin) and small cities (Bolzano) with high concentrations of women migrants employed as domestics, caregivers and housekeepers. To shed some light on the dimensions of their work: foreigners living in Turin at the end of 2011 numbered 124,172 (13.6 per cent) out of a total population of 906,874. Female foreigners come mostly from Morocco, Peru, China, Albania, Moldavia and Philippines.[16] In Bolzano,

13 The legal definition of 'care worker' is 'anyone who is a non-EU citizen and works as an employee in a family in which there are dependent people or members affected by pathological ills'. Author's translation from the original: '[chiunque sia] occupato alle proprie dipendenze personali di origine extracomunitaria adibendolo ad attività di assistenza a componenti della famiglia affetti da patologie o handicap che ne limitano l'autosufficienza' For more information on Law 189, art. 33 (30 July 2002) see Italian Parliament 2002.

14 The financial bill specifies '[care workers are] employees for non-autonomous people in their daily reproductive labour'. Author's translation from the original: 'addetti alla propria assistenza personale nei casi di non autosufficienza nel compimento degli atti della vita quotidiana' For more information on Law 311 (30 December 2004, see Italian Parliament 2004.

15 The ILO Convention became law on the 5th of September 2013 (De Nesi 2013).

16 Data elaborate by Divisione Servizi Civici, Ufficio di Statistica-Osservatorio Socio-economico (ILO 2013). The ILO Convention became law on the 5th of September 2013 (De Nesi 2013). See also: (Divisione Servizi Civili, Ufficio di Statistica -Osservatorio Socio-economico e redazione editoriale n.d.).

at the end of 2011 the foreign population was 44,362 (8.7 per cent) out of a total population of 105,774. Sixty-three per cent of the total foreign inhabitants (44,362) are women from the Ukraine, Albania, Morocco, Russia and Moldavia, who arrived thanks to family-reunification. And 16.5 per cent are of Pakistani or South East Asian origin.[17]

In particular, Turin exemplifies the decentralization of public, social and immigration services, such as the renewal of residence permits, and provides services through a mix of voluntary associations and the communitarian sector. Turin has a leftist tradition that differentiates its local policies in three ways. First, a 'specificity approach' towards immigrants reveals a *reactive* policy style, i.e. immigrants have to be dealt with through *specific* policies and *ad hoc* institutions, as was the case for mainstream Italian social policy at least until the 2000s. Second, the government has adopted a 'mixed' approach to welfare encouraging the involvement of voluntary organizations and local institutions in delivering social services, particularly to immigrants, and the development of specific patterns of social integration. Third, communitarian organizations and the voluntary sector are polarized between leftist-feminist organizations such as the intercultural centre *Alma Terra* and the Catholic Church that sponsors organizations such as *Caritas Femminile*.[18] In Turin, local social policy requires a 'willingness of negotiating solutions directly with all the other public and private actors already active around specific issues' (Caponio 2000: 81). Furthermore, as a big European municipality, Turin participated in European and international projects designed to facilitate the accommodation of cultural difference that have led to common strategies for immigrants' recognition and participation.[19]

The city of Bolzano is a Northeastern Italian town on the border with Austria in the autonomous Province of Bolzano with specific criteria for accessing permanent residency. The municipality acquired its autonomy in 1948, when Italy became a Republic, after the defeat of the Monarchy and the exile of the Savoia royal family in the Second World War. The Province of Bolzano has been declared

17 A significant percentage (43 per cent) of the total foreign residents in Bolzano come from Germany. This is due to the Germanophone origin of the city (see a short explication below in the section) (ASTAT – Ufficio Statistico Provincia Autonoma di Bolzano 2012).

18 For more references see Caponio et al. 2000, Caponio 2009 and Trifiletti 2009.

19 In the mid-1990s in the context of international developments, Turin participated in projects such as the UNESCO project: Multicultural Policies and Modes of Citizenship in European Cities (MPMC), promoted in 1996. Eleven cities took part: Amsterdam, Antwerp, Athens, Barcelona, Birmingham, Brussels, Cologne, Liege, Marseille, Milan, Oeiras (Lisbon), Paris, Rome, Stockholm, Tel Aviv, Turin and Zurich. In 2001, thanks to a contribution of the Italian government and a number of European foundations, the International Research Network on Interethnic Politics and Migration launched the Ethnobarometer programme which reviewed local policies in managing ethnic minorities in nine European cities: Lisbon, Rotterdam, Stockholm, Brussels, Manchester, Mannheim, Toulouse, Murcia and Turin. For more references see http://www.unesco.org/most/p97.htm and http://ethnobarometer.org/ (accessed on 14 April 2010).

autonomous because of its historical status as a territory of the former Austro-Hungarian Empire and its proximity to German-speaking countries. Italy obtained the Northern Provinces of Bolzano and Trento, as well the region of Friuli-Venezia Giulia (in the East), from the former Austro-Hungarian Empire in 1919, after the First World War. In 1972, the Province of Bolzano acquired more legislative power in the fields of health, immigration, education, schools, labour, tourism, transports, road networks, construction, handicraft, fishing and agriculture.

After completing interviews in Turin and Bolzano, and by comparing these two diverse management systems, this chapter sheds light on a topic that has received little attention so far. On the one hand, the leftist and metropolitan city of Turin has a long tradition in welcoming flows of immigrants and providing services to new arrivals, as expressed in its mixed approach (leftist and Catholic organizations) to providing services. On the other hand, Bolzano is a small and autonomous town that 'selects' its foreign migrant workers, supplies them directly with integration tools, such as linguistic training courses (German and Italian are taught), primary education for illiterate adults, and financial support as part of a 'social citizenship' package. The unique and respective management systems of these cities inform my selection of these sites for this research.

Methodology and Interviewees

Six in-depth interviews with migrant women were completed in December 2009. Respondents were selected on the basis of snow-ball references. They were mothers with high levels of education (which is consistent with the last wave of migrant workers, who arrived in the last half of the 1990s and the beginning of the 2000s), and are employed in unskilled jobs despite their qualifications. All the interviewees were married, three out of six to Italian men, and all are between the ages of 30 and 65. They all arrived with regular documents. Four of the six arrived between 1999 and 2009, following the economic crisis in Europe, the accession of several Eastern European countries into the European Union and short stays in other European countries. Two interviewees came to Italy in 1985, through the family-reunification programme and in 1994, after a mass migration of Albanians toward South and North Italy. All but one of the interviewees now lives with her children or adult sons or daughters in Italy. Some of the children were born in Italy and in one case an unaccompanied boy joined his mother through family reunification. Another woman lives with her adult son in Italy, but he was born in the country of origin.

All my interviewees acquired postsecondary training in their countries of origin and were employed in an industrial factory, in the service sector, in catering, or in an educational institute before their departures for Italy. The interviews with these migrant women reveal that all of them worked as live-in or live-out domestic workers when they first arrived in Italy (or in the first country of arrival, as is the case of one interviewee who moved from Spain to Italy). Two out of six are still domestic workers, but they are working for a pool of families on an hourly basis in

Turin. One interviewee lives with the disabled person for whom she cares. Three of six interviewees gained further educational training in Italy, which allowed them to leave domestic work and work for the migrant women's association *Donne-Nissà* in Bolzano as a secretary, accountant and educator, respectively.

All the interviewees discussed their intentions to ultimately change fields (but also the difficulties therein) and work either in the social services for migrants, as cultural mediators, or in the health sector, as licensed practical nurses.[20] Some of the migrant women argued that being engaged in the labour market in a foreign country is a sign of 'knowing how to go on', knowing how to cope with the difficulties of entering a segmented labour market, not being passive actors, and being responsible for the well-being of their families abroad and/or at their destinations. Some of the women interviewed have achieved some social mobility thanks to improving their knowledge of Italian and taking advantage of on-going training. They have been able to leave the domestic/care sector for employment as an officer, cultural mediator and nurse. In fact, enhancing their qualifications and language fluency allowed the women to upgrade their social status and move beyond the domestic/care sector.

Before turning to the interviews themselves, I will briefly introduce the six interviewees. *Doina* is a Romanian 37-year-old live-in domestic worker. She arrived in Sicily in November 2009, after having spent two years and three months in Madrid as a live-in care worker. She left Romania on her own, leaving her adult son and daughter with her husband. She has two sisters, one who lives in Italy and one in Spain. This interview was conducted in Spanish, since her knowledge of Italian was limited.

Lidia is 34 years old and comes from Poland. She came to Italy for the first time 10 years ago and before getting married to an Italian man, she travelled back and forth between Poland and Italy. She settled in Turin seven years ago and has a five-year-old child. For two years, she worked as a cleaner for different families. Previously, she worked as a live-in domestic worker, waitress and babysitter for another Italian employer.

Ileana who is 30 years old arrived in 2002, after Italy, along with other European countries, abolished the requirement for a valid visa for Romanian citizens to enter Italy. She left Romania alone, leaving her young child with her parents. After a year and a half, she obtained a valid resident permit, and through a family reunification policy, she was allowed to bring her child to Italy. She married an Italian man and they have two young children. After her third pregnancy in 2007, she began working as a cleaner and domestic worker for a pool of families.

Irene is 61 years old and left Argentina, her country of origin, after the last economic and financial crisis there in 2001. She left her third adult son

20 In Italy, migrant women are employed as Operatrice Socio Sanitario (OSS), after having completed 1,000 hours of training organized by the regions with municipalities. The training includes studies in social and health systems, in order to professionalize domestic assistants and authorize them to work in hospitals, retirement and nursing homes.

in Argentina and joined her husband and her two adult sons, who migrated to Tuscany before 2001. She was first employed as a live-out domestic worker for a family. In 2003, she and her family moved to Bolzano where she was able to obtain additional education that allowed her to look for a job similar to her previous employment as a teacher in Argentina. Nowadays, she works as a secretary at *Donne-Nissà,* the association for foreign migrant women.

Bahija is a 45-year-old Moroccan woman who has been living in Italy for 24 years. She came to Italy through the family-reunification programme, after her husband left Morocco at the end of the 1970s. She has three children, two of whom were born in Italy. Bahija experienced poverty at the very beginning of her migratory project and had no place to live. She worked as a cleaner and this work allowed her to learn Italian and subsequently enrol in secondary school. Now she works as a counsellor for *Nissà-Care* at the *Donne Nissà* migrant women's association and studies for her secondary school degree.

Fatbardha is 60 years old and originally from Albania. She has been living in Italy for 15 years. After getting married to an Albanian man and having three sons, all of them born in Albania, she left Albania on her own. Later, her husband and sons joined her in Italy. She was employed initially as a care worker and became a cultural mediator after gaining further training and language classes. Now she is responsible for the kindergarten *Mafalda*, an intercultural kindergarten for native and foreign children from 0 to 6 years of age, organized by the *Donne-Nissà* association. As well, Fatbardha is a counsellor for the *Nissà-Care*[21] service help desk, which offers assistance and counselling to care workers who are mostly migrant and newly arrived women.

Analysis of the Interviews

The personal narratives of women interviewed for this research illustrate how the experiences of migrant women are influenced by their positions at the intersection of multiple identity categories including gender, migrant status and labour market status all of which are interpolated with prejudices and stereotypes concerning

21 Association Donne-Nissà is a non-profit organization founded in 1995 and since that time it has led projects financed through the public funding of the Autonomous Province of Bolzano, the Social Services and Health Office, the Equal-Opportunity Unit, the Department of Labour and Social Security and the European Social Found of the European Commission. The association was created by and for foreign women living in the province of Bolzano. Besides the organization of cultural events, the association offers several services, from helping foreign women find work to language training. It has organized a kindergarten, called Mafalda, for children of migrant and Italian women, to assist with bridging and accommodating ethnic diversity. Since 2006 the association has created the Nissà-care consulting counter in order to meet offers of and demands for care and domestic workers.

ethnic minorities.[22] As occurs in other European countries, the Italian labour market is mostly segmented on the basis of ethnicity (Reyneri 2004, Ozyegin and Hondagneu-Sotelo 2008). Foreign workers are employed in low-skilled labour: construction, seasonal work, domestic care, agriculture, tourism and manufacturing. Even though the foreign labour force is better educated than in the past, their degrees, qualifications, experience and skills are not acknowledged and/or not sufficiently valued in Italy.

The sections that follow examine: 1) the social consequences of the migration process; 2) the support networks that facilitate migrants' entry into the local job market; 3) women as active subjects and 4) the patterns of employment as a live-in or live-out worker and 5) future plans.

1) The Social Consequences of the Migration Process

Four of the women decided to migrate alone, leaving their children in the care of their parents and/or spouses or other relatives. In the countries of origin these relatives balance the 'welfare and the well-being' of the kin and children left behind. The labour of care, nurturing and loving is mainly in female hands, especially those of grandmothers, and in rare cases, care tasks are undertaken by husbands. Some migrant women benefitted from Italy's family reunification policies. As the experiences of Ileana and Irene demonstrate:

> I came to Turin alone with a friend of mine in 2002. I had known a man from Turin and I decided to come here because it's closer to my country, it's better to arrive there so when I want to go to Romania, it's nearer. I left my first child with my parents and I didn't see him for a year and a half. He joined me thanks to the family re-union policy in 2003. (Ileana, 30, Romanian)

> I joined my husband and two out of three sons in Italy in 2001, after the last economic, financial and political crisis in Argentina. The third son has always stayed in Argentina, trying to 'resist' the crisis. (Irene, 61, Argentinean)

In the case of Doina, after more than two years of separation, she hopes her husband will join her soon. She describes it like this:

> I have lived alone in Madrid for two years and three months. I came to Italy because I have a sister who works as domestic worker. I might stay alone until March 2010 and then my husband might join me … I have a son of twenty and a daughter of seventeen who have stayed with my husband in Romania. (Doina, 37, Romanian)

22 McCall claims that complexity is managed 'from the analysis of a social location at the intersection of single dimensions of multiple categories, rather than at the intersection of the full range of dimensions of a full range of categories' (McCall 2005: 1781).

The international division of reproductive labour[23] generates care chains, wherein female relations such as grandmothers, adult daughters, sisters and aunts become responsible for childcare and household chores. In other cases, migrant mothers pass down their care responsibilities to less privileged migrant women. The care chain not only frees men of household work in the country of origin but also frees female employers in the destination countries. It has the potential to create strains between women in households in the homeland. Based on my interviews, Ileana and Doina, moved alone and left their children and husbands behind. The childcare and care of other needy family members was taken up by female relatives of the older generation, including grandmothers and other relatives. While the care deficit is seen to at the migrants' destinations, such as in Italy, a 'welfare' system based on grandparents and other relatives is created in the countries of origin to address the care deficit in that site. This arrangement forms new meanings of motherhood 'from afar'; it expands mothering to encompass breadwinning 'from afar' (Hondagneu-Sotelo and Avila 1997 and Parreñas 2008b). Rachel Parreñas argues that '[In] the [global] international transfer of reproductive labour, women do not subvert but instead pass on their reproductive labour responsibilities to women less privileged. Consequently, the burden of reproductive labour poses challenges to, instead of supporting, solidarity between women' (2008b: 17). In this chapter, I illustrate just one case of a practice of 'motherhood from afar', since my other empirical findings were based on mothers who raised their children in Italy, or joined adult sons in the destination country or reunited with children under the age of 18 thanks to family reunification policies.

The decision to migrate depends on socio-economic opportunities and access to the destination countries. The spatial distance, the criteria for obtaining a national visa and residence permit, and human smuggling operations influence the accessibility of each destination. The greater the spatial distance and the more restrictive the entry policies, the more important the infrastructure of care in the country of origin that facilitates illegal immigration becomes.

2) The Support Networks that Facilitate Migrants' Entry to the Local Job Market

Kin and friendship relationships are 'support networks' for hosting and orienting new migrants. In the field of domestic work, job offers are circulated by 'word of mouth' among migrants who share information with friends and relatives about families who are interested in hiring domestic workers. While some interviewees experienced an initial deskilling through migration, they generally found it easier to work as domestics as a first step prior to entering the Italian job market. As my case studies indicate, some migrant women have succeeded in leaving the

23 Reproductive labour refers to the work of raising and caring for children as well as to the housework, care giving and nurturing required to sustain the lives of other families. In care work literature, the '3Cs', cooking, caring and cleaning, are synonymous with the label *reproductive labour*.

domestic sector to work for a migrant women's association. Three of the six women work for the *Donne-Nissà* association and one might consider their trajectories as 'success stories', since they have left the domestic sector. This is the case for Irene, who takes advantage of the professional expertise acquired in her country of origin as secretary of the association. This is also the case for Fatbardha, a 60-year-old woman from Albania who was a live-in domestic worker when she first arrived in Italy and now works as a counsellor and manager of the kindergarten *Mafalda*. Bahija, a 45-year-old woman from Morocco, who is employed as an accountant and counsellor on care work at the *Nissà-Care* counter at the *Donne-Nissà* association, also was a domestic worker upon arrival in Italy.

3) Women as Active Subjects

An agent-centred approach towards domestic work considers women as capable of acting in their own self-interest, rather than being mere victims of global inequalities and objects of commodification. Such an approach underlines that the migration process has multiple features: not only does migration function to fulfil an economic strategy in order to maximize resources and minimize the time spent abroad, but it may also encompass 'instrumental' jobs (i.e. that are useful and are followed by better jobs) that migrants may take upon arrival, at the beginning of their insertion into the labour market. An agent-centred approach regards migration as a conscious choice that may be characterized by empowerment and personal achievement.[24] Emphasizing migrant women's agency draws attention to 'the social, political and economic power structures at the national and international level, which limit and influence [women's] actions' (Zontini 2004: 1114). As Irene explains:

> My immigration pattern has been an adventure and a personal 'challenge' and I lived it with optimism. Before immigrating, I had never been outside Argentina and when I left, I took four planes by myself! And this has grown me up. At that time, I was 52 and I was only permitted 35 kilograms of baggage: what do I carry in merely 35 kilograms of my 52 years of life? I did not carry any photos, because it hurt me too much; actually I did not carry too much stuff. The first time I was here, I was afraid of losing my identity, taking the bus and going outside alone. I did not know the habits and customs of here and I was afraid of speaking Italian, because for me it was like losing my identity. (Irene, 61, Argentinean)

24 The agent-centred approach underlines that the 'choice' of being caregivers is not always a constraint, but can represent an opportunity for self-reliance. However, one also has to recognize that not everyone who works in the domestic sector necessarily wishes to be incorporated into civil society as a 'domestic worker', due to the 'invisibility' of this work and the neglected rights related to it.

4) Patterns of Employment as a Live-in or Live-out Worker

Despite their success finding and keeping jobs, half of the interviewees, namely, Doina, Lidia and Ileana, are still working in the domestic sector, two as live-out domestics and one as a live-in. Some care workers either chose or are forced (by the birth of children, for instance) to move to other occupations, usually live-out or hourly-paid cleaners or domestic workers. For example, Doina, who works as a live-in domestic worker, recently arrived in Italy from Spain, where she was a live-in domestic worker for a family in Madrid. Irene, on the other hand, was a full-time live-out worker for a family in Tuscany where she settled after migrating from Argentina. Lidia and Ileana, decided to work for a pool of families, cultural associations, or restaurants. Often, workers who have multiple families as employers supplement their earnings from full-time jobs by taking on additional work during their free time. Lidia, for instance, was a cleaner in a cultural association but she worked additional hours as a babysitter and waitress in the bar and restaurant of the association. Ileana, alternately, had a five-hours-per-day work contract with a family employer but was working eight hours per day for the same family. For the additional hours she was paid 'off the books'. For women who remain in the domestic sector, the tendency is to move away from live-in work to work as an hourly-paid cleaner or domestic worker. This is the case for Lidia and Ileana, both married and with little children. They prefer to have multiple employers and to be hourly-paid cleaners and to pay their own social security contributions while working for several employers. Working as an hourly-paid cleaner is convenient because it offers more flexibility and manageable arrangements with regards to family, personal time and work balance. As Lidia and Ileana state:

> If I stay in Italy, I would like to quit domestic work (and find another job), but I would have problems reconciling working hours with the school life of my child. (For now), to be a cleaner is the best temporary solution (for me) in order to manage the work and family balance. (Lidia, 34, Polish)

> To be a cleaner allows me to balance the organization of my hours in regards to the family-work equilibrium (and the hours of the kindergarten). (Ileana, 30, Romanian)

As the women left live-in work for hourly-paid work, they had to deal with reconciling their work hours with the care of their own family and their children, as do all women who balance family and paid work. Thus, being an hourly paid domestic worker is a strategic way for these women to deal with the issues of balancing the care needs of their families with work outside the family. For Italian working women, substituting the reproductive labour of foreign women for their own labour, as new family needs develop, is their strategy for creating more time for themselves and their families.

5) Future Plans

My interviewees disclosed their intention to either change work or acquire additional training in order to work in other sectors, such as health services, social services for migrants, unions, Catholic associations such as *Caritas*, and voluntary associations. Working as a cultural mediator in the unions or in voluntary associations is an important achievement because the women feel that they act as a 'bridge' between different cultures; they are able to understand the problems of their fellow migrants and render them intelligible to Italian institutions, as is the case for Fatbardha and Bahija. One of the main concerns for migrant women who are legal residents in Italy and informally employed as domestic workers is having a regular labour contract that guarantees social assistance, social benefits and the right to a pension. As workers for a 'patchwork of families', Lidia and Ileana expressed concern that they do not hold a regular labour contract.

> I am taking evening courses organized by the Red Cross in order to join its Voluntary Medical corps. It takes six months. After that, I would like to get a degree as a licensed practical nurse. I would also like to continue with my studies and get a degree in accounting. (Ileana, 30, Romanian)

Lidia's desire to go back to Poland is strong and her professional expertise acquired in Italy will be an advantage in Poland, where she might have a better life. For the moment the choice to remain in Italy is a 'necessity' for her child and his future, rather than an opportunity for her to gain professional promotion. As she points out:

> The idea is to go back to Poland and change job because there I have a family network and I know better the 'milieu', with the professional expertise gained in Italy I would have a better life there ... Living here is necessary for the sake of my son. In Italy I [don't] see [a positive future], here [it seems to me that] there is work but not [money]. (Lidia, 34, Polish)

Here it is important to underline that being a care and domestic worker represents a *temporary choice* or a *strategic and functional decision* that allows migrant women to draw together migratory patterns that may otherwise have opposing goals. Some women express their intention to *climb the economic ladder* and find employment for which they are more qualified; others transform the domestic job from full-time, live-in work to a part-time activity. Still others hope for family reunification, while some plan to migrate to other Western countries or return to their countries of origin.

The Care Worker Mobility Model

Care worker migrants are typically, but not exclusively destined for the unskilled labour market. Countries such as Moldavia, Ukraine, and Russia, are currently a flourishing export base for (live-in) domestic workers, but the intensity and rapidity of the drain on care work at home may decline in the near future. The temporality of care work in the destination country means that care workers are likely to return to their countries of origin. As well, if the pattern that I have uncovered in Italy persists, then many women are only using care work as a step to a higher skilled form of employment and will move from domestic work to other occupations.

My interviews reveal that migrant women in the domestic work sector have specific working trajectories. The heterogeneity of immigrant flows and the articulation of economic and social life among migrants have produced new patterns of labour market insertion and rapid labour mobility out of care and domestic work. In most cases, women migrants consider the care and domestic sector as instrumental for achieving social mobility and better job opportunities. As soon as language requirements are met or further education is achieved, migrant women 'succeed' by leaving the domestic sector and obtaining employment in other sectors. Their departure creates openings for other newly-arrived women who are willing to do care and domestic work as their entry point into the labour market.

The ethnicization of domestic labour, which is already highly gendered influences the duration of the migratory project. Ethnic prejudices often reflect cultural stereotypes about minority women. For example, Eastern Europeans, mainly Romanians, Ukrainians, Moldavians and Polish, as well as Filipinas, Peruvians and Ecuadorian women are preferred as both live-in and live-out caregivers in relation to Moroccan women (Zontini 2004). Irene, a Latina, experienced this 'ethnic stratification' and discrimination:

> I was a cleaner, [but I was employed] without a legal employment contract. The lady [for whom I worked] was already cared by a live-out Ukrainian woman. After four months of cleaning, the lady needed more help due to her worsening health conditions and she needed a live-in care worker. The lady's family wanted to hire a Polish live-in worker, because [in their opinion] Polish women are more patient and open-minded. I wasn't her live-in caregiver, I was [just] a live-out domestic worker. Once the family hired the Polish domestic worker, I [left the job and] moved [from Toscany] to Bolzano. (Irene, 61, Argentinean)

She describes the gender hierarchy that Parreñas says is '... based on race, class and nation [which] establishes a work transfer system of reproductive labour among women' (2000: 577). Some women are defined as better able to engage in the temporal and spatial separations needed to accommodate the reproductive labour and care work required in Italy and in many other countries. In summary there are two mobility scenarios to which my research points. First, domestic work has poorer and less regulated labour conditions and longer work hours that newly-arrived migrants are more likely to accept. Live-in domestic service constitutes the 'fastest' way of getting a job and is situated at the beginning of the process of integration. Nevertheless, domestic work is abandoned at the first opportunity of a better job, which normally comes once an immigrant becomes a legal resident (which is usually achieved after five years in Italy) (Colombo 2007). Second, care migration affects not only external migration (i.e. from the departing country to the destination; or from a first country of destination to a second one), but it also affects internal migration in the country of destination. Based on my interviews, many Eastern Europeans, including Romanians and Poles engage in step-wise and circular migration. Doina moved from Madrid to Sicily, while Lidia travelled back and forth from Poland to Italy several times before her settlement in Turin. Here is how Lidia explains her internal and regional 'mobility':

> The first job I found when I arrived in Rossolini, near Siracusa in Sicily, was as a live-in care worker for a self-sufficient elderly person. I was employed without a contract. I stayed there for four months, and then I moved to Milan for two months. After that I came back to Rossolini for just one month before going back to Poland for one year ... [and so I went back and forth]. (Lidia, 34, Polish)

Conclusion

My findings show how two Italian cities (Turin and Bolzano) are tackling the care deficit and how they rely on the availability of foreign workers for low-skilled jobs. The employment of migrant domestic workers fills the care deficit in Southern European countries as women's participation in the labour force increases, the population ages, and new household structures replace the nuclear family. Restrictive migration policies that limit migrants' entry, along with ad hoc liberal legalization amnesties have strengthened the ethno-stratification of domestic labour. The growing migration flows toward Southern European countries have a variety of origins. My interviews demonstrate that certain migrant women who perform domestic and care work are preferred (i.e. from South America and Eastern Europe). Gender, class, religion and ethnicity are criteria of selection for migrant women and demonstrate how discrimination contributes to stratified inequalities in the domestic and care sector.

To conclude, I argue that the Italian social assistance system relies on the systematic availability of foreign workers to care for dependent people and to do household work. Personalized family-based care allows families to hire foreign eldercare assistants because families are also reluctant for moral reasons or unable for economic reasons, to hospitalize siblings and elderly family members. In this chapter, I have analysed care work from an intersectional perspective to consider how gender, ethnicity, and migrant status interconnect to shape the experiences of migrant women. I attempted to clarify the social, cultural and economic forces that promote the ideology of women's domesticity for reproductive labour and encourage women's migration. Migratory processes engender relations of inequality, vulnerability or detachment between women. Once women migrate on their own, they start a care chain of kin and siblings at home that connects the care and domestic sector with the transnational movement of women. When women arrive at their destinations, they face a labour market characterized by segmentation and ethno-stratification that identifies them as appropriate for and locates them in care and domestic work. I argue that migrant women are positioned in this labour sector, because on the one hand, Italian families are more inclined to hire a foreigner to provide care due to a lack of affordable social services for elderly; and on the other hand, migrant women act strategically to achieve their migration goals by working as care givers or domestic workers.

Chapter 5

The Magic of Migration, Immigration Controls and Subjectivities: The Case of Au Pairs and Domestic Worker Visa Holders[1]

Bridget Anderson

Immigration controls have rather magical qualities in policy and academic debates around migration and work: now you see them, now you don't. They tend to come to the fore in discussions and analyses of exploitation and vulnerability, when 'illegality' is typically used to rationalize the abuses endured by many migrants. Yet they disappear when migrants are 'legal', with the assumption that migrants, once admitted, work under more or less the same conditions as citizens. Immigration controls are perceived as being sorting mechanisms, or more generally, a tap that is switched on and off depending on national interests. But they are moulds rather than taps, producing workers with certain types of relation to the labour market, and residents with certain types of relations to citizenship and social institutions, and I will argue that we ignore them at our peril. It is important to denaturalize immigration controls and in particular to consider the impact they have on employment relations. However, immigration controls are not in themselves sufficient to understand the different experiences of life and work that migrants have, and they are located and produced not only by economic relations, but also by specific historical and social conditions. These conditions and controls also interact with particular individual circumstances to help shape subjectivities, all of which go towards understanding differential experiences and the interpretations of those experiences.

In this chapter I consider the inter-relationship of immigration and subjectivities with reference to migrant domestic workers and au pair visa holders in the UK. Private households are particularly illuminating with respect to these questions as they are sites where the social construction of 'labour' is revealed and contested, and where the relation between work and the creation of social lives and social relations is particularly clear. Migrants working in private households are directly imbricated in the creation of social life and relations, the blurring of the boundaries between citizen and non-citizen, between productive and reproductive

1 This chapter is based on the earlier 2009 publication: 'What's in a name? Immigration controls and subjectivities: The case of au pairs and domestic worker visa holders in the UK', *Subjectivity* 29: 407–424.

work. The nature of the relationships between these two groups of visa holders and their host families/employers therefore make a particularly interesting site for the explication of the relation between gendered subjectivities and migratory and employment processes.

I will first consider the social and legal construction of the figure of the migrant and then the particularities of the status of au pair and domestic worker visa holders. I will examine how and why it is that, despite these two groups doing the same kinds of tasks, the ways in which these tasks are imagined and the relationships produced can be very different. It will be seen that immigration controls play a crucial role in this. However, I will also illustrate and discuss why it is that immigration controls are not in themselves sufficient to understand the experiences and living and working conditions of these groups, and show that these arise from particular social and historical circumstances. I will argue that it is the interface of these conditions and circumstances with life stages and subjectivities that explain the varied experiences of different visa holders, and that this is crucial to grasp in order to appreciate possibilities for collective action.

Who Counts as a Migrant?

The figure of the migrant is first and foremost constructed by the state. While the impetus to move is by no means simply a consequence of state politics or of capitalism, the control of movement, its channelling and endless categorization, is in part a manifestation of state relations to both capital and labour (Hardt and Negri 2000, Linebaugh and Rediker 2000, Moulier Boutang 1997). The legal subject of the migrant is created by immigration controls and by citizenship legislation. However, 'the migrant' is not simply a legal construction, and there are multiple ways and scales by which this figure is imagined, defined and represented (both in the abstract and in the particular). It is not just the state, but a wide range of other actors, including academia, the media, NGOs, trades unions and the daily practices of individuals (both citizens and non-citizens), that work with and against each other to construct and identify who counts as a migrant (Anderson 2013).

The figure of the migrant is riddled with contradictions and this is not merely an outcome of loose popular usage vs rigorous political definitions. In the UK's public debate, government documentation and research, a 'migrant' is often defined as 'foreign born' (House of Lords 2008, Migration Advisory Committee 2008). This is quite different from the legal construction of the migrant. As well as including British citizens born abroad as migrants this also means that a person can *never* cease being a migrant even if they acquire British citizenship. The figure of the migrant is also racialized. Consider the term 'second generation immigrant', which implies that people born in the UK to British citizens are somehow 'immigrants'. It reveals how blurred the line is between 'immigrant' and 'ethnic minority' as in most large-scale datasets only those people who are identified as 'ethnic minorities' can be identified as 'second generation immigrants' because surveys typically do not ask for parents' country of birth.

The migrant is also a spectacular figure that can be summoned for political purposes (De Genova 2002, Hampshire 2008). A key principle identified by the UK state for effective border controls is 'reassure and deter'. Border controls must be visible in order to deter potential illegal immigrants and 'to provide a level of reassurance to the public that the border controls are successfully tackling the perceived threats' (Cabinet Office 2007). Some mobilities are more alarming than others, and come to epitomize challenges to immigration regimes: the 'bogus asylum seeker', 'the welfare scrounger', the 'foreign prisoner', etc. all have a political dimension. State action is targeted on these and other populations that are seen as posing particular problems and it ostensibly aims at efficiency and ensuring that the movement of 'legitimate' migrants is facilitated. But it is also a political exercise, as the UK Home Office's document on 'Enforcing the Rules' cited in the introduction states:

> From our analysis of detected overstayers, some may be doing so inadvertently, of whom many are thought to be young and from countries with reasonably high GDP per capita and perhaps with high levels of education. Anecdotal evidence suggests that these groups do not intend to stay long term in the UK and require low levels of encouragement to return home. Some groups overstay deliberately as a way of evading immigration controls and some of these may then go on to make an unfounded asylum claim (Home Office 2007: 10, Anderson 2013: 123).

So, while illegal migrants are a particular cause for concern for reasons of security and criminality, and because they allegedly undermine employment conditions, those from wealthy countries potentially cause less harm, and therefore those from poorer countries should be targeted instead. The implementation of immigration control is in practice highly differentiated, and that differentiation, while ostensibly national, also has a racialized element.

The challenges and contradictions around the definition of 'migrant' similarly apply to 'migrant worker', a term which is itself highly gendered. This is not only because immigration controls and practice reveal the gendered nature of receiving states' labour markets and the gendered notion of skill (Anderson and Ruhs 2010, Kofman et al. 2000). In the same way as the law helps to construct the figure of the migrant and the domain of immigration and citizenship, so too it helps create the domain of employment and of the family. Beyond that, whatever counts as 'work' – and indeed the very separation of 'work' from 'life' in the first place is also codified in control and practice – must thereby deal with inevitable contradictions. This is manifested in the au pair (not work)/domestic worker (work) distinction, but runs throughout immigration controls. For instance, people who hold dependant visas (in practice predominantly female) are not imagined as 'migrant workers' even though they usually have full access to the labour market. While this can be advantageous for some people, it can cause problems for others.

Take for example, the case in December 2008 of a Chinese woman who was on a visitors' visa and staying with her sister in Oxfordshire. She was deported on the grounds that looking after her niece meant that she was working as an unpaid nanny (Bardsley 2008) – i.e. even though she was 'part of the family' and (reportedly) taking great pleasure in her time with the baby as well as her sister, this still counted as work for the purposes of immigration control. One should again recall the racialized nature of implementation: would this have been the same had the aunty been a white US citizen visiting a white UK national?

Who counts as a migrant, then, like who counts as a worker, depends partly on who is doing the counting and partly on what the purpose of the counting is, but it is clear that in general the subject of the migrant is an object of concern and consequently his/her mobility must be monitored and constrained. The subject of migrant is racialized, gendered and classed, such that (for example) those who are coming to work in the UK as financiers or as university professors are not generally constructed as migrants. In this respect there is an element of tautology in the concentration of migrants in low waged work, as those foreign born people (or even non-citizens) in high waged work are often not imagined as being 'migrants'.

One crucial result of these contradictions is that many of those who in one set of discourses are considered to be migrants are not subject to immigration control, and therefore do not fit with the policy armoury of immigration controls that are designed to 'manage migration'. This has become particularly obvious since European Enlargement in 2004.[2] The UK has subsequently seen intense popular and policy concern with migrants from the new EU member states ('EU 8 nationals'[3]). As the impact of the economic crisis deepens, this concern has widened to include citizens of the EU 15[4] – hitherto not viewed as being a cause for concern – and manifest in the slogan 'British jobs for British workers'. However, EU citizens, whether EU 15 or EU 8, are not subject to immigration controls, and British labour markets, like their European counterparts are indeed nationalistically reserved, but for European, rather than British, citizens. A protectionist logic is fundamental to immigration controls, but the borders are European not British. Thus within a European context 'British workers' cannot be protected by their 'Britishness', but arguably could be by a more generous British government interpretation of the Posted Workers Directive, and improvements in British collective wage setting mechanisms (ACAS 2009).

2 On 1 May 2004, 10 new countries (Cyprus, Estonia, Hungary, Poland, the Czech Republic, Slovenia, Latvia, Lithuania, Malta and Slovakia) became members of the EU enlarging the membership to 25 countries.

3 EU 8 nationals are migrants from Estonia, Hungary, Poland, the Czech Republic, Slovenia, Latvia, Lithuania, and Slovakia.

4 The EU 15 countries are Austria, Belgium, Denmark, Finland, France, Germany, Greece, Ireland, Italy, Luxembourg, Netherlands, Portugal, Spain, Sweden, and the United Kingdom.

The Case of Au Pairs and Domestic Workers

The position of migrants who do domestic work in private households sheds light on how state legislation and rhetoric manage and reproduce the contradictions around what counts as family, and what counts as work. It is important to consider the more general social context whereby domestic work in private households is highly gendered. This work, though low status, is often rhetorically valued, especially when it involves care of children (Cox 2006, Hondagneu-Sotelo 2001). Like soldiering, care work is a key site for the production of nationhood, yet interestingly (as with soldiering) this is not a sector that is considered to be unsuitable for non-citizens. Indeed, neither domestic nor military labour is conceived as being a sector where jobs are 'taken' from British workers. When it comes to domestic work it is rather the opposite: paid domestic work is seen as facilitating the employment of British women. However, although being valued in rhetoric as priceless, such work is not valued economically. It is one thing to acknowledge the value and dignity of the work in theory, and another to actually pay for it.

Non-citizens who are working in private households may be doing so quite legally as they may well have permission to work on a variety of visas (student, working holidaymaker, dependant etc.). However, in the UK there have been only two types of visa that permit *entry* specifically to do domestic work: the au pair visa and the visa given to domestic workers who enter the UK with their employers (the latter may be tourists, on business, or resettling UK nationals etc.). This chapter will consider the case of these two groups of visa holders, i.e. people who have entered legally in order to work in private households. Nevertheless, it is important to bear in mind that this is also a sector where there is a considerable amount of informal working, and often migrants and citizens may both therefore not be working 'legally' with reference to employment law.

The cases considered are based on two research projects that were undertaken at the Centre on Migration, Policy and Society (COMPAS), University of Oxford between 2003 and 2006 (COMPAS 2006). The first project was on Filipino caregivers and explored the living and working conditions and employment relations of Filipinos working in hospitals, in care and nursing homes and in private households, principally through 60 semi-structured interviews with the carers. The second project examined the impact of EU enlargement on the living and working situations of migrants from East and Central Europe working in low wage occupations. It included a survey of 106 au pairs and 267 host families before and after EU Enlargement. In depth interviews were conducted with six host families, five au pair agencies and 19 au pairs. It should be noted that the UK visa arrangements for both groups of workers have changed substantially since this research was conducted. Unless otherwise indicated, the descriptions of immigration rules refer to this period only.[5]

Immigration Controls and the Creation of Categories of Entrant

Eliska, from the Czech Republic, came to the UK in 2003 on an au pair visa. Marisa is from the Philippines, and entered the UK in early 2005 with her employing family, having spent just over two years with them in Dubai. Both of their means of entry were conditioned by their citizenship, gender and class. Eliska had been working in a multinational company as an accountant but wanted to learn English to further her career. She decided to come on an au pair visa (before EU Enlargement in 2004 Czech women constituted the largest nationality of au pair visa holders). At that time the au pair visa was only available to certain European nationalities and to people who were aged between 17 and 27.[6] Given that it was only a few weeks before her 28th birthday, Eliska could not wait, but had to 'risk it' and take the first available family. She did not want to 'be' an au pair, but rather this practicality was according to her 'the cheapest and the easiest way to get here'. This was the case for most of the au pair visa holders interviewed, some of whom on arrival in the UK began to work in sectors other than private households (Anderson et al. 2006). Even though several interviewees alluded to the relative cheapness of the route, it could nevertheless still represent a considerable financial investment. In Eliska's case the agency and travel cost 12,000 Czech crowns[7] which she had to borrow, paying an additional 12,000 in interest. At the time of her first interview, Eliska had not yet managed to repay this loan.

Marisa entered the UK as a domestic worker accompanying her employer. She had originally migrated from the Philippines to Dubai having trained as a nursing aide, explaining: 'I couldn't afford to become a nurse anyway. I thought OK, fine, I will become a nursing aide … because we knew back then that was the fastest way to get a job'. Similarly to Eliska, Marisa felt that providing some form of paid care offered the best opportunity for legal migration. She would have much preferred to have gone to Canada but this required a 6 month certification course and because she came from a farming family that did not own land this was simply not a viable option. Consequently, she borrowed 20,000 pesos[8] from someone she described

5 In 2012 the only immigration status available as an au pair was to Romanian and Bulgarian ('A2') nationals. They had to have an Accession Workers' Card, like other workers. This tied them to host families but did not give them the right to the minimum wage. The domestic workers' visa was for a maximum of 6 months, non-renewable, with no right to change employer.

6 Au pair visas in the UK were only issued to women up until 1993 (Anderson et al. 2006).

7 Approximately $650 CAD.

8 Approximately $475 CAD.

as a 'loan shark' in order to cover her medical fees, agency fees and travel from her village to Manila. At the time of interview she had repaid this money and was remitting most of her income to pay for her nieces' and nephews' education.

These women were given legal permission to enter because in Eliska's case, she was of the right demographic and nationality, and in Marisa's case, she had the right employment history and experience. Yet it is clear that while recognizing that immigration controls are imposed categories that are constructed by the state, neither Eliska nor Marisa were simply objects of immigration controls, nor were they victims of forces beyond their influence. Immigration controls are engaged with and contested in specific instances and forms, and are affected by migrants at individual and collective levels. Moreover, the fact that there was a legal channel of entry was regarded as an indicator that there was a demand for migrant women to do this kind of work. Indeed, immigration controls required them to have a position as a condition of entry. It might be argued that this in theory afforded them a level of security, but neither job was particularly desirable, and Marisa was required to sign a second, harsher contract when she arrived in Dubai.

Nevertheless, despite the hardship of their work both women, constrained and facilitated in their different ways by class, nationality, age, and other factors, were able to use immigration controls instrumentally. They were not paid domestic workers who decided to emigrate; they were women who decided to work in private households as the easiest way of obtaining legal work abroad. However, the parameters set by constraints and facilities are not fixed, but shift even at the level of individuals. Marisa does not present coming *to London* as her active choice; her Dubai employers spent every winter in London, and she explained that in 2005 she simply came with them:

> They hold passport, they make decisions, they hold my money and my salary. Everything. They just brought me along. I just was hanging on to them the entire time. Following what they did. I had no idea of anything. I had no idea how long they would be here.

Both Eliska and Marisa were, at the time of interview, spending their time doing the same kinds of physical tasks, looking after children, cleaning, washing and other household work. This is more generally the reality for au pairs and domestic workers. Yet, despite performing similar tasks, the model ostensibly imposed by immigration controls as a suitable relation describing the performance of these tasks is quite different. Au pairs must be treated as 'part of the family' and are not constructed as workers by immigration controls. Domestic workers, in contrast, are considered to be 'employees' and are so constructed. Immigration controls therefore play a crucial role in determining the relations of (re)production in the context of live-in domestic labour.

Immigration controls are not a neutral framework facilitating the sorting of individuals into particular categories according to their intentions and identities, but rather they *produce status*. This requires us to conceptualize immigration controls as being not simply about conditions of entry across borders, but about conditions of stay (Sharma 2006). Once non-citizens have entered the UK, providing they have done so within the law, they are subject to particular conditions depending on their visa status. This often impacts on their employment relations (Anderson and Ruhs 2010). In the case of au pairs and domestic workers the nature of their relationship with host families/employers is not constructed in a vacuum, arising simply as a result of different personalities and expectations, but is partly moulded by immigration controls. Host families and employers choose certain visa holders partly anticipating the different types of relation that these signify (Anderson 2007). It is anticipated that the immaterial (gendered) labour of au pairs and domestic workers will produce particular and different types of relations.

Au pair visa holders were expected to 'help with housework' and childcare for up to five hours a day, five days a week, and to be prepared to babysit twice a week. They had to live with the family and be treated as 'part of the family'. However, precisely what is meant by being 'part of the family' is extremely hard to define, given that 'families' are imagined as nuclear and highly exclusive (as evidenced in immigration controls where the interpretation of family member for the purpose of reunion is extremely restrictive). The term 'au pair' itself indicates that the au pair is an equal, and 'part of the family' is often used to denote equality. On the one hand this is a somewhat dewy-eyed view of families. As has long been acknowledged au pairs hold far from equal places in families that are structured around status and hierarchy. However, in practice both au pairs and host families often used notions of equality and family membership in contrast to servitude. Thus being considered part of the family distinguished the au pair from a service relation: neither au pairs nor host families wished this relation to be one of a servant (Cox 2006, Stenum 2009). However, for the purpose of immigration controls (and also, significantly, for minimum wage legislation), being 'part of the family' was in opposition, not to being a servant, but to being a *worker*. So as far as immigration controls go this was not a route to employment (which would demand all sorts of other requirements), and for participants (host families and au pairs) it was (and is) not contractual or fully commodified.

In practice a key indicator for being 'part of the family' was the amount of money that was earned: limited commodification, it seems, means limited money. An au pair is not paid a wage but is given 'pocket money'. The Immigration Directorate's Instructions on au pairs at the time of interviews defined a 'reasonable' amount as being up to £55 a week claiming that 'any sum significantly in excess of this might suggest that the person is filling the position of domestic servant' (IDI 2004: Annex A paragraph 4). Interestingly, minimum wage legislation is itself somewhat more nuanced. In 2002 an Indian woman (who was not on an au pair visa) took her employing family to court to demand payment of the minimum wage, which they refused to do because they claimed they treated her as part of the family. The judgement, which found against the family, hinged on what being 'part of the family' actually included. It was found that 'had the Applicant been treated as a member of the family there would have been many more photographs of her with the family', and it was noted that when she was included in photographs it was only when she was with the child she was caring for, or she was in the background.

In contrast to au pairs, domestic workers entering the UK accompanying their employer were constructed as workers. Employers had to demonstrate evidence of written terms and conditions of employment. They also had to undertake to provide a separate bedroom for their worker, or, if they were not to live in, to ensure that the worker had access to adequate accommodation. While in the UK the migrant was subject to employment protections, including the minimum wage and also, in theory, had access to employment tribunals and could join trade unions. But a crucial requirement was that they were *not* 'family workers' i.e. are not 'employed to live as members of the family'. Nevertheless, domestic workers in our study often indicated that they would like to be regarded as part of the family, and often sought to develop this relationship by giving care that they felt was appropriate to a family member. They almost invariably used the phrase as un-problematically indicating that they were treated with respect. It was never used negatively, but was considered the most desirable kind of arrangement, even though it was sometimes associated with lower wages:

> They were a good family. They were well educated and they were friendly. It is just that the rate of pay there is so much different to that of the pay here … I was already like a member of their family or at least that is what I felt … . They said they would raise my salary but I thought that would be a bit embarrassing if I accepted a higher salary from them.

This demonstrates the ways in which immigration controls lay out the kinds of relation that au pairs and domestic workers work under, but in practice these are only formally discernible through tangible markers such as pay, hours and physical living arrangements. While host families and employers may select particular groups of visa holders in anticipation of particular types of relations, these relations may be challenged by migrants, and indeed by the practices of the host families and employers.

Out of Control: Gender, Age and Subjectivities

The importance and the limitations of immigration status in structuring the experiences of migrants are revealed in an apparent contradiction. In many ways a domestic worker visa seemed to have advantages over an au pair visa. In practice, according to the immigration criteria devised to differentiate the hours, salaries and the nature of their relationship to host families/ employers, many 'au pairs' could be equally well designated 'domestic workers'. It is notable that the practices of host families in our research did not conform to immigration instructions regarding pay or hours, with au pairs reporting their average weekly 'pocket money' as being £68 and average working time as being 30 hours a week (though it was often significantly more than this). It is possible, then, to argue that (somewhat perversely) this indicates that au pairs were often effectively doing the work of domestic workers but that this went unrecognized in terms of status and protection.

Yet despite the greater employment protections afforded to domestic worker visa holders, and the vulnerability of au pairs in terms of employment rights, there seemed to be greater evidence of employer abuse of domestic worker visa holders than of au pair visa holders. For example, although the research studies were not directly comparable, it is notable that a 2008 report found that 34 per cent of domestic worker visa holders had had their passports retained, while in 2004 our survey found that only 1.5 per cent of au pairs had had their passports held by their employer. Moreover, while our survey found that au pairs earned below the minimum wage this was nevertheless more than many domestic worker visa holders actually earned (Anderson et al 2006, Wittenburg 2008). Thus arguably the apparent protections offered by being recognized as a worker in terms of immigration legislation are more limited than it first seems.

It is true that there is a difficulty in implementing employment rights in private households. So while immigration provisions in theory gave domestic workers access to certain protections, in practice these could be extremely difficult to implement, especially as workers were usually unaware that they had these rights, or did not know how to enforce them, and were also often faced with other practical and personal obstacles. However, while the difficulty of implementing rights partly explains how it is possible to abuse domestic workers, it does not explain the discrepancy in experiences (and in responses to these experiences) between au pair and domestic worker visa holders. That is to say that, while being crucially important factors, neither immigration controls nor the vulnerability of people in private spaces are sufficient to explain the diversity of experiences of migrants working in private households.

In order to begin to understand this one must consider exactly who enters under particular visa regimes. Domestic labour is women's work, and, as currently commodified in Europe, it is deeply racialized. Gendered and racialized subjectivities are reinforced by national legislation and by individual family practice, as well as by the discursive work of agencies and media. So certain nationalities are promoted by agencies and their employers as being typically 'docile', 'friendly', 'good with children' etc. This practice thus communicates not only what these groups are like but also what the work requires. However, while some attention has been paid to the importance of race and nationality in structuring this labour market, less attention has been given to the role of age and life stage. These are nevertheless important aspects of demand: older women are preferred by some as they are considered more motherly (particularly if they have experience as mothers); sometimes younger women are seen as more suitable companions for children (Anderson 2007).

Age is a relatively unexplored feature of immigration controls, and yet it nonetheless can be significant. In Tier 1 of the new UK immigration system for example, an inherent bias against younger workers in a Points Based System that awards points on the basis of earnings and level of qualifications is recognized and those aged under 28 are given 20 additional points (those under 31 are given an extra five points). There are age limitations on particular visa categories, and as has been seen in Eliska's case, in order to enter as an au pair a person must be of a particular age. They must also have no dependants and indeed among all the au pairs interviewed only one was sending earnings back to people who depended on her for an income.

While au pairing has its legal beginnings in the Strasbourg Convention of 1969, as a practice it has its roots in 'life-cycle service'. In the early modern period of northwestern Europe late marriage meant a long gap between puberty and marriage, and an estimated three fifths of English young people in the sixteenth–eighteenth centuries were sent to work in other households. In some respects the life-cycle servant of early modern times has been replaced by the modern day student as a period of protected transition from the family home to adulthood. For the majority of life-cycle servants this was a transient phase, and while elites did not send out as many young people as they hired, much movement was lateral or nearly lateral across classes and relations were familiar. Young people moved into the homes of others of the same, or perhaps slightly higher, social status and they were regarded as 'junior members', subordinate but integral (Cooper 2004). They performed a range of tasks including: hauling water, doing laundry, gathering wood, and looking after children. These tasks were gendered, with childcare being predominantly the job of female life-cycle servants. This scenario bears a remarkable similarity to the way that the au pair regime is imagined, i.e. as a movement of young people, now consisting of mainly females who are child-carers, and as being transient, and also between equals. For example, one middle class family could host an au pair and send their daughter as an au pair to her parents' family. (Though arguably, this started to change as numbers of women from the Czech Republic and Lithuania were beginning to enter the system.)

Au pairing is therefore very closely linked to life stage in immigration practice and in the imaginations of the au pair and the host family. It is an arrangement whereby one person's stage in the life cycle, as young, without dependants, inexperienced, and flexible, fits another household's life stage – as overstretched, and in need of 'help' with demanding young children. The practice is not anticipated as being permanent. Life-cycle service indeed is and always has been open to abuse, and while there may be commonalities in tasks performed it is a different model from that of the domestic worker as an employee.

Thus au pairs were often young women at a certain life stage with no clear migratory project (Anderson et al. 2006, Búriková 2006). As Eliska stated:

> I wanted to learn English, where was I to go? An English speaking country. I was limited mainly by the age limit and my age was still OK for Britain and it was also financially available for me. And that is about it.

These women were often concerned to emphasize their youth, and life stage and the fact that they were carefree and had choices. Those who had been an au pair for a while were equally concerned to locate this role within their 'youthful' experience: 'I want to take my chances and make most of them. And when I run out of chances and opportunities I will come back'. Their position, as footloose, young and free could be contrasted with host mothers, often perceived as frazzled, limited by domestic responsibilities and sometimes jealous of their au pairs' freedom. They were mobile, not just across borders, but also (unlike host mothers) within families. When there were problems with host families most of them felt able to move on relatively quickly. As Eliska explained: 'If we did not get on well, I went. Why stay with them? We would only get on each other's nerves'.

The majority of those entering on domestic worker visas came from further afield, from places where travel is more expensive, often from Asia (the Philippines, India and Indonesia account for nearly two thirds of entries). They were usually women with children or other dependants. Most were remitting a large portion of their wages and had migrated from developing countries often in order to financially support their families. They had a far greater age range than au pairs, with some of them being in their late 60s.

This is not the model of life cycle service, but is closer to that of the nineteenth century English domestic worker, where those who were resident were physically and psychologically more distanced from the families they lived with, and class rather than life stage was the determining factor of one's role in the family. The middle and upper classes were no longer providing servants, even before the post-World War I decline, and poorer houses increasingly had no paid workers at all. Race rather than class perceptions now underpin these relations (though it should be remembered that class was often highly racialized (Anderson 2013). Nevertheless the fact remains that these families would no more consider 'exchanging' their children with the households of those providing servants than British families would consider sending their sons and daughters to work as domestic workers for, say, Indian families in India.

Domestic workers then tended to couch their descriptions in terms of 'suffering' undertaken, not to further their own projects, but to support their families. Indeed some could be critical of their female employers, going out to work and leaving their children, when, unlike migrants, they could afford to stay at home and be 'proper' full time mothers. Those migrants who were mothers were often concerned to explain how it was that they were good mothers and to reconcile this with their migratory project.

> Since the day I left the Philippines to work abroad the time I have spent with my daughter has only been measured in months … I don't really think of myself, I just think of my daughter. I pride myself in thinking at least I was able to finish her education and go to college. (Filipina domestic worker visa holder aged 49)

Thus costs of failure in the migratory project could be high, and often not just for the individual concerned. Differences in migration motivation, household responsibilities and life stage have implications for labour mobility. For those with dependants and far from support networks, losing a job (and potentially not securing another one) could have serious consequences, not just for the individual but for their dependants (Wittenburg 2008). The risks attendant on moving within the labour market can act as a significant constraint, even if legally one has the possibility of so doing. Contrast Eliska, quoted above, with Marisa, remembering that both were equally free in law to move households:

> I guess the only reason I lasted for six years is because that honestly I needed the money. That's why no matter how much hardship I was experiencing no matter what they did to me I never complained. As long as my body could take it I would push onward.

Migrants' subjectivities, their sense of responsibility and the dependence of others (often highly gendered), have an important constraining effect on how people use their mobility (Federici 2004).

Temporariness and the Future

Subjectivities are not confined to the present, but are concerned with the future, with potential, with where one is going as well as where one is. How this relates with the temporal nature of immigration controls is also important in understanding the differential positioning of au pairs and migrant domestic workers. Au pair visas could not be renewed and were valid for a maximum of two years (with a possible six month extension). Visa holders could not acquire residence rights over time. Thus being an au pair was inevitably associated with temporariness. This temporariness was part of what made it tolerable. Martina was typical in her attitude:

> for all girls from Slovakia coming here for the first time, I fully recommend the work of an au-pair because it is a good starting position for them to get higher as they can later find a job of their dreams. So I am strongly for girls coming here as au-pairs, yet they shouldn't get taken advantage of and they shouldn't stay in the families, definitely not more than a year.

Thus the enforced temporariness of au pairing was typically not regarded as a problem, as it was not regarded as a 'job' that the visa holder wanted to remain in for a prolonged period; rather it represented a chance to come to the UK and to live a different kind of life for a while. As for its employment aspects, au pairing was, at best, a chance to look around, find some accommodation, improve one's English and make some contacts, rather than being an indicator of the type of employment the au pair imagined in the future. Au pairs were keen to emphasize their education, their aspirations, their breadth of experience and possibilities. Many au pairs implicitly and explicitly expressed the sense that 'This is not all that I am'.

For most of those on domestic worker visas, even if domestic work was not a 'job for life' it was certainly not temporary work, and their stay in the UK, if not permanent, was not imagined as being short term. Unlike au pair visas, domestic workers' visas at that time were renewable, and after four years (changed to five years in 2006) a visa holder could apply for permanent residence.[9] Thus domestic workers have an incentive to invest effort in the promotion of the *dignity* and value of their work. Rather than, 'This is not all that I am', the implication, sometimes expressed was: 'This is what I do, and it has value'. The effect of this investment has been apparent in the organizing of migrant domestic workers in many countries, often (as in the UK) over matters to do with non-recognition of their work for the purposes of immigration control. Direct engagement with immigration controls can be, as we have seen, about individual decisions instrumentalizing control – it is manifest, for example, when people (citizens and non-citizens alike) report migrants to the authorities as being 'illegal'. It is also manifest in legal cases, where non-citizens assert demands to remain, to work, and to be joined by families etc. But immigration controls may also be contested collectively. Domestic workers, while being in a difficult position to organize themselves have nevertheless managed to forge political organizations. For example, in the UK an organization was developed that built upon individual acts of resistance (such as escape from employers) and enabled domestic workers to assert themselves as political actors. They demanded rights and forged citizenship by demonstrating, to themselves, employers and the wider public that they were working (Anderson 2010, Papadopoulos et al. 2008, Rancière 2004). Workers showed that they were not just 'helping' but were contributing socially and economically to households and to the wider society; that they were not simply 'girls' but were women (and men) who were often sustaining extended families back home. This also asserted their legitimacy as public actors, their right to be heard and to be treated with respect, and it was accompanied by the demand that this labour be recognized as a route to formalized citizenship (Gordon and Lenhardt 2008).

It is not that au pairs did not recognize the demanding nature of the physical (and emotional) work of being an au pair, but that they were clear they were seeking to move on quickly from this work. They had little incentive to invest in achieving recognition of their work as labour, and tended to see it as drudgery rather than as being 'honourable labour' (Brace 2004).

> Therefore I don't consider au-pairing a job because you are living with those people, eating with them, using their electricity, water, heating and you should

9 This changed in April 2012 when domestic work became aligned with other 'low skilled' temporary migrant work.

> be a part of the family, not just work. That's why I admire people that are able to do the au-pairing for longer than a year. I am almost finished now, but the lady that comes to the family instead of me is 37, a Portuguese, and she's been an au-pair for seven years. So when I saw the lady, I just stood with my mouth open and I can't understand at all how she can be an au-pair after 7 years, but that's none of my business.

Conclusion

A focus on immigration controls is critical for two reasons. Firstly, they delineate the 'problem' by ostensibly identifying the migrant who is the subject (or object) of the debate in the first place. Secondly, it is assumed that immigration controls provide the answer to the problem (rarely are they perceived to be the source of the problem). An understanding of how immigration controls function, in all their tedious legal nitty-gritty, is important for an understanding of the experiences of migrants. However, it is not sufficient. Examining au pair and domestic worker visa holders reveals firstly that mobility is deeply affected by interdependencies and more specifically by caring responsibilities. Gendered and aged subjectivities are crucial elements of this. Secondly it demonstrates that some migrants may have little investment in being considered a 'worker' – even if this has the potential to bring them improved wages and working and living conditions. Indeed, they may not even consider themselves to be 'migrants' at all, however they may be classified in the official statistics. Understanding the relation between subjectivities, history, social imaginations and immigration controls throws new light on the different experiences and positionings of non-citizens and citizens within nation states.

Acknowledgements

Thanks to Lourdes Gordolan, research assistant and interviewer in COMPAS project *Filipino Careworkers* and to Martin Ruhs, Ben Rogaly and Sarah Spencer for their permission to use data from the COMPAS research project *Changing status, Changing lives? The socio-economic impact of EU Enlargement on low-wage migrant workers in the UK* (funded by the Joseph Rowntree Foundation and the Economic and Social Research Council (ESRC). I am grateful to Jenny Newman, Ben Rogaly, reviewers of an earlier version of this chapter, my co-editor of the 2009 *Subjectivity* Special Issue: Conflicts of Mobility: Migration, Labour and Political Subjectivities (Volume 29, Issue 1), Rutvica Andrijasevic, and the *Subjectivity* editorial board, for their helpful comments on previous drafts of this chapter.

Chapter 6
The Use and Abuse of Domestic Workers: Case Studies in Lebanon and Egypt

Ray Jureidini

Much of the literature on domestic work focuses on the inequalities and paradoxes of women from poor countries traveling to serve families in rich developed nations (see Ehrenreich and Hochschild 2002, Zimmerman, Litt and Bose 2006). Less known and understood are the histories and experiences of middle- and upper-class households in so-called developing countries that draw on local, regional, and increasingly global sources of female labour for their families (Cheng 2006). This chapter presents information from two surveys of migrant domestic workers – one in Beirut, Lebanon and the other in Cairo, Egypt. The aim here is to examine the social profiles of migrant workers who are recruited through two very different procurement and placement systems and to evaluate their living and working conditions and the types and frequency of abuses perpetrated against migrant domestic workers. To what extent are the vulnerabilities of female domestic workers a function of being migrants?

Background

Paid domestic workers are in a unique employment relationship that has both occupational as well as personal elements that are clearly identifiable in Arab states. The juxtaposition of the personal and professional is at the heart of the problems that face many domestic workers and their employers. Paid domestic workers, whether local or foreign, are mostly strangers who must learn to deal with the family dynamics of the household in which they work, from the position of being simultaneously close, but distant, familiar, but unknown (Simmel 1950); in a permanent yet irreconcilable dissonance, or what Gamburd (2000) terms 'marginal insiders and intimate outsiders'. She may come from, and represent in the imagination of family members, a different race, class, ethnicity, or nationality that is variously subservient, comfortable, or threatening.

Throughout the Middle East, and for many generations, middle and upper-class women have had live-in domestic help. Domestic workers have often played critical intimate roles within Arab families (Joseph 1999), but there has been a significant shift in the origins of domestic workers – from local and regional Arab women (and girls) to Asian and African migrant women (Jureidini 2009a). Currently, the Middle East contains the largest migrant population in the world, taking into account regular and irregular migration, as well as refugees and asylum seekers (Baldwin-Edwards, 2005) amounting to around 20 million migrants, developed over the decades following the fourfold price increase of oil in 1973. This event resulted in the migrant workforce of the Gulf states exceeding the number of nationals (Castles and Miller 1998, Hertog and Dashti 2010, Jureidini 2005). The Middle East has also become the largest source and host of refugees, constituting around 42 per cent of the total world refugee population (Fargues 2007).

Around half of the world's 90 million migrant workers are women (Moreno-Fontes Chammartin 2005) who now most often migrate as the major breadwinners in their families, rather than following their husbands. In the Middle East, these women, primarily in private household domestic work, come mainly from Nepal, India, Pakistan, Bangladesh, Philippines, Sri Lanka, Indonesia and Ethiopia. With 1.2 million migrant domestic workers employed in Saudi Arabia (Human Rights Watch 2008) and 600,000 in the United Arab Emirates (IRIN 2006) alone, it is estimated that there may be around 3 million migrant domestic workers in the Middle East.

Largely invisible in the private realm of the household where law-enforcement agencies are reluctant to intrude, domestic workers are very vulnerable to abuse and exploitation. Often quite ignorant of the country where they are going to work and rarely speaking the local language, many live in conditions that are akin to slavery or labour indenture. Three aspects of their living conditions violate basic human rights, namely: 1) violence or the threat of violence; 2) restrictions on their freedom of movement; and 3) economic exploitation (see Jureidini and Moukarbel 2004). These problems arise from the *kafala* system of employment sponsorship[1] and partly because in most Arab states, domestic workers, whatever their tasks, are not covered by labour law. In Egypt, as well as in Saudi Arabia, Kuwait, Lebanon and the United Arab Emirates, labour laws exclude domestic workers (Human Rights Watch 2007). In Egypt and Lebanon, domestic work is explicitly excluded because it is classified as a 'personal' relationship, not as an employment relationship.

Violations against migrant domestic workers in the Middle East are now almost legendary with daily reports in newspapers in the Gulf countries and in the sending countries. Outrage from these incidents has led the governments of some sending countries to ban migration to specific receiving countries. Some recent examples include the decision by the Philippines government in January 2008

1 *Kafala* sponsorship means an employer must take full responsibility for the foreign employee who may not leave the sponsor without leaving the country, or gaining government approval. To do so renders the guestworker an illegal alien liable to arrest, detention and deportation. The employer-sponsor, or *kafeel*, must inform the government of any change in the employment contract status of the worker (such as breach, renewal or expiry) and is responsible for the cost of repatriation upon completion of the contract (see Longva 1997).

to prohibit recruitment of Filipinas by Jordanian employers (GMA News [Pinoy Abroad] 2008). Filipinas were also banned from going to Lebanon following the war in July–August, 2006. In 2006, the Philippines government introduced three measures to reduce the attractiveness of Filipinas to the Middle East labour market, requiring a minimum salary of $400 per month for Overseas Filipino Workers, limiting domestic workers' contracts to two years or less, and banning the payment of wages to placement agencies in the host country.[2] Sri Lanka also stopped housemaids from going abroad after 2008, arguing that preference should be given to the out-migration of skilled workers such as nurses. The government also released a proposal to ban the migration of all women with children less than 5 years of age and to require that mothers of older children register a plan for their proper care before the women were allowed to leave the country (Human Rights Watch 2007).[3] Despite such bans and restrictions, the flow of migrant domestic workers to the Middle East has continued unabated. In time, sending countries typically back down from bans and threats, because of the billions of dollars in foreign currencies that are annually remitted back to them.

In 2005–06 in Beirut and 2007 in Cairo, two surveys of domestic workers were conducted to provide a) demographic profiles of the various nationalities involved and b) some statistical evidence on the extent of human rights violations perpetrated against them. The two countries are very different with respect to the systems of procurement and placement of domestic workers. In Lebanon, a highly organized system of contracts restricts entry unless employment is pre-arranged through registered agencies. All foreigners in the country are the responsibility of the General Security Forces that operate a detention centre for women who have absconded from their sponsor/employers and are thus illegal residents. With a small population of four million, approximately one in three to four Lebanese households employ a migrant domestic worker, and almost all households employing domestic workers rely on their recruitment by agencies from outside the country. Thus, it is not surprising that the hiring and employment of domestic workers have become major public issues. In Egypt, by contrast, most domestic workers are recruited locally from Egyptian nationals, refugees who are resident in Cairo, and irregular migrants from Africa. There are few women from the Philippines and Indonesia, because of a general ban by the Egyptian government on the entry of foreign domestic workers. In Egypt, domestic work is not seen as a public issue, in part because Egypt is a much larger country than Lebanon with a population of over 79 million and Cairo is an enormous city of over 17 million people with high levels of poverty and live-in domestic workers employed only in wealthy families.

---

2 These measures have only been partially successful. While domestic workers may sign two-year contracts in order to leave the Philippines, on arrival in Lebanon, agents often force them to sign 'replacement contracts' that specify lower wages and for three years (see Jureidini 2010).

3 After serious objections by Human Rights Watch on the grounds of discrimination, these proposals were withdrawn.

Lebanon

The local and regional sources of domestic labour for Lebanese households became globalized during and after the Lebanese civil war (1975–90) which caused an abrupt exodus of Egyptians, heightened the reluctance of Palestinians to work, and reinforced the unwillingness of Lebanese employers to employ locals (see Khalaf 2002, Traboulsi 2007). From 1990 to 2006, the main sources of domestic labour in Lebanon were Sri Lanka, the Philippines and Ethiopia (see Jureidini 2004, 2005). The racialization of domestic work is exemplified by the reference of Lebanese to a *Sirilankiye* as a domestic worker, regardless of her nationality (see Jureidini and Moukarbel 2004). At the time of the survey conducted in 2005–06, there were estimated to be roughly 160,000 female migrant domestic workers in Lebanon, mainly from Sri Lanka (100,000), the Philippines (30,000) and Ethiopia (30,000). Since 2006, the proportions of these nationalities have changed, with Ethiopians and Nepalese replacing the Filipinas and Sri Lankans who did not return (Jureidini 2011).

Private agencies in Lebanon contract with agencies in the sending countries to bring migrants into Lebanon. Employers pay the Lebanese agents between US$1,500 and US$3,000 and the employee signs a contract with the employer. The standard 'Contract of Employment for Domestic Helpers from Sri Lanka in the Middle East Countries' stipulates the salary, working hours 'not exceeding 12 staggered hours per day'; that the employer is to provide free passage to and from Sri Lanka; that arrangement and payment of the visa/work permit is the responsibility of the employer along with suitable living quarters and adequate food, medical services (health insurance is compulsory by law); and conditions of termination. 'Special provisions' prohibit the employee from being required to work anywhere other than in the employer's residence; and require that the employer 'shall treat the employee in a just and humane manner. In no case shall physical violence be used upon the employee' (OHCHR 2009).

The regulation and monitoring of recruitment and placement agencies in Lebanon has been a problem since the civil war. The criteria for an agency license are not clear and no knowledge or character tests are required. Agents must place a $33,500 non-interest bearing guarantee with the government's Housing Bank (*Bank de l'Haxxbitat*). For this, they are able to bring 150 migrants per year into the country. However, with some 310 licensed agents in Lebanon, only around 44 are operating as genuine agents with an office and staff. In 2006–07 the Lebanese Ministry of Labour closed 15 placement agencies on grounds of violations of workers' rights including physical abuse (TIP Report 2007), although some were only temporary closures. There is a continuing judicial reluctance to bring criminal charges against both employers and agents in Lebanon (see TIP Report 2007, Jureidini 2003, Huda 2006b) although the first successful prosecution of an employer was completed in December 2009 (see below).

In 2004, a brief survey of newspapers revealed 52 reports of violence against migrant domestic workers. Between January 2007 and August 2008, Human Rights

Watch (2008) reported the deaths of 95 migrant domestic workers in Lebanon. Most were classified as suicides (40); falls from high rise apartment buildings (24); accidents, mainly car or drowning (nine); carbon monoxide suffocation (five); murder (two); natural causes, such as heart attack, cancer, disease (14); and one unknown cause of death. The majority of deaths were Ethiopian (67 per cent), Filipina (16 per cent), Sri Lankan (10 per cent), Bangladeshi (4 per cent), Madagascan (1 per cent), Eritrean (1 per cent) and Nepalese (1 per cent). Typically, police and General Security investigations of these deaths are inadequate and therefore lack credibility (see Jureidini 2003, Human Rights Watch 2008). Finally, in December 2009, the first case against an employer was successfully prosecuted. It took some three years of action by the legal department of the Caritas Migrant Center before the employer was sentenced to 15 days in prison and required to pay US$7,200 in compensation to the employee who was physically beaten in public when she tried to escape from her employer's car.

Egypt

Egypt differs from most Arab countries that host organized migrant contract labour. In recent years it has received many thousands of refugees from sub-Saharan Africa. At the time of writing, the most numerous are from Sudan. Although Egypt has restricted foreign workers' access to local labour markets, there is a general tolerance for refugees and other African residents who are working without permission, notwithstanding deportations and *refoulement* of Sudanese and Eritreans (Amnesty International 2008). By all accounts, most domestic workers in Egypt are Egyptians, although there are some suggestions that Egyptian women are increasingly reluctant to undertake paid domestic work. Some contract migrant domestic workers are present in the country, mainly from the Philippines and Indonesia. We do not know the populations of Egyptian, Sudanese, Ethiopian, Eritrean or Nigerian domestic workers in Cairo, as they are not identified in large-scale labour or household surveys or in the census.

For thousands of refugees in Cairo, domestic work is the only employment available to them and a crucial source of income for their survival. Indeed, many domestic workers have become the main breadwinners for their families. Local agencies in Cairo operate to place migrants, refugees and Egyptians in domestic work. Indeed, almost half of the interviewees in the survey said they were placed in their current households by an Egyptian agency. For example, at All Saints Church in Zamalek, the mainly Sudanese and Eritrean refugee women are offered a two week course on domestic work, as well as placement.

There has never been specific legislation in Egypt to facilitate the entry of migrant domestic workers. Domestic maids were not mentioned in Egyptian law until 2003 when Labour Law 2003 (Article 28) stipulated that foreign workers must have a work permit *before* entering the country. Article (4G) of the same law states that domestic work is an exception to the labour law and that normal 'restrictions on terminating the work contract don't apply to the employer in this case'. What is important is the explicit recognition of the private and personal nature of the relationship within the household. Paid domestic work is not a 'proper' form of labour (perhaps it was also not accepted as 'productive' labour), so labour law does not apply; nor does the law of contract.

Egypt's reservations to the 1951 Refugee Convention have been generally understood as not granting rights to employment in Egypt for refugees, resulting in refugees being forced to rely on the informal sector where they are easily exploited. Refugees must obtain work permits from the Ministry of Labour, but in practice they are difficult to obtain, thereby forcing refugees into irregular employment. In 2006, the Egyptian government reiterated its strict control of foreign domestic workers. There has been recent pressure, however, for the Egyptian government to address foreign and local domestic worker issues. As a signatory to the UN Migrant Workers Convention which came into force in 2003, the Egyptian government made it clear that all rights and obligations pertaining to foreign labour in the country are the same as those of its own citizens (UN CMW 2006: par 17). It would seem, however, that these provisions did not apply to migrant domestic workers employed in private households, because the Labour Code excludes their recognition as employees and thus their protection. However, in 2007, the government indicated it was looking into ways to modify the 'Labour Code to enhance the status of domestic workers, to give them more dignity and to provide a formal framework for such work' (MWC Committee 2007: par. 41).

Finally, there have been prosecutions of abusive employers of Egyptian domestic workers. The most prominent was in 2001, when the film actress, Wafaa Mekki, was sentenced to 10 years imprisonment for severely injuring her Egyptian maid (Allam 2001) Their significance, however, has been acknowledged by Egypt's longstanding and vibrant film industry, where a number of Egyptian films depict relationships with domestic workers from various perspectives (see Jureidini 2006).

Methods: An Evaluation

Separate but related surveys of domestic workers were conducted in Beirut and in Cairo to learn about the social characteristics of domestic workers, their working conditions, and human rights violations. The aim was to survey foreign female domestic workers to learn their age, marital status, number of children, education and religion and to document human rights violations as reported by migrant domestic workers themselves. To contact domestic workers who work in private homes, who live with tremendous restrictions on their daily movements, and may not know the local language or their rights, we relied on interviewers from the same ethnic groups as the domestic workers, many of whom were or had been domestic workers themselves, and convenience sampling. Neither survey is representative, as the sampling was purposeful, not random. Nonetheless, it is believed to be the best sample possible, given the particular circumstances of migrant domestic workers in the Middle East.

In the 2005–06 survey of 610 migrant domestic workers in Beirut, the sample consisted of 201 women from Sri Lanka, 201 from the Philippines and 208 from Ethiopia who were interviewed with questionnaires translated into Sinhalese, Tagalog, and Amharic. To avoid the bias that employers would only permit domestic workers who were treated well to be surveyed, many of the interviews were conducted on Sundays in and around churches where domestic workers were known to attend and in Dowra, on the outskirts of Beirut where they go shopping and where there are cafes and small restaurants to serve them. Interviews were also conducted in the apartment buildings of the interviewers themselves or in adjacent buildings. Since many domestic workers were not allowed to leave the house,[4] many were interviewed across the balconies during the day when the employing families were away.

In Cairo, the sample consisted of 116 Filipinas, 62 Indonesians, 125 Sudanese, 129 Ethiopians, 118 Eritreans and 82 Nigerians.[5] An additional 149 Egyptian domestic workers were included as a control group. The aim of the survey was to replicate the survey previously carried out in Lebanon. The questionnaires were translated into the respective languages of the interviewees, although the Filipinas were interviewed in English. The survey sample was around 5.4 per cent of the population of Filipinas in Egypt and 12.4 per cent of the population of Indonesians in Egypt.

The seeds for the snowball sample were domestic workers known personally to each of the interviewers. Interviews were conducted whenever and wherever it was most convenient and private, which included the homes where the domestic workers worked. Egyptian workers generally refused to be interviewed at their places of work, so most interviews were conducted with them at public places such as parks and bus stops. Most Filipinas were interviewed at the churches they attended, in the houses they worked or at their own apartments in the case of freelancers. Indonesians were interviewed at an Indonesian restaurant with the permission of the owner. Ethiopians and Eritreans were interviewed before or after church services and in their own homes while Nigerians were mostly interviewed during traditional weekend community gatherings at the home of the principal Nigerian interviewer.

Demographic Profile of Domestic Workers

The ages of domestic workers in the two countries are similar to each other and to the age distribution of the working population, with an emphasis on young women in their twenties (Table 6.1).

---

4 Indeed, 31 per cent (N=137) of respondents in Beirut reported that they were not allowed outside the apartment.

5 The different numbers were due to the ability to conduct the interviews within the time deadlines of the study.

Table 6.1 Age by nationality (per cent)

Beirut	18–20	21–30	31–40	41–50	>50	N
Sri Lankan	2	41	34	19	4	200
Filipina	1	35	40	18	7	200
Ethiopian	5	90	5			207
Total	**3**	**56**	**26**	**12**	**3**	**610**
Cairo						
Egyptian	14	47	26	13	1	149
Filipina	1	26	40	27	12	116
Indonesian	2	24	56	8		62
Sudanese	2	23	48	15	2	125
Ethiopian	2	69	28	2		129
Eritrean	2	78	18	3		118
Nigerian	7	74	17	1		82
Total	**5**	**52**	**31**	**10**	**2**	**781**

Compared with other nationalities, Filipinas in Cairo and Beirut were older with more women over 50 years of age, while Egyptians, Ethiopians, Eritreans and Nigerians had larger numbers of young adult women in their twenties. The Ethiopians in Beirut stand out as a much younger population than the other nationalities. They are also more likely to be single, a marital status that caused the Lebanese government to ban Ethiopians from entering the country in 2004, ostensibly because the Ethiopian recruitment agency was over-charging Lebanese placement agencies and employers. However, although it was not publicly stated, the ban was also instigated by evidence that many young Ethiopian women were engaging in prostitution. The ban was lifted following the 2006 Israeli invasion that resulted in a large demand for domestic workers.

Again, the marital status of domestic workers in each country was also similar (Table 6.2).

Table 6.2 Marital status by nationality (per cent)

Beirut	Never Married	Married	Separated	Divorced	Widowed	N
Sri Lankan	23	54	9	7	8	201
Filipina	45	39	8	1	7	201
Ethiopian	81	9	5	2	2	208
Total	**50**	**34**	**7**	**4**	**5**	**610**
Cairo						
Egyptian	50	30	5	7	7	149
Filipina	45	39	8	1	7	201

Indonesian	29	55	3	10	3	62
Sudanese	18	56	7	7	11	125
Ethiopian	78	15	2	2	3	129
Eritrean	80	13	3	4	0	118
Nigerian	42	46	6	5	1	82
Total	**48**	**36**	**6**	**5**	**5**	**781**

Around half had never been married and just over one third were married at the time of the interview. Consistent with their youthfulness, Ethiopians, and Eritreans were more likely to have never been married compared with other nationalities; while Sri Lankans, Indonesians, Sudanese and Nigerian women were more likely to be married. There were slightly more divorced Indonesians and widowed Sudanese than in other nationalities, however, the differences are small.

The overall number of domestic workers with children in the two countries was almost identical. However, consistent with the age and marital status differences, fewer Ethiopians and Eritreans had children (Table 6.3).

Table 6.3 Percentage of women with children

Beirut		
Sri Lankan	67%	(N=201)
Filipina	57%	(N=201)
Ethiopian	12%	(N=208)
Total	**45%**	**(N=610)**
Cairo		
Egyptian	44%	(N=149)
Filipina	70%	(N=116)
Indonesian	63%	(N=62)
Sudanese	68%	(N=125)
Ethiopian	18%	(N=129)
Eritrean	19%	(N=118)
Nigerian	51%	(N=82)
Total	**46%**	**(N=781)**

Although Nigerians were quite young (74 per cent were in their 20s), almost half were married and with children. In Beirut, only 3 per cent of respondents had their children with them. As Lebanon does not allow family members of migrant domestic workers to accompany them or permit family reunion, these are most likely children who were born in Lebanon. In Cairo, by contrast, of the migrant women who had children, some 47 per cent were with them. Almost 60 per cent of Sudanese mothers, who are mostly refugees, had their children with them.

A glance at Table 6.4 reveals that the educational attainments of Egyptian, Sudanese and Sri Lankan women were less than those of the other nationalities. Of the Egyptian and Sudanese women, 85 per cent and 66 per cent, respectively, had not completed high school. One third of the Sudanese indicated that they could not read or write in their first language. In contrast, almost half of the Filipinas (47 per cent) and Nigerians (45 per cent) had undertaken some post-secondary studies. The educational attainments of the Nigerian domestic workers are noteworthy as they were all live-in and 'economic migrants' rather than refugees.

Table 6.4 Educational attainments of respondents (per cent)

Beirut							
	Sri Lanka	Filipina	Ethiopia				
None	4	–	1				
Partial Primary	30	–	10				
Completed Primary	20	2	9				
Partial Secondary	39	1	24				
Completed Secondary	5	16	26				
Partial Post-Secondary	1	23	10				
Completed Post-Secondary	1	58	20				
(N =570)	(165)	(197)	(208)				
Cairo							
	Egypt	Filipina	Indonesia	Sudan	Ethiopia	Eritrea	Nigeria
None	11			18	1		
Partial Primary	23			10	3	4	
Completed Primary	17	4	5	18	9	4	2
Partial Secondary	33	16	11	20	25	25	2
Completed Secondary	5	33	34	19	57	55	50
Partial Post-Secondary	10	30	29	9	5	8	
Completed Post-Secondary	1	16	21	6	2	3	45
(N = 781)	(149)	(116)	(62)	(125)	(129)	(118)	(82)

Although almost one quarter (23 per cent) of interviewees had less than a primary education or had just completed primary schooling, 34 per cent had completed their secondary schooling and one fifth (20 per cent) had some post-secondary training.

A majority of migrant domestic workers in Beirut (69 per cent) identified their religion as Christian, while, in Cairo, the majority of domestic workers were Muslim (Table 6.5).

Table 6.5 Religion of respondents (per cent)

Beirut	**Christian**	**Muslim**	**Buddhist**	**Hindu**	**N**
Sri Lankan	11	3	79	7	(191)
Filipina	93	6	–	1	(197)
Ethiopian	97	3	–	–	(197)
Total	**69**	**4**	**25**	**2**	**(595)**
Cairo					
Egyptian	14	86	–	–	(146)
Filipina	92	8	–	–	(116)
Indonesia	23	73	2	3	(62)
Sudanese	58	42	–	–	(125)
Ethiopian	92	8	–	–	(129)
Eritrean	93	7	–	–	(118)
Nigerian	33	67	–	–	(82)
Total	**60**	**40**	**0.1**	**0.3**	**(778)**

The 11 per cent of Sri Lankans identified as Christians may have been inflated by our decision to conduct interviews at Christian-run shelters for those who had run away from their employers. In Cairo, the proportions of Christians are high among Filipinas, Eritreans and Ethiopians. The same trends are apparent among employers; 60 per cent of the employers in Beirut were Christian, while 67 per cent of employers in Cairo were Muslim. The religions of employers and domestic workers do not always match. In Beirut, 44 per cent of Christian domestic workers were employed in Muslim households, 54 per cent in Christian households and 2 per cent in Druze households; 59 per cent of Muslim domestic workers were employed by Muslims; 70 per cent of the Buddhist Sri Lankans were employed by Christians. In Cairo, 64 per cent of Christian workers were employed in Muslim households, while 70 per cent of Muslims were employed by Christians.

Working Conditions

The working conditions of migrant domestic workers are influenced by their legal status in the countries where they work. Between Cairo and Beirut, there are marked differences in the legal status of the surveyed women that may also affect their working conditions, e.g., wages and work hours, and their reports of human rights violations. In Beirut, 75 per cent of respondents lived-in with their employing household (Table 6.6).

Table 6.6 Employment status of respondents (per cent)

	Live-in	Freelance	'Runaway' (not employed)	N
Beirut				
Sri Lankan	66	26	8	(200)
Filipina	84	12	4	(200)
Ethiopian	75	19	6	(208)
Total	**75**	**19**	**6**	
N =	(458)	(116)	(34)	(608)
Cairo				
Egyptian	42	58		(149)
Filipina	58	32	10	(116)
Indonesian	50	45	5	(62)
Sudanese	18	82		(125)
Ethiopian	54	46		(129)
Eritrean	32	68		(118)
Nigerian	100			(82)
Total	**48**	**50**	**2**	
N=	(372)	(395)	(14)	(781)

Those who were 'freelancing' had previously been on contract, but had left their employers and were working as domestic workers part-time, some for more than one household. Almost all freelancers are working illegally as they do not have a legitimate sponsor. Some have a sponsor who regularly renews their permits, although this is an illegal arrangement, for the sponsor (*kafeel*) should be their exclusive employer. These women usually pay a commission to their sponsors and pay for their own residency permits and insurance. Women classified as 'runaways' (not working) are those who had absconded from their employers but were not employed. These women were most likely to have been interviewed in shelters (safe houses) of NGOs or their embassies.

In Cairo, 85 per cent of all foreign workers surveyed stated they were working illegally. Excluding those from the Philippines and Indonesia, 98 per cent said they were working illegally (i.e. Sudanese, Eritrean, Ethiopian and Nigerians). Almost all Sudanese, Ethiopians and Eritreans were refugees with blue cards (i.e. UNHCR registered refugees), yellow cards (UNHCR registered asylum seekers), files under appeal, or closed files (refugee status denied by UNHCR) that rendered them ineligible to work in Egypt. Approximately half (57 per cent) of the Filipinas, one third (34 per cent) of Indonesians, six Ethiopians (5 per cent), two Sudanese, one Eritrean and one Nigerian in the survey had work permits. Even the women who reported that they had work visas were only eligible to work on contracts that specified their employers, places of employment and duration of contract. The 14 domestic workers who had open-ended permission to work were married to Egyptians. Approximately half the domestic workers in Cairo were living in their employers' households. The exceptions were the Nigerians, all of whom were live-in workers, and the Sudanese and Eritreans, most of whom did not live-in.

Wages and Remittances

As is well known throughout the Middle East, the services of Filipina domestic workers come at a premium, as they are generally the highest paid and have the most prestige. This was the case in both Beirut and Cairo (Table 6.7). It is noticeable, however, that in Cairo a significant proportion of Indonesian workers also receive wages above US$400 per month. These women are most likely to be employed by senior government officials, military and personnel of foreign corporations and embassies who can arrange work visas and are obliged to pay higher wages. In Cairo, the high proportion of Egyptians and Sudanese who received relatively low wages can be partly explained by part-time employment, because most had their children with them. While there would seem to be a correlation between level of education and wage levels, this is not the case. There is no consistent explanation for the differential wage rates, other than agents' and employers' vague notions about competency, reliability and trustworthiness, language (whether or not they can speak Arabic or English) and physical attractiveness, as some employers and agents have admitted (Jureidini 2010).

Table 6.7 Wages per month (per cent)

Beirut									
	<$100	$101–150	$151–200	$201–250	$251–300	$301–350	$351–400	>$400	(N)
Sri Lanka		57	11	11	7	7	6	2	(183)
Philippines		16	29	17	17	6	10	5	(186)
Ethiopia		40	19	14	17	7	2	1	(201)
Total		**37**	**20**	**14**	**14**	**6**	**6**	**3**	**(570)**
Cairo									
Egypt	31	44	22	2	1				(148)
Philippines	2	6	16	16	15	13	6	29	(110)
Indonesia	5	39	10	3	9	3		31	(59)
Sudan	43	36	11	7	1	2			(124)
Ethiopia	1	7	25	12	20	20	9	6	(128)
Eritrea	2	7	33	15	32	12			(118)
Nigeria			6	51	31	12			(82)
Total	**14**	**20**	**19**	**14**	**15**	**9**	**2**	**8**	**(769)**

Many more migrant domestic workers in Beirut than in Cairo are supporting families in their home countries through remittances. In Beirut, the majority of respondents (85 per cent) sent money monthly to members of their families, whether they were never married (82 per cent), married (85 per cent), separated (95 per cent), divorced (75 per cent) or widowed (97 per cent). Ninety-three per cent of Filipinas remitted money compared with 81 per cent of Ethiopians and 80 per cent of the Sri Lankans. In Cairo, less than half, 42 per cent, of all migrant domestic workers sent monthly remittances to their home countries although more separated and divorced women, 61 per cent and 64 per cent respectively, made monthly payments. There were also significant differences in the proportions paying remittances between the different nationalities. While 84 per cent of Filipinas, 61 per cent of Nigerians and 56 per cent of Ethiopians sent money home, this was the case for only 37 per cent of Indonesians, 32 per cent Eritreans and 2 per cent Sudanese. The low rates of remittances in Cairo by some groups of women were due partly to their refugee status, having their families with them in Egypt and no immediate family members remaining in their countries of origin.

Hours of Work

In Beirut, restrictions on domestic workers' freedom of movement experienced by almost one third of the women who were interviewed are not just rules imposed by employers, they also reflect the length of the women's work hours (Table 6.8). Sixty-five per cent of respondents worked 11 or more hours per day; 42 per cent worked 13 or more hours per day; 31 per cent worked 15 or more hours per day and many added that they were 'on-call' 24 hours a day (Jureidini 2005).

Table 6.8 Hours of work (per cent)

	Beirut[6]	**Cairo**	
	Live-in	**Live-in**	**Freelance**
Per day	%	%	%
<8	7	12	2
8	9	5	2
09–10	19	6	6
11–12	23	9	20
13–14	11	19	27
15–16	21	20	19
17–18	8	14	13
19–20	2	6	9
Unlimited	0	9	2
N	458	372	395

6 Information about hours of work and time off is not available for women who freelance in Beirut.

In Cairo, the work hours for live-in domestic workers are equally long with 78 per cent working 11 or more hours per day, 49 per cent reporting 15 or more hours per day and 29 per cent working 17 or more hours per day (Table 6.8). Surprisingly, freelance workers in Cairo reported equally long hours of work with 90 per cent working 11 or more hours, 43 per cent working 15 or more hours per day and 24 per cent working 17 or more hours per day.

In addition, close to 40 per cent of respondents worked seven days a week, regardless of whether they were live-in or freelance (Table 6.9). Most of the others had 24 hours or less of rest during the week. The similarities in work hours between live-in and freelance workers in Cairo are surprising. Domestic workers appear to have little or no social protection, even those who are Egyptian.

Table 6.9 Regular time off (per cent)

	Beirut	Cairo	
	Live-in	Live-in	Freelance
	%	%	%
None	34	43	38
Once a week	42	40	49
Twice a week	6	10	10
Every two weeks	4	2	2
Every four weeks	2	2	1
Only with family	2	3	0
Anytime	2	0	0

Another crucial aspect of domestic work concerns the places where live-in domestic workers sleep. Domestic workers who have their own rooms may be more comfortable but a solitary room is a double-edged privileged. It affords workers protection from the rest of the household, but it also creates opportunities for sexual harassment and other forms of abuse out of the purview of family members (see Jureidini 2006). In Beirut and Cairo, most live-in domestic workers had their own rooms, 60 per cent and 51 per cent, respectively. The working days of those who sleep in the kitchen, living room, or other space that is used by family members are extended because the worker is forced to stay up until all other family members have gone to bed, which in many Arab households can be well after midnight.

Human Rights Violations

Beyond their working conditions, migrant domestic workers suffer a wide range of human rights abuses that violate international agreements. One of the most common complaints of migrant domestic workers and their advocates is the withholding of passports by employers that violates women's rights to freedom of movement. In Beirut, over 90 per cent of migrant domestic workers had their passports held by the employer. Not surprisingly, live-in workers were more likely than freelancers to have their passports held by their employers. In Cairo, however, perhaps because of the preponderance of refugee domestic workers, the study found only one quarter of workers had their passports held by their employer. Interestingly, however, most of those whose passports were held were Filipinas (44 per cent) and Ethiopians (43 per cent). Like the Filipinas, the Ethiopians whose passports were being held were those who had come to Egypt specifically to do domestic work and who had been recruited and placed by agents. No Nigerians reported having their passports held even though the majority (82 per cent) said that they had come to Egypt specifically to work and half had used the services of an Egyptian employment agency. It seems Nigerians were able to keep control of their passports unlike Filipinas and Eritreans, but in a context where labour migrants from these countries expect passports to be withheld.

Harassment: Yelling and Name-Calling

Abuse in the form of yelling and name-calling is also widespread in Beirut and in Cairo where 52 per cent and 59 per cent of respondents, respectively, reported being yelled at. Yelling included abuse such as 'I'll cut your tongue out' – 'I'll kill you' and '*Touf a la rasik*' (I spit on your head). In Beirut and Cairo, the female employer was yelling and threatening in 75 per cent and 73 per cent of cases. Respondents gave a number of reasons for being yelled at including work-related mistakes, being late, the children's behaviour, language difficulties, slow work, the worker's requests for money or food, other work-related disagreements, and 'no reason'. Many respondents did not understand why they were being yelled at or they accepted that the employer was just 'in a bad mood'. While yelling may be seen as a normal response to mistakes in the workplace, frequent and derogatory yelling is a serious form of intimidation and abuse. It is often difficult to determine how seriously the above statements are invoked, however, in most of the reported instances, yelling constituted threats of violence.

In Beirut, there was little difference between the nationalities of workers who were yelled at while in Cairo, more Sudanese (82 per cent) and Egyptians (71 per cent) complained about yelling. The impact of yelling was more hurtful for workers whose cultures frown upon and actively suppress yelling – i.e., Filipinas, Sri Lankans, Indonesians and Sudanese.

Interviewees were also asked, 'Are you called names?' In Beirut, 31 per cent and in Cairo, 30 per cent said 'yes'. The most common taunt in both countries was *hmara*, meaning 'donkey' or 'stupid'. In Beirut, the other names used were *hayawany* (animal), *sharmuta* (whore), *wisikha* (dirty), and *kalbi* (dog/bitch). In Cairo, similar names were used, but they also included *abed* (meaning slave). There were also racist taunts; for example, Africans were called *Kalb Aswad* (black dog), *Ya Khara* (you shit), *ya aswad* (you black one), *bint al wiskha* (dirty girl), *bint al kalb* (daughter of a dog) and *honga bonga* (no translation). Egyptians were more likely to be called *sharmouta* (prostitute), *hayawana* (animal), *hashara* (insect), *khanzeera* (pig), *sorsa* (cockroach) or *fallaha* (peasant). Female employers were mostly responsible for this type of abuse. Seventy-four per cent and 51 per cent, respectively, were reported to be the female employers in Beirut and in Cairo. These names clearly indicate status degradation and racist attitudes towards the migrant domestic workers in their households.

Physical and Sexual Abuse

Physical abuse is damaging in and of itself and it establishes a constant threat of further violence in the future. In Beirut, 14 per cent of all survey respondents said they had been physically abused and in Cairo, 27 per cent of respondents said they had been physically hit, which was almost double the incidence reported in Beirut. In both countries, slapping, hitting with an object, pushing, punching, kicking, hitting with a shoe, pulling ears and burning with a cigarette were reported. Some respondents also indicated they were spat on. Consistent with other studies around the world, most hitting was perpetrated by the 'madam' of the household, that is, the female employer (70 per cent). Despite the similarities in patterns of abuse, there are differences in the frequency with which abuse is reported by individual nationalities in the two cities. Of those who reported being physically abused, there were no differences between the three nationalities in Beirut, but in Cairo the percentages reporting physical abuse varied with 63 per cent for Indonesians, 35 per cent for Sudanese, 34 per cent for Eritreans and 25 per cent for Egyptians.

Interviewees were also asked if they had experienced any kind of sexual harassment where they worked. This kind of abuse is typically under-reported because of shame and stigma, so interviewees were also asked whether they knew of others who had been sexually harassed or molested. The proportion of those who said 'yes' to the second question rose substantially. The types of incidents reported included demanding sex, verbal harassment, touching, exposing genitals, showing pornographic films and materials, and attempted and actual rape and gang rape.

In Beirut, 7 per cent of respondents reported experiencing some form of sexual harassment. When asked if they knew of others who were sexually harassed, 23 per cent said 'yes'. A slightly higher proportion of Sri Lankans (10 per cent) reported sexual harassment and abuse than Ethiopians (8 per cent) and Filipinas (4 per cent). In Cairo, 10 per cent of interviewees complained of sexual harassment with larger percentages of Indonesians (27 per cent) and Sudanese (15 per cent) reporting sexual abuse. When respondents were asked if they knew of others who were sexually harassed, 18 per cent said 'yes'.

Typically, the perpetrators of sexual harassment were the male employers, sons of the employers, other male relatives of the employers and in one case, the father of an employer. In three cases in Cairo, the abuser was a single male employer. In Beirut this did not arise because it is illegal for a single male to sponsor a migrant domestic worker in Lebanon (see Jureidini 2002). Job loss often results from complaints about sexual harassment. Typically, those who were subjected to sexual harassment were threatened with losing their jobs, physical violence, being sent home or being sent to prison to maintain their silence. One interviewee said: 'The husband comes to my room every night for sex. I can't say no because he gives me money and helps me with many things'.

Combining the data from Beirut and Cairo reveals that only 15 per cent of the male employers who were physically abusive towards the domestic worker were also physically abusive with their wives. Of the female employers who were physically abusive towards the domestic worker, only 18 per cent were themselves physically abused by their husbands. Although it may not be entirely conclusive, these two surveys suggest that there is no, or only a weak, relationship between physical abuse in the family and physical abuse against domestic workers. The non-sexual physical abuse of domestic workers by female employers cannot be easily attributed to the general patriarchal subordination of women in the Middle East, for there is little empirical evidence that male violence towards their wives and women generally contributes directly to the physical abuse of migrant domestic workers.

Conclusions

The poor working conditions of migrant domestic workers in the Middle East are well known and they mirror those in other countries. The two surveys here provide a detailed demographic profile of migrant domestic workers in two Middle Eastern countries and offer some sense of the extent of violations of their human rights (both individually and structurally). In Beirut and Cairo, relatively young populations of women (most between 20–40 years of age) from Asia and Africa are employed as domestic workers. Almost half of them are separated from children who remained in their home countries and except for Indonesians, Sudanese and Nigerians in Egypt, the majority were sending money home to their families. Only the women from the Philippines and Indonesia had done some post-secondary school education or training, while most Sri Lankans and Egyptians had only completed primary school.

Collectively, most domestic workers earned between US$120–175 per month. In Egypt, the majority (85 per cent) of foreign domestic workers were working illegally, but with impunity. Half of them lived independently from the households where they worked. While three quarters of the sample surveyed in Lebanon were living in the household, 19 per cent were freelancers, working illegally and thus, tenuously. With families dependent upon their earnings for survival, many domestic workers are vulnerable to abuse and often tolerate difficult and arduous working conditions. Most are working 11 or more hours per day, with at least one quarter reporting they work 15 or more hours per day, and generally with little or no time off.

Rights abuses included withholding passports, particularly in Beirut, psychological abuse such as being yelled at (56 per cent) and being called derogatory names (30 per cent), physical abuse (21 per cent) and sexual abuse (9 per cent). Although the findings reveal that only a minority of domestic workers are psychologically, physically and sexually abused, the large numbers of migrant domestic workers in the Middle East mean the absolute number of women who are suffering rights abuses is very large (e.g. 10 per cent of 3 million = 300,000).

The conditions under which domestic workers live and work are unregulated and they are not protected by labour unions. In Lebanon, migrant domestic workers are not allowed to form or belong to trade unions that may negotiate collectively on their behalf and under the *kafala* system they cannot withdraw their labour without serious repercussions. In this sense they are 'unfree'. In Egypt, while most are able to leave their employers, and, in principle, may join existing trade unions, almost all migrant domestic workers are working illegally and are unable to bargain collectively. Egyptian domestic workers cannot join trade unions because they are not even recognized as being employed. Isolated and vulnerable within private households, domestic workers are difficult to organize. International efforts to bring about more regulation and protection of this widespread occupation include the Convention for Decent Work for Domestic Workers approved at the 100th Annual Conference of the ILO in June 2011. By March 2014, the convention had been ratified by thirteen countries including Argentina, Germany, Ecuador, Italy, South Africa, the Philippines, Mauritius, Costa Rica, Guyana, Uruguay, Bolivia, Nicaragua, and Paraguay. By accepting domestic work as 'real work' and not simply an extension of unpaid household and care work, the ILO convention recognizes domestic workers as workers in a formal employment relationship, acknowledges the skills involved in domestic work, and codifies domestic workers' rights to organize and join trade unions and to establish decent conditions of work as well as the right to and access to training.

The findings from surveys in Beirut and Cairo confirm that attention to various rights including freedom of movement, the right to change employers, freedom from harassment, physical and psychological abuse, and sexual exploitation and the right to decent living conditions is essential to improve the living and working conditions of migrant domestic workers. In countries such as Lebanon, recruitment and placement agents for migrant domestic workers need to be better regulated and the state must intervene seriously in cases of abuse and death. For without proper regulation – with legislation and contracts – the state must be held responsible for the moral hazard of ultimately encouraging abuse, exploitation and human trafficking.

PART II
International Domestic Work and the Family: Remaking Femininity and Motherhood

Chapter 7

Unravelling Privilege: Workers' Children and the Hidden Costs of Paid Child Care[1]

Mary Romero

Introduction

Workers' children often suffer the consequences of our society's low minimum wage, lack of health care and child care benefits, inflexible work schedules, as well as required overtime. These conditions are commonly experienced by the children of the working poor and lower-middle-class who occupy a wide range of low-wage dead-end jobs. However, when factory or office workers are required to remain on the job after hours the benefits to the employer and costs to the worker are camouflaged with layers of economic exchange. In contrast, the children of parents employed in domestic service and the rest of the low-wage caring industry frequently experience a special stigma and form of exploitation. They see first-hand, not only the material abundance and fortunate circumstances of the children of privilege, they experience directly the exchange of inequity. The higher quality paid reproductive labour the employers' families receive produces as a direct consequence less unpaid reproductive labour in their own families. In other words, when a household worker is asked to stay an extra hour to watch the employer's child or to do additional cleaning, this takes an hour from her own child, her ability to provide 'quality' time or do reproductive labour in her home.

I want to conceptualize child care as a scarce resource in order to address inequities and privileges maintained by the failure to address the need for care giving with the fundamental restructuring of society. Limiting the discussion to the ways that care work is normatively linked to gender (Cancian and Olikder 1999) and measuring the disproportionate care giving between men and women within the family (Blair and Lichter 1991) erases the imbalances between families. The current crisis in work and family is not only the result of women entering the labour force, the gendered division of domestic labour, and the devaluation of care giving but it is related to numerous social changes that occurred simultaneously.

In order to reveal the hidden costs of paid reproductive labour in employers' homes, I examined the 'mothering' of domestics and nannies' children (Romero

1 This chapter is a shorter version of: 'Unraveling Privilege: Workers' Children and the Hidden Costs of Paid Child Care', Symposium on The Structures of Care Work, *Chicago-Kent Law Review* 76 (3): 101–121 (2001).

1997). This research uncovered both micro and macro linkages between paid and unpaid reproductive labour and related systems of privilege and domination made necessary by inadequate assistance for all working families. In this chapter, I will argue that reforms and proposals ignoring the working conditions of women paid care workers presuppose gender essentialism (Harris 1999) while perpetuating ideological assumptions about the nature of caring that reinforce the status quo (Wildman 1996). I will briefly reiterate major themes in the work and family conflict literature and note their linkages to earlier feminist debates on the 'politics of housework' (Malos 1980), and the social construction of contemporary mothering. I will then consider how hiring a domestic or nanny enables middle-class women to enter the labour force while retaining aspects of mothering central to her class and gender identity by shifting oppressive aspects of care giving, thus reproducing stratified social relationships.

I begin by analysing how care processes and social relationships embedded in the hiring of nannies expose class privilege and the social curriculum of class relations that socialize employers' and workers' children to their social positions. I then examine care work in the worker's family from the standpoint of the children (D. Smith 1999). Like the employers' children who might accompany their mothers and fathers to college campuses, law firms, science laboratories and hospital wards, the children of domestic workers are socialized by helping their mothers clean apartments, private houses and small office buildings. In each instance the children are exposed to their mothers' work status and are treated accordingly. I will summarize my own research on private household workers and their children (Romero 1997), while building on the legal and social science literature on in-home workers classified as domestics, nannies, au pairs, caretakers, and babysitters. Interview data that I collected from the adult children of domestic workers facilitates rethinking care giving as a nationally and global need rather than a private family issue. I argue that solutions to society's care needs structured around individual responsibility and purchasing power reproduce a stratified nation of racialized, classed, and gendered American families. I conclude with a call for proposals that engage in the fundamental restructuring of the economy.

Uncovering the 'Nature' of Unpaid and Paid Child Care

The care crisis depicted in recent legal and social science feminist writings has revived arguments that are reminiscent of the 1960s and 70s debates on the 'politics of housework' (Malos 1980). The debate began with the conceptualization of care work as women's unpaid labour relegated to the private sphere of the family (Kimmel 1996, Roberts 1997). It continued by identifying the inequalities that women as caretakers experience as employees (Williams 2000, Blau and Ehrenberg 1997), and noted the absence of public support for care giving (Michel 1999, Rose 1999, Heen 1995). The theoretical similarities bring us full circle, forcing a reconceptualization of the essence of care (Cancian and Oliker 1999).

Care Work, Parenting and Motherhood

During the last four decades of women's increased participation in the labour force, there have been significant increases in men's contribution to family care (Coltrane and Galt 2000), nonetheless the burden of care work in the family remains on the shoulders of women (Sheldon 1992). Married women with children not only do a greater share of domestic work (Coltrane and Galt 2000), but are responsible for major household tasks that are the most time-consuming and less open to postponement. Not surprisingly, working mothers report less leisure time and experience higher levels of stress than their husbands (Hochschild 1989). Simultaneously, there is increased promotion of 'family values' and male responsibility while strong essentialist beliefs about women as caregivers and mothers are emphasized, and caring for children is represented as natural, universal and unchanging (Coltrane and Galt 2000). Traditional male roles as protector, provider and leaders are central tenets in the conservative defence of traditional fatherhood while nurturing remains a nearly exclusive feature of mothering, and more generally, of womanhood: 'all women need to be mothers, that all mothers need their children and that all children need their mothers' (Oakley 1974: 186).

Contemporary views on socially appropriate mothering constitute 'a gendered model that advises mothers to expend a tremendous amount of time, energy, and money in raising their children' (Hays 1996: 54). In her book, *The Cultural Contradictions of Motherhood*, sociologist Sharon Hays identified the prevailing ideology of motherhood prescribed by child care experts, and accepted by mothers, as advocating child-centred, emotionally demanding, labour-intensive and financially draining methods. The increasing emotional dimension of motherhood transfers household tasks and childcare from 'real' work to a 'labour of love' and builds on the ideological foundation inherited from the 'cult of domesticity' and the 'cult of true womanhood'. Principles of scientific management applied to homemaking, along with the growing industry of child rearing manuals, teach a middle-class working mother to adopt the mother-manager model that requires her to devote herself to arranging activities that further her children's development and monopolizes 'quality' time with her children.

Substituting Mothers

Sub-Dividing Care Work

Private household workers are distinguished from nannies along the lines of housecleaning and childcare; however, job descriptions do not necessarily fall neatly into these separate categories (Wrigley 1995, Anderson 2000). Live-in domestics and nannies have the most difficulty maintaining boundaries between housecleaning and childcare, but all private household workers struggle against increasing workloads that blur the distinction. Live-in positions incorporating both childcare and housework lend themselves to particular abuse because of the unregulated work hours, expectation of emotional labour, and the vulnerable status of the worker (Colen 1995). Emotional labour is more likely required of domestics assigned care giving tasks (Sussar 1991): 'The domestic is ... an extension of, surrogate for, the woman of the house' (Rollins 1985: 183) and consequently they were frequently expected to fulfil the psychological needs of their employers and families (MacDonald 1998). Based on her analysis of various work situations, Judith Rollins concluded that employers expecting emotional labour hire women to relieve them from the burden of housework and to enhance their own feelings of superiority. Applying Rollins' analysis to the specific case of live-in nannies, hiring a surrogate is an ideal strategy for maintaining child-centred, emotionally demanding, and labour-intensive mothering, while shifting the burden from one's own shoulders. Domestics and nannies are relegated the more physical and taxing part of child work while employers upgrade their own status to mother-managers (Rothman 1989).

Working Conditions

The structure of the occupation, characterized by the informality of negotiations conducted in the privacy of the employer's home and lacking definitive contract criteria (Sussar 1991), affords considerable opportunities for employer abuses (Romero 1997) and makes it difficult or impossible for workers to organize (P. Smith 1999). While employers in domestic service engage in similar self-interests as other employers – increasing the amount of labour and decreasing its value – they resist other dimensions of employment: (1) acknowledging that when a private household worker or caretaker is hired, their home becomes the employee's workplace; (2) accepting the worker as an employee rather than an extension of the employer's roles as housewife or mother; and (3) actively resisting practices of modern work culture. Domestic labour may be priceless, but employers are unwilling to pay very much for it (Romero 1992).

While intimate relationships between employees and employers have been material for novels, films, and myths, studies indicate that such relationships are much more exploitative than personally or financially rewarding to workers. Judith Rollins (1985), Evelyn Nakano Glenn (1986), and others counter popular media depictions of maids and butlers. Rather than treatment as 'one of the family', the occupation is characterized by everyday rituals of verbal and spatial deference (Romero 1992). Rollins argued that the rituals functioned to affirm and enhance the status of employers and their families. Bridget Anderson (2000: 19–20) asserted that:

> The employment as a paid domestic worker ... facilitates status reproduction, not only by maintaining status objects, enabling the silver to be polished and the clothes to be ironed, but also by serving as a foil to the lady of the house. The hired productive worker is reproducing social beings and sets of relationships

> that are not merely her own but also deeply antagonist to her own interests. Her presence emphasizes and reinforces her employer's identity – as a competent household manager, as middle-class, as white – and her own as its opposite.

By purchasing the low-wage labour of other women in order to substitute for the unpaid labour of wives and mothers, employers are engaged in the social reproduction of their family status; that is, social reproduction of privilege based on gender, as well as class, race, sexuality, and citizenship.

Labour Market Dynamics

Both micro and macro-levels of analysis demonstrate how racialized-gendered-immigrants and non-migrants (Abramovitz 1996, Law 1983) are positioned on the continuum of household labour as domestics, nannies, and au pairs; and differentiated by wages, benefits and overall working conditions. At a micro-level, employee and employer social networks (Romero 1992, Glenn 1985) and employer preferences (Wrigley 1995, Rollins 1985) shape local domestic labour workforces. Employee and employer networks are evident in the residential clusters of racialized and immigrant domestics and nannies throughout the country. Different populations of workers frequently become stereotyped as ideal employees for housework, childcare or for live-in positions (Mattingly 1999). Past work experience or skills are less likely to be the basis for hiring private household workers than personality (Romero 1997). Racial and ethnic preferences for housework versus childcare, as well as women's willingness to do the most work for the least pay, are common criteria used to hire domestics. Consequently, paid domestic labour is not only segregated by gender but is stratified by race and citizenship status; higher status individuals are employed at the top of the market and individuals with the lowest status are employed in the least favourable working conditions. Macro-level analysis of labour-market dynamics indicate that areas with the highest levels of income inequality employ the largest number of private household workers in the country (Milkman 1998). Immigration and welfare policies control the flow of low-wage workers available for domestic and nanny positions. Restricting government subsidies and opportunities for legal work status or citizenship, ghettoizes specific populations of women in domestic service (Mattingly 1999, Chang 2000).

Revealing Privileges Embedded in Paid Care Work

Mothering and the Boundaries of Paid Care Work: Who is Caring for the Maid's Children?

The childcare arrangements made by private household workers and nannies are similar to those of other poor and working-class mothers in the US: mothers and fathers juggle work hours in order that one parent can be home with the children;

they call upon relatives or siblings for help; they give older siblings responsibility for childcare and domestic labour; sometimes they are forced to leave the children alone, or in a few cases, take their children to work. Changes in work and school schedules require flexibility and contingency plans, but the absence of available and affordable childcare greatly limits the options available to paid workers.

Live-in positions pose severe restrictions making it difficult and sometimes impossible for domestics to mother their own children. The circumstances forcing working mothers to accept live-in positions underscore the irony that 'to be good mothers, women leave their children to migrate' (Colen 1989: 172–173). Women accept live-in positions during periods of economic crisis or during a transitional process to residing in the US. Occasionally, women find employers who are willing to accept their children (usually one child) as part of the live-in arrangement. Two children of domestic workers that I interviewed described mothers who were employed as live-in workers and had arranged to keep their children with them full-time and one mother who kept her daughters with her on weekends. One child remembers:

> It was extremely hard for her to spend the weekend away from us where we didn't really know anyone here. I spent most of the time during weekends with my father, but so then as she got to know the Patrona we were able to go there with her and spend the weekend with her, and she really liked us and she actually liked us to talk to her two children – the little girl was five and the little boy was two or three. She liked us to speak to them in Spanish. They were fluent in Spanish and French and English. She really liked having us around, so we would go. We would go to the park.

Both began by sharing the maid's quarters with their mothers as small children and as the employers' children left for college and vacated their rooms, they moved into their own rooms. In both cases, employers were unable to pay a full-time salary thus requiring their mothers to do day work throughout the neighbourhood, and then return to clean and pick-up after their live-in employer. The arrangement was maintained through most of the women's working lives because living-in with one employer and doing day work allowed the workers to enroll their children in neighbourhood schools that were some of the best in the country (Romero 1997). However, in each case, the boundaries between family and work were blurred and the distinction between paid and unpaid reproductive labour disappeared.

A growing number of working women employed as domestics and nannies are engaged in transnational mothering. The following account of children who spent a number of years with their grandmothers while their mothers were employed as live-in domestics, exemplifies the conditions, personal sacrifices, and family disruption posed in transnational motherhood. When Sophia Miller was 12, her mother migrated to New York from St Vincent, leaving her for four years. Once her mother obtained a green card, she was able to send for her daughter and son. Years later, as a college student, Sophia still felt the loss and rupture in the mother–daughter relationship. The following quote points to the personal cost of transnational mothering.

> Those four years I went through a lot of changes and she wasn't there. I think growing up I didn't really need her as much as I needed her during that four years when she left. So like, I don't know there's things I would've liked to talk to her about and she wasn't there, and now she's around I really don't have that need for her as much as I did back then, and I that's something I can't get over you. I keep saying, 'Well you weren't around. You were never there'. I've kind of resented her at first ... 'Why isn't she coming back [I asked my grandmother]. 'She said she was going to be gone for a month'. She was gone for four years. We resented her for that for a while, I really did.

Time spent at work, the demand to work late, and requests to take work home are all factors influencing the rearing and socialization of the workers' children. The circumstances of child rearing for immigrant and poor women employed as household workers differ from those of their employers. Middle-class children may not spend much more time with their working mothers than the children of domestics, but they are provided a parental substitute. A quote from Edward Miller points to this distinction: 'I only experienced her (mother) from I guess 5:30 to 8:00 at night, for three hours of the day, because we had to go to bed at that time, at eight or eight-thirty at night and the little white kids got to benefit from her all day'. Live-in as opposed to day work is the major factor shaping domestic workers' mothering. Employers' requests for employees to work in their own homes changes the quality of time spent with the employees' own children. Cooking, sewing and childcare may not be entirely opposed by workers because they can care for their own children while earning money. However, these tasks extend the number of hours engaged in paid labour and shift the cost of equipment and electricity to the worker. Bringing the employer's reproductive labour into the employee's home may also include the children's unpaid labour if they assist their mother in ironing, cooking and babysitting.

Boundaries marking paid and unpaid care giving were significant in identifying the divisions between work and family. Mother-manager was a distinguishing feature of parental activities. William Taylor noted several kinds of employer's requests that crossed the line from paid child care to parenting activities.

> My mother took care of these kids. I think the girl and I were the same ages, and I used to go over once in a while. This woman (employer) just kind of turned over her house to my mother and she ran it. This woman kind of depended on her (mother) for all these little things in life that we normally take care of. But she (mother) just kind of took over the house, took over the kid. She (employer) would say look, 'could you take the kid out' – I don't remember the kid's name – 'and get clothes, school clothes'. So then my mother would get in the car and

> they'd go out and she'd buy her school clothes for the year. She (employer) would leave them money to buy school clothes for the year.

However, at times the boundaries were crossed and domestics' children recognized that they had indeed been the principle caretaker throughout the lives of the employers' children. Edward Miller described his mother's parenting role: 'She (mother) actually raised their kids. And she knew more about what was going on in their lives than they [employers] did'.

Social Reproduction: Learning About Privilege

Domestic service involves the social reproduction of class, as well as gender and race privileges in both employees' and employers' families (Anderson 2000, Rollins 1985). Ascribing the parent's social status to children is a form of social reproduction that links family and work. It takes a peculiar form in domestic service when adolescent children are called upon to augment or replace their mother's paid labour. This is a strategy women doing domestic labour are forced to use to handle family emergencies or illnesses when they fear being fired or losing pay if they miss work. Because they do not receive sick pay or leave, they frequently have no one but family members to call upon. Wages and benefits (or the lack thereof) establish the economic conditions that contextualize child rearing and socialization. Like other poor and working class children, the years of dependency for the children of women in domestic service are restricted to early childhood rather than extending into adolescence and early adulthood (Elkin and Handel 1984). Children of domestics take their place in the division of household labour with increasing responsibility as they reach adolescence. Unlike upper and middle-class children, these children were expected to engage in household tasks. For the most part, age was the major determining factor in the amount of work they did; and secondly, was gender. Gender was reported to shape the allocation of tasks in families in cases where the oldest child was female; gender was less a factor in families where the eldest child was a son or when all the children were male. The presence of another adult family member, a father or relative, also affected the redistribution of household chores. Of course, children's involvement in domestic work was dependent on the number of hours mothers spent away from home and the family's financial means.

The following accounts illustrate how children learn about privilege. Edward Miller's image of the employer's son clinging to his mother as he cried and the knowledge that he was allowed to express such ownership over his mother was a powerful message of class and race domination, as well as privilege.

> I remember going with my father, I guess I must of been four years old, because I could actually physically stand up on the seat, back then they didn't have car seats and seat belts and all of that, so I would drive with him standing up on the seat, the front seat of this forty-seven chevy we had and we went over to

> the house where my mother worked, the white family that my mother worked for and this little boy, this little white boy about my age was crying his eyes out because my mother was leaving and I remember feeling a twinge of jealously and downright anger because I had been taught never to cry when my mother left because that was something she had to do. So I had already been trained not to express that kind of emotion, 'get used to it, your mother has to go to work'. And here is this little white boy expressing all of this anguish and emotion because my mother was leaving him. My father had gone to pick my mother up from work and she was trying to excuse herself from the little brat and he was crying his eyes out. And I am sitting there watching this and I couldn't cry, I wasn't supposed to cry. So that was first hint of caste and class differences, and culture and all that.

Recounting the complaints her mother made about an employer's child, Linda Duran learned parents' different class expectations and the extra work that privilege meant for her mother:

> They're too submissive, you know, the kids run wild. One kid has a room full of stuffed animals. Evidently they're all over the dresser and the bed and the floor and this angers her because she's got to pick them up to dust underneath it and that sort of thing. 'The kid's too damn old to be having all this stuff in there anyway' and 'I don't understand why they have to have so many'. 'The kid is twelve and why do they have teddy bears'. She decided that the kid's not growing up fast enough. So she does talk about it, usually when it affects her work somehow.

Domestic service is a source of knowledge for the workers' children to learn the folkways, mores, norms, values and racial etiquette of class, gender, whiteness, and citizenship. Rituals and practices of deference that characterize servitude are powerful tools of instruction to teach privilege. Answering evening telephone calls from employers exposes children to the linguistic deference common in domestic service: e.g., referring to the worker by her first name while formally addressing the employer; domestics referred to as 'girl', 'my girl' or Maria; and the Anglicization of first names for easier pronunciation. Workers' children experienced spatial deference when they accompanied their mothers to work as helpers or as domestics themselves. They are frequently the recipients of employers' 'gift-giving' of old clothes and other discarded items (Rollins 1985, Romero 1992). The nonreciprocal nature of the interaction and the quality of the exchange is an important lesson in privilege. The system of gifts and favours that shapes the personalism of the relationship into a strategy of oppression is brought home to domestics' children when mothers feel obligated to comply with every employer request. While many of the interviewees recognized that domestic service offered employment in a labour market that held limited options for their mothers and attributed employers' generosity for their additional clothing and opportunity, they still felt strongly that their mothers were frequently manipulated. For instance, in the following account Alex Conrad describes how the employer pressures his mother to work on the holidays by implying she owes a debt.

> This judge (employer) I mentioned, he was instrumental in our lives, my brother got a scholarship to college because he pulled strings. My brother's very bright, but it helped that he could pull some strings. But years later, this woman – the judge was dead – this woman (judge's wife) would call my mother and say, 'would you come out on Saturday and work'. One time she called, it happened that we were home for the holidays and I got angry and my brothers got angry and, 'No. We don't want you to go'. And this woman would invoke, 'after all the judge did for you'. Our response was, 'tell her that your son the college professor and your son the lawyer said that we want you home for the holidays and not going out cleaning her house'. There was this real tension between just the fact that we felt that early on, but we could play her elitist games now and argue back. My mother felt obligation and she felt bad for this woman.

In summary, I found that while the adult children of private household workers did not necessarily understand class and racial stratification, they learned their place in it. Experiences with employers, their children, the peculiar customs and rituals of deference, and the low wages found in domestic service accentuated the significance of class and race in their lives.

Work, Family, and Capitalism: Reproducing the American Family

Affordable child care remains a private and family problem rather than a public issue requiring a public solution. Upper-middle-class families can afford personalized service to augment the limited child care options. As long as the discussions about reproductive labour remain outside the public arena and are characterized as 'a battle between the sexes', our conceptualizations of work and family conflict stagnate. By contrasting motherhood and childhood in the employer and employee family, the divisions of work and family are revealed as social issues that transcend the purely personal. Both employer and employee families have childcare needs but their purchasing power present completely different options placing the children of domestics at an enormous disadvantage. Stories of domestic service told by workers' children accentuate the unequal distribution of reproductive labour at the societal level. Social scientists have restricted their analysis to the family unit which does not capture the ramifications that poorly paid domestic labour and child care has on other sectors of society, particularly the workers' families. The ideal American family depicted in Norman Rockwell drawings and later updated with the two career families and Take your Daughter to Work Day exists because certain groups pay the price. Caring for children is not priceless in our society but usually relies on the cheapest labour available (Roberts 1997). Immigration policies and declining welfare benefits assure professionals of a ready pool of low-wage workers.

By hiring private household workers and nannies as substitute mothers under inferior working conditions, employers are purchasing services crucial to both the reproduction of their families and to the social reproduction of privilege. Rather than challenging the everyday rituals that affirm patriarchy in the home, such as the gendered division of household labour, the work is simply shifted to a poorly paid female employee. The system of privileges available to employers and employees determines child rearing and socialization while reproducing class differences. When immigrant mothers employed as live-in nannies are restricted to the most basic 'mothering' agenda of sending money home to house, feed and clothe their children, while they simultaneously sell their labour as caregivers to middle-class women engaged in intensive mothering, 'quality' time and activities enhancing cognitive development becomes a privilege not a right. Child care policies and programmes that are not inclusive of all mothers, regardless of class, race or citizenship, maintain a system of privileges that relies on subordination.

Chapter 8

Domestic Disturbances: Immigrant Workers, Middle-Class Employers, and the American Dream in Los Angeles

Susanna Rosenbaum

On 25 October, 2012, Marina Krim, a mother in New York City, came home to find every parent's worst nightmare: her two-year-old son and six-year-old daughter had been stabbed by their nanny, Yoselyn Ortega, who although still alive, had slashed her own throat (Ruderman and Santora 2012). While the reason for the stabbing remains unclear, Ortega, a Dominican-born US citizen, was apparently facing financial ruin – her nanny salary and additional income earned selling jewellery and beauty products was barely enough to pay the rent for an apartment shared with three family members. The story immediately became front-page news, as horror and panic spread among all of the families in New York City who employ some sort of stay-at-home childcare. Parenting blogs blew up; some individuals expressed concern and sorrow, others bemoaned the necessity of hiring a nanny and decried working mothers as greedy, while still others faulted the mother for failing to notice that her nanny was 'psycho'. Still another set of discussions focused on the nanny's deficiencies and inevitably called up racist sentiments. On urbanbaby.com, one particular thread stood out. Titled 'I think mexicans [sic] have a violent and bloody culture underlying a lot of other stuff', the conversation proceeded as follows:

> » oh, so she was mexican??
> » More violent than OUR culture???
> » no probably not
> » Well, that explains it. Mexicans are the root of all evil. No other culture or race has ever done harm or committed evil in this world. Just them goddamned Mexicans. Fuckin' taco eaters. Que bueno que no sea una de ellos.
> » she could be from any latin country, really.
> » She's from the DR. Get your prejudices in light with facts!
> » Oh, I have a whole different set of prejudices with that crowd (Urbanbaby.com Thread 2012b).

I begin with this story not to underscore its anomalous nature, but rather to underline its opposite: none of these responses is remarkable. An extreme reaction to an extraordinary instance, it nevertheless contains all of the tropes that characterize childcare issues in the contemporary US. Mother-blame *always* works itself into any discussion of nannies, and this event seemingly substantiated every fear parents have about entrusting their children to someone else's care. Even more, as we see in the above exchange, the national-cum-racial distinction between caregivers and employers, or rather, the homogenizing representation of this difference was at the core of the discussion. Commenters were not sure if the nanny was Mexican, Dominican, or 'from any Latin country, really' – her precise country of origin not nearly as important as her generic 'Latin' foreignness. They completely disregarded that Ortega is an American citizen, an official classification that could not mitigate her essential otherness.

In my fieldwork among immigrant domestic workers and their native-born employers in Los Angeles, I repeatedly heard similar sentiments. Much like the above contributors, the employers I met in LA always returned to the subject of immigration when talking about their domestic employees. Whether weird or wonderful, callous or caring, reckless or responsible, the immigrant women who worked in their homes were always, decidedly, *not* American. In this chapter, I argue that employers' insistence on foreignness helped to alleviate the awkwardness of domestic service. Hiring immigrant women to work in their homes allowed middle-class Angelenos to pursue the American Dream; at the same time, however, it forced them to grapple with the inequalities, inconsistencies, and complicities required to sustain this Dream. That is, to secure their own 'Americanness', they grew increasingly reliant on global processes of migration and paid care work. This disrupted employers' sense of self as well as the mythology of the American Dream. Here, I analyse employers' attempts to manage these contradictions, emphasizing how their discomfort with and discursive constructions of domestic workers illuminate the limits of the American Dream. In so doing, I highlight the concomitant production of the domestic sphere with domestic, or national, borders.

Domestic Service and the American Dream

> All you ladies who put your career and money above your children, this is what can happen. And don't give me the old tired you 'can't afford not to work', which really means 'I dont [sic] want to give up my current lifestyle and move or cut back on the manicures and what have you … (Urbanbaby.com Thread 2012a).

In the wake of the 'killer nanny', the usual denunciations of working mothers became particularly trenchant, but I argue, these sentiments are not atypical. They foreground the well-known difficulties of juggling work and family life and point to the enduring elusiveness of 'having it all'. In contemporary American society, women are required to be both full-time mothers and full-time workers, the first fulfilling the imperatives of femininity while the latter underpins a socially recognizable and respected identity. They are caught in an impossible dilemma that renders *all* of them inadequate, whether they engage in full-time paid employment, part-time work outside of the house, or opt to be stay-at-home mothers. As one mother in LA explained, 'Everything about being a mother is fraught with guilt. If I put my kid in daycare, I'm guilty, if I have a nanny, I'm guilty, if I stay at home – guilty, if I work – guilty …'.

Parenting ideologies aside, many mothers have no choice but to engage in paid employment – their families' middle-class lifestyles, their American Dreams, more dependent than ever on two incomes. In the US 'middle-class'[1] remains an amorphous and ideologically all-inclusive category, since almost everyone claims this status. Classifying oneself as middle-class thus serves less as predictor of income level than as indicator of being a full and respected member of society. For being middle-class is crucial to fulfilling the American Dream, and this accomplishment recursively reveals that an individual is the right kind of person, in possession of the fundamental qualities of 'Americanness' – discipline, determination, and a fierce work ethic.

The American Dream posits a classless, middle-class society and pledges success for anyone willing to work hard. According to Berlant, the Dream 'promises that if you invest your energies in work and family-making, the nation will secure the broader social and economic conditions in which your labor can gain value and your life can be lived with dignity' (1997: 4). Presuming equal and limitless opportunity, the Dream places responsibility on the individual and attributes any failure to personal deficiency (e.g. Fischer 2010). As such, it binds middle-class status to national belonging, distinguishing the proper national subject through her aspirations. In this formulation, middle-class identity is less about a particular level of income than a set of goals, or as Sherry Ortner (2003) terms it a 'project': an open-ended and enthusiastic quest for a better life, regardless of financial status. This ongoing pursuit spans generations, as each cohort must outdo its predecessor, part of an assumed *progression*, a forward movement that continually enhances and expands the prerogatives of 'Americanness'.

Yet this Dream is only sustainable through foreclosure, for its very possibility is premised on its limits. The physical labour of those on the outside supports the lifestyles of those on the inside, and this boundary is constructed by denying entry to particular ethnic, racial, religious, or national groups (Sennett and

---

1 Defining middle-class in the US is a thorny endeavour. Some scholars use occupation rather than income to define the middle class, or sectors within it (e.g. Ehrenreich 1989, Ortner 2003, Devine 2005). Others argue that occupation is not necessarily a good indicator of class status, as the meaning of different occupations has shifted over time (e.g. Walkowitz 1999, Bledstein 2001). Moreover, even individuals whose occupations would position them as working class, continue to identify as middle class (e.g. Halle 1984, Zussman 1985). I rely on self-ascription, since every employer I encountered placed herself in the middle class. Further, as Ortner points out, middle class often 'means simply all those Americans who have signed up for the American dream' (1998: 8).

Cobb 1973, Lowe 1996, Lamont 2000, Liechty 2003, Ortner 2003, Lipsitz 2006). Liechty asserts,

> [o]ver the centuries, slavery, steady influxes of vulnerable immigrant populations, and more recently, highly productive migrant labor populations … have all served as a kind of shifting human extractive frontier (hidden within the nation) that has helped make possible the 'classless' middle-class American lifestyle (2003: 10).

These boundaries are necessary and necessarily invisible, erased through the fiction of equal and infinite opportunity. As such, a lack of success reveals only individual shortcomings, a person's inability to be 'American'. The processes of middle-class, then, produce 'Americanness' by separating those who achieve from those who do not – who *cannot* – into 'Americans' and 'others', internal or otherwise.

Consequently, the Dream is fraught with as much peril as possibility. In fact, every employer I met in Los Angeles, primarily white women in their 30s, 40s, and 50s, fretted about her economic position (Newman 1988, Ehrenreich 1989). Whether pushed to the precipice or not, all of them felt broke, afraid that they would not be able to maintain their standard of living. Life in LA was expensive, rendering uncertain their financial futures. Further, to recognize themselves as successful, they had to guarantee that their children would become middle-class adults. However, this outcome was never certain, as middle-class status is not automatically reproduced; parents cannot pass it on to their children, so it must be attained all over again by the next generation (Ehrenreich 1989, Ortner 1991, Devine 2004).

Individuals did everything they could to facilitate this process, but what it took to prepare children continually expanded. In turn-of-the-millennium LA, raising a successful child required a range of activities, from intellectual stimulation and academic enrichment, to participation in team sports, a nice house, a constantly-expanding number of consumer goods, and vacations to far-flung places. As basic needs inflated, so did expense, often pushing families past their financial limits. More and more, providing for children required two incomes and a great deal of time. Shuttling children from one activity to the next organized parents' lives and this without including the requisite 'quality' time one had to allot kids.

As a result, the tensions between home and work magnified, exacerbating an already precarious situation. Kristen, a white, 38-year-old mother of two who worked as a legal secretary, characterized her life as a 'constant battle':

> this is where a big chunk of the dilemma comes from – being a parent and living, living in this city and trying to raise your children in the best way you can … what you're saying, the juggling, the balancing, there is no balance. Something is always giving. Whether it's me giving myself up, whether it's my kids giving

> up their parents ... Something is always giving, and as time goes on, you find that more and more things are giving (Kristen, personal interview, 2003).

Part of the problem was the conflicting demands, the impossible choice between earning a sustainable living and spending time with your children:

> you can't be expected to be there and not be there at the same time but that's what we are expected to do as parents ... . It's this total line between what we in society are saying, these are our expectations of you as a parent, despite the fact you're working full time, you still have to do these things (Kristen, personal interview, 2003).

For Kristen, as for many others, domestic service provided a short-term, stop-gap solution. Paying someone to clean and/or take care of the children eased the stresses, permitting parents to work late or travel for their jobs; it also liberated individuals from housework, and in turn, afforded more time for their careers, to enjoy their kids, or to take up additional leisure activities.

But this did not solve the conflict, merely papered it over, bringing other inconsistencies into sharp relief. A majority of employers expressed deep discomfort with this occupation, since it suddenly made their privilege visible, challenging their middle-class status. After all, to be middle class is to be ordinary, to be ambitious, hard-working, and successful but to remain disciplined and modest. While the belief in American exceptionalism emphasizes the singularity of the nation vis-à-vis the world, 'ordinariness' remains crucial to being a desirable member of the nation (e.g. Lamont 1992, 2000, Kefalas 2003, Devine 2005). And, it is this defining principle that domestic service throws into question: the presence of a domestic employee, usually a Spanish-speaking immigrant woman, forces middle-class employers to see the economic and social disparities that uphold their lifestyles.[2]

For employers, the possibility of inequality, the idea that their success was somehow less than fully earned, was disruptive – so much so, that many struggled even with the decision to take on a domestic employee. For instance, Allison, a 39-year-old African American lawyer and mother, explained her reluctance to hire someone:

> I'm not about being *grand* or being, *you know*, I want my things to be nice, and I worked hard to be in the middle-class. It wasn't obvious that I was gonna be here, and I'm not ashamed of it or embarrassed about it, but it's not like, you know, I didn't need to have the biggest house on the block or the fanciest deck and a new car, and all that kind of stuff, right? It's important to me that my

2 Berlant maintains 'the affective fantasy of the normal requires activation of what Sedgwick calls "the privilege of unknowing" the social costs to others of a general sense of personal freedom' (2008: 9, cf. Berlant 2011).

> house, that we behave in ways that are civil to one another and that we *talk* to each other … . We say *thank you* and *please* to each other … . And, so then I can say to [my daughter] when she does something, we don't talk to each other like that (Allison, personal interview 2003).

Seven months pregnant and working full-time, Allison had grudgingly, and temporarily, contracted someone to clean her home every two weeks. She believed that she should be able to handle all of her commitments and considered herself a failure for her inability to do so. Although she was proud of her upward mobility, she feared losing her moral centre. Did she really need help or had she succumbed to the decadence and indolence of the upper classes? She was not certain. More importantly, she wanted to ensure that her daughter learned the proper values and worried that exposing her to domestic service would produce an attitude of entitlement rather than the expectation of hard work and self-disciplined ambition.

Similarly, Kate, a white, 40-year-old stay-at-home mother, recalled that she had had to convince herself to bring in someone to clean. Kate hated housework, and as the mother of a two-year-old and a nine-month-old, had little time to devote to it. Nevertheless, it felt 'strange' to hire someone, and her husband had to talk her into it, pointing out that she would have more time to enjoy her kids if she did not have to worry about cleaning. He understood her hesitation, for he had felt the same way when he first paid someone to mow the lawn:

> So the same kind of internal dialogue that I had with myself for internal, you know, cleaning, household cleaning, that he had for himself. I guess giving up that was kinda like I don't know, like he would be much better than, kinda like a doctor, and I was the same way, like why should, you know, do I deserve this luxury of having somebody come in? And I even feel bad that they're cleaning my house, even though I'm paying them and helping them … . No, I guess I don't … I guess I feel good, I mean they're probably making a decent living. They seem like they are. I guess I would have to kinda catch myself, because like why would I feel … meaning like I don't respect that work? I mean who likes to clean other people's dirt, but they do a really good job and … I'm just so happy with them, cause I'm like 'oh my house is clean' (Kate, personal interview, 2003).

Realizing that they could turn to domestic service, both Kate and her husband had experienced a shift in the ways they thought about themselves. This was unfamiliar territory, as they had both grown up in middle-class families where their moms did the housework and their fathers tended to the lawn. In hiring someone, both experienced a moment of unwelcome recognition that had required, and continued to call for, a reworking of the terms. After all, neither was used to such 'luxury' and neither wanted to feel 'much better than, kinda like a doctor'. Kate had accepted her newfound position as employer, simply because it made her life much easier. Still, a twinge of discomfort remained as she wrestled with her newfound status, and she struggled to remind herself: 'I guess I don't feel … I guess I feel good, I mean they're probably making a decent living' (Kate, personal interview, 2003).

Reframing the Dream

Kate's and Allison's quandary reveals not only the inherent contradictions of the American Dream but the ways these shaped employers' relationships to domestic service. Although paid domestic employment has a long history in the US, it was relatively new for the employers I met, and it evoked palpable unease in most of them. They could not reconcile the idea of employing a 'servant', and they clung to their middle-class status, fiercely rejecting any association with wealth and its excesses. Their disquiet took various forms, ranging from unsolicited, flat-out denials of privilege to more nuanced perspectives but always revealed a necessary struggle to redefine themselves as ordinary and ethical. Some, like Kate, pointed out that they were 'helping people' earn a 'decent' living. Others asserted that they had a special bond with their domestic employees, deflecting structural inequalities by personalizing the relationship. However, often in the same breath, they would make sure to point out that these women were immigrants. These two statements are intimately connected.

Take Carla: 47, white, and mother of two, she had employed three different nannies over the years, a Filipina woman, a Salvadoran woman, and one who was 'the blonde, blue-eyed all-American girl'. What was amazing, she told me, was that the Salvadoran and the Filipina nannies did whatever she asked. Rosa, her current nanny would 'do everything – nothing is beneath her, literally, not that I would demean her'. Conversely, the 'American' had had an attitude problem: 'it was a little bit the air she gave, you know'. The difference, Carla concluded was that 'when they're immigrants, they have an expectation of what they think that they can accomplish when they get here, so they're not looking to, you know …' (Carla, personal interview, 2003).

Carla did not consider her demands excessive but reasoned that the 'blonde, blue-eyed All American girl' was selfish. For her, this difference turned on the distinction between 'immigrant', or Salvadoran, or Filipina, and 'American' nannies. Drawing this boundary, Carla sidestepped her own privilege, displacing it onto the 'American' nanny's impertinence. Yet, what made her experiences with the 'American' unpleasant was not just the nanny's reluctance to do what she was asked but what this refusal highlighted: as an 'American', the nanny had the same rights as Carla. By contrast, if she hired an immigrant woman, Carla would not have to worry about infringing on another's prerogatives. What Carla never mentioned was whether Rosa or the other nanny were or were on the path to becoming American citizens. It made no difference: to her, 'American' clearly meant 'blonde and blue-eyed'. This is a common conception, permanently denying immigrant workers access to the benefits of 'Americanness'.

The legal and ideological associations of whiteness with 'Americanness' are long standing. Indeed, whiteness was a requirement for naturalization until 1952 (Haney-Lopez 2006) and, as Carla's comments indicate, remains visual shorthand for 'Americanness'. Whiteness, however, is not fixed but flexible, its content changing and changeable over time (e.g. Warren and Twine 1997, Yancey 2003, Zhou 2004). As scholars have shown, different ethnic groups have been 'whitened' through economic integration and class mobility (e.g. Roediger 1991, Ignatiev 1995, Brodkin 1998, Jacobson 1998). I do not mean to elide the importance of race, or to reduce race to class; rather, I hope to emphasize how the 'Americanness' of employers requires racializing the category of 'immigrant' – an insuperable distinction, a fixed 'foreignness' (e.g. Hondagneu-Sotelo 2001, Lamont 2000, Romero 2008) that underscores who is entitled to the American Dream and just where the 'shifting human extractive frontier' (Liechty 2003: 10) is located. These differences are often constituted through immigration laws which

> provide a 'magic mirror' into the nation's collected consciousness about its perceived national identity – an identity that marginalizes poor and working immigrants of color and denies them full membership in American social life (Johnson 2009: 2, cf. Gordon and Lenhardt 2007).

Cheryl, 35, African American, and expecting her second child, similarly shifted class anxiety onto national, ultimately racialized terms. She had hired a local cooperative of domestic workers to clean for her but was less interested in this group's ideals than in good service. Cheryl found that the co-op was effective in weeding out the women who did not clean well or had negative attitudes. She had tried other cleaning services, but they had had a different manner, more 'white bread'. They were very expensive and acted as though they were doing you a favour, she told me. Cheryl did not want to be one of those people who treated their 'cleaning people like servants', but she certainly took note of unwarranted surliness: 'I think, you know what though, I think I'm just weird with that. I'm weird with help, because I never want to make it seem like, you know, "go do that"; or *you know what I mean*?' She explained:

> I don't know what it is, I mean, I grew up like in boarding schools and stuff, and so I had friends who had servants, and I just never really liked the way, you know, it just all came across. *You know what I'm saying*? It just, you know, all came across, really, *you know*, but I just, it was never really my thing (Cheryl, personal interview, 2003).

Co-op members, on the other hand, cleaned well and had a cheerful demeanour. Still, her husband was convinced that they hated him and always left the house while they were there. She said,

> I mean, it's that whole thing, between, you know, the Hispanic working population, feeling like the gringos, and you know whatever, whatever. 'Oh hi, hi, hi' and as soon as they turn around their backs, they're like you know. Or just like when you walk into an Asian nail salon ... that same mentality ... and he swears, I mean, he's half joking, but he's like don't fool yourself (Cheryl, personal interview, 2003).

Cheryl could not name the problem. Lacking a vocabulary to talk about privilege, she resorted to phrases like 'you know what I mean?' or 'you know what I'm saying?' Certainly we know what she was saying; we all know about class but have trouble speaking it. Instead, we shift it onto idioms of nationality and race, both of which 'function as sites of displacements of class, and as crypto-class discourses' (Ortner 2003: 51). These slippages confirm the abiding overlap among categories of race, class, and nation. In the US example, middle-class is inextricable from ideas of whiteness and 'Americanness' – together they form the unmarked norm, the privileged subject against whom everyone else's deviance is measured. Significantly, while racial, ethnic, and national *differences* are more easily acknowledged, whiteness, as the norm, remains unsayable.[3] According to Lipsitz,

> since the passage of civil rights legislation in the 1960s whiteness dares not speak its name, cannot speak on its own behalf, but largely advances through a color-blind language radically at odds with the distinctly racialized distribution of resources and life chances in U.S. society. (2006: 250 n4)

The illusion, or delusion, of colour blindness functions in much the same way as the denial of class difference – both fictions naturalize and erase inequality through the language of merit (e.g. Brown et al. 2003, Doane and Bonilla Silva 2003, Lipsitz 2006). Foreignness, on the other hand, remains utterly marked and unproblematically singled out, particularly in a context of increased political polarization over immigration.

Not surprisingly, then, Cheryl found a way to express difference through national categories. For instance, her use of 'white bread' to describe other cleaning services signals both whiteness and 'Americanness'. Phrases such as 'white bread' critique whiteness as empty and insipid, while at the same time, confirming it as unmarked norm. Used as synonym for boring, blandness, normal, 'white bread' verifies the inherent correspondence between whiteness and 'Americanness'.

In a similar vein, Cheryl drew a meaningful equivalence between the 'Hispanic' women who cleaned her house and the 'Asian' women who work in nail salons, for in both cases, she could not understand what the women were saying. This

---

3 Frankenberg (2001) asserts that the unmarked nature of whiteness emerged at a specific historical conjuncture and insists that we attend to the varying contexts in which whiteness is and has been indeed radically visible (cf. Hartigan 1999).

verified her suspicion that their foreignness was immutable, an unbridgeable chasm. Referencing nationality, Cheryl explained away any suggestion of exploitation or unfairness on her part. The co-op's members had a 'good' attitude, she declared. They wanted to be there; as immigrants, they could not really ask for more. They knew that, and Cheryl knew that, and thus both parties understood how the relationship should work.

As necessary 'others', immigrants are crucial to the processes of 'Americanness', essential to marking boundaries (Chock 1994, Coutin 2000, de Genova 2005, Honig 2001, Ngai 2004), and though often invisible, the household remains a principal site for the creation of 'domestic' borders (Kaplan 1998). Historically, racially or ethnically marked women have provided the main supply of paid domestic labour in the US. Although the ethnicity, race, or national provenance of the women who performed this work has varied according to region and historical moment, they have always belonged to groups 'placed in a separate legal category from whites, excluded from rights and protections accorded to full citizens' (Glenn 1992: 8, cf. Katzman 1979, Tucker 1988, Palmer 1989, Barnes 1993, Thornton Dill 1994). The concept of 'illegality', often projected onto all Mexican and Central American immigrants whether they have legal documents or not, further rigidifies these lines (see Ngai 2004, De Genova 2005, Romero 2008, Rubio Goldsmith et al. 2009, Johnson 2009). In the present, the operative distinction is not one between full citizens and internal 'others'; instead, we find 'Americans' and (dangerous, encroaching, illegitimate) foreigners, outsiders who cannot expect *any* rights or protections.

Conclusion

Thus, taking on a domestic employee does more than secure the material grounds of 'Americanness'; it actively reconstructs and redefines the very possibility of membership in the nation. Through the quotidian exchanges of domestic service, employers generate a logic of exclusion that not only reaffirms their position on the inside but also domestic workers' place on the outside. Characterizing domestic workers as forever foreign, intrinsically inassimilable, employers categorically excluded domestic workers from the benefits of membership. More than rhetorical sleight of hand, this particular constellation of equality, access, and 'Americanness' reveals the limitations of the American Dream. It also has real, material repercussions, reproducing the inequalities that underpin a middle-class lifestyle. Invisible to employers, these disparities are illuminated through domestic service, precisely because of its location in the home. As they collide, unwillingly, with these realizations, employers begin to articulate what was once perhaps practical knowledge, recreating – and deepening – the naturalized difference of immigrant women. As such, they elucidate how the global and the foreign remain indispensable to the construction of 'Americanness' and the American Dream.

Chapter 9

Family Separation and Reunification Among Former Filipina Migrant Domestic Workers and Their Adult Daughters in Two Canadian Cities

Conely de Leon

The Philippines is one of the largest organized exporters of human labour in the world (Guevarra 2010). The mass exodus of Filipinos to over 190 countries has resulted in a 'crisis of care' involving the separation of reportedly millions of children from their migrant parents (Parreñas 2005). Particularly striking is the disproportionate number of children being separated from their mothers, a phenomenon which is directly attributable to the high demand for Filipinas in the global labour market- a reflection of the feminization and racialization of contemporary migrant labour. For example, in Canada alone, Filipinas constitute over 90 per cent of migrant domestic workers and caregivers (Kelly et al. 2009). Moreover, the Philippines has been named Canada's top source country for immigrants (Friesen 2011). Given the strong presence of Filipinos in Canada, particularly Filipina migrant labourers, it is both necessary and urgent to build on academic research that speaks to these unique global trends. Leading theorists on the subject of migrant domestic labour in Canada and the United States have primarily focused on the socioeconomic and political struggles of migrant women of colour (Silvera 1983, Giles and Arat-Koç 1994, Macklin 1994, Bakan and Stasiulus 1997, Colen 1995, Romero 1992, 2002). More recently, Canadian feminist geographer, Geraldine Pratt (2004, 2012) and theorists such as Sedef Arat-Koç (2001), Rhacel Salazar Parreñas (2005a), Pierette Hondagneu-Sotelo (2001), and Mary Romero (2011) have shifted attention to the experiences of the families of migrant domestic workers of colour. Family separation continues to be an important issue in the transnational migration literature, particularly in studies of migrant parents and children from Central and Latin America, the Caribbean, and the Philippines.

In this chapter, I will build on the work of these leading theorists by tracing the ways in which long-term family separation affects the children of former Filipina domestic workers into *adulthood*. Specifically, I wish to provide a snapshot of the relationships between Filipina mothers and adult daughters before, during and after reunification. I insist that a focus on adult daughters is necessary due to the highly gendered, sexualized, classed, and racialized processes at work in systemically circulating and reproducing a demand for Filipinas in the domestic and care industry. Moreover, I have chosen to focus on the adult daughters of former migrant domestic workers in an attempt to destabilize existing Canadian stereotypes of Filipinas that are persistently one-dimensional and highly misogynistic. The stereotypes of Filipinas as nannies and housekeepers adversely affects their socio-economic and political realities in Canada, as reflected in the high rate of deprofessionalization among Filipina workers in Canada (Pratt 2004, Kelly et al. 2009, Coloma et al. 2012). In this chapter, I also engage with, as well as challenge, these harmful stereotypes in order to develop a nuanced and heterogeneous understanding of Filipinas' lives. By exploring Filipina mother-adult daughter relationships, we may begin to ask important questions about what it means to grapple with gendered, sexualized, classed and racialized stereotypes, and their generational impact on mothers and adult daughters over time, particularly in terms of how they navigate post-reunification tensions and attempts to re-build intimacy. Drawing on in-depth, one-on-one interviews with Filipina adult daughters and their mothers in Toronto, Ontario and Montreal, Quebec, this chapter will investigate key transitions in the lives of research participants by firstly, examining the initial moment of family separation; secondly, exploring some of the key challenges to immediate reunification; and lastly, focusing on activism as a way of fostering a sense of community among migrant workers and their families, establishing awareness of the structural causes behind systemic family separation, and rebuilding relationships between mothers and their adult children. The empirical data presented here was collected over the course of two years, from 2006 to 2008, and was part of my Master's thesis research. The case studies presented in this chapter explore the intimate complexities and nuances of post-reunification family life. Such an intimate analysis allows us to pay close attention to the ways in which global migration processes operate at macro and micro levels, including that of 'the family'. As Yeoh et al. (2005) suggest, attention to 'the family' as a potential unit of analysis offers insight into the transnationalization of families.

Research Participants and Research Sites

Dating back to the 1950s, various recruitment methods have been adopted by the Canadian federal government to encourage the migration of foreign domestic workers of colour to Canada. They began with the Caribbean Domestic Scheme, the first programme to mark Canada's 'gradual transition from a predominantly white labour pool in domestic service to one in which the majority were women of colour' (Macklin 1994). Canada has continued to recruit temporary foreign domestic workers under the 1981 Foreign Domestic Movement (FDM) and the 1992 Live-in Caregiver Program (LCP). In my own research, each mother participant migrated to Canada as a hired domestic worker under the FDM. Both adult daughters were sponsored by their mothers in the early 1990s, landing in two major destinations for FDM and LCP migration and settlement: Toronto and Montreal (Kelly 2006). One of the mother-adult daughter pairs lived in Côte-des-Neiges, Montreal and the other pair lived in Scarborough, Ontario, an eastern suburb of the Greater Toronto Area (GTA). Although I did not originally intend to conduct interviews outside Ontario, finding research participants in Côte-des-Neiges, Montreal allowed me to explore two distinct geographical areas of Filipina migration and settlement within Canada.

Since little research on family separation and reunification in Canada has traced the experiences of the children of former migrant domestic workers into adulthood, I have elected to highlight the experiences of two Filipina adult daughter-migrant mother pairs who have been reunited in Canada for over 10 years. This 10-year mark served as a standardizing technique for adequate assessment and evaluation of the potential challenges faced by adult daughter participants after reunification. In addition, the 10-year mark was ideal for the purpose of this study because it allowed me to explore some of the enduring effects of separation, as well as some of the important transitions in the adult lives of the two daughters.

Participant Profiles

Lourdes and Aurora

When Lourdes' mother, Aurora, was recruited illegally to work for three months as a domestic worker in Brunei, she was detained and forced to remain there for roughly six months before being released. In 1986, after completing a two-year contract as a domestic worker in Singapore, Aurora returned to the Philippines for a brief family visit and in 1988, migrated to Canada under the FDM. After six long years, Lourdes was reunited with her mother. For Lourdes, life in Canada was challenging. She dropped out of school for the first time when she was 17 years old. She worked a series of low paying jobs until she finally decided to pursue a degree in nursing. Now at 29 years old, Lourdes is married, has a five and a half year old son, and works full time as a nurse. Aurora, now in her late 60s, still works part-time as a live-out caregiver for her elderly employers in Montreal, Quebec.

Chris and Tessie

When Chris' mother, Tessie, migrated to Singapore as a domestic worker in 1986, Chris was 11 years old. From Singapore, Tessie migrated directly to Canada under the FDM. Tessie and Chris were finally reunited in 1994 when Chris was 19 years old. Adjusting to life in Toronto presented many challenges for Chris. To get away from recurring arguments and familial tensions, Chris moved to Ottawa for four years but ultimately returned to Toronto in order to be with her family. She is now 33 years old and works for a government agency. She lives with her partner and family in a home co-owned with her younger sister. Her mother, Tessie, is currently in her late 50s and works as an office cleaner, along with her husband.

Situating Myself within a *Pinay*[1] *peminist* Framework

As a Toronto-born, second-generation Filipina born to a working class family, I foreground a *Pinay peminist* (feminist) theoretical and qualitative methodological framework in this chapter, a framework advanced by Asian Pacific American Studies scholar, Melinda L. de Jesus who defines *Pinay peminism* as 'a specific form of feminist theory rooted in the Filipina American experience ... one that radically repudiates white feminist hegemony' (2005: 5). For de Jesus, *Pinay peminism* aims to resist the marginalization of scholarship by feminist theorists of colour within the field of Women and Gender Studies as defined by white liberal feminism. It further aims to resist the marginalization of Filipina voices in the otherwise patriarchal fields of Asian American Studies and Filipino American Studies. Although rooted in Filipina American experiences, I strategically invoke de Jesus' *Pinay peminism* as a useful entry point for articulating a framework grounded in the gendered identities, subjectivities, and situated knowledges of Filipinas who have migrated to Canada. There is an important political project which *Pinay peminists* like de Jesus are engaged in and that is the project of transforming and building scholarship on Filipina lives. I wish to insist that Filipina feminists provide insights that other feminist scholars do not provide in light of powerful critiques by many indigenous women and women of colour on the ways in which the lives of gendered and racialized Others tend to be written *about*, which implicitly suggests that they themselves are incapable of *writing theory*. In other words, their ability to theorize, to contribute to epistemological production is not validated or recognized, thus it is imperative that I interrogate *which* women's lived and embodied experiences and knowledges are being privileged within the academy and other types of knowledges and experiences are being silenced. As Alexander and Mohanty argue:

> The key to claiming epistemic authority for people who have been oppressed in a particular way stems from an acknowledgement that they have experiences-experiences that people who are not oppressed in the same way usually lack- that can provide them with information we all need to understand how hierarchies of race, class, gender and sexuality operate to uphold existing regimes of power in our society (1996: xl).

Here, then, I must insist on the utility of Filipina feminist scholarship. In this chapter, I deliberately invoke the work of de Jesus and other Filipina feminist scholars in an attempt to think through issues of gendered migration and its impact

1 Colloquial term for Filipina.

on Filipino families. The need for more robust feminist scholarship that insists on the importance of naming and identifying the stories of Filipinas at this historical juncture is necessary not simply because there is a significant dearth in feminist scholarship on Filipina lives in Canada, but because this dearth signifies the continued underrepresentation of Filipino women in Canadian society, as well as in Canadian institutions such as the academy.[2] As de Jesus states:

> Despite our ubiquitous presence throughout the diaspora, Filipinas remain contingently visible: as nameless, faceless overseas contract workers, sex workers, and mail-order brides scattered across the globe. We are seen as objects of a sexist, imperial ideology, yet we remain invisible as subjects and agents. Filipinas are simultaneously everywhere and nowhere (2005: 3).

Exploring the possibilities of Filipina feminist studies as a valid field of study in Canada is part of a strategic move towards establishing an epistemological standpoint committed to critically analysing what is currently known and not known about the lived experiences of Filipinas in Canada and elsewhere in the world, and towards identifying the ways in which Filipina feminist forms of knowing are useful in both academic and non-academic settings. Commitment to prioritizing critical issues of concern identified *with* our communities in order to resist processes of dehumanization is another necessary aspect of understanding what Filipina feminist scholarship and activism might look like. This is the driving force behind this chapter, which strives to foreground the perspectives, practices, and lived and embodied experiences of the adult daughters of Filipina domestic workers in Canada. Thus, by exploring the relationships between Filipina migrant mothers and adult daughters, as well as their journeys toward community activism, we may begin to develop more diverse understandings of Filipina lives across generations.

The FDM and the Growth of *Pinay* Activism in Canada

Implemented in 1981, the Foreign Domestic Movement (FDM) marked a surge in the recruitment of Filipina domestic workers in Canada. Under the FDM, it became mandatory for migrant domestic workers to have prior experience in domestic and care work, and complete two years of live-in work in Canada in order to be eligible for permanent residency (Macklin 1994: 18). This two-year live-in requirement kept migrant domestic workers locked in temporary and precarious positions, as well as under constant threat of deportation. Moreover, FDM applicants who had spouses and dependants were routinely denied entry into the programme. The

2 According to Coloma et al., 'scholarship on Filipina/os in the Canadian context is decidedly more recent and more limited in scope. A shorter immigration history has meant a shorter incubation period for both cultural and academic production' (2012: 12).

programme was designed to ensure that applicants lived and worked in the country as 'single people' therefore guaranteeing systematic family separation (Arat-Koç et al. 2001: 20). The surge in the recruitment of 'single' Filipinas to Canada under the FDM led to the construction of homogenizing images of Filipino women as docile, meek, and subservient and thus 'best suited' to domestic and care work.[3] Anna Romina Guevarra writes of this notion of 'suitability' in the context of labour brokering activities among domestic employment agencies in the Philippines. She argues:

> They sell Filipinas by promoting a discourse of productive femininity rooted in culturally essentialist logic in which the Philippines is a natural source of a cost-effective and desirable workforce that has innate caregiving abilities, is multiskilled, and is educated (2010: 125).

Guevarra further argues that Filipinas' 'added export value' highlights a racialized form of labour power that is used to construct Filipinas as ideal care workers, thereby justifying their continued recruitment as domestic workers and caregivers (2010: 125). But these images are challenged by Filipina domestic workers who have a long and active history of resistance against domestic worker abuse. With the significant increase in Filipina domestic workers in Canada, several vibrant and thriving migrant workers' organizations designed to improve the working conditions of Filipina domestic workers in the country including INTERCEDE, Filipina, *Migrante* Ontario, United Filipino Mothers, *Pilipinong Migrante sa Canada* (Philippine Migrants Society of Canada), and the Philippine Women Centres of British Columbia, Ontario, and Quebec emerged. Their history is often masked by the rhetoric of Canadian multiculturalism claims to:

> assist in the development of strategies that facilitate full and active participation of ethnic and cultural communities ... and improve the ability of public institutions to respond to ethnic and cultural diversity by assisting in the identification and removal of barriers to equitable access and by supporting the involvement of these communities in public decision-making processes (*Kalayaan* Centre 2008).

These claims re-create the national mythology of Canada as a just, diverse and benevolent nation that 'accommodates' the needs of ethnically and culturally diverse communities of people in Canada even as federally regulated programmes like the FDM render the lives of temporary Filipina migrant domestic workers and their families precarious. Moreover, such multiculturalist claims refuse to acknowledge the heterogeneous and nuanced lives of Filipinas who actively fight for the rights and welfare of Filipinos in Canada. It further ignores first and

3 For an historical analysis of temporary foreign domestic worker schemes in Canada, see Macklin 1994.

second generations of Filipino youth who have founded and sustained activist organizations in Canada such as *Kabataang Montreal* (Montreal Filipino Youth) and *Ugnayan ng Kabataang Pilipino sa Canada* (Filipino Canadian Youth Alliance), which operate, in part, to provide support, programmes and services to the children of migrant domestic workers. The racialized recruitment of Filipina domestic workers to Canada reveals some of the ways in which Canadian domestic worker policies have systematically curtailed the rights of migrant domestic workers of colour and fostered long-term separation from their families.

Nonetheless, Canada remains a popular destination for migrant domestic workers because it is one of the few countries that offers the possibility of permanent settlement (Parreñas 2005). The journey toward permanent residency and family reunification is long and tedious. According to a collaborative research project conducted by INTERCEDE and Sedef Arat-Koç, a domestic worker can include her dependants in her permanent resident application forms, provided that the entire family passes medical and criminal checks (2001: 106). If one member of the family does not pass any one of these 'background' checks, sponsorship can be delayed for several months and even years. According to Pratt, the average number of years that families may remain separated is six to eight years (2008: 12). Additional complications may increase the length of family separation. For example, dependants over the age of 19 who are not registered as full-time students are not considered eligible for sponsorship. Additional financial challenges include expensive application and 'right of landing' fees. Moreover, the Canadian government's Eurocentric, heteropatriarchal definition of 'the family' ignores extended kinship networks among migrant families. As Arat-Koç et al. argue:

> The conception of 'family' as defined by Immigration Canada involves an imposition of a narrow, western and heterosexist definition of the nuclear family ... it is important to remember that for many domestic and caregiver workers, separation from parents, siblings, same-sex partners, or other intimate friends have been as difficult and as devastating (2001: 23).

Indeed, the realities of separation and reunification precipitated by overseas labour migration involve far more expansive definitions of 'the family'. As we shall see in the next section, the issue of family separation and the challenges that come with it pertain to a host of messy and complex extended kinship networks.

Lola, Ina, Anak:[4] Family Separation Across Generations

In sharing their experiences of separation from their daughters, Tessie and Aurora both revealed that they had experienced varying degrees of separation from

4 *Tagalog* terms for grandmother, mother, child.

their own mothers. Tessie grew up living in an extended family household while separated from her adoptive mother, who often migrated to other parts of the Philippines to seek work as a labandera[5] or as a domestic worker and nanny. While separated from her mother, Tessie lived under the primary care of six women; her aunts and their close friends, until she completed high school. Tessie never knew who her biological mother was. In fact, Tessie did not realize that the woman who adopted her was not her biological mother until she was much older. She explains: 'The mother that I know of is not my mother. And yet the mother that I know never said that I was not her child … Who really are my parents?' (Tessie, personal interview 2007). Not only has Tessie experienced prolonged separation from her adoptive mother, but she has also experienced the shock of discovering that the person whom she believed to be her mother for most of her life was not, in fact, her 'real' mother. Similarly, Aurora was adopted by other family members after her father's sudden death and her mother's remarriage. She recounts:

> I was an orphan at the age of two. Our father passed away in a motorcycle accident. We were seven in all and our youngest sister was only three months old at that time. We were given away. I lived with my grandma and my aunties (Aurora, personal interview, 2008).

Despite being so young, Aurora had to grow up living with the loss of her father, and her subsequent separation from her mother and siblings. In sharing this painful childhood memory, Aurora insists, 'I didn't have a happy life' (Aurora 2008). It was, in fact, Aurora's grandmother who made the final decision to forcefully separate Aurora from her mother and siblings. She explains:

> My grandmother was very upset with her for getting married again so we were not allowed to see her. We were only allowed to see her once a year during Christmas time. You know, our Philippine tradition is- we have to kiss the hand of your in-law or mother-in-law. I remember she used to brush her hand away (Aurora, personal interview, 2008).

Here, Aurora is observing interactions between her paternal grandmother and mother. Kissing the hand of an elder is a culturally significant sign of respect. Aurora notes the symbolic expression of a mother-in-law's rejection of her daughter-in-law through the brushing away of her mother's hand. In this scenario, Aurora's paternal grandmother expresses disappointment in her daughter-in-law for remarrying only a year after her son's death. Aurora's paternal grandmother ultimately disowns her, takes her seven children from her and redistributes them among extended kin. This severance from and loss of multiple family members during Aurora's childhood touches on the challenges that she experiences with her daughter later in life.

5 *Tagalog* term for laundress.

For Aurora's daughter, Lourdes, and Tessie's daughter, Chris, some of their most vivid memories involved the moment at which they were separated from their mothers, or as Pratt terms it, 'the moment of departure' (2001: 30). The moment of departure is an important moment to examine in the lives of children 'left behind' by migrant mothers, for the moment of departure signifies a moment of loss. Significantly, both Chris and Lourdes reported not being told that their mothers were leaving them. In coping with the impact of separation from their own mothers, both Tessie and Aurora may have chosen not to inform their daughters of their departure to avoid potentially re-living a painful past. Chris recalls the day her mother, Tessie, left her when she was 11 years old:

> I remember it vividly. It was a school day. I was ready to go to school and I'm like, 'Okay, bye Mom! I'm going to go to school now'. And it was just a regular day and she's like, 'Oh wait, wait, wait before you leave uh give me a kiss'. And so I kissed her and then I left. And then I came back home and after a few more weeks or months, I found out she was in Singapore (Tessie and Chris, personal interview, 2007).

Here, Chris recalls an ordinary day and a seemingly out-of-the-ordinary request for physical affection from her mother. In a similar fashion, Lourdes recounts the moment of separation from her mother at the tender age of five:

> All I know is that she left 'cause I am used to her leaving.[6] And then, I don't know, for some reason, I just understood that she's not there anymore, that she left for somewhere else, that she's not coming back (Lourdes, telephone interview, 2008).

Although Lourdes does not have tangible proof that her mother has left, she nonetheless displays an awareness of her mother's absence. Loss and separation, as experienced by Chris and Lourdes, are sudden and unexpected resulting in belated and severe emotional scarring reflected during the post-reunification years. The sudden and unexpected departure of their mothers caused subsequent trust issues complicated by recurring feelings of betrayal and resentment. For Chris and Lourdes, separation from their mothers is the context for understanding the deep sense of loss experienced by both sets of mothers and daughters, as well

---

6 When Lourdes mentions being 'used to her [mother's] leaving', she is referring to the type of work that her mother used to perform as a travelling manicurist/pedicurist. For the most part, this type of travelling consisted of very short trips within Quezon City. On the other hand, Aurora's work abroad forced her to be away from home for much longer periods of time. Technically, Aurora migrated to three countries to perform domestic work: Brunei, Singapore, and finally, Canada. But as mentioned before, the work that Aurora was contracted to perform in Brunei turned out to be illegitimate. Nevertheless, the bogus work opportunity separated Aurora from her family for several months.

as the moments of intergenerational tension and conflict that mark the post-reunification years.

Post-Reunification: The Immediate Years

For Lourdes and Aurora, Chris and Tessie, the immediate years following reunification were identified as a particularly difficult time of adjustment. According to Suárez-Orozco et al., reunification is 'a time of mixed feelings [as well as] excitement about the prospect of reuniting with loved ones and a new life' (Suárez-Orozco et al. 2001: 3). Indeed, this particular understanding of reunification is reflected in my own research findings. Recalling the period of separation between herself and her mother, Chris shares, 'When times [were] really difficult I just [thought], "Oh well, there's going to be an end to this because we're going to be reunited with the whole family and it's going to be a good life over there"' (Tessie and Chris, personal interview, 2007). Here, Chris alludes to the ways in which migrant mothers may mask the harsh realities of life 'abroad' for the sake of their children. As it turns out, reunification does not bring Chris the 'good life' she expects. The very day she and her mother are reunited, Chris is forced to face the reality of her mother's life in Canada. She recounts:

> We came at 11:00 at night. She took us to her workplace and it was a hotel.[7] We just came and she's working already! I almost cried 'cause I'm like, 'What?! We're still poor in Canada?' We're already poor in the Philippines and I was thinking, but she promised! She said we were gonna have all these good things (Tessie and Chris, personal interview, 2007).

Chris' description of her first day in Canada highlights the shock often experienced by the children of migrant mothers upon reunification. It further underlines the systematic process of de-skilling that inevitably locks temporary foreign domestic workers and caregivers in similar underpaid positions as live-out house, hotel, and office cleaners (Chang 2000). This is precisely the case with both Chris and Lourdes' mothers, Tessie and Aurora. Upon reunification, both Chris and Lourdes found that their mothers worked for more than one employer to make ends meet. Faced with the realities of life in Canada as the daughters of former domestic workers, Chris and Lourdes expressed feelings of betrayal by their mothers. As Chris shares, 'I thought at the time, well, she lied. She said all these things and it's not the truth. It wasn't what I expected- not even half of it' (Tessie and Chris, personal interview, 2007). Indeed, Pratt, in collaboration with the Philippine Women Centre of British Columbia (PWC-BC), argues that Filipino youth previously separated from their migrant mothers often express feelings of 'betrayal, of vulnerability … of bewilderment, of inexplicable fear,

7 In the early 1990s, Tessie was working for a major hotel chain as a housekeeper.

of not understanding the sudden departure of one's mother' (2012: 60–61). Such complicated feelings of betrayal and frustration cause children who have lived through prolonged separation to experience greater difficulty reconciling with their migrant parents. It is important to note that these responses to immediate family reunification are not unique or isolated. As Pratt et al. argue, familial challenges during the reunification period are 'not from inherent deficiencies of these particular individuals or families, or within the Filipino community, but as a direct result of the period of family separation regulated by the Live-in Caregiver Program (1992)' and its predecessor, the Foreign Domestic Movement (1981) (2006: 46).

When recalling the immediate years following reunification, both Lourdes and Chris identified recurring moments of conflict and tension between themselves and their mothers. In conversations with both mother and adult daughter participants, tensions between mothers and daughters often erupted in hurtful verbal exchanges. These verbal exchanges, born out of feelings of disappointment and resentment towards their mothers during the initial period of separation even drove Lourdes to run away. Lourdes recalls, 'When we used to live in the same apartment we used to fight a lot' (Lourdes, telephone interview, 2008). Her mother, Aurora, confirms: 'She doesn't listen to me so we have a big argument. One time, she even ran away. I said, 'If you don't want to listen to me, get out!'' (Aurora, personal interview, 2008). Later on in the interview, Aurora recalls a particularly tense moment between her and Lourdes: 'She doesn't listen to me when she was a teenager. One time she came home late. I really have to slap her face and pull her hair. She came home at three in the morning with a friend. I was very tough with her' (Aurora, personal interview, 2008). Aurora's and Lourdes' combined recollections of the immediate years following reunification expose the types of struggles that can emerge from prolonged separation. Arat-Koç in collaboration with INTERCEDE state:

> In addition to problems of establishing trust, love and intimacy, reunification was often a time of difficulties in establishing authority over children … children were not likely to accept the authority of their mother, who was often like a 'stranger' to them. As mothers tried to fulfill their new role, some children resented, resisted and rejected this (2001: 34).

Indeed, Aurora's attempts to regulate her daughter's behaviour after being separated from her for a decade underscore some of the troubling details of family life after reunification. Having spent eight years living a relatively independent existence, Chris also found it challenging to adhere to her mother's demands. Chris shares, 'We were just fighting all the time, my Mom and myself. I just got used to making decisions myself' (Tessie and Chris, personal interview, 2007). As the eldest child in her family, Chris was used to making decisions about the family's finances and other practical household responsibilities during separation. Here, Tessie describes what she believes is her first fight with Chris in Canada:

> One time, I don't remember exactly what was the issue, we were screaming at each other and then finally she speak out and said, 'What do you expect me to do? I grow up so young. I was forced to become mature!' I think that was our first fight here [in Canada] (Tessie and Chris, personal interview, 2007).

In order to survive, children like Chris learned to mature quickly as they tended to take on greater familial responsibility. Recalling the times when her mother sent remittances 'back home', Chris shares, 'The arrangement was my Dad was going to receive the money that she's sending to us [but] because of the gambling and the drinking, I had to take over at a fairly young age. I was pushed to be mature' (Tessie and Chris, personal interview 2007). Chris' story is supported by Parreñas who describes Filipina daughters of migrant domestic workers as 'dutiful daughters' who tend to take on 'far more responsibility … in the maintenance of immigrant families' (2005a: 109). Clearly, the life Chris led in the Philippines conflicted with the life she was suddenly expected to conform to in Canada. This ultimately drove her to move out. Recalling the years she spent living in Ottawa, Chris shares:

> I remember when I was in Ottawa and they [Mom and Dad] continued fighting because my Dad would still gamble and drink. I just tell them [to] separate already 'cause you're killing your kids, you're affecting myself and my sister. I believe the family affects the individual in a lot of ways. Always fighting affects your self-esteem, your interaction with a lot of people (Tessie and Chris, personal interview, 2007).

For Chris, her father's drinking and gambling became a significant source of concern both during and after separation. And while father–daughter relationships are not the primary focus of this chapter, it is important to recognize that Chris' memories of her father point to the challenges that long-term separation can have not only on the children of former domestic workers, but also on their spouses/partners. Indeed, in recalling the persistent fights between her mother and father, Chris reflects: 'They were earning [money] but couldn't really save. My Dad will be like, "This is my money and I'm going to do whatever!" And my Mom's like, "Stop gambling already so we can start saving for your children!"' (Chris, personal interview, 2007). For Chris, her father's habits served to heighten familial tensions during the immediate years following reunification

In her analysis of familial and financial tensions across three generations of Japanese domestic workers and their husbands, Evelyn Nakano Glenn states, 'Money spent on alcohol … drained off scarce income. Thus the conflict over drinking often involved a deeper conflict over control of family resources' (1986: 213). In comparing the effects of her parents' fighting to 'killing' Chris demonstrates an acute awareness of the devastating impact that persistent conflict over financial resources can have on previously separated families, and particularly on the self-esteem of family members. As Portes and Rumbaut confirm, such 'harsh experiences can produce enduring negative consequences – first, in lowered self-esteem and heightened alienation' (2001: 130).

Pinay Activism and the Journey Toward Post-Reunification Reconciliation

I now wish to reflect on Chris and Lourdes' respective journeys toward reconciliation with their mothers. It has been 14 years since Chris and Lourdes first arrived in Canada. Over this period of time, each daughter participant acknowledged that some of the challenges they experienced immediately following reunification diminished considerably as a result of their involvement in Filipino activist organizations.

Lourdes is a founding member of Kabataang Montreal (KM). The Filipino youth outreach group and drop-in centre was formed in Côte-des-Neiges, Montreal in 1999. One of KM's key objectives is to address the needs of Filipino youth who have undergone separation from their mothers, often former or current live-in caregivers and domestic workers in Canada. One of the leading members of KM describes the organization as 'a progressive, politically active organization that deals with the realities [of] drugs, teen pregnancy, ethnicity, [and] parental problems' (Lejtenyi 2003). As Lourdes confirms: 'There's other Filipino youth [groups] but this was the only politically aware organization that's involved [in their] rights and welfare' (Lourdes, personal interview, 2008). According to a cover story in the alternative newsweekly, *The Montreal Mirror*, 'Most of the members have similar histories. [They experience] the confusion, isolation, and family strains common among many immigrant families' (Lejtenyi 2003). KM's commitment to fighting for the rights and welfare of young Filipinos in Canada enabled Lourdes to find meaning and a sense of belonging among a group of Filipino youth who had also experienced family separation. Through KM, Lourdes expresses heightened awareness of her situation as one child out of many who had been 'left behind': 'Right now I can relate, I can really understand why it [separation] happened. It's when I joined KM. That's when they explain why the separation had to take place' (Lourdes, personal interview, 2008). Working with KM helped Lourdes understand her mother's reasons for leaving the Philippines. Her involvement in mass protests and community projects aimed at fighting against discriminatory Canadian foreign domestic worker policies helped her name her childhood pain and understand the structural causes behind it. Similarly, Chris explains her own involvement in Filipino advocacy groups as part of an important process of rebuilding her relationship with her mother. She shares:

> It's a big contribution to my relationship with my Mom. Now she's like a friend. [If] there's some disagreement we can just try and talk – not the yelling. Before it was like, 'I disagree and you took me to Canada and I don't want to go here!' (Chris, personal interview, 2007).

This is, of course, not the case for all children of Filipina migrant domestic workers. Some find it far more difficult to cope with the challenges of family separation many years after reunification. Clinical depression and suicide are more serious examples of what can happen to youth who have experienced long-term separation from their migrant parents.[8] Like Lourdes, Chris' experiences with Filipino advocacy groups strengthened the bonds between herself and her mother, Tessie. Chris now sees her mother as a friend. Over the course of time, Chris and Tessie have learned to deal with their disagreements in more constructive ways. Chris continues:

> Now I understand why she left me, why she left us in the Philippines. It was also understanding it was a big struggle. It was very difficult for her to leave us. So that in itself was a big relief, you know, after realizing all those things (Chris, personal interview, 2007).

Chris is able to gain perspective on the urgent reasons behind her mother's sudden departure. Recall that during the immediate years following reunification, Chris resented her mother for leaving her. This realization has allowed Chris to reconcile differences with her mother over time. In fact, Chris adds that she was introduced to Filipino community advocacy groups through her mother whose own story of activism is worth highlighting here. Tessie recounts:

> I started organizing the United Filipino Mothers just basically to share experiences- your joyful moments, your hurting moments. I did not have any understanding of advocacy. I just see the spirit -that there's power in the community (Tessie and Chris, personal interview, 2007).

Tessie was intent on creating a space where mothers who immigrated under the FDM could gather to share their experiences, as well as their frustrations. Tessie's advocacy work helped nurture what she calls the 'spirit' of the Filipino community in Toronto and encouraged her own daughter to get involved in Filipina activist endeavours. Chris affirms: 'Introduction to this group of people was through her and also these other support groups. But it was already in me because of what I experienced back home. I thought, "I have to do something"'. Chris emphasizes that she already possessed a desire to 'do something' for her community based on her own struggles coping with family separation. She further explains: 'What helped was my four years of living away from home, trying to find myself, plus more exposure to community building in Ottawa' (Chris, personal interview, 2007). During the four years that Chris lived in Ottawa, she joined a community organization called *Pilipinong Migrante sa Canada* (PMSC). PMSC was formed in 1996 as a support group for Filipino migrants and their families.

8 For more information on depression and suicide as it affects daughters of Filipino immigrant parents in California, see Wolf 1997 and Arat-Koç et al. 2001.

Chris highlights her leadership role in PMSC: 'I got exposed to the *Pilipinong Migrante sa Canada* or PMSC. I had a good understanding of how it worked because of [what] my Mom went through and so I would give out orientations [and] workshops'.

Chris recognized that her activist work not only established a broader understanding of her own personal, socio-economic, and political challenges in Canada as the daughter of a former domestic worker but also empowered her and enabled her to help others work through some of these same challenges. Chris states:

> Before it was just too personal but then I got exposed to all these other children who were separated, and parents or mothers who came to the program, and how that wasn't their choice to leave the country or leave the family. I got a better understanding and so, it's solved (Chris, personal interview, 2007).

Chris' and Lourdes' involvement in Filipino-based community organizations enabled them to meet others facing similar struggles, allowing them to feel a greater sense of belonging among fellow *kababayans*.[9] Indeed, many of the relationships that they have built through these organizations are some of their strongest. Significantly, Chris and Lourdes have both found their present partners through their activist work. In the following excerpt, Lourdes describes her relationship to her husband as it relates to their involvement in KM: 'We have the same story. He was separated from his Mom too so it made our relationship more stronger 'cause we're politically aware of what's going on' (Lourdes, telephone interview, 2008). It is evident that the relationships Lourdes values most are strengthened by a political awareness around issues faced by migrant Filipino communities. Chris reflects on her own relationships in similar terms: 'My friends were the other participants too 'cause I can only relate to children who were born and raised in the Philippines' (Chris, personal interview, 2007). What this accomplishes is a symbolic connection to the familiar, to 'home', to the land from which they were torn. These organizations and the relationships nurtured therein thus serve as strategic sites of empowerment, belonging, and healing. Moreover, Lourdes and Chris' participation in the formation and preservation of Filipino community activist organizations in Ontario and Quebec allowed them to thrive in supportive environments surrounded by other Filipinos who have similarly coped with the pain and frustration associated with long-term family separation. Their involvement enabled them to build lasting bonds of friendship with other Filipino migrant families but most importantly, nurtured possibilities of post-reunification reconciliation between themselves and their mothers.

9 *Tagalog* term for fellow Filipino, compatriot or townmate. In the contemporary moment, the term is also used to unite fellow Overseas Filipino Workers (OFWs) and their families.

However, the journey toward reconciliation among previously separated mothers and adult daughters is never stable or clear cut. As mentioned earlier in this chapter, the effects of long-term family separation do not simply end once families are reunited. Rather, they persist and manifest in different ways and across generations. The following excerpt from my interview with Lourdes showcases a particularly striking recurrence of loss and separation between herself and her own five and a half year old son. When Lourdes decided to go back to school to become a nurse, she decided to keep her day job in order to support her family. But her decision to go back to school came at an emotional cost to herself and her family:

> That's when I felt the separation in my head. I'm like, this is what happened between my Mom and me. The only difference is I'm here with my son but I don't spend time with him because I'd work in the morning and go to school at night. The only day I see him is Friday night and Sundays. When you work and go to school, you're really tired. You don't have patience anymore. I felt the separation 'cause he doesn't even come to me. He always goes to his Dad. I was telling myself, this is so unbelievable. Like, I'm already here with my family but yet there's a separation (Lourdes, telephone interview, 2008).

The deep sense of loss that can be experienced by those who have been separated from their parents due to overseas labour migration is recalled by Lourdes through her son. His inability to recognize her as his mother adds another complex layer to the challenges of rebuilding family lives across generations.[10] Lourdes seems to re-live the moment of loss and separation from her mother through her own child. This narrative points to the intergenerational impact of separation and underscores some of the challenges of rebuilding relationships over time. Indeed, the process of healing and reconciliation is a long one but one that seems to be made possible through critical awareness of the overall negative effects of long-term family separation. Lourdes' absence from her son's life during these critical years forces her to recall the years she was separated from her own mother. Ultimately however, the lessons learned through her work with KM move Lourdes to prioritize her relationship with her son over her family's financial needs. Indeed, soon after realizing that her full time schedule was negatively impacting her family life, Lourdes decided to quit her day job to focus on rebuilding a relationship with her son. After committing to spending more quality time with him, she shares, 'I think the bonding or the closeness started maybe two years ago' The fact that Lourdes' relationship to her son has only transformed within the past two years suggests that the journey towards reconciliation and healing is far from over. In this instance,

10 Clearly, long-term separation has a generational impact that is deserving of greater theoretical attention. Moreover, the path to healing and reconciliation is a long one but one that is made possible through critical awareness of the overall negative effects of long-term family separation. This experience is specific to Lourdes and her family and is not meant to be a generalization applicable to other families who have experienced long-term separation.

Lourdes recalls a deep sense of loss and separation from her mother through her own child – an example of some of the long-term effects of separation experienced by the adult daughter of one former domestic worker. While this moment recalled by Lourdes is specific to her and her family and is not necessarily applicable to other families who have experienced separation, it draws attention to the long-term effects of family separation that warrant greater theoretical attention.

Conclusion

Drawing on one-on-one, in-depth interviews with two former Filipina domestic workers and their adult daughters, this chapter examined long-term intergenerational effects of separation both during and after reunification. As highlighted in the stories of Chris, Tessie, Aurora, and Lourdes, the effects of separation do not simply end with reunification, but rather continue to affect familial relationships across generations.

This chapter also explored the possibilities of post-reunification reconciliation through *Pinay* activism. Lourdes' and Chris' involvement in organizations like KM and PMSC helped them understand the reasons why they were separated from their mothers. Being able to identify some of the structural causes behind systemic family separation helped to rebuild their relationships with their mothers and work through particularly difficult times. Their activist pursuits also enabled them to meet other Filipino migrant youth, fellow *kababayans*, thereby nurturing a sense of belonging and empowerment to take on leadership roles in their communities. Their mothers' own involvement in various community-building strategies also points to the collective efforts of mothers and adult daughters to establish a sense of 'home' and rootedness in Canada. Further, in examining key transitions in the intimate lives of Chris, Tessie, Aurora, and Lourdes, I have also attempted to foreground a *Pinay peminist* framework not only to underscore their perspectives, as well as their lived and embodied experiences in Canada, but also to highlight the contributions of *Pinay peminist* scholarship and activism. In doing so, it is my hope that we may begin to develop nuanced and heterogeneous understandings of Filipina lives in Canada and empower our communities to resist ongoing processes of dehumanization and marginalization.

PART III
Emotional Labour and Intimate Care Work

Chapter 10

On the Road and on Their Own: Autonomy and Giving in Home Health Care in Quebec

Deirdre Meintel, Sylvie Fortin and Marguerite Cognet

Introduction

The transformation of wage work in the context of globalization has involved, among other things, the extension of precarious, poorly paid employment with few social benefits (Castel 1995), especially for service jobs that correspond to what was once women's domestic work. In Canada as elsewhere, home health care has emerged as a low status field where labour is predominantly female, often foreign-born and of visible minority status (Aronson and Neysmith 1996, Cognet 2003). Home care is increasingly important in the Canadian health system, yet those who deliver it are pressured by the contradictions between caregiving and economic constraints, between the officially public, state-supported character of the health system and its increasing privatization, between the traditional notion of care as a private, mostly feminine concern, and its emergence as a public issue (Tronto 1993).

The restructuring of health care in Canada is occurring in the wider context of globalization that is transforming women's work, including unpaid child care and volunteering (Neysmith 2000), as well as wage work (see Bakan and Stasiulis 1995, Ng 2002, Stasiulis and Bakan 2003). Our research has shown that restructuring of the health sector in Quebec has accentuated gender and ethnic stratification by creating a veritable two-tier home health care labour market; immigrant women of colour are less likely than non-immigrants or male immigrants to find home care jobs in the public sector, which is characterized by better working conditions than private agencies.

In this article we examine how the same factors that structure the labour market, i.e. race, gender and immigrant origin, are articulate, in life on the job for home health workers in Quebec. Called 'family and social auxiliaries' (*auxiliaires familiales et sociales*), they give home care to the elderly, handicapped and chronically ill. Their jobs are badly paid, especially in the private sector, low status and often difficult; moreover, we find that incidents of racism and sexual harassment by clients are not uncommon. Nevertheless, nearly all home care workers we contacted express great attachment and commitment to their work; in fact most say they 'love' their work. Pride in giving service well and satisfaction at being able to turn 'difficult' clients around are recurrent themes in the narratives we collected. Given the notorious levels of dissatisfaction among nurses in Quebec (Lévesque 2002) and Canada (Canadian Nursing Advisory Committee 2002: 8 *et passim*), such attitudes are all the more intriguing.

Besides looking at how race and gender issues play out on the job, we seek to understand why *auxiliaires* are so attached to their work. Hochshild's (1983) discussion of emotional labour does not, we think, take us far enough in understanding the workers' perspectives, nor the strength of their positive feelings about what they do. Recent discussions of the classic notion of the 'gift' (Mauss 1960 [1925]) offers new avenues of understanding why caregiving can provide such satisfaction to those who perform it, despite its social denigration. The relative autonomy of the work – largely a factor of the caregivers' mobility within the city and physical distance from their institutional base – appears crucial, because autonomy is a necessary condition for the 'giving' that goes 'beyond the call of duty'. Moreover, giving is often embedded in an 'economy of gratitude' (Hochshild 2003) that brings meaningful reciprocity to the worker. Following Tronto (1993), we argue that the commitment of the *auxiliaires* to their work should not be construed as false consciousness, but rather as a valid assessment of its importance. Finally, we raise the question of how the devotion of these workers may condition the political struggle for more just recognition of the value of home health care work.

Home Care in Quebec

Under the pressure of rising costs and the growing health needs related to the aging of its population, Canada implemented a number of reforms in health care aimed at rationalizing the health system beginning in the 1980s. Among these are policies aimed at reducing or eliminating hospitalization, often through home health services (Cognet and Fortin 2003). In Quebec, the health system has undergone a radical reorganization of health care in favour of community- and home-based services over the hospital-centred model of the past, in the name of lowering costs (Contandriopoulos et al. 2000).

A network of 147 public health and social service centres (*Centres locaux de services communautaires*, or CLSCs) provides basic health care services in Quebec, including 29 in Montreal. Home health care is generally free of charge to clients; it accounts for about 40 per cent of CLSC activities, and 30 per cent of their expenditures (CACC 1995). In 1994, 90 per cent of home health services was provided by public institutions; but since then, rising demand along with insufficient funding for the public health care system has led Quebec, like other Canadian provinces, to subcontract to private agencies, including multinationals based in the United States.[1] The three CLSCs that were partners in our research subcontracted some 60 per cent of their home care activities to such agencies in the years 1999–2001.

Home care workers in Quebec are estimated to be about 8,000 (Boileau 2002); high turnover, along with the fact that some workers are employed by more than one establishment, makes it difficult to arrive at an exact figure. Some 30 private agencies offer nursing services and home health care assistance in Montreal. Locally-owned agencies tend to be small (five to 10 full-time employees, along with a roster of on-call workers, typically numbering around 200) and are often owned by a health professional-turned-entrepreneur; multinational agencies employ up to 500 workers.

The Research[2]

An exploratory pilot study of home health care workers (Meintel et al. 1999) was carried out at a CLSC located in a highly multiethnic[3] area of Montreal (pop. 1,853,489 in 2002;[4] the population of the wider metropolitan area was 3,426,350 in 2001 according to Statistics Canada). The largest CLSC in the city, it serves a geographic sector of the city whose population numbers some 127,000. Based on interviews and field observations, the pilot study showed striking differences among home care workers regarding training and rank as well as considerable diversity in terms of national origin. The pilot study led to a

1 Subcontracting health care to private agencies is currently much debated in Quebec, and has been highly contested by health care professionals (Séguin 2003). See also the following websites: http://radio-canada.ca/regions/abitibi/nouvelles/200312/10/003-manif-hopitaux.shtml; http://mesnouvelles.branchez-vous.com/communiques/cnw/LBR/2003/10/c9458.html.

2 We gratefully acknowledge the financial support given by the Conseil Québécois de Recherche Sociale, the Centre de recherche et de formation du CLSC Côte-des-Neiges and Immigration et métropoles. Our sincere thanks to Eleonore Kofman and Wenona Giles for their invaluable comments on earlier versions of this article. Researchers include Deirdre Meintel (director), Marguerite Cognet (managing director), Robert Sévigny, Jean Renaud and Rachad Antonius. The interviews were conducted by Laurent Raigneau and Barbara Fournier. Géraldine Moissière and Marie Noëlle Fortin assisted with the analysis and offered helpful comments.

3 One third of the population of the general urban area where this CLSC operates are members of visible minority groups (mainly of African, Caribbean and Asian origin). Forty-four per cent of the area's population are foreign-born (Bernèche et al. 2002).

4 All percentages and population figures for the city of Montreal proper and its districts (*arrondissements*) that appear in this section are taken from Ville de Montréal, Bureau des relations interculturelles. They were compiled by a team composed of F. Bernèche, J. J. Mongeau, S. Giroux, J. Archambault, and M. Riendeau, under the direction of D. Rose, INRS Urbanization, Culture et société, February 2002, available at: http://www2.ville.montreal.qc.ca/diversite/portrait.htm.

broader study (1999–2002) that was oriented to elucidating how factors such as national origin, visible minority status and gender figure in the way home health care workers are integrated into the job market and the health system as well as in relations with other health care personnel and clients. (Unlike physicians, *auxiliaires* usually speak of 'clients' rather than patients; 'client' is the official term used by CLSCs to describe the recipients of home care services.)

Field research was carried out in three CLSCs,[5] representing the public sector, and three private home care agencies, representing the private sector. The agencies were already working with the CLSCs in the study on a subcontracting basis. All three CLSCs serve sectors of Montreal that have a substantially higher proportion of immigrants than the city average of 26 per cent (Canada Census 1996). The two added for the present research are in the middle range of clientele size for Montreal CLSCs, serving populations of 52,000 and 69,000, respectively. As for the three private agencies, the largest is a US-based multinational; the other two are locally owned. Extensive subcontracting by the CLSCs[6] means that home care workers in both private and public sectors serve largely the same clientele.

Taken together our six sites provide a pool of about 600 homecare workers, 146 in the CLSCs and approximately 450 in private agencies. (The latter figure is approximate because of the fluidity of the labour force in the agencies.) Our study is based on field observations of meetings and work in clients' homes, a questionnaire sent to 280 *auxiliaires* and answered by 181 (41 per cent of them in the private sector), and interviews with 40 home care workers. The interviews were carried out in French by two assistants, one male (an immigrant) and one female (a Francophone Québécoise). *Auxiliaires*, immigrant and non-immigrant, provided feedback on our methods and findings at every stage of the research, in meetings and conferences as well as informally.[7]

Eleven men and 29 women were interviewed about their experiences on the job, perspectives on their work and relations with clients and other practitioners. Of the 40 interviewees, 23 are foreign-born, including 13 from Haiti. Eight of the 40, evenly divided by gender, have university degrees; seven of these are foreign born. Most of the native-born workers are not originally from Montreal but from smaller towns and rural villages in Quebec. Typically, those born in Quebec have entered home health care via a personal contact – friends or family members doing similar

5 One condition of our research in these CLSCs was that their names not be published, so as to assure the anonymity of those who participated in the study.

6 According to Laforest and Amzallag (2000), the proportion of home care hours subcontracted by CLSCs ranges from zero to 40 per cent. However, the CLSCs in our study subcontracted up to 60 per cent of home health care and services to private agencies (Cognet and Fortin 2003). Each CLSC has considerable administrative autonomy in deciding how its resources will be used, including how much home care will be subcontracted to the private sector.

7 An African women's association called Solidarité Femmes Africaines used our research results in a public theatrical presentation.

work; however, younger *auxiliaires* have sometimes been attracted to the field via more formal channels, such as conferences or publications. The analysis presented here is mainly based on the interviews, as framed by the more general analyses of questionnaire and observation data carried out under the direction of Marguerite Cognet (2002, 2003, 2004). After a brief presentation of our findings on how this labour market is stratified, we turn to our main concerns. First of all, how are experiences on the job conditioned by gender, national origin and racialized status? To what extent do these workers perceive discrimination? How do they interpret it and react to it? How does it affect their feelings and perceptions around the job? And finally, how do we explain the highly positive feelings expressed by nearly all those interviewed about their work?

Racial, Gender and Ethnic Stratification in Home Care

Statistics on the ethnic/national origins of *auxiliaires* are not available; however, of the 181 questionnaire respondents, 47.5 per cent are foreign-born, whereas immigrants make up 26.7 per cent of the city's active population (CAMO 2001, p. 43). Of the immigrant respondents, 62 per cent work in private agencies. Though no data exist for *auxiliaires* in general, almost half of our questionnaire respondents are of immigrant origin, and of these, over 60 per cent are of Caribbean, usually Haitian, origin. Over 15 per cent of employed Haitians in Montreal work in the health and social service sector, where they earn only 83 per cent of the mean salary (CAMO 2001: 189).

Cognet and Fortin (2003) have demonstrated that the reorganization of the health sector has helped reinforce social and professional stratification along the lines of gender and national origin, creating a veritable two-tier health care labour market: *auxiliaires* working for private agencies earn only about half as much for the same work as those employed by CLSCs; i.e. about $7.10 an hour, 20 cents over the minimum wage, versus an average of $15/hour for their peers in the public sector. Moreover, CLSC workers have much better job security, belong to a union, enjoy better supervision and on-the-job training, and have more contact with other types of health professionals. Agency workers have almost no professional support and no job mobility, except for what pay increases they can negotiate – something men are better positioned to do than women, male home care workers being scarce and much in demand. Most would prefer to work for a CLSC. Their reasons include better pay, better benefits, better supervision and more contact with other health professionals around the care of clients, as well as shorter distances to travel between clients (Cognet and Fortin 2003).

Informal patterns of discrimination described by Cognet and Fortin (2003) limit access to public sector jobs in home health care by visible minority immigrants, especially women from the Caribbean. The formal training for work as an *auxiliaire* is a course of 960 hours; however, many older native-born and some of the immigrant men and women working in this field have not taken such a course; some have taken one of 600 hours that qualifies them as an assistant for clients, *préposé au bénéficiaires*. Our data indicate that access to CLSC positions is highly unlikely for an immigrant without the 960-hour course, and immigrant workers interviewed report that French–English bilingualism is often required of them as well. (Native-born workers did not mention such a requirement.) Questionnaire results show that White immigrants are far more likely than immigrants of colour to work in CLSCs, at almost the same rate as the (White) native-born. Cognet's analyses (2004) have shown that differential access to CLSC positions cannot be explained by factors such as prior training or language competence; rather, colour is the determining factor. Women from the Caribbean are concentrated in the agencies even more than their male counterparts; one reason may be that the men in question (and not the women) are often deskilled, educated professionals. Also, male workers are needed by CLSCs to work with male clients, as CLSCs tend to allocate clients to *auxiliaires* by gender; often religious Jews and Muslims request an *auxiliaire* of the same gender.

It is extremely rare that immigrants are given supervisory positions in the CLSCs we studied. These positions do not call for prior training and bring little monetary benefit, but they allow more frequent contact on a collegial basis with health professionals. Discrimination is not endorsed by the CLSCs and is in contradiction to their stated aims of social solidarity and respect for cultural differences. Nevertheless, the practice whereby outgoing supervisors propose a replacement from their own personal network makes for structural discrimination that keeps immigrants (including those of colour) out of such positions. Similarly, Tania Das Gupta shows that 'subjective' promotional procedures and 'ad hoc' methods used to fill leadership positions keep Black hospital nurses out of management in Ontario (1996: 83).

The *Auxiliaires Familiales* and their Work

Given the preponderance of women in this occupation, the feminine form is generally used in official documents. Officially the *auxiliaire*'s work is composed of tasks oriented to daily life activities, particularly in the domestic sphere, that the client cannot carry out independently (Gouvernement du Québec 1994). The *auxiliaire* may identify needs and communicate them to nurses and others involved in the client's care. She (he) may help out with children, diet, hygiene and other matters that concern the physical well-being of the household, and may occasionally accompany clients on errands outside the home, to the doctor's or the bank, for example. Official definitions give a rather narrow job description, but in practice the tasks these workers may be asked to do is almost unlimited. On the basis of field observations, Cognet and Fortin (2003) have divided *auxiliaires*' work into three general types: (1) direct personal care and assistance relating to hygiene (giving baths and shampoos, for example) and bodily functions (eating, excretion), giving physical and social support; (2) care of the client's environment (light housework, cooking, giving moral support to family caregivers, etc.); and

(3) administrative and institutional tasks (organizing their workday, coordinating with other caregivers, observing the client's and family's changing needs, transmitting relevant information to other personnel and performing domestic chores in the establishment where they are based). For example, *auxiliaries* in CLSCs may be asked to clean the refrigerator at the nurses' station or clean up a meeting room after other employees have used it.

Work Relationships

Most of the *auxiliaire*'s activities are based on another form of work, which is difficult to quantify or itemize; that is, relational work with clients, with family caregivers, and other health personnel involved in the client's care (Armstrong 1994, Neysmith 1996). Here we examine different levels of interaction where the *auxiliaire*'s relationship skills are critical for clients' welfare: with clients, professionals involved in the client's care and others in the family. Later we examine some of the issues that come up in work relationships such as sexual harassment, racial prejudice, and cultural differences and how *auxiliaires* handle them.

Our interviewees emphasize the importance of establishing trust with patients in order to assure quality of care:

> It's a whole deal to negotiate, to be accepted … If the client isn't ready for you to give them a bath the first day, for sure you don't just come in, bing bang … when it comes from them, often they are really happy, they're satisfied, they appreciate you … I help her get dressed … it's important to put on her little earrings for her before I leave, she always looks nice, it's so good for her morale … I follow their rhythm … If I came today, and she (client) is weak, tired, maybe she can't take a bath today, then it'll be a wash-up at the sink … (Marielle,[8] born in Québec, late 40s, part-time employee, CLSC)

The first encounter is crucial:

> The minute you get there, you shake their hand … Already she's starting to trust you … You start to talk … 'How was your day?' … She knows you're not just going to cook and leave. That doesn't do anything for her. Whereas the exchange, the talk … I tell myself it is balm for her soul … and she will say that she's had a good day … (Marie, born in Haiti, agency employee, contracted by a CLSC)

---

8 All proper names of auxiliaires are pseudonyms. Those born in Quebec are of Franco-Québécois background, with French being their mother tongue, unless otherwise indicated. For reasons of confidentiality, age is not mentioned except when pertinent. The region, rather than the country, of origin is given in cases where the latter might identify the informant.

Whether *auxiliaires* work for the private or the public sector, they are inevitably obliged to bend the 'rules' of strict role definition about what to do for clients, in the interest of preserving the rapport necessary for good care (cf. Goffman 1959, 1961). Negotiating with clients about whether she will wash the kitchen floor, cut hair or give a pedicure oblige the worker to make choices based partly on official definitions of the job, partly on the *auxiliaire*'s desire to maintain smooth relations with the client and to oblige her (him), as well as on safety considerations: for example, one *auxiliaire* refused to give a pedicure to a diabetic, knowing that this requires specialized training. It should also be kept in mind that dissatisfied clients can ask the worker to leave or make a complaint to her employers.

Coordination and negotiation is a regular part of the *auxiliaire*'s task. Family members may ask her to do household chores that are not part of her job, while health professionals may pressure her to take on skilled tasks normally done by a nurse (giving medicine) or an occupational therapist (exercises). The latter type of activity, called 'delegated acts', is a somewhat contested zone; *auxiliaires* must weigh requests by nurses or others on the care team against the risks for themselves and clients.

> I observe medication and keep an eye on it … (recounts discovering a mistake by the pharmacy for a client's medication and reporting it to the nurse) … but I don't give medication, that's an act for a nurse to perform … I protect the client and I protect myself … I don't give eye drops … but some *auxiliaires* do. (Danielle, 54 years old, born in Quebec, CLSC employee)

Finally, the home care worker must communicate with the professionals involved in the client's care, most often nurses, occupational therapists or dieticians, as well as with the heads of the team of *auxiliaires* and the multidisciplinary team. For example, abuse of the elderly is likely to first be noticed by the homecare worker, who spends far more time in the client's home than any other category of health personnel. Because they have greater access to other professionals, CLSC workers are better placed than agency employees to bring such problems to the attention of those able to intervene.

Relations with clients and other types of health personnel are strongly coloured by the low status of *auxiliaire* work among the general public. One woman says her friends and family see her work as 'collecting shit'. Several African men in the study allow their relatives in Africa to believe they are nurses. Immigrant men from African and Haiti recognize that the work they are doing is considered women's work in their milieu of origin; for both genders, the fact that what they do is traditionally unpaid kinship work means that family and friends may see it as not 'real' work, or at best, 'dirty' work. (However, some of those interviewed, both immigrant and native-born, were influenced in their choice of occupation by *auxiliaires* in their immediate family or close personal network.) The stigma attached to the job may explain why there are almost no Canadian-born children of immigrants among the workers in the study.[9] As for clients, while many express great appreciation for the services these workers provide, some, including immigrants, refer to the *auxiliaire* as 'the maid' (*la bonne*) or 'the charwoman' (*la femme de ménage*) and treat her with less deference than other health care personnel who come to the home. This seems especially true for the Haitian women in the study. Some clients (including Haitians; see below) find it 'natural' that a person of colour, especially a woman, who is providing a service in their home, be regarded as a servant or a cleaning woman (see Collins 1990: 43).

While home care workers usually react to clients' perceptions as a professional challenge, they find non-recognition by co-workers (e.g. nurses) more difficult to contend with. Many complain of being ignored, not listened to, 'put in their place' as several expressed it, in their contacts with nurses, social workers and other professionals. Being asked to clean up after others in the institution where they are based reinforces the *auxiliaires*' sense that their work is not given just recognition in team settings. As one put it,

> You feel that you're not taken into account, you feel there are limits, they make you feel … it's like, 'You've done your job, that's enough, I'll take care of the rest, and it's mine' … Even if it is you who is there every day, who knows the problems, who's trying to reassure the client … There are others who adore us, who respect us, who take us into account … (Claudine, born in France, CLSC employee)

The quality of inter-professional relations is highly variable by context, ranging from non-existent in private agencies to highly collaborative in the CLSCs. Agency workers often say that they hardly ever see other *auxiliaires* except when they pick up their paycheck. Occasionally, an accessible supervisor gives needed support and recourse in case of difficulties, but there is usually no interaction with other categories of health personnel involved in the client's care. By contrast, *auxiliaires* working in an experimental CLSC programme of prevention-oriented care for the elderly met regularly with nurses and other personnel, had access to patient files and felt more part of an interdisciplinary team than is usually the case. According to one *auxiliaire* who held a supervisory position, experience in this programme led several to continue their education. The programme was later discontinued for budgetary reasons, though administrators hope to incorporate some of its components into CLSC practice.

9 In research done in Toronto, Giles (1993) has described how women of Portuguese background born in Canada reject manual labour ('dirty' work) only to accept low-level service jobs that are often no better paid or more secure than the jobs in factories done by their mothers, who arrived in the 1950s and 1960s, but are seen as 'cleaner'. We have noticed similar trends in other long established immigrant groups in Montreal. This does not necessarily predict what will happen with today's immigrants who are more often of urban origin and better educated than earlier arrivals.

There is reason to believe that the public sector may be coming to resemble the private in some disquieting ways. For example, budgetary restrictions have led to the elimination of interdisciplinary meetings and even meetings among *auxiliaires* in certain CLSCs, and to their reduction in others; in some CLSCs, home care workers no longer have the access to patients' files that they had in the past. Such changes would make any problems encountered by home care workers, such as elder abuse or sexual harassment, all the more difficult to track and report.

On-the-Job Issues of Difference and Diversity

In this section we look at various issues that arise in on-the-job relationships between home care workers and clients such as sexual harassment, anti-immigrant stereotypes, racial prejudice and cultural and religious differences. In so doing, we will look at how, in the face of such difficulties, *auxiliaires* manifest agency, or 'the socioculturally mediated capacity to act' (Ahearn 2001: 112). The family metaphor surrounding what home care workers do is epitomized in their official title, normally shortened to '*auxiliaire familiale*'. Indeed, some of the women describe their work in familial terms, as being 'what a mother might do', or 'like a daughter would do'. For most of the foreign-born and the older women, such designations indicate closeness and indispensability to the client, but several younger women reject them as unprofessional. Because of the associations of their work with women's traditional labour, some immigrant male *auxiliaires* believe they are stereotyped as gay.

Both genders are affected by sexual harassment, though in different ways. Many of the women have experienced inappropriate touching by male patients; by their accounts, verbal firmness is usually sufficient; otherwise, they will ask that a male *auxiliaire* be sent in their place. Patients' wives are occasionally jealous and, once again, professionalism is the preferred strategy. None of those we contacted mention harassment as *auxiliaires* by colleagues or superiors, who are likely to be female in any case. Some male *auxiliaires* worry about being accused of harassment themselves and so feel ill at ease bathing female clients. (CLSCs usually assign home care workers according to the gender of the client/patient, but agencies do not necessarily make such distinctions.) Frequently though, female *auxiliaires* express pleasure in working with male colleagues and clients, and vice-versa.

Women of colour are also more likely to experience the negative conditions of agency work mentioned earlier: having more difficult and aggressive clients, greater distances to travel between jobs, and finally, the stigmatization of working for agencies. This last is generalized among health care workers and clients alike: the CLSC may threaten to transfer a difficult client to an agency. Workers in both the private and the public sector believe that such transfers are standard, and give agency workers a more difficult clientele. It is not a matter of *policy* on the part of CLSCs to send difficult clients to the agencies, but workers' impressions suggest that it is a matter of informal practice. Many CLSC *auxiliaires* believe that those working for the agencies are not only severely underpaid and more pressured for time, but also ill-trained, and less conscientious. It should be added that the stigmatization of agency work seems particularly widespread among Haitians; one woman interviewed lets other Haitians believe that she works in a home for the elderly rather than for an agency.

Whether in agencies or CLSCs, women, especially Black[10] women, report being pressured to do housework beyond what has been agreed upon. One of the men interviewed thinks that women are more pressured to do household tasks; on the other hand, he says, men are asked to do heavy lifting that is not part of the initial agreement (e.g. to move furniture).

Being an immigrant can be just as important as race, according to 'Matilda', a Caribbean-born worker who used to work for an agency and is now employed by a CLSC:

> Sometimes I feel they look down on me, but I'm used to it, since when I came to Canada, from my school days here (in a small Quebec town) ... The other day, we were five *auxiliaires*, including me, one from Peru, another was from Chile. The one from Chile, says the same thing, she is used to encountering people who make judgements.

Indeed, a home care worker born in Latin American whom we interviewed reports being labelled a 'job thief'[11] by clients on several occasions.

Although immigrants of any origin may experience anti-immigrant prejudice at some point, the weight of discrimination is most keenly felt by the Haitian-born, possibly because they are the 'visible minority' that is most numerous in the home care sector.

Most Black workers have encountered a racially prejudiced client at some point. Institutional responses to racism is varied; one CLSC in the study refuses clients who insist on having a White caregiver; another tries to accommodate the client when possible, as do private agencies for the most part. What is most

10 In the Canadian context, 'Black' is a heterogeneous social category that includes those of dark skin colour who are of African, Caribbean or African-American origins; defined in this way, Blacks account for 5.7 per cent of the Montreal population; however, they are 12.5 per cent of the city's immigrants and only 2.9 per cent of the native-born (Bernèche et al. 2002). It does not include those of Asian background. The frequently used term 'visible minorities' is applied to a wide range of groups, including Blacks, as well as those of many other backgrounds including Latin American, Middle Eastern, South Asian, Korean, Japanese, Philippino, etc. 'Visible minorities' account for 18.7 per cent of the Montreal population; they include 48 per cent of the city's immigrants and 7 per cent of the native-born (Bernèche et al. 2002).

11 This accusation was reported by only one *auxiliaire*; however, immigrants have often been stigmatized as being '*voleurs de jobs*' (job thieves, in Québécois parlance). However, it is widely recognized that Quebec needs immigrants to compensate for the low birth rate and maintain the province's demographic weight in Canada.

striking about the narratives of racist incidents in the interviews are the workers' detached and professional responses, of which the following is a typical example:

> When I replaced another *auxiliaire* who was sick, I heard that she didn't like Blacks. I said, 'It's not my problem if she doesn't like Blacks. One can't like everybody!' So when I arrived at the (client's) home, I said, 'It seems that you don't like Blacks'. She was shocked, she didn't say a word. I said, 'Myself, I don't have anything against you, I like you just the same even if you don't like me. I'm here to help you. Even if you don't like me, it's not a problem, the service is to help you' ... I spent a good six months with her ... (Cecile, born in Haiti, agency employee)

In yet another case, the client indicated to the CLSC that she did not want to have a Black health care worker, but the person available happened to be a Haitian *auxiliaire*. Finally, the client agreed and the women had a frank exchange:

> She told me she had had experiences ... she was afraid of Blacks ... She was afraid because I was Black and in her mind, we don't wash. When she told me that, I laughed. I found it funny ... She asked if she was insulting me. I said, 'Not at all!' ... I asked her how many races she thought there were. She looked at me completely surprised ... Then she said, 'I don't know and I don't want to know, but I've had my bath, I'm very happy with it, and if you want to come again, it doesn't bother me'. (Yvonne, born in Haiti, CLSC employee)

Discrimination experienced by Haitians at the hands of other Haitians is often mentioned; sometimes this is seen as a matter of hair type and darker versus lighter colour, sometimes as a matter of social class. Many of the Haitians interviewed speak of avoiding or refusing Haitian clients, who are likely to try to treat them, they say, as domestics. Émile, an agency employee born in Haiti, categorically refuses to take Haitian clients, after two unpleasant experiences. He holds that, for Haitians, 'if you are not a professor, a doctor or a lawyer, you do not have an honourable profession'. Like several of his peers, he suspects that Haitians would treat a White worker better than a Haitian.

When asked about racism, many *auxiliaires* told us of experiences with clients such as those just cited. However, few mentioned structural discrimination around hiring. Oscar, a South American refugee with a university degree, is employed by an agency and works under contract for a CLSC. He reports that he was refused employment in a CLSC on the grounds of 'lack of experience', whereas others (Quebec-born Francophones) without experience were hired. Sometimes discrimination is acknowledged by the worker and seen as the price to be paid for migration. Several speak of the agencies as 'giving a chance' to immigrants, of being a 'springboard' to something better. This may be overly optimistic; almost half of the immigrant women who responded to the questionnaire had at least 10 years' Canadian experience in home care (Cognet 2002), and most were still working in private agencies.

Auxiliaires, Quebec-born and immigrants alike, object to how certain immigrant clients treat them. Émile, for example, finds Eastern Europeans condescending ('They dictate to you'). Another Haitian male *auxiliaire* finds immigrants generally 'more demanding' than native-born Québécois. A CLSC worker recounts the following incident involving a client from North Africa:

> The client said, 'You are not to look at me in the eyes. You are to look at the floor when you talk to me' … I said, 'Yes. You are right. I owe you respect. You also owe me respect. And no, Madame, I will not look at the floor. I am not a dog. Do we understand each other, Madame?' … She said, 'You'll have to go'. I said, 'No problem'. I left. (Jocelyne, born in Quebec)

Many of the workers consider ethnocultural variety one of the interesting aspects of their occupation. (Recall that most participants born in Quebec grew up in ethnically homogenous environments.) Religious and cultural observances around food and meals are respected insofar as possible; in one CLSC with a large elderly Jewish population of Eastern European origin, some of the home care workers attended classes about kosher practices. Cultural difference is usually approached in pragmatic terms, first of all in terms of language and communication, given the necessity of establishing rapport with clients:

> The woman didn't speak my language. At one point the client said, '*leche*' … *Leche* means 'milk'. I wrote it down, I took notes when she told me a new word … I can communicate (with the client) a bit, a few words now (in Spanish) … but you can always talk with your hands … (Manon, CLSC worker, born in Quebec)

Loving One's Work

Given the physical and psychological demands of the job, its often denigrated status and low pay, not to mention episodes of racism and sexual harassment, how can the 'love' of their work spontaneously expressed by almost all those interviewed be explained?

> I began with a three-month trial period; I'm still there now. Not only do I love it, I don't want to change at all … (Yvonne, born in Haiti, CLSC employee for 15 years)

'Love' is in fact the word our interviewees most often used to describe how they feel about their work. As many put it, 'You *have* to love it to be able to do it'. Home care workers tend to invoke a non-utilitarian logic when describing their work (Cognet 2002); that is, they speak not of monetary gain or social prestige but rather describe their feelings about the work in terms of personal pride and satisfaction in the care they give. Indeed, some use the word 'vocation' to describe what they do. The interviews give abundant evidence that meeting the emotional and intellectual challenges of the job are sources of pride and satisfaction for the *auxiliaires*. For example, one of the youngest we interviewed, a Quebec-born CLSC home care worker in her early 20s, says:

> Preparing nice fast little recipes, cooking them well, that's fun, I like that ... It's using your imagination ... when you see that there's not much in the fridge or in the cupboard, and they have to eat ... Me, I like it to be done well, I'm a perfectionist ...

Another woman working in the public sector relates how she got an Alzheimer's patient who would not open the front door but would do so by singing. The woman opened the door and the worker sang the whole time she worked with this client. A Latin American agency employee who arrived in Canada with a university degree tells how she has dealt with difficult clients:

> Most of my clients, even if they are aggressive, I have a special touch with them, I brainwash them! (Laughter). There's a man who used to be a journalist; he's obese and has a nasty disposition ... but I manage to have a good relationship with him ... Then there's a woman, very difficult, very aggressive ... but she asks for me, I'm the only one she can stand, she can't stand the others ... I manage to control my feelings, relax, laugh at myself ...

'Love' for the work seems to be the case as much for agency workers as for those in the public sector, and applies as much to the overqualified as to others. Three of the 40 individuals interviewed (one woman and two men) came to their present occupation after long careers in other fields; still others did so by force of circumstances; e.g. the deskilling that is so often part of the migrant experience (notably for the men from Africa and the Caribbean). For a great many others – most of the women – work in this field has followed less satisfying experiences in equally low-paid jobs, in manufacturing or sales-related services. Despite these different occupational trajectories, almost all the workers speak in terms that connote a wellspring of motivations based on service to others, responding to the needs of others, finding pride and satisfaction in providing for those needs even when the other is racist, sexist or otherwise difficult to deal with. Some of the younger *auxiliaires* envisage an eventual change of occupation, given the physical demands of their present one, but virtually all hope to go on working in human services (typically, social work).

The question of what motivates these workers and gives them satisfaction is all the more interesting given the very high levels of dissatisfaction in another highly feminized health occupation – nursing. According to a recent survey by the Quebec Order of Nurses (*L'Ordre des infirmie`res et infirmiers*), 62 per cent are unsatisfied in their work (Lévesque 2002), mainly because of the way their skills are used and the low value accorded their profession by others. It is possible that the family metaphor that surrounds the *auxiliaires familiales* reinforces a kinship ethic. However, there is much to suggest *auxiliaires*' perceptions are not all that different from nurses'.

First of all, it is important to distinguish between 'job' and 'work'. According to the Quebec study, most of the nurses who would like to change jobs would prefer to work in the CLSCs rather than hospitals. Likewise, the home care workers in our study would generally prefer working in CLSCs rather than in hospitals, old age homes or private agencies. Though, as we have pointed out, the public sector is very much affected by privatization of health care, it still offers working conditions that promise not only better pay and security but also more satisfactory conditions for work than what obtains in other contexts. Home care workers who had worked in hospitals, for example, often complained that they were rushed in their work and unable to care for patients in a humane way. Several had in fact been fired from hospitals for being 'too slow' in their work.

A study of hundreds of nurses, practical nurses and home health aides in Saskatchewan cites autonomy as the most important factor in practitioners' morale. By the same token, a report on nursing across Canada mentions 'lessened autonomy' as a major issue for nurses (Canadian Nursing Advisory Committee 2002: 29). A Saskatchewan study of job satisfaction among registered nurses, licensed practical nurses and home health care workers finds that autonomy and interaction with clients and other caregivers outranks pay for all three groups (Williams et al. 2000).

Mobility and its Implications

Spatial distance from the institution that employs them is a major factor in the *auxiliaire*'s autonomy. Working alone with clients outside the walls of the institution seems to confer a sense of agency that is in itself rewarding; *auxiliaires* typically speak of themselves as being 'on the road' (*sur la route*) constantly and 'on their own' with clients. Though they mention the need for support from other professionals, they take pleasure in the autonomy of their work.

> I couldn't stand the 9 to 5 in an office anymore. I needed to get close to people. We (*auxiliaires*) are not surrounded by nurses but we can call them if there is a problem … We're on our own. You go, you make your own work plan … It's a wonderful autonomy … It's often unpredictable … We move around, we're alone. Of course you have to call in if there is a problem … (Marielle, born in Quebec, former secretary, part-time CLSC employee)

Distance from the institution means that supervisors generally leave the decision to perform small services not included in the formal definition of the job to the discretion of the worker – cutting hair, preparing a snack for the client, taking out rubbish, etc. For their part, workers reason that such services facilitate rapport with clients, contribute to their well-being, or simply 'make them happy'. As one woman remarked, 'It's not part of my job, but she likes it when I make her a coffee and a little snack before I leave'.

The flip side of geographical distance is the workers' spatial and social marginalization in the institution. The areas reserved for home care workers that we observed in CLSCs are set away from those of nurses and social workers, uninviting and impersonal with fluorescent lighting, the lack of voice mail and limited telephone access in a windowless room. The worker is not allowed to leave personal objects or adornments. All this makes for what Augé would call a 'non-place' (1992), a space devoid of meaning and personal investment. For their part, *auxiliaires* do not seek more or better space in the CLSC, probably because their marginality to the institution helps legitimize the autonomy they find in mobility and distance from it (Meintel et al. 1999: 30–32). In any case, they regard the real locus of their work as 'on the road'.

Private sector employees spend even less time in the institution that employs them as compared to public sector workers. For them, the degree of geographical mobility required by the job adds special burdens. They travel longer distances than CLSC workers because, unlike CLSCs, agencies are not organized on a geographical basis and have a much less localized clientele. Moreover, travel is at the agency worker's expense, whereas CLSC *auxiliaires* receive a public transport pass and travel time is factored into their schedule. None of the women in agencies have cars, unlike their male colleagues. Furthermore, agencies do not deposit paychecks in employees' bank accounts as do CLSCs, which means yet another unpaid trip for the worker.

Despite such drawbacks, mobility allows a degree of personal initiative that *auxiliaires* find satisfying. As we have seen, they make ample use of it to do more than the job requires for their clients. Of course this margin of initiative holds disadvantages for workers. Clients may not distinguish between essential and discretionary services, and will expect the same from others (e.g. a vacation replacement caregiver). Taking personal initiative can carry risks for which the worker will be held responsible, e.g. lifting a patient who is too heavy. Performing extra services may put the worker under stressful time pressure, especially those working for private agencies. The stress is all the more acute given that *auxiliaires* believe that such 'extra' services are essential for doing their job well.

The emphasis so many home care workers give their autonomy is a clue, we believe, to understanding better their readiness to go beyond what contractual obligations require on a day-do-day basis in their jobs. Recent discussions of 'the gift' – a form of social action for which autonomy is a *sine qua non* – help us better understand these caregivers' perceptions and motivations.

The Gift and Wage Labour

Mauss' notion of 'the gift' (1960 [1925]) has enjoyed a renaissance in recent years, notably in the work of sociologists such as Godbout (2000) and Caillé (2000), and anthropologists such as Godelier (1996) and Saillant and Dandurand (2002). This current of thinking holds that a great deal of human action cannot be explained by utilitarian motives. It has generated interesting analyses of volunteer work (Cellier 1995), self-help groups such as Alcoholics Anonymous (Godbout 2000), and issues surrounding motherhood, e.g. surrogate motherhood (Layne 1999), adoption (Ouellette 1995) and foster mothering (Tahon 1995). Generally speaking, the activities analysed as forms of the 'gift' are unremunerated ones associated with biological and social reproduction. We suggest that it can also be understood as including voluntary acts of service in the context of salaried work.

The fact that the health care worker is paid a salary does not take away from the spirit in which the work is done; indeed, the day-to-day realities of the job involve innumerable gratuitous acts of service that go beyond contractual obligations. For many *auxiliaires*, the wage work they do is imperceptibly blurred with volunteer work. Many call clients on weekends, visit former clients and bring special treats to those in their care. Several say they hope to do similar work as volunteers when they retire (see also Stone 1999, on visiting nurses, cited by MacDonald and Merrill 2002).

Furthermore, the 'gift' takes many forms that are unrecognized in the contractual relationship between worker and employer, and yet are essential to the successful caregiving. This has been noted by several researchers who have studied those whom Kittay calls 'dependency workers', i.e. those who give care to individuals who would otherwise be 'bereft of life-sustaining resources' (Kittay 1999, p. 31), e.g. immigrant domestics (Colen 1986, 1995) and camp monitors for the mentally handicapped (Robitaille 2004). As Godelier has noted, 'The gift is becoming … an objective, socially necessary condition of social reproduction' (1996: 293).

Care and Recognition

Like Ungerson (1999: 599), who has studied personal assistants to disabled people, we see the *auxiliaire*'s work as involving emotional labour, but of a different kind than the commodified emotion discussed by Hochshild (1983). We are more concerned here with the feelings toward clients and about the work that appear unforced and genuine. Hochshild's recent work on 'the economy of gratitude' (2003) helps to understand better the reward system involved. As the author points out, 'Crucial to a healthy economy of gratitude is a common interpretation of reality, such that what feels like a gift to one person feels like a gift to another' (2003: 105). Developing a satisfying interaction with clients who are initially hostile or difficult seems to provide particular satisfaction (see also Ungerson 1999, Robitaille 2004). We have seen that *auxiliaires* find challenge and creative expression in the aspects of their work that involve 'giving': singing to calm a disturbed patient into accepting service, creating appetizing meals with the ingredients at hand, and so on. Moreover, home care workers find the appreciation shown by clients very satisfying, something also noted by Robitaille (2004). A smile or a word of thanks from the client are taken as return gifts and ample reward. Yet, as Das Gupta has pointed out in her work on nurses, what is 'appreciated' by patients and their families is not the same as what is 'valued' (1996: 74).

Tronto (1993) argues that care of all kinds (for the elderly, the sick, children, the environment, our 'world', in short) has been tied to subordinate status and to a peripheral dimension of social life. But now, the author argues, caregiving can no longer be seen as a private activity; the notion of a separation between public and private life that was conceivable in the nineteenth century can no longer be sustained (1993: 151). Similarly, in a study of caregiving in the family, Saillant and Dandurand (2002) have argued that the 'gift' itself must be given due public recognition as a form of social practice.

Tronto refuses to dismiss the commitment and value that caregivers attach to their work as a form of 'false consciousness'; rather, she argues, 'caregivers can see an essential truth about the value of care' (1993: 117), even though this does not negate its peripheralization in society as a whole. While fully agreeing with Tronto on this point, it is worth asking whether *auxiliaires* and other caregivers' practices of 'giving', of providing service beyond their contractual obligations, are an obstacle that prevents them obtaining more just recognition for their work. MacDonald and Merrill (2002) argue that for mobilizing child care workers, 'intersubjective recognition', or what we might call the reciprocity evoked by the gift (appreciation by clients and other practitioners), is as essential as institutional recognition (redistribution).

As we have seen, the privatization of home care work in Canada in recent years has accentuated structural criteria of job market stratification, including racialized differences, gender and national origin. Working conditions in the private sector limit the freedom of *auxiliaires* to provide optimal service; meanwhile, conditions of work in the public sector are becoming more similar to those in the private sector. In this context, the quality of care that clients receive will necessarily be compromised. We agree with MacDonald and Merrill's call for 'a more robust and inclusive definition of recognition' that addresses not only economic issues but those of intersubjective recognition (2002: 75). Such a definition would not violate *auxiliaires*' perceptions of their work, but rather validate it. And, as MacDonald and Merrill (2002) suggest, intersubjective recognition can be a powerful basis of solidarity between givers and receivers of care in the struggle for justice.

Chapter 11

A Politics of Intimacy: Citizenship Rights, Emotion and the Making of Israeli Children

Maya Shapiro

> Our connection to this is personal: It began when my grandmother, who is 95 and a Holocaust survivor, made us promise that we would take care of her 'granddaughter' Purita – her Peruvian caretaker's little girl … As the August deportation deadline drew near we prepared about 75 hiding places for children … I felt personally responsible. My grandmother was saved from the Holocaust by a Polish woman who hid her for two and half years. I'm not making a comparison here, but there's this ongoing womanly grace happening here, and perhaps my grandmother is also trying, in her way, to pay the world back in kindness.
>
> (Noa Maiman, anti-deportation activist, quoted in Wieler-Pollak 2009b).

> I feel Israeli in my heart and in my soul.
>
> ('Rabbi' Eliazar Cruz, 11-year-old son of migrant careworkers from the Philippines living in Israel, quoted in Kraft 2009).

On 30 July 2009, in a statement released by the office of Prime Minister Benjamin Netanyahu, the Israeli government declared a three-month suspension on the deportation of 1,200 children of migrant workers. These children, born in Israel to women with expired or invalid visas, had no formal status in Israel, and many also lacked status in the countries to which they were slated for deportation. Their mothers had come from villages, towns and cities all over Asia, Africa and Latin America, and had settled mostly in Israel's commercial centre of Tel Aviv in order to work as caregivers and domestic workers in the homes of Israeli citizens.

While the 30 July statement was embedded in a much longer campaign on the part of the Israeli government to rid the country of its 'illegal' residents, and the responses on the part of migrants, activists and allies were similarly part of many years of struggle against policies that criminalize migrants, the suspension and the ensuing reaction to it had the effect of renewing and reinvigorating the debate on citizenship, migration and belonging in the Israeli context. What happens when 'temporary migrant' women, employed to do various forms of domestic and reproductive labour for Israelis, choose to build their own homes and families in the places where they live and work? How are their Israeli-born children classified in this 'ethnic republic' (Zolberg 2000) where citizenship is based on religion and not place of birth? How do these classifications draw from, and contribute to the long-standing social and political divisions that characterize Israeli society? And how can the rights of migrant workers and their children be framed and struggled for in this context?

The questions raised by the potential deportation of the non-status children of migrant caregivers and domestic workers are not unique to Israel. Indeed, in a time in which the 'global care chain' (Hochschild 2000) is expanding and becoming more institutionalized, while 'guest' or 'temporary' labour recruitment programmes continue to be based on the assumption that migrant women will not settle and raise families in the host country, these questions have taken on new meaning and immediacy around the world. Migrant worker women, as has become strikingly apparent, often reject the notion that they should be temporary. They do not just work, but also live, engage in relationships, and have children in the places they migrate to. As such, policy-makers, service providers, entrepreneurs, journalists, activists, artists and academics, who wish to understand more about migrant worker women and to establish effective policies around migrant work, can no longer ignore the domestic desires, choices and practices of these women as they develop in the host country.

As the epigraphs illustrate, the Israeli case is a particularly compelling example of the ways in which the domestic lives of domestic workers have become relevant to the political milieu of the migrant-receiving country. This is because the ever-present themes of nationalism, belonging and the continuing importance of history that pervade Israeli politics and social life (and that have become more salient still in recent years) have engendered a new trend in the discourse that applies to these women and to citizenship in Israel more generally. Unlike similar debates in the country's past, the ongoing campaigns for and against the deportation of the children of undocumented workers have focussed intently on emotional ideals that describe how experiences of empathy, solidarity, a love of country and an appreciation of collective histories are central to the behaviour of both migrants and hosts as they strive to determine who deserves the rights associated with membership in the nation state. Months of demonstrations, media coverage, and a general mobilization of activity around what it means to be, and indeed *feel* Israeli have brought to light the ways that discourses of emotion and intimacy have become an integral part of current discussions about belonging and citizenship.

In this chapter I use debates surrounding the Israeli-born children of migrant workers to examine the ways that a politics of intimacy characterizes discourse and practice on the rights of migrants in exclusionary citizenship regimes. My aim is threefold. First, I will establish links between anthropological literatures on citizenship, emotion and intimacy in order to emphasize the range of ways that migrants and hosts construct and are assigned personal and emotional profiles that help define their behaviour, social positioning, and political potential in local settings. Second, I will describe the special significance of these profiles considering how changing patterns of migration and continued tensions regarding the preservation of a Jewish State have highlighted differences between and among migrants in this context. Finally I will draw on previous scholarship and participant observation of the campaign to grant citizenship to the children of migrant workers to demonstrate the ways that migrants, politicians and advocates of various kinds have recently instrumentalized these profiles to connect relations of intimacy to nationalism and policy decisions regarding who deserves citizenship.

The Politics of Intimacy, Citizenship Studies in an Emotional Age

Increases in the rates, flows, and scope of global migration have corresponded with the development of new tropes of national exclusion and inclusion while exposing and elaborating upon existing frameworks concerning who has access to the rights and obligations associated with membership in the nation-state. The ever-expanding and interdisciplinary study of citizenship has attempted to track these changes by establishing new theoretical categories that capture the fluid nature of how rights become relevant on the ground. Literature on post-national citizenship (Soysal 1994, Sassen 2002) suggests that increasingly significant international conventions, framed in the language of universal human rights, can act as guarantors of important forms of entitlement for migrants, even in the absence of formal citizenship. Theoretical explorations of substantive or 'negotiated' citizenship (Stasiulis and Bakan 2005, Levitt and Glick Schiller 2004) have both expanded upon, and challenged this idea, positing that established forms of belonging and citizenship rights are 'not granted or conceded from above but are, in an essential respect, constructed from below' (Balibar 2004: 48) when migrants' access to social services and community organizing takes form at the level of personal interaction with citizens and service organization personnel.

Research has referred to how factors such as race, gender, and class affect the ways that migrants and citizens engage in these personal interactions and develop identities that emerge out of them (see Goldring 2001, Preibisch 2004, Ilcan and Basok 2004). But these factors must be considered more carefully and with greater attention to the nuances and patterns that they produce in migrants' interactions with one another and with citizens. Beyond those associated with race, gender and class, questions remain regarding how, why, and to what end one's nationality, age, labour market positionality and citizenship status also shape migrants' relationships. New scholarship in this area would begin to address migrants' conceptions of their futures and indeed the potential for such futures to be realized in the migrant-rccciving country.

An exploration of emotion discourse and emotional norms as they shape migrants' interactions and struggles for rights offers a useful and novel entry point into expanding citizenship studies in this direction. As experiences and behaviours that 'not only represent but create social reality' (White 1990: 47) emotions are a key, if often neglected, element of studying processes of globalization and mobility (Svasek and Skrbiš 2007). A nascent body of literature that explores 'potent sources of emotions' (Skrbiš 2008: 236) for migrants has focused on the ways that 'experiences of adjustment, settlement, nostalgia, a shattered sense of belonging, renewal, loss, discrimination, abrupt endings, new beginnings and new opportunities' (Skrbiš 2008: 236) contribute to migrants' establishment of personal (Mar 2005), familial (Coe 2008) and political (Steyn and Grant 2007) profiles that become central to their identities, ways of behaving, and interpretation of what is possible in the host country.

Foundational to these studies is an understanding of the migrant self as 'multiple' and 'relational', owing its formation to an acknowledgement of 'past, present, and future experiences and environments' (Svašek and Skrbiš 2007: 371) and an engagement with the emotional norms prevalent in those conceptual and physical spaces. When developing relationships with various actors in the host society, migrants may feel 'forced' to express their feelings in 'newly coded ways' (Skrbiš and Svašek 2007: 375) that match, contrast, or otherwise 'play into' host society ideals and expectations. Migrants may also, however, experience and express emotions in strategic and/or conscious ways as they respond to their own readings of host society norms and of the labels that are ascribed to them.

Scholarship on migrant caregiving and domestic work has been especially helpful in demonstrating how emotional norms govern the ways that migrants behave both inside and outside the workspace. Close contact with members of the host society that is established and developed through 'emotion work' and the adoption of 'conventions of feelings' produced within the work environment (Hochschild 1979: 564) both enables and encourages the development of emotional behaviour as it extends beyond what is necessary and required for professional conduct. Filipina live-in domestic workers in both Hong Kong (Constable 1997) and Taiwan (Lan 2004), for example, may enact a particularly moralistic, religious and/or de-feminized persona on their days off as well as on workdays in order to assuage female employers' jealousy as well as societal paranoia regarding men's potential for infidelity. In a similar vein undocumented Mexican eldercare workers in the United States become well-versed in elderly employers' personal and collective 'narratives of suffering' (Ibarra 2002: 337) while they begin to prepare and enjoy for themselves foods and pastimes that 'produce comfort' in this context (Ibarra 2002: 332).

As is evident from these studies, emotional conventions and expectations produced in the workplace (especially when that workplace also happens to be a private home) are directly related to norms that are relevant in society more generally. Chinese sexual mores or American-style empathy, for example, may have particular applications in domestic and care work, but these norms are also significant in wider social, political and moral contexts where they shape, as they are shaped by, the day-to-day interactions of those who live in the society.

Participating in these interactions and 'fitting in' by way of developing emotional habits is thus especially important under conditions of 'emotional capitalism' in which the 'private self' is increasingly performed publicly and 'harnessed to the discourses and values of the economic and political spheres' (Illouz 2007: 4). According to Illouz, the popularity of psychological and therapeutic interventions in advanced capitalist societies has meant that the expression of emotional norms is not only highly valued in particular societies, it may also become a marker of class position and a tool for social advancement in the long term.

> If cultural capital is crucial as a status signal, emotional style is crucial to how people acquire networks, both strong and weak, and build what sociologists call social capital, that is, the ways in which personal relationships are converted into forms of capital, such as career advancement or increased wealth (Illouz 2007: 67).

As emotional norms become important parts of social capital, it is not just the private self that is rendered public in various ways, but private relations (between two or more people) that are also acted out in ways that draw from and create social meaning. Interactions between people and within and among groups therefore become as significant in economic and political discourses and practices as do individual expressions of emotion norms.

It is in this way that intimacy, defined primarily in popular as well as academic literature as descriptive of private sexual and/or emotionally-laden relationships between two people, is also reconfigured under conditions of emotional capitalism. Where emotions and relationality are publicly and overtly expressed, the intimate does not only occur between two individuals but potentially between any number of people in a social network who share (or imagine that they share) a particular closeness that can be expressed through a common emotional style and mode of emotional expression. As they are increasingly relevant to social networking, intimate relations can be understood as emotional interactions that have the capacity to both reflect and delineate membership in various kinds of social groups.

Ethnographers note that employers who describe domestic workers as 'one of the family' (Anderson 1997, Romero 2002, Lan 2006, Hondagneu-Sotelo 2007) show that intimacy is both overtly expressed and indicative of membership in a group. The use of family metaphors in these situations also, however, points to the double-sided nature of intimacy as a relation that includes as many obligations to the group as it does privileges. Workers who identify (or are identified) as especially close to their employers are therefore asked to stay extra hours or provide additional services 'for love and not money'. Their loyalty is both created, and continuously reinforced, through expressions of their membership in the family unit.

What I define here as a politics of intimacy borrows from this analysis and describes the processes by which discourses and displays of emotion and emotional engagement become useful as political tools that, in this case, contribute to migrant and host society conceptions of who is, or may become, members in the nation state. These processes separate migrants into distinct groups according to their perceived and real levels of intimate engagement with hosts and the host society.

Domestic workers, equipped with the emotional tools of the society through their specialized proximity to the emotional realm, have privileged access to, and are active in creating, local ideals of intimacy. But just as they must bear the responsibilities, emotional debts and extra commitments of intimacy in the private homes in which they work, so too must they take on such responsibilities on a national level. Indeed, while processes that make up the politics of intimacy draw on already established emotional engagements, they may also create new engagements that engender as much obligation as they do privilege. These engagements may place both migrants and hosts in a position of responsibility to the nationalist framework that they claim an intimate part.

In the remaining sections I will develop this point by describing the ways that the development of an international labour recruitment programme in Israel is especially embedded in the contentious politics of nationalism and belonging in this context. As such the influx of non-Jewish, non-Palestinian migrants from various parts of the Global South has set the stage for new 'emotional hierarchies' (Illouz 2007: 4) to map onto the social, economic and ethnic hierarchies that already characterize Israeli society. These hierarchies have become significant in debates over whose personal experiences connect them most intimately to societal norms and ways of feeling.

After a brief overview of the Foreign Worker Program (FWP) and implications for patterns of legal and illegal immigration to Israel, I will describe how an emotionally-situated nationalism that is expressed through a politics of intimacy has been invoked in discussions of the granting of citizenship rights to the Israeli-born children of migrant workers.

Ethnographic Context: Foreign Workers as Israel's other Other

In the late 1980s, the Israeli government responded to a 'crisis point' in the labour force by convening the Knesset to implement the Foreign Worker Program (FWP) (Drori 2009: 8). Initially considered by state officials to be an 'undesirable' situation, likely to create 'social problems' that were too cumbersome for the society to bear (Ramon 1988 quoted in Raijman and Kemp 2007: 31), shifts in attitudes towards the international recruitment of workers have been linked directly to the outbreak of the 1987 Intifada and the changes in Israeli policy and social life that emerged out of this period (Roer-Strier and Olshtain-Mann 1999, Semyonov et al. 2002, Levine 2009).

For decades prior to the Intifada ('uprising' in Arabic), Palestinian 'migrant' workers – those who lived in the West Bank and the Gaza Strip, did not have Israeli citizenship, and crossed borders in order to access worksites – had provided a pool of cheap labour that helped build and sustain Israeli agricultural and construction industries (Farsakh 2005). At the start of the Intifada, however, intensifying political and social unrest began to prevent Palestinian day labourers from regularly attending work in towns and cities across the border. Measures taken by the Israeli Defence Forces (IDF) to heighten security at the borders led to periodic closings of key checkpoints, long line-ups, and the systemic harassment of would-be workers. At the same time, violent skirmishes among Palestinians within the territories were on the rise as members of the Intifada leadership began to pressure those working in Israel to boycott their jobs and join the active resistance against Israeli political control (Raijman and Kemp 2007: 33).

The Intifada represented and also encouraged a marked escalation of conflict, mistrust and division between Palestinians and Israelis. As the long-standing employment relationship between these two parties declined, a labour recruitment programme that would reduce Israel's dependence on Palestinian workers and indeed assert this severance of ties in ways that would resonate as a consequence of Palestinian violence, became increasingly attractive in Israeli political circles (Levine 2009: 81). The FWP, an unprecedented opening of Israel's national borders to non-Jewish migrant workers from various parts of the Global South, thus became the newest manifestation of shifting (yet always dialogical) ethnic and class identities within Israel. As a low-wage workforce that was neither Jewish nor Palestinian, foreign workers came to constitute a novel Other in the Israeli context, the markers that were initially defined less by who they were, than by who they were not.

Caregivers and Domestic Workers

While at first only applicable to agriculture and construction, the FWP soon expanded to include a caregiving component in which migrants from South and South East Asia were recruited to provide home-based care for elderly and/or dependent individuals. This development in the programme did not come as a direct result of the Intifada, but was rather catalyzed by a combination of factors including increases in worldwide labour mobility, local developments in the Israeli economy, and demographic shifts in the population. Specifically, the migration of elderly Jews to Israel in the 1980s and 90s had contributed to already high rates of aging in Israeli society. At the same time Israeli healthcare industries were undergoing processes of privatization that made various goods and services that were once taken for granted less accessible to the middle class (see Filc 2004 and 2005). As the children of elderly people were gradually less able or willing to care full time for their parents because of their own economic responsibilities, work lives, and social expectations, there was an increased demand for a flexible and private workforce of caregivers who would live and work in the homes of infirm elderly people and provide 'on-call', individualized service.[1]

1 With the implementation of the 1988 Nursing-care Insurance Law, the Israeli National Insurance Institute (the Israeli social security agency) responded officially to these shifts, authorizing the distribution of financial support to 'disabled elderly' who required 'home visits' from staff who could assist in bathing, dressing and home management (Bar-Giora 2007:11). Currently, Israelis wishing to employ a foreign worker for caregiving must be deemed 'dependent' by an evaluation process administered by the Ministry of the Interior (Drori 2009: 57).

The incorporation of caregiving in the FWP has been especially significant for the growth of Israel's migrant worker population and for the development of identity markers within this population. As a result of various social, political and economic factors that have increased the need and desire for home-based eldercare work in Israel, caregiving is the fastest growing sector in the FWP, and the only one that there is no formal cap on the numbers of visas that can be issued. The predominance of women in the FWP is therefore steadily increasing as caregivers (still mostly women migrants) now constitute 70 per cent of all foreign workers in the country (Zohar 2009).

The inclusion of this new labour sector into the FWP has also contributed to the complex ways that migrant workers become viewed as integral to Israeli social and nationalist interests. As it had formerly been women's work that took place in government-run institutions and required particularly intimate engagements with Israeli citizens, eldercare was part of the informal and unregulated employment sector described above only in the rarest of cases. These new FWP participants, hired specifically to work in the private homes of Israeli citizens, were therefore immediately distinguishable from their Palestinian migrant worker predecessors not just through predictable channels of racialization (specifically that the foreign worker caregivers were not 'Arab'), but through the ways that their gender, labour type and the location of their work and social lives brought them into a different kind of contact with Israeli citizens and Israeli society.

In the past two decades, more migrant women from the Philippines, India and Nepal, have begun circulating in neighbourhoods outside of the migrant worker hub of South Tel Aviv, learning and becoming fluent in Hebrew, and developing relationships with their employers and the elderly people with whom they live and work. As migrant women have also set up and settled in their own neighbourhoods, established community newspapers, and created and maintained religious and social organizations in Tel Aviv and other urban centres, these participants of the FWP have come to occupy labour and social positions understood and presented as distinct from those occupied by Palestinian workers before them. In short, while Palestinian workers from the Territories were more likely to 'go home at night' (Freedman 2005), or else remain 'spatially segregated' when they did stay in Tel Aviv for longer periods of time (Portugali 1993: 14), FWP participants and women caregivers in particular, have made themselves increasingly visible to Israelis, constituting a part of the national imaginary in ways that non-Jewish workers had never been before.

Recent ethnographic scholarship that examines the integration of female migrant workers into Israeli economic and social spheres addresses the ways that their perceived value to the nation and implicit distinctiveness from former Palestinian workers has resonated on a variety of different levels. Research on the use of 'compassion imagery' and rhetoric within Knesset committee debates on migrant labour in Israel highlights governmental representations of migrant caregivers as necessary to the alleviation of suffering and pain of elderly and incapacitated Israeli citizens, and indeed to the country's ailing healthcare industry in general (Efrat 2006). A series of Israeli films made in the last few years such as *Jellyfish* (Geffen 2007) and *Noodle* (Shemi and Menahemi 2007) have similarly popularized the image of migrant care workers and cleaners as contributors to Israeli society who neglect their own family obligations in order to fill the domestic positions that allow Israeli women to work outside the home and pursue creative and professional endeavours.

In a more direct communication of their connection to Israeli social norms, Filipina women working in Israel may identify and represent themselves as 'politically active Christian Zionists' (Liebelt 2008: 567) who express a love for Jewish holidays and a belief that Israel is the rightful homeland of the Jews. Expressions of loyalty to the state and its causes are also evident in journalistic and personal accounts of migrant workers' opinions on the Israeli/Palestinian conflict. Migrants may articulate fear or mistrust of Palestinians in ways that match or even supersede the negative feelings expressed by many Israelis. They 'side with' or 'root for' Israel and Israelis (Derfner 2002) as they underscore their own vulnerability with respect to random violence (specifically bus bombings, some that have killed or injured migrant workers), and economic downturns associated with the conflict (Derfner 2002).

Visible but Vulnerable, First and Second Generation Migrant 'Illegality'

Despite the social visibility and professed political loyalty of some FWP participants, however, it is impossible to overstate the lack of power of both documented and undocumented labour migrants in Israel with respect to being able to stay in the country on a permanent basis. Following a citizenship regime based on the principle of *jus sanguinis*, or the right of blood, there is almost no possibility within the FWP (or indeed for non-Jews more generally) of obtaining full citizenship in the Israeli nation-state. Workers can therefore be characterized as 'permanently temporary' (Freedman 2005) due to the fact that their legal status in the country, and as participants in the FWP, has over the course of the programme's existence been placed in the hands of either the employer, or the labour placement agency who carries the permit for each worker employed. Because of this indentured labour system, women migrants who work as caregivers lose their legal status 90 days after the person for whom they care dies, if they quit, or if they are dismissed for any other reason. When these women are not able to use official channels to find another employer within this time period[2] they will often join women who have lost their legal status for other reasons in search of under

2 Both migrant workers and migrant worker advocacy organizations report that employers prefer to hire caregivers from outside the country as opposed to those already living in Israel (personal communication Dec. 17 2009; Kav LaOved and Migrant Forum Asia 2009).

the table or illegal employment as domestic workers, cleaners, and caregivers for children and the elderly.[3]

While the notion of migrant 'illegality' has become normalized in the Israeli and especially Tel Avivi context, where estimates suggest that approximately 50 per cent of the 180,000 migrant workers who live in Tel Aviv lack legal status (Hotline for Migrant Workers 2009), the issue of 'illegal' children (born in Israel to migrant women with no legal status) is a concern that has emerged with the changing demographics of the programme. As more migrant women, both documented and undocumented, settle for longer periods of time in Israeli cities, the rate at which these women become pregnant and give birth to children who do not have status in the host country has become a political and social concern. Israeli policy now formally states that pregnant migrants are 'requested' to either send their baby to their home country, or leave Israel with their baby no later than 14 weeks from the date of the birth (Central Bureau of Statistics 2009).[4] Contracts drawn up by manpower agencies may also stipulate that women migrants can lose their jobs, and consequently their legal status, if they become pregnant and give birth while employed in Israel. Despite such draconian rules and guidelines that render the Israeli-born children of migrant women illegal, and/or entirely stateless in cases where the origin countries of their parents demand residency rights in order to grant citizenship, women have continued to raise their children and develop communities in the country that they live and work.

Discussions over whether or not the children of migrant workers could achieve full status in Israel first became fodder for political debate in 2003 when then Minister of the Interior Avraham Poraz spearheaded and waged a 'battle over naturalization' (Kemp 2007: 679) that would address the possibility of granting formal status to the Israeli-born children of migrant workers and undocumented residents of Israeli cities. On 26 June 2005, the government formally announced its decision that a select group of the children of migrant workers, those who

3 The growing population of migrants who live in Israel without formal documents or citizenship status have arrived at their illegal status in any one of the following ways. Migrants become illegal if they complete their FWP labour contracts and choose to continue living in Israel without a valid permit. Migrants become illegal if they leave the employer to whom their work permit is tied. Migrants who enter Israel on tourist visas become illegal after the three month deadline of this permit. Migrants who come across the Egyptian border in order to claim asylum are illegal until such time as they obtain official refugee status (only guaranteed for some migrants from specific countries).

4 In a controversial ruling reported on 13 April 2011, Supreme Court Justice Ayala Procaccia voided the Interior Ministry regulation that migrant workers would stand to lose their visas 90 days after giving birth. Citing both local employment equity laws which prevent discrimination against pregnant women and mothers, and international agreements calling for the protection of migrant workers' rights, Procaccia stated that both options in what was referred to colloquially as the 'baby or visa' regulation 'violate [migrant womens'] constitutional right for parenthood and harm her financial prospects severely' (Procaccia quoted in Glickman 2011).

were born in Israel, over 10 years old, speak Hebrew, and had been schooled in the Israeli education system, would be granted permanent residency, and then citizenship at the age of 21 or upon completion of mandatory army service.

Deportation, Demonstration and the Identification of 'Israeli Children'

While the 2009 plan to deport 1,200 children of migrant domestic and care workers and the ensuing discussion over their potential for becoming Israeli citizens was not the first of its kind in Israel, the debate that followed resonated more overtly with the Israeli public than it had in previous years and took a decidedly different tone. Whereas the 2005 decision to grant residence to migrant children was proposed in language that emphasized the 'one-time', and case-by-case nature of granting residency rights to children of migrant workers (Kemp 2007), the current discussion could no longer be based on the claim that such a policy would be unique or exceptional. Reasons for granting residency rights have therefore been phrased in more emotionally-situated nationalism that is less about the technical aspects of who meets specific requirements for citizenship as it is about who deserves rights based on their ability to identify with Israel as well as perceived and contested Israeli values. Unlike the 'politics of numbers' that characterized, and in fact proved 'crucial' (Kemp 2007: 681) in the previous debate over how many children could be granted residency and then citizenship, the 2009 debate emerged as a politics of intimacy, centred on a series of themes that describe what forms of emotional expression and self-identification are necessary to be Jewish, Israeli and a citizen.

When I arrived in Israel on the first of August 2009 to begin fieldwork on eldercare work in the FWP, it was one day after the announcement to delay the deportation was made. My research focus quickly shifted as I came to discover that the children who were slated for deportation occupied a primary niche in any and all discussions of migrants' rights and migration policy. Far from being isolated in the predictable venues of parliamentary committee meetings and migrant service centres, these discussions spilled over into the popular media and onto the streets of Tel Aviv, where people previously uninterested or unengaged in the issue of migrants' rights were finding new avenues through which they could participate in activities for or against the deportation.

Over the course of the next 13 months I participated in demonstrations, meetings, fundraisers, concerts and other public events all focused on the question of whether or not children of migrant workers should receive status in Israel. At the same time I engaged in the everyday activities implicated in those fundamental questions, accompanying migrant women to appointments at pre-natal health centres, daycares, legal aid offices, government ministries, migrant service centres and to children's parties, religious events and community gatherings. Throughout the process I spoke formally and informally to dozens of migrants, politicians, activists, advocates, service providers, community leaders, academics, journalists, and neighbours and friends of mine about their relationship to this issue and to the broader questions it represented.

The following sections highlight this social and political climate as I observed it in both public and private venues over the course of the first five months that the government was to decide on the fate of 1,200 children of migrant workers. The privileging of both emotion discourse and rhetoric meant to invoke emotion demonstrates the ways that rights are understood and (re)presented as entities that are either earned or granted based on the personal qualities and sentimental commitment to nationalism of both migrants and hosts. Three themes emerged as significant; the emotional engagement of the children in wanting to be Israeli, the emotional engagement of Israelis in reinforcing and legitimating their own imagined Israeliness, and the anti-emotional (or alternative emotional) response meant to centre the debate in rationalist politics.

Children's Emotional Engagement; Nationalism, Love of Country and Army Service as an Expression of Loyalty

On 30 July, in a letter addressed to Interior Minister Eli Yishai and subsequently released to the press, President Shimon Peres[5] described a recent visit to Bialik-Rogozin, an elementary school in South Tel Aviv that was attended by a number of the children of migrant workers who are slated for deportation. Referencing both his own and the children's emotional experiences to justify his public support for the children to stay in Israel and receive status, he wrote, 'I felt they had an appreciation for Israel, where they were born. I heard Hebrew ring naturally from their mouths. I felt their connection and their love for Israel and their desire to live in it, to serve in its army and to help to strengthen it' (Shimon Peres, quoted in Weiler-Pollak, 2009d). The statement was made at the beginning of the three month period that the government would convene on the issue of the children of migrant workers. November first would mark the end of the decision-making period and the point that the children and their parents would receive the news of their status.

Peres' rhetorical linking of usefulness to the state with love of the state mirrored that of migrant workers themselves, many of whom have created, adopted and perpetuated similar claims about being at the service of Israeli endeavours and goals. Two months after the publication of this letter, with the November first deadline fast approaching and media coverage of the debate for rights was gaining momentum, the themes of appreciation, love, and care for Israel emerged in a context that was distinct, but directed toward the same purpose. At the 2009 Miss Twinkle Star Beauty and Folklore Competition, a local pageant run by

5 In Israel's parliamentary system the presidency has a mostly ceremonial and symbolic character, though current President and elder statesman Shimon Peres, like others before him, has used his post to take a stance on contentious issues.

some members of Tel Aviv's Filipino community, that was dedicated this year to issuing 'a statement of thanks to the State of Israel' (Weiler-Pollak 2009a), mistress of ceremonies Hermina Ocampo emphasized that one of the purposes of the pageant was to '... show the decision makers that we have something to offer and to contribute to the country ... I hope that they will recognize our many talents and that it will touch their hearts, and they will understand that all of us here are Israeli' (Ocampo cited in Weiler-Pollak 2009a).

Central to 'touching the hearts' of both policy makers and the general public has been an emphasis on the desire and enthusiasm that the 1,200 children in question have to defend the nation. If the connection between citizenship and service in the Israeli Defence Forces (IDF) was at all ambiguous in the past, the 2005 decision to give residency rights to select children of migrant workers clarified the pragmatic as well as ideological and sentimental significance of the army within this debate. According to the technical terms of the residency rights now held by these children, full citizenship status for them and later for their younger siblings and parents would be tied to enlistment in the army (Kemp 2007). As a defining principle of what it means to be the most loyal kind of Israeli, service in the army is implicitly understood as a necessary element of what children of migrant workers would be obliged to do in order to earn their citizenship rights.

Because it was taken for granted that migrant children would serve in the army, the 2009 campaign highlighted not just their understanding of this responsibility but their emotional engagement in fulfilling it. Echoing a common refrain among supporters of migrant children, Rotem Ilan, one of the founders of Israeli Children, an activist collective established in direct response to the 2009 threat of deportation, emphasizes both the inherent Israeliness and the deep feeling associated with the children's response to serving in the army.

> Their love and passion to be good citizens is just amazing. I say many times: They're more Israeli than a lot of my friends. If I ask them, 'what do you want to be?' they say they want to be soldiers, they want to protect Israel. They love this country. They're a part of it (Ilan, quoted in Estrin 2009).

The emotional engagement with civic and military responsibilities that was apparently displayed by children of migrant workers was posited as being 'more Israeli' than that which Israelis themselves feel and express. Such a paradox was additionally significant because of the wider political atmosphere surrounding migrants' rights activism in this case. As will become apparent below, many of the most active anti-deportation activists were also heavily involved in the struggle against Israel's military occupation of Palestinian lands, and some had themselves refused army service in explicit resistance of IDF operations that serve this end. It was perhaps because many of these activists (full Israelis in the legal sense of the word) were aware of how their own actions against, or critiques of the IDF distanced them from Israeli mainstream society and bodies of government, that they perceived a strategic importance in promoting the children's particular desire to serve in the army.[6]

Even when Israeli activists did not make use of this strategic potential (as a small number refused to do on principle), some migrant activists continued to make public statements that connected the desire to serve in the IDF with the argument that their children were just like all their (Jewish Israeli) friends. Ambivalence on this issue was ever present, as was the case when I interviewed a Filipina woman who initially told me that her daughter (an eight year old girl, born in Israel and on the list of children slated for deportation) was 'absolutely' going to serve in the IDF. After thinking for a moment she then modified her response to say that the girl would serve only if she wanted to and if she came to the decision to when she was drafted (personal communication, 15 December 2009).[7] Other women I spoke to informally about their children's participation in the army however, inevitably expressed that such service was an important civic duty and something that everyone did. They all assumed that their children would want to serve if given the opportunity.

Striking a balance between portraying Israeli-born children of migrant workers as both normative and exemplary, fully Israeli but also Israeli plus, was been central to generating popular support for the struggle. Indeed, as was consistent with the paradoxical nature of migrants' intimate position in Israel, 'Israeli Children' (non-citizen children of migrant workers) were counted as part of an imagined national family, while they were simultaneously called upon to prove their love for its institutions, members and practices in ways that Jewish Israeli children (actual, and taken-for-granted members of the imagined national family) seldom have to do.

Narratives of Compassion: 'Jewish Values', Living History and Humanitarianism over Politics

Israeli citizens were not, however, emotionally complacent or inactive in this struggle. Nor did they serve simply as a reference point against which non-citizens

6 A 2008 campaign, spearheaded by Defence Minister Ehud Barak and IDF Chief of Staff Gabi Ashkenazi, to wage a 'war on draft evasion' and actively promote army service as a central tenet of Israeli nationalism provides concrete evidence for activists' and migrants' assumption that this is a particularly timely issue and consequently a key point in the struggle (see Harel 2008).

7 While there is no concrete data on this as of yet, a migrants' rights advocate who is in touch with the children of migrant workers given formal residency status in 2005 told me that all those who are now 18 or older (and therefore eligible for service in the IDF) have been 'eager' to serve in the army and in particular to be employed as 'fighters'. Only one girl out of an estimated 20–50 did national service in a hospital instead of basic training because there were an unusually high number of female applicants that month and the army did not accept her (personal communication, 13 January 2010).

were evaluated and judged. While a politics of intimacy is a concept that can be used to describe migrants' construction and expression of self as emotionally prepared and well-suited to become a citizen, it is also useful in describing the ways that migrants and members of the host society actively reinforce moral and emotional ideals about those who are *already* citizens. Defining an intimate Other requires a definition of the intimate collective that such a person can be incorporated into, in this case one well versed in what it means to be Jewish, Israeli, and humanitarian.

Throughout the campaign to grant residency to the children of migrant workers politicians from various levels of government gave voice to a rising discourse in the Israeli public that Jewish values (variously defined, or not at all defined) were integral to the determination of a citizenship policy and of politics more generally. In his attack on Minister of Interior Eli Yishai of the Shas party, Meretz Party Member of Knesset Haim Oron stated concisely that the 'brutal and shameful decision to deport children ...' indicates that Yishai and his fellow members of Shas 'have forgotten what it is to be Jewish' (quoted in Weiler-Pollak 2009b).[8] Days later, Defence Minister Ehud Barak contributed his own statement to the debate as he implicitly drew connections between religious, political, and humanitarian behaviour as all part of the Israeli sense of self. 'It is our Jewish, national, moral and human obligation to keep the children in Israel' (Jerusalem Post 2009).

While neither Oron nor Barak elaborated on the specific characteristics that Jewishness entailed, it is easily assumed from the discussions that followed that they were both referencing the commonly-stated truism that being Israeli and Jewish carries with it an inherent understanding of oppression. An editorial in the left-leaning national newspaper, *Haaretz* published online within the same week as both these statements were issued puts it more succinctly: 'A country that was founded by the children of refugees and migrants is obligated to show an extra degree of sensitivity – especially when it comes to children' (Haaretz 2009a). Rhetoric on Jewish values and Jewish obligation as these play out in the Israeli national context therefore did not just have to do with tenets outlined by religious texts: it also included important cultural references such as emotional qualities and capabilities (like 'extra sensitivity') that were associated with having a collective history of expulsion and exile.

Migrants contributed to the image of Jewish Israelis as especially sensitive in their own justification for both participating in a political campaign against deportation, and in developing expectations that it would be successful. Describing to me why he attended an 'Israeli Children' demonstration in Jerusalem, a migrant

8 This comment, and those like it, must also be understood as yet another manifestation of an old and ongoing Israeli debate on 'the Jewish character' of the state, its politics and its politicians. Since the 1990s the liberal, middle-class and secular Meretz party and the ultra-orthodox, working-class Mizrahi Shas party have been perceived as oppositional on this issue and as such have traded accusations on each other's Jewishness and understanding of the principles of Judaism.

worker from the Congo who did not want to be identified by name, told me that Jews were 'compassionate people' whose own experiences of discrimination necessarily made them sympathetic to the plight of others who have suffered discrimination (personal communication, 18 November 2009). Months later, at a rally against neo-liberal social policy that was put on by socialist-Zionist youth movement HaShomer HaTza'ir (the Youth Guard), and dedicated in 2009 to the anti-deportation struggle, African community leader Edwin Brownie made similar connections. His rhetorical linking of Jewishness and the historical oppression of the Jews to the sense of empathy that he hoped to see from relevant politicians is worth quoting at length here.

> Children who are born here are denied [basic rights] because they say it is a Jewish State, yes. But what is the meaning of the Jewish State? … The meaning of a Jew, has a spiritual meaning. So if Israel will act in such a horrible way against these children you see before you today, then I will not accept it. Because God has said that we should not, that Israel should not oppress or molest children who are born in this country. Why? Because Israel was once in a foreign land in Egypt and God with his mighty hand brought them into this country … We are pleading please Bibi, Eli Yishai you have once traveled to another country before. And now you are born in this country. Please love the children. Look into the eyes of these innocent children and give them their rights.

By directly addressing Prime Minister Benjamin (Bibi) Netanyahu, and Minister of Internal Affairs Eli Yishai, and associating them personally to the past struggle of the Jews in 'another country' and to the present struggle of non-Jews in Israel, Brownie was perpetuating the use of historical narratives as living entities in Israeli politics.

As evidenced by the quote that begins this chapter, public statements about the Holocaust also served as narratives of individual and collective experiences in both the past and present. In Israel, it has never been uncommon to hear political debates that draw in explicit or implicit terms on the Holocaust as an event that is both nationally shared, continuously relevant and of course, highly emotional. As the anti-deportation campaign accumulated supporters, various organizations that had previously been unaffiliated with the plight of migrant workers began to issue their own statements on Jewish responsibility as a product of experiences in the Holocaust. An especially well-reported statement came from Zeev Factor, the head of the Centre of Organizations of Holocaust Survivors.

> You have a moral obligation, especially in light of what happened to the Jewish people. These are children who only know this country and speak our language, and a child must not be deported from the land in which he was born solely due to his origins – this is a lesson engraved in our flesh (Branovsky 2009).

Here the evocative imagery of something being 'engraved in flesh' can be understood as both a literal and figurative reference, alluding on one hand to the concentration camp tattoos and physical violence done to Jews throughout the Holocaust, and on the other hand to the lingering psychological effects of the break-up of families, massive loss of life, and refugee experience that followed. In a collective statement addressed to Prime Minister Benjamin Netanyahu, a group of representatives from Holocaust survivor organizations further emphasized the ways in which their position on the issue was felt on both visceral and emotional levels. 'We the Holocaust survivors have special difficulty ignoring the choked feeling and the shame (of not taking a moral and political position on granting citizenship rights to the Israeli-born children of migrant workers)' (Branovsky 2009).

References to the historical oppression of Jews and especially the Holocaust were significant in this context because they both related migrants to citizens (in that they shared experiences of subjugation and cruelty), and placed citizens in a position of responsibility to refrain from inflicting the same suffering on others as that which had been inflicted on them. Intimacy was created both through the likening of experiences, and through the incorporation of migrant workers into a discourse that occupied a particularly emotional position in the national consciousness.

Anti-Emotion Discourse

The use of emotional language and establishment of intimacy in this context however, did not go uncontested. Perhaps the most interesting element of the debate regarding granting citizenship to the children of migrant workers was the resistance to emotion discourse that came from activists and politicians in both the pro-deportation and anti-deportation camps. These activists, for very different reasons and in light of different goals, advocated for the debate to be more in touch with political structures and demographic patterns, rather than with the sympathy and sentimentalism expressed by the examples cited above.

Pro-Deportation Activism and the Push for Rational Thought

In response to the anti-deportation activism that was growing in scope and numbers throughout September and October, a group of residents of the southern neighbourhoods of Tel Aviv (those sections of the city in which a majority of migrant workers live) mobilized to voice their pro-deportation or anti-migrant stance. These residents who have historically been the most marginalized and poorest neighbourhoods of Tel Aviv began to organize their own demonstrations and to appear at anti-deportation events in order to distribute information outlining their opposition to granting residency rights and citizenship to both the children of migrant workers and to migrant workers in general. Their argument was framed as one that dismissed emotion as a factor in deciding who should stay in the country and who should be sent away. Sentimentalism, as was their claim, was the modus operandi of a wealthy elite unaware of the real political implications of granting citizenship to migrants.

On the evening of one of the first fundraising events held by the anti-deportation group 'Israeli Children' I was given a flyer by a middle-aged man who told me that he was protesting the event. Standing outside the venue in the rain with his young son, the man explained that he was attempting to educate those who were there to support the migrants' cause. The flyer, entitled 'The Chorus of Hypocrites' stated that it was written on behalf of residents of South Tel Aviv and directed readers (who were presumably coming from elsewhere in the city) to 'free themselves from the influence of the media and to consider *rationally* whether these children and their families would not be better off returning to their homeland' (emphasis mine).

The flyer critiqued the 'emotional manipulation' of the Holocaust to serve the interests of wealthy Tel Aviv residents. In a refrain that would reverberate throughout the pro-deportation campaign, the man explained to me that the hypocrisy of the elite rested on the fact that these residents from the north of the city benefited from the employment of migrants while not having to endure the negative elements (defined here as crime and poverty) that migrants were bringing to the places in which they live. North Tel Avivis, he told me, could have their houses cleaned for them during the day and then return at night to a neighbourhood free of migrants, all the while congratulating themselves on their charitable feelings towards the downtrodden.

While their own rhetoric played on alternative and perhaps equally emotional discourse, not the least of which was propagating fearful imagery of migrants bringing violence to Tel Aviv communities, many residents of the southern neighbourhoods made frequent references to the disjuncture between a liberal, leftist agenda and the reality of what was happening on the ground. In opposition to what they call the 'yafey nefesh' (literally 'good souls', but akin to the English expression 'bleeding hearts'), they view and express their position as pragmatic as opposed to idealist. As such they presented themselves in confrontations with their political opponents as protectors of the 'real' threat, in this case, the fragile demographic balance (often described as a 'numbers game') that ensured the maintenance of a Jewish majority in Israel.

In a similar attempt to frame the debate in rational as opposed to emotional terms, long time right wing politician and Interior Minister Eli Yishai, pleaded with Israelis to 'not have naïve, bleeding hearts' that would cause them to ignore the calculated political behaviour of migrants in 'using' their children to secure their own status in Israel (Jerusalem Post 2009). Yishai, consistently an adamant advocate against granting citizenship to children of migrant workers, at once reinforced the image of Israelis as especially moral and sentimental, while emphasizing the need for the government to make political decisions based on demographic concerns as he saw them developing in the future.

> It is no secret that if we continue to abandon the borders and allow the entrance of foreigners into the country and don't – call it what you will – deport, remove or return them to their homelands or if we are too 'good-natured', as too many of us are, in a few years we will find hundreds and thousands of them here, and that is a threat to the Zionist project in Israel. We will lose our country. (Yishai quoted in Friedman 2009)

Throughout a series of interviews on Army Radio, Yishai employed distinctions between 'us' and 'them' to neutralize or reverse links that had been made between migrants' rights in Israel and the history of Jewish oppression. He was also clear in his repeated references to the capacity of migrants to manipulate and 'exploit the *kindness* of the state of Israel' (quoted in IRIN 2009, emphasis mine), that Israelis could be victimized by migrants who themselves were all too aware of the potential to abuse Israelis' excessive emotional character.

Shortly after making these comments, in January 2010 Yishai took his advocacy for the pro-deportation cause a step further, attending a 'tour' of the area around Tel Aviv's Central Bus Station and southern neighbourhoods in order to consult with the local population about the problems that they were having with migrant and refugee residents. The tour, bringing together Yishai, a local unit of the Oz deportation squad, and Finance Minister Yuval Steinitz, focused explicitly on the economic toll that the activities of undocumented migrants were having on local businesses. Several of what Yishai's handlers called 'street meetings' were organized and managed by the entourage, and emphasized citizens' frustration with the rise in illegal businesses and the increasing prevalence of undocumented people profiting off local residents. The discourse of money problems, and particularly of undocumented people's evasion of taxes, reinforced the rationalist 'numbers game' rhetoric already established by Yishai's earlier focus on demography.

Over the course of the next several months, pro-deportation activists both inside and outside the government continued to level sensational and damning accusations against undocumented people (the most dramatic and controversial being Yishai's claim that migrants were bringing diseases to Israel).[9] Pregnant women and new mothers became especially important symbols of migrants' strategic efforts to take advantage of Israeli benevolence. As one Israeli man, the owner of a kiosk outside the Central Bus Station once told me about the Filipina women he had met, 'They're playing us. Having babies all over the place and doing it with anyone who has a drop of citizenship. They know that because we

9 Yishai's 10 October statement, that workers 'will bring with them a profusion of diseases: hepatitis, measles, tuberculosis, AIDS and drug [addiction]' (quoted in Haaretz 2009b), provoked strong reaction from rival politicians and citizens alike.

are Jews and we've suffered so much as outsiders as well … that we will feel sorry for them and we will let them stay'.

This man's presentation of migrant women as opportunistic, willing to craftily manipulate their bodies and indeed their entire lives in order to 'play' Israelis, exposes the deep sense of threat felt by Jewish Israelis living in south Tel Aviv. At the same time however, this attitude also defined these women as active agents in ways that much of the humanitarian discourse (supportive of the migrants' cause) did not.

Anti-Deportation Activism and the Push for a Broader Politics of Inclusion

While their political positions could not be more different from those of Yishai and his supporters, many anti-deportation activists also became interested over the course of the campaign in moving the citizenship debate from the sentimentalist discourse that forced migrants into a particular emotional mould, to a more politically-defined struggle about what rights were inherent and deserved by all residents of Israel. Their focus was not on humanizing individual workers but on politicizing their cause by contextualizing it in the language and ideals of their more expansive critique of the state's exclusionary policies.

In a public statement, unique in its focus and tone, deputy mayor of Tel Aviv Yael Dayan expressed this position. 'Whoever is in our territory deserves our services … It's not a question of grace, it's really a question of right. It's not doing them a favour and it's not how moved we are by these little children …' (quoted in Kalman 2009). Dayan was referring here to a set of Tel Aviv municipality decisions, implemented in the early 2000s, that emphasizes 'urban citizenship' by giving migrants access to rights that were tied to their residence in the city (see Kemp and Raijman 2004). She clarified in this statement her critique of granting rights and services to migrants based on emotional frameworks or sentimentality. What mattered fundamentally was where migrants lived, not who they were or how they made others feel.

As is mentioned above, other anti-deportation activists were critical specifically of using emotion-laden tropes of intimacy in order to prove the worth of migrant children as potential citizens. While this population of activists was relatively small and this commentary far less common in public venues than those of the pro-deportation camp, a few levels of the critique emerged out of an ethnographic study of events around the anti-deportation movement. Some activists demonstrated ambivalence about the over-individualization of migrants' rights that was typified in media portrayals of particular children as high achievers who deserved citizenship based on their merit. As they counted their engagement with non-citizen migrants in Tel Aviv as congruent with, or following from, years of battling structural issues (including but not limited to city infrastructure and housing inequalities) these activists came to resent the focus on 'helping' one particular child. Their conflict was ongoing. Even as they facilitated the media's connections to human interest stories, they discussed amongst themselves whether or not such stories directed readers to the appropriate issues at hand, namely the rights of all migrants.

Dov Khenin, a member of Knesset in Israel's Hadash party and a former mayorial candidate in Tel Aviv's Ir Lekulanu (City for All) party, expressed this position in the various public appearances he made in support of granting the children residency rights. His speeches inevitably emphasized that the question of children's deportation was really about 'broader' politics. Like Dayan, his main concern was with municipal policies and practices, but he also brought forth inconsistencies in the recruitment of migrant workers, a set of policies managed at the national level. Stating frequently that the deportation debate was 'not just about the children', he challenged the public to consider in more expansive terms what sort of society they wanted to create.

Still other activists opposed the use of emotion rhetoric on the grounds that it relied on and indeed promoted what they saw as a racist Zionist national agenda. A few such activists who became especially involved in the anti-deportation campaign were the same people who were attending weekly protests in Palestinian villages against the military occupation of those lands. Israel's denial of rights to migrants, as they saw it, followed logically from the state's exclusionary and violent policies toward other oppressed minorities. Aligning migrants' struggle for citizenship with long-established tropes of Zionism as opposed to aligning them with Palestinians' struggle for freedom and sovereignty was therefore unacceptable to this small group. Even as it had the potential to (and, in fact, did) garner support from a wider audience within Tel Aviv's Zionist left, the tactic of dressing children up in military uniforms and Israeli flags had the doubly negative effect of drawing attention away from the politics of the Military Occupation of Palestinian Territory while contributing to its underlying ideological causes.

Considering these conflicts, it was common early in the 2009 campaign to hear discussions, debates and even the sharing of jokes among some anti-deportation activists, advocates and NGO workers regarding what kinds of actions went 'too far' in pushing a Zionist agenda. As they worked toward stopping the deportation they also held meetings in which they considered the sorts of political collaborations and/or emotional discourse refocused or diluted the struggle, or the conceptual associations that obscured the principal goal of demanding full rights for *all* migrants (not just children) and indeed all individuals residing within the borders of Israel/Palestine. For some activists, establishing personal and emotional profiles for migrants and hosts that reinforced nationalistic, Zionist, and implicitly exclusionary frameworks, effectively harmed their broader and longer-term goals of challenging these ideologies and providing a space where rights could be granted regardless of emotional or sentimental compatibility with the host society.

Actors on both the left and right thus expressed opposition to the particular politics of intimacy that characterized the 2009 anti-deportation campaign. While their motives and foundational ideologies were different, the respective interests of these movements (sometimes also defined as pro and anti-Zionist) were equally damaged by the use of discourse that portrayed migrant children and Israeli citizens as intimately connected to one another through shared emotional norms.

Conclusions

In this chapter I have explored some ways in which emotion and intimacy are significant, if often overlooked aspects of how citizenship rights are imagined, understood and discussed in advanced capitalist societies. If, as Chang and Ling state, migrant domestic work is the 'intimate other' of 'techno-muscular capitalism' (2000: 27), or the hidden processes that underlie and support better-known forms of globalization, then migrant domestic workers are themselves the intimate Others who enact these processes. Their relationships and conceptions of self are therefore fundamental to trends in politics and the changes that these trends bring about.

My analysis of the 2009 pro and anti-deportation campaigns regarding Israeli-born children of migrant workers demonstrates how struggles for substantive and formal citizenship increasingly developed into a politics of intimacy whereby citizenship rights were defined as flexible entities, granted based on the capacity of migrants and hosts to experience and express common emotional norms. While highlighted and/or exaggerated in times of direct struggle, the rhetorical and pragmatic association of some migrants (and not others) as intimate Others was a process that drew from and contributes to draw from the personal and emotional profiles that both migrants and hosts construct and are assigned as they participate in social life.

These observations expand on an aspect of the literature on domestic workers that begins to explore the specific ways in which migrants develop emotion and relationships in the migrant receiving country. In *Love and Gold*, Hochschild notes that though it is like other precious resources that are sought out and mined for a particular kind of profit, love is not 'simply extracted from the Third World and implanted in the First; rather it owes its very existence to a peculiar alchemy that occurs in the land to which it is imported' (2002: 24). I have argued here that the alchemy that can be observed in Tel Aviv is one that has been created through the coming together of local cultural matters, immediate political concerns, and the historical and current position of domestic workers and their children in this society. Further that in the case of undocumented women and their children struggling for residency and citizenship rights, the local 'production' and 'assembly' (2002: 25) of the resource of intimacy has long term implications.

Far from offering a *carte blanche* to migrants, intimacy is a double-edged sword, involving various expectations and demands that migrants must fulfil. Such demands are particularly marked for children as they are educated from a young age to develop and express emotions that emphasize their intimate connection with the host country and its particular brand of nationalism. Much like their mothers whose roles as caregivers and domestic workers who are defined as 'part of the family' involve expressions of exaggerated loyalty toward their employers, migrant children who are characterized as intimate Others may find themselves in a position of emotional indebtedness to the state that has accepted them (against obvious odds, or else odds that are made obvious) as one of its own.

The Israeli case presents an example of an advanced capitalist and ethno-national state in flux struggling on one hand to support neoliberal reform by recruiting low wage foreign labour, and on the other hand to retain a religiously homogenous population by imposing strict controls on immigration and citizenship. Despite the many particularities of the Israeli social and political situation, however, questions and patterns associated with the ways in which emotional discourse and practice are being used in debates concerning belonging are becoming ever more significant around the world. Additionally, issues around the status of children born to migrants who have lost their own status are increasingly relevant as more migrant women settle, have children, and strive to create communities in the places in which they live and work.

Postscript and Acknowledgements

Since January 2010, when this paper was written and submitted for publication, a number of significant changes have occurred in Israeli migration policy and in the political climate of migrant activism in Tel Aviv. I address and analyse some of these changes in my doctoral dissertation (see Shapiro forthcoming). Interested readers may also refer to the engaged and long-term research of journalist, Mya Guarnieri (http://www.myaguarnieri.com/category/foreign-workers-in-israel/) for updated information on the situation of migrant workers in Tel Aviv and Israel. Special thanks to Matan Kaminer for his insightful comments on the earliest draft of this paper.

PART IV
Questions of Regulation and Protection

Chapter 12

Toward Particularism with Security: Immigration, Race and the Organization of Personal Support Services in Los Angeles

Cynthia J. Cranford[1]

In-home personal support work is the paid work of assisting old and younger adults with physical disabilities[2] with bathing, dressing, eating, going to the toilet, and other activities of daily living including light housekeeping. Like other paid domestic work, generally this work is precarious that is, insecure, low paid with few benefits, little regulatory protection and poor working conditions. Like most paid domestic workers, personal support workers are women of colour who are largely, but not exclusively, immigrants. Some argue that paid domestic work is inherently oppressive due to a highly asymmetrical racialized class relationship between employer and employee (Kaplan 1987, Rollins 1985). In contrast, others locate domestic workers' precariousness in the organization of employment, suggesting that a more contractual employment relationship or less familistic state policies would improve domestic work (Bakan and Stasilius 1997, Cheng 2003, Coser 1973, Fudge 1997, Glenn 1986, Romero 1992). Despite their differences, both sets of scholars locate the insecurity of paid domestic workers in particularism as opposed to universalism. The first set of scholars focus on the particularistic, ascribed characteristics of the workers, especially the social locations of race and class, as the main determinant of precariousness. The second set of scholars view a particularistic employment relationship as a key determinant of precariousness, that is employment based on a personal rather than contractual relationship.

---

1 Associate Professor of Sociology, University of Toronto, 3359 Mississauga Road North, Mississauga, ON L5L 1C6, c.cranford@utoronto.ca. I wish to thank the study participants for taking the time to speak to me and also to Steve Sidawi. I also thank the staff at the Personal Assistance Services Council (PASC) and the Department of Public Social Services (DPSS), the Editors of this volume and Rob Wilton for helpful comments on previous versions of this paper. The analysis in this paper, however, does not necessarily reflect the views of the PASC, DPSS, ILCs, the LTCWU or the private sector owners and managers.

2 Disability is broadly defined to be the socially constructed mismatch between an individual and the environment that results in disabling that person, including the lack of adequate personal supports (Morris 1993). It therefore includes difficulties in activities of daily living faced by young and old people with disabilities. I do not focus on children.

In this chapter, I extend the debate about the determinants of precariousness in paid domestic work by focusing on one aspect of particularism, namely employers' particularistic hiring strategies. Specifically, I focus on employers' use of subjective, personal characteristics of workers and recipients in the hiring process. In contrast to the number of important studies that focus on domestic workers' experiences, my goal here is to 'study up' (Messner 1996) in order to understand how people with power organize one form of paid domestic work. I use a comparative study of in-home personal support services in the public and private sectors of Los Angeles County, drawing on in-depth interviews with government representatives, employers and worker and disability activists.[3]

This case allows us to question key assumptions in the literature on paid domestic work due to three differences between personal support work and other domestic work: the social location of recipients, organization of employment and organization of resistance. Firstly, this case allows us to examine the relationship between vulnerable workers and recipients who are also vulnerable along the dimension of ability and, in the public sector, class and often race. Given the intimacy of the services, disabled citizens seek choice over who provides them based on particularistic criteria such as personality and seek long term relationships. Secondly, the organization of personal support work includes state, private agency, as well as household level actors, who introduce a version of particularism with varying influences on personal support workers. Thirdly, my study also includes an innovative organization of resistance in the public sector, whereas the private sector is devoid of collective resistance, allowing for an examination of the impact of this understudied dynamic on precarious employment.

My comparison of the highly precarious private sector to the significantly less precarious public sector demonstrates that a particularistic organization of employment is not a necessary determinant of workers' precariousness. Both sectors organize employment around particularistic criteria with very different

3 In the private sector, I interviewed 18 owners or managers of non-medical, personal support companies licensed to provide 'custodial' or 'maintenance' care. In order to understand better their distinct niche, I also interviewed one company that specialized in cleaning services and one licensed to provide medical services. In the public sector, I interviewed 29 key informants including: five administrators from the County office of the Department of Public Social Services (DPSS) who manage the In-Home Support Services (IHSS) Programme and five social workers who implement programme polices; three staff (including the Executive Director) and five board members from the Los Angeles 'Public Authority' (called the Personal Assistance Services Council or PASC), a non-profit agency with an employment registry and the employer of record for collective bargaining purposes; four unionists from the Long Term Care Workers' Union (LTCWU), including the President of the Los Angeles local; and seven disability advocates, five of whom were Executive Directors of Independent Living Centers (ILCs), an ILC staffer and a long-time activist. Most of the disability advocates and PASC board members were also recipients of some form of PAS. IHSS data was provided by the In-Home Support Services Programme for 2006.

effects on workers. Furthermore, a comparison of the racialization of particularism shows that asymmetry in social location is not a sufficient cause of precariousness. Particularism in the less asymmetrical private sector is often, but not always, explicitly racialized in the private sector, but it is tolerated in the public sector as well. I show that a key factor limiting precariousness in the public sector is a resistance based on employment security in the labour market rather than job security with an individual employer.

Los Angeles is an ideal site for a study of the relationship between particularism and insecurity since as a 'negative' case it reveals the conceptual components key to explaining insecurity (see Burawoy 1991). Los Angeles is most different in terms of the organization of resistance. Since the early 1990s it has been the site of a 'new unionism' whose experimentation with re-regulating outdated labour laws, alliances with other social movements and community-based tactics has brought some of the most successful organizing drives, especially in the immigrant-dominated service sector (Milkman 2000). This experimentation is more extreme than in other cities, like San Francisco, or countries, like Canada, where labour still has a seat at the table and where union density is not as low. The organization of domestic employment is more informal in Los Angeles than in countries with contract labour programmes, such as Canada, including a large number of undocumented immigrants and extreme lack of regulation (Hondagneu-Sotelo 2001). As we shall see, informality extends to in-home personal support. Finally, the existence of a large private sector alongside a means-tested public sector for personal support results in diverse social locations among personal support recipients, in terms of class and race. Social locations of workers in this sector are shaped by the overwhelming majority of Latinos among immigrants alongside newer Filipino and Caribbean migrations and a longstanding, and class polarized, African American community (James et al. 2000). After a review of the relevant literature on social location, organization of employment and organization of resistance as determinants of insecurity, I examine how these factors impacted insecurity differently in the Los Angeles public and private sectors. I conclude that particularism for recipients and security for workers is possible under certain conditions.

Social Location, the Organization of Employment and Resistance

Social Location

Scholarship on paid domestic work identifies employers' use of particular, ascribed characteristics of workers, as a key determinant of worker precariousness, including employment insecurity, low pay, little regulatory protection and poor working conditions. Coser (1973: 39) argues that only workers with 'multiple status disabilities' such as those who are racialized, foreign and female, will consent to the low pay and poor working conditions of domestic work today. As a result, wages are tied to particular employers. Others emphasize that basing wages on workers' ascribed characteristics is made possible by extreme asymmetry in the racial and class locations of employers and workers (Dill 1988, Kaplan 1987, Rollins 1985). Citizenship is an increasingly important axis of inequality that funnels women into insecure, low paid domestic work (Bakan and Stasilius 1997, Hondagneu-Sotelo 2001). Particularism based on ascribed status on the one hand, and extreme asymmetry between worker and recipient on the other are merged in the direct householder-domestic relationship. In personal support work, however, reference to ascribed vs. achieved characteristics is present but relations are less asymmetrical because the recipients' social location is different. Disability is not only a stigmatized location in Western, capitalist society but it also brings bodily vulnerability. A quest for particularistic hiring can be based on these vulnerabilities instead of class privileges (Morris 1993).

The Organization of Employment

One distinctive aspect of the organization of paid domestic employment is how certain people are matched to certain jobs and how many employers they have. Studies of live-in contract labour programmes, such as those found in Canada and some parts of Asia, document extremely exploitative working conditions (Bakan and Stasilius 1997, Fudge 1997, Constable 2002). Unlike indentured contract workers, immigrant workers find their jobs after arrival and are thus 'free' to quit resulting in better wages and conditions (Glenn 1986, Hondagneu-Sotelo 2001). Romero (1992) argues that workers who do 'job work' for multiple employers where they would sell not their person (as in pre-industrial relations) or their labour power (as in industrial capitalist relations) but rather specific cleaning services to customers as professional contractors are able to earn a better living than workers with one employer. Securing multiple employers may also have an impact on personal support workers. Much depends on the ability to find sufficient, jobs to make a living. Hondagneu-Sotelo (2001) finds that securing multiple paid domestic jobs in Los Angeles is still highly dependent on recommendations from employers, who keep wages low by sharing information. These studies show that the move from a particularistic relationship with a single employer to contractual, employment relationships with multiple employers is a key way to limit workers' precariousness. Personal support workers also have multiple employers but, unlike job workers, their employers may include organizations.

Domestic work organizations also use particularistic criteria in hiring or matching with varying implications for workers. Studies find that agencies appeal to, and often construct, particularistic, and racialized, criteria to match workers to recipient preferences (Bakan and Stasilius 1995, Hondagneu-Sotelo 2001, Lobel 2001). The racialization of particularism is problematic because it can result in exclusion of certain groups from this type of work, or paying workers of colour less within it. These studies find that while workers can technically choose their clients, given their need for work and lack of information they have less choice than the recipients/clients. While lack of power in the labour market results in insecurity and low wages, some studies suggest that the profit motives, economic resources and stability of nanny employment agencies that cater to wealthy clientele result in some upgrading of this work at least in comparison with the direct householder-domestic relationship (Hondagneu-Sotelo 2001, Lobel 2001). There is need for more research in this area, however.

Personal support work is a hybrid of domestic service, temporary agency work and self-employment bringing many difficulties to workers. Like the temporary help industry, private sector personal support is organized by a triangular employment relationship between an agency, a client and worker (Vosko 2000). Temporary agencies want to maintain a middleman employer role so they not only control workers' access to initial jobs, but often penalize workers for turning down jobs (Vosko 2000). The difference between personal support and temporary agency work is that the client is generally a recipient of personal services in her/his home, making this relationship similar to that of domestic service. The indirect relationship between worker and recipient/client is not recognized under labour law and, coupled with the location of the work in the home, this allows agencies to consider the workers to be self-employed contractors, rather than employees, although their legal basis to do so is shaky (Cranford 2005, Lobel 2001). Since neither the self-employed nor domestic workers are able to bargain collectively, their ability to organize for employment or wage security is limited.

In the public sector, the organization of employment is historically more like a public form of domestic service (Boris and Klein 2008) but today it resembles a hybrid between domestic service and self-employment. One might assume that recipients' particularistic preferences would not trump workers' security when employers are non-profit but public sector studies suggest otherwise. Neysmith and Aronson (1997) argue that (Ontario) government contracted agencies try to appease elderly recipients' preferences for white workers, like in the private sector, but they often cannot given the largely immigrant women of colour workforce available for this low paid work. Furthermore, public sector studies show that when the two state roles of regulator and funder are combined precariousness for workers can increase, such as when the state simply declares workers to be entrepreneurs thus denying them collective bargaining rights (Boris and Klein 2008, also Fudge 2005). Today, some public personal support recipients hire their own workers, but workers in this situation are more likely to have multiple employers and this hybridity between domestic service and contract work also often results in their classification, or treatment, as self-employed with no right to unionize (Cranford 2005). In addition, employment studies of public personal support work note the importance of more macro-level political and economic factors, like funding models and levels, on workers' security (Aronson and Neysmith 2001, Boris and Klein 2008).

The Organization of Resistance

Early studies of domestic work focus on individual resistance to psychological domination in the relationship between employer and worker (Dill 1988, Kaplan 1987, Rollins 1985). However, challenging precarious employment also requires collective efforts. There are now several studies of community unionism among paid domestic workers. Community unionism operates at the small group levels often in workers associations or workers' centres (Cranford et al. 2006, Fine 1998). Community unions/associations provide tools to help domestic workers reform labour law and enforce fair working conditions (Elvir 1997, Hondagneu-Sotelo 2001, Velasco 1997). These interventions are important but insufficient.

In order to provide security to home-based workers with multiple clients/employers, we also need, what Fine (1998) calls, a 'labour market unionism'. Labour market unionism is organizing the entire labour market for a particular good or service and thus includes models of union representation and bargaining that go beyond the single employer, worksite based industrial model (Cobble 1991, Fudge 1997, Vosko 2000). Occupational unionism links representational rights, wages and benefits to an occupation, not a single employer, and seeks control over the labour supply through a hiring hall. Thus it allows employer discretion on firing but places workers in a new job (Cobble 1991). In order for it to work for those with little economic power or skill recognition, however, occupational unionism must be legislated (Fudge 1997).

In order to bring security to personal support workers, labour market unionism must be coupled with a social movement unionism able to address more macro-level political and economic conditions. Social movement unionism is here defined as coalitions between social movements around labour issues. In the public sector, it takes the form of improving the quality of work in order to improve the quality of service but this linkage is also relevant for the private sector (Johnston 1994, Kumar and Schenk 2006). Coalitions can also take issues into the court of public opinion where workers with less power might gain recognition (Velasco 1997, Wilton and Cranford 2002). Studies on the Los Angeles public sector identify the importance of both new regulations to foster a labour market unionism and coalitions between workers and recipients to pressure the state to increase funding (Boris and Klein 2008, Delp and Quan 2002, Rivas 2007).

Social Location in LA Personal Support Work

In the private sector, disability, often age-related, is the key axis of social location that disadvantages recipients. The private sector companies in this study specialize in long-term, extensive care to seniors with physical frailties, cognitive disabilities (Alzheimer's or dementia) and those in need of companionship. The workers, in contrast, are able-bodied and middle-aged. Along the axis of gender, recipients and workers are similar. Company estimates range from 90 per cent to 100 per cent women recipients, since 'the women outlive their husbands' (C15),[4] and 70 per cent to 95 per cent women workers. On other axes, however, the recipients have more social power than do the workers. Generally, the recipients are middle class or wealthy. In contrast, the workers are working poor (Table 12.1: Wages, recipient fees, employment status and benefits). Reflecting the relationship between race, citizenship and class most recipients are white, US citizens. Most companies have a mix of immigrants and US-born workers of colour and some also hire white and Black Americans. Immigrants include Filipinas, (East) Indians, Belizeans, Mexicans, Central and South Americans, those from the Caribbean and Tongans. All owners and managers claimed their immigrant workers were 'legal'. However, there are likely some undocumented workers in this sector, albeit probably less than in the direct householder-worker relationship. A few owners admitted that immigration law only requires them to see a social security card, not to check whether it is a valid one, and a thriving industry in false papers allows undocumented workers to be employed in a range of low wage service sector industries in California (Cornelius 1989).

In the public sector, by contrast, the axes of inequality between recipients and workers are outnumbered by similar locations lacking power and privilege. The public sector has more young adults with disabilities than the private one but, like in the private sector, most public sector recipients are seniors with age-related physical and cognitive disabilities while most workers are middle aged and able-bodied.[5] In addition to disadvantages of disability and/or age, recipients in the public sector are below the poverty level since this is a means tested programme. Unlike in the private sector, here there is less similarity in terms of gender. Women are the majority of recipients, at 64 per cent, but men make up a significant minority. Available figures report that 83 per cent of the workers are women.[6] The public programme will also pay family members to provide the services, and roughly half of recipients choose family providers.[7] Recipients include all different races and ethnicities but African Americans and Latinos are over-represented, compared to their per cent in the population, at 20 per cent and 26 per cent, respectively, while

4 In brackets I include the number I assigned to the interview to maintain anonymity. C stands for 'company'; D for 'disability advocate'; P for PASC; U for Union; IA for IHSS administrator and IS for IHSS social worker. See also fn 3.

5 According to 2006 IHSS data, roughly 4 per cent of recipients are 17 or under, 33 per cent are 18–64, and 63 per cent are 65 or older (21 per cent are 80 or over and 5 per cent are 90 or over).

6 Figures on recipients are from 2006 IHSS data (see fn. 3). Figures on workers are from a University of Southern California survey of 1,230 home care workers in Los Angeles County (Cousineau 2000 cited in Delp and Quan 2002: 3).

7 Statewide, 49 per cent of workers are recipients' family members (Doty et al. 1999 cited in Delp and Quan 2002: 3). In California, family members can be spouses or children but their funding is insecure because it is not subsidized by the Federal government, although funding for more distant relatives does in part come from Federal funds.

Table 12.1 **Wages, recipient fees, employment status and benefits**

	Worker Wages		Recipient Fees		Status	Benefits			
	Hourly	Live-in, daily	Hourly	Live-in, daily		Health	Dental	Vision	Retirement
Private Sector									
Company 1	$9–15	$110–150	< $25	missing	Employee	no	no	no	no
Company 2	$8–10	$80–100	missing	missing	Employee	missing	missing	missing	missing
Company 3	$9	$65–75	$16–18	$160–180	Employee	yes, > 3 mo.	no	no	yes, 401K
Company 4	$9.50	$90	$16–$18	$160	Employee	yes, > 3 mo.	yes	no	yes, 401K
Company 5	$12	$100	$15	$130	Contractor	no	no	no	no
Company 6	$10–$12	$100–150	$12	$100–120	Both*	no	no	no	no
Company 7	missing	15–20% mark up	missing	15–20% mark up	Both	missing	missing	missing	missing
Company 8	$9	$110–120	$13–$15	$150	Both	no	no	no	no
Company 9	$9	$95	$15	$150	Employee	no	no	no	no
Company 10	$8–12	N/A	missing	missing	Both	yes, FT	yes, FT	yes, FT	yes, FT
Company 11	$8.50–9.50	N/A	$15–25	N/A	Employee	no	no	no	no
Company 13	$10	$80	missing	missing	Employee	no	no	no	no
Company 14	$8–9.50	$90–110	$17.50–20.50	$170–210	Employee	no	no	no	no
Company 15	$9	$100	missing	missing	Employee	no	no	no	yes, co. plan
Company 16	$8–10	missing	$15–18	$160–180	Employee	no	no	no	no
Company 17	$10–15	highly variable	$23–27	$230–260	Employee	yes			yes, 401K
Company 18	$10–12	$100	missing	$170–$210	Both	no	no	no	no
Company 20	$10–11	$130	missing	missing	Employee	no	no	no	no
Public Sector	$9.00/hr	N/A	N/A	N/A	Multiple employers	yes	yes	no	no

Note: employers 12 and 19 are medical and cleaning companies, respectively.
* The company uses both contractors and employees.

whites are over-represented, at 36 per cent.[8] In terms of language, 42 per cent speak English, 18 per cent Spanish, 16 per cent Armenian, 7 per cent Chinese, 5 per cent Russian, 2 per cent Vietnamese, 2 per cent Korean and 1 per cent Cambodian and these smaller groups are predominant in some parts of LA County. There are more Latino workers than recipients: 40 per cent of workers are Latino, 25 per cent African American, 7 per cent Asian and 27 per cent 'white' (including 14 per cent Armenian or Russian) (Cousineau 2000, cited in Delp and Quan 2002: 4). In order to receive these services, one must be a US citizen or permanent resident. Officially the workers must be eligible to work in the US and have a social security card to get paid (http://www.pascla.org/homecare-registry). However, interviews suggest undocumented workers are present in this sector, if less prevalent than in the past. The recipient is responsible for checking workers' documents but, like in the private sector, enforcement is rare.

The Particularistic Organization of Employment in LA Personal Support Work

Private Sector: Degrees of Racialization in the Match Making Process

> We are very clear with people that we match because of personal characteristics. So when they ask for a specific race and not a specific race, we really deep dive into what are the characteristics … 'Well they're polite and they don't talk back and they cook good'. Fine, let's look – and those are the priorities, and we get somebody that cooks. That's legal. I mean that's legal and it's also, you know, ethically to stereotype a whole country based on your experiences … Somebody that's that bigoted or whatever, they can leave … There are some traits of different cultures that are more consistent within a culture and we'll look for those traits (C17).

The opening quote is full of contradictions – this manager does not tolerate blatant bigotry, but matches on personal characteristics and believes certain traits coincide with certain cultures. A match between which services are needed and workers' skills and availability are the 'priorities' but the recipients' 'preferences' are also central to a good match (C17). In the private sector, recipients do not interview, hire or directly choose the worker(s); instead the company tries to guess who they might like and send out someone compatible. Although the companies mediate the recruitment and hiring process, they do not eradicate the racialization of personal preferences found in the direct householder-domestic relationship and sometimes they reproduce it.

The goal of the companies is to match 'compatible' recipients and workers in order to ensure a good relationship. Given the interpersonal nature of the work and

8 2006 IHSS data (see fn. 3).

its location, there has to be a 'bonding' (C8) between workers and recipients; they have to 'click' (C15). As one owner says, 'I'm just trying to match the recipient with the caregiver to ensure it's a successful relationship … It's in your home, in your face, all day … So it has to be somebody that you at least like' (C13). Owners, managers and staff try to tap into the wide array of personalities and temperaments using proxies such as occupation, disability and age as well as the stereotypes that go along with them. They say some recipients want a worker who is 'a little more forceful and kind of aggressive to tell them what they need to do', while the 'aggressive' worker would 'clash' with a recipient who wants to direct their worker (C18). 'Personality' also includes the owner/manager's judgment on work ethic and attitude. Generally, companies pre-clear workers who they think 'would fit a number of situations' (C13) including different personalities.

Making a 'compatible' match includes matching the recipient's preference for a worker of a given sex, reflecting the gendering of this work. The predominance of women workers is in part due to recipient's gendered preferences, owners and managers say. As one owner says 'first of all, we're talking about the home. So it's a little bit more private and so they're more comfortable with a female taking care of them' (C1). Some men are 'very private; they'll only want a male' (C17). Sometimes it is the family that wants a male caregiver (C14). However, the over-concentration of women is also related to the low pay. A large company with wealthy clientele that offers good wages and benefits has 'some great men' (C17) but most companies say they have difficulties finding 'a good male caregiver' (C13).

Most of the companies allow recipients to pick a worker based on race or ethnicity, or change one based on racial preferences. A common sentiment is 'there's a lot of prejudice in the senior population still' (C15), although several say it is often the family's preference. One manager shows me a 'classic example' of a note in a recipient's file that says 'my mother has always been afraid of Black people. Please do not send a Black caregiver' (C3). One mentioned recipients who say not to send 'brown' people (C8). Others mentioned lack of preference for Filipinas (C14; C15). Some recipients ask companies not to send 'people of colour' (C1) or people with an accent (C6).

The way owners and managers react to recipients' or their families' racial preferences vary.[9] At one end of the spectrum are companies that gave examples of reinforcing them. Two companies say they openly ask recipients about their racial preferences as part of the needs assessment. For example, one white owner says they get many requests for the 'ideal caregiver – a white middle-aged woman' but has a code word for this ideal worker to get around discrimination laws (C15). Some companies recruit white workers when requested. For example, one Filipino manager said when recipients ask for someone without an accent he finds someone 'real American' for whom they charge the recipient double since white workers charge more (C6). These owners and managers speak explicitly, often unprompted,

9 The three reactions mark events, not static positions in stable categories.

of their own stereotypes about the nationality of the ideal caregiver. Several agree that Americans were not brought up to do in-home care work. One elaborates on how she thinks African Americans feel care-giving is beneath them (C5), while another cautions that one has to be careful hiring whites because they 'can be pretty much white trash' (C15). Views on which immigrant workers are ideal vary widely. One white owner views Mexicans as 'too subservient' and thinks Filipinas are just out to gain citizenship and economic security by marrying the recipient (C5). Another white owner's description of the 'immigrant market for caregiving', includes statements that Filipinas are 'brought up from infancy to take care of their elders', while Mexicans 'have that in their culture, but not quite as much' (C1).

At the other end of the spectrum are companies that describe instances of challenging recipients' racial preferences. For example, one African American manager tells recipients who 'play the race card' that 'as long as I'm giving a qualified caregiver, it really doesn't matter what colour their skin is'. She tries to convince them to accept African American caregivers which sometimes results in the recipient abandoning long held racial prejudices (C4). Similarly, a Filipina owner recounts asking a recipient who wanted a white worker to try a Filipina first and, smiling, reports that the recipient agreed and now eats rice (C8). One white owner said he would turn down an account if the recipient insisted on a white worker (C14).

Most owners and managers are in between these extremes of reinforcing or challenging recipients' racial preferences. They are uncomfortable with recipients' racial preferences but feel they are part of a good match. As one white owner said, 'I'll still work with that person who is Chinese but I'll work them on another home, because I don't want to discriminate, but if the family says "I don't want somebody Chinese", I'm not going to give them somebody Chinese' (C10). Several say they match by recipients' racial preferences so as to not put a worker 'in a situation of hostility' (C16). Racial stereotypes were not explicit in this group. For example, one white owner felt that Belizeans were 'a caring kind of group of people … and dependable' but also said 'there is good and bad in every race' (C17). Despite the lack of explicit racial thinking, by allowing race to be a match criterion companies often fall down a slippery slope of cultural stereotyping, as is evident in the opening quote.

These varying reactions to recipient racial preferences can be explained by the structure of specific labour markets and the company's place within it. The race of the owner/manager is not simply correlated with challenging employers' racial preferences. Owners and managers of colour are included in all three categories of reactions and several white owners say they do not act upon recipients' racial preferences. Instead, those who challenged racial preferences had in common their provision of services in the South Bay – a region of LA County with a concentration of African American working class and poor neighbourhoods juxtaposed with wealthy white ones. Indeed, a white South Bay owner admits he would pass up an account due to racial preferences not because he wants to 'do everything perfectly' but because it is 'too hard to manage' since he 'has more people of colour than are just white' (C14).

The organization of the private home care market suggests that particularistic employment relationships are not necessarily detrimental to workers. Some companies challenge their racialization while still adhering to personal criteria, although others allow and encourage racial stratification in employment and pay. The contour of local labour markets plays an important role in modifying or exacerbating, racial preferences and in their implications.

Public Sector: Continuities and Changes in Racialized Hiring

> The clients say many things. But the option is what's available. We have someone who doesn't speak English very well, she or he has a car, is willing to work the hours that you want and do the things that you want. Do you want to consider that person, or these people?' So it's up to them (P2).

Public personal support services in California, called In-Home Supportive Services (IHSS), follows one type of 'consumer directed' model, namely the 'independent provider' (IP) mode, where no agency mediates the employer roles of hiring/firing and supervision. Public sector recipients hire and fire the worker(s) and most recipients' hire family, friends or friends of friends. A registry run by the non-profit Public Assistance Services Council (PASC) was set up to address recipients' problems finding reliable workers. And recipients also use registries provided by Independent Living Centres. As the quote from a PASC representative above suggests, these poor, often non-white recipients have racial preferences but, unlike wealthy and upper middle class private sector recipients, they are less able to implement them, given low funding levels and available workers.

Particularism as recipient choice over who to hire allows for a good relationship between recipient and worker, say disability, IHSS and PASC representatives. Given the intimate nature of service, connection is imperative. As one disability advocate says 'if you need an attendant to help you with the personal needs like showering, you really need to build a confidence level between you and the attendant' (D4). Similarly, an IHSS representative says if the recipient knows who is entering their home he/she is 'comfortable with the person so the bond is there' (IA1). In addition to ease, hiring one you know is viewed as 'a matter of trust' (IS7), and able to make recipients feel more 'comfortable and secure' (IA9).

Some public sector recipients have racial preferences for certain workers, as in the private sector. A PASC representative says many recipients 'invariably ask for an English speaking person' (P2). And Armenians and Chinese are underrepresented on the registry since they 'normally only work for people of their own country' (P2). At the same time, reflecting the correlation between disability and poverty, disability advocates who are also recipients of personal supports say many recipients prefer Latina immigrants, especially recently arrived, undocumented ones, because supposedly they will do more for less than those born in the US.

The registries designed to provide recipients with more recruitment options also allow for particularistic criteria. The PASC and ILC registries provide a list of people for recipients' to interview based on several objective criteria, including the number of funded hours, service needs, time of need and location (P2). Preferences of recipients who use these registries can also include gender, language and race (P2; D2). Preferences for women workers are not as strong for this population as for the private sector one, likely because there are more male recipients.

PASC representatives, IHSS personnel and disability advocates neither reinforce nor challenge recipients' racial preferences but are complicit with them. Like some private sector employers, both white and non-white public sector respondents felt the racialization of preferences was part of establishing the essential good relationship between recipient and worker. A non-white PASC board member says that racial conflict is 'weeded out at the beginning' when the recipient calls the registry and says they 'want a Black person or a Spanish person' (P8). And this respondent reasoned that if a recipient does not want to hire a Black worker, for example, they should not have to. 'I think that would not be a good match because they didn't want that person in the first place' (P8). PASC representatives are more likely to talk about language than race, but in Los Angles lack of a certain level of English language and a Latino accent is a key way Latino immigrants are racialized (Hondagneu-Sotelo 2001). English-speaking recipients request English-speaking workers but PASC does not have a sufficient number of English- speaking workers to fit with their preferences. Like the private companies, PASC says it does not discriminate against workers. 'The thing is you can't say well, you don't apply because you're from this group' (P2), said a PASC representative. Yet PASC representatives also do not challenge recipients' racial preferences. The representative continues: 'So what we have to do is wait-list some folks … We don't go through the entire application process otherwise we would have just too many folks that cannot be hired' (P2). Similarly, the director of one ILC said: 'the recipient picks who they want; we don't have anything to do with the process' (D2). Given the large number of Latinos on the registry, reflecting their majority among immigrants, it is they who are most often wait-listed.

Unlike private sector companies, however, these non-profit registries do not have a profit-driven interest to please recipients thus they do not reinforce recipients' racial preferences, manufacture elaborate racial stereotypes, or try to guess which groups will match best with which recipient. At the same time, unlike some private sector companies, for whom a differently racialized labour market (that includes African Americans and Filipina immigrants) encourages them to challenge recipients' race preferences in some instances, these non-profit intermediaries do not have such a structural push because they do not seek to maintain a mediating role. Instead, they believe the opposite: that the recipient should have control over hiring and firing and even if that includes racial preferences they should not, or cannot, intervene.

These data suggest that the social location of disabled, poor and often racialized recipients, resulting in less asymmetry with the workers, is not sufficient to challenge the racialization of particularistic employment. Even in the public sector racialization slips into particularistic hiring, and civil society organizations do not, or cannot, challenge it given more macro level realities such as the IP model of provision and low funding levels. The consequences of racialized particularism, however, are different in the public and private sectors.

Private Sector: Particularism and Insecurity

The private companies establish a very casual relationship with the workers, whether they treat them as contractors or employees. The former type of company considers workers closer to entrepreneurs who should bear all the risk for a reward of autonomy. Companies with employees are not so different in that they too offer only temporary employment. Twelve of the companies in my study hire the workers as employees. Only one employer admits that she treats all the workers as contractors but five say they have a mix of employees and contractors. Several companies specialize in a distinct form of live-in work, where recipients can receive extensive, even 24-hour care, but from more than one worker, thus resulting in a given worker living in only certain days a week. Private sector workers who are considered employees have the right to unionize and bargain collectively, while those considered contractors or domestics are prohibited from doing so. None of the companies in my study were unionized, reflecting a lack of union presence in the private sector.

Insecure Employment

> If we have hours, they get work; we don't have hours, they don't get work. We consider that to be like a registry almost (C14).

As the opening quote suggests, workers' jobs depend on recipient needs. These companies, however, mediate that relationship for a profit. Like employment registries they take little employer responsibility, but the operative word in the opening quote is 'almost'. These companies are more like temporary agencies in that they want to keep workers on as employees, albeit casual ones.

Owners and managers describe a very insecure employment relationship. As one manager says, 'my caregivers are per diem employees. They can decline any offer; they can accept any offer … It's not a set schedule unless they actually get in there and get a case and it works out' (C4). Another manager reveals a bundle of contradictions when she says 'we hire them on, what we call, full-time temporary ongoing basis' (C16). They work full-time hours but do not have full-time employment. The relationship is both temporary and ongoing. The company wants the relationship to be ongoing because they wanted to ensure they have the workers when they have clients. But they want the employment contract to be temporary so they have no commitment to the workers in between clients.

Companies justify the workers' insecure status with reference to flexibility of recipients' needs, but the companies' profit interest is what results in a precarious employment relationship. One owner describes great fluctuation in employment: 'it changes because if the client expires, we'll start all over again to build up their 40 hours ... So at any given time, the client says "I don't need her today, can you cancel her", we do and that means that she may or may not get another client to replace that one' (C16). The owner or manager decides who they call for a given case, based not only on client needs, but also management ease. One owner expresses the frustration of several when she says, 'we get people – they only want to be with nice people ... they only want to work within three seconds of their home ... and all these things ... Well, you know, that's nice and if we have somebody but the more open people are ...' (C17). As another owner says, 'those people that are more flexible and help you more, now when something comes up you're going to ask them first' (C10). In this sense, workers have a choice of cases, but the consequences of their choice could be limited employment.

Security hinges largely on individuals' training and skill. Owners and managers refer to the importance of skill in gaining employment security. As one owner said, 'the more skills you have to work with, the more challenging people, the more likely you are going to get cases' (C17). Building skills, however, is largely left up to the individual worker. To maintain their certification, workers need to upgrade their training by taking additional courses. Licensed home health agencies are required to offer this training for free but these non-certified personal support companies are not and do not.

In an effort to gain employment security, workers seek jobs from multiple home care agencies, nursing homes or hospitals and some work both for companies and directly for recipients. A couple of companies boast that they can put a worker to work the day after an assignment ends. More commonly, however, even those 'always working' generally have 'a week break or something until something else comes up' (C9), while others are 'taking time off' (C3) or (unpaid) 'vacation' (C4). A few companies say they are able to give people full-time hours but immigrant workers are 'driven' (C10) and 'amazingly industrious' (C3) and want to work more than full-time hours. The decision to take multiple jobs is related to insecure wages.

Wage Insecurity

> We start them at $9.00 an hour. (Author: Do you give them raises or?) It depends. It's case by case. I don't have a policy because they, like I have one, she's at $11 and she's been with me for three and a half years. She was with the same recipient up until three months ago when the recipient passed. ... If they're really stable and they do their job, I have no problem giving them raises. And a lot of times a recipient will call and say 'she's doing such a good job. I'll pay more; give her a raise'. I have one at $15. The recipient insisted. And I said

> 'ok well I'm going to have to charge you $25.95 an hour'. And she said 'that's fine' (C15).

Hourly wages range from $8 to $15 per hour, and 'live-in' rates from $65 to $110 per day. Some companies change their rate to the recipient, and pay to the worker, depending on the difficulty of the case. Companies generally only give raises or bonuses based on merit to 'the girls who deserve it' (C1) or to those who meet the nearly impossible goal of being 'stable' when recipient's needs and preferences change (C15). If they consider workers employees, companies must contribute to payroll taxes (unemployment, workers' compensation, disability and old age pension), while companies who use contractors seek to evade these costs. Companies who treat their workers as contractors say they pay the worker more so they can buy their own benefits; however the cost would be great for a single worker. Few of the companies with employees significantly contribute to benefits for these part-time, temporary workers (Table 12.1). Pay is linked tightly to recipients' needs. Few companies pay workers for travel time in between recipients. Long hours of work are common in this field but workers are rarely paid overtime. They can work up to five 12-hour shifts a week for a total of 70 hours for a single company (generally with two different clients) with no overtime pay and long hours are particularly common in 'live-in' work. Furthermore, legislation does not permit workers to add up time with multiple employers to measure overtime more accurately.

Insecure Working Conditions

> 'If it's not safe I will hear from the caregiver and get them out of there!' (C5).

Enforcing fair working conditions is largely left up to the individual worker. Recipients with 'live-in' workers are supposed to provide 'adequate, decent, and sanitary' lodging with one's own bed and 'wholesome' food on top of the general charge for services.[10] Support from the company is present but it is weak because it is balanced against their commitment to their paying customers and because the work is done at the recipient's home. For example, following a worker complaint, one owner is planning on visiting the recipient to ask if he could 'at least let the worker sleep 6 hours' (C3b). Another owner said, the live-in workers are told they work only eight hours a day 'and we presume that's going on' (C13). The main recourse workers have is to quit the case. As discussed above, however, quitting may jeopardize further placements.

Companies with employees are liable if workers are injured on the job, so they do practice self-regulation here but, as with employment standards, it is weak. Health and safety issues abound in this home-based personal work. The greatest risk to workers is lower back strains from transferring or lifting people. Also

---

10 See: Section 10, Wage Order 15 (State of California-Department of Industrial Relations 2007).

common are slips while helping people to bathe or shower, or go to the bathroom. Sexual harassment of women by male care recipients or family members is another safety concern mentioned by several owners/managers. Companies catering to wealthy clients generally visit the home to do an 'environmental' assessment (C1) or a 'safety check' (C4; C15) that includes suggestions for grab bars in the shower, a transfer chair in the bathtub, a walker, a hospital bed, a Hoyer lift, a bedside commode or port-a-potty, and getting rid of slippery throw rugs. Most companies try to eliminate heavy cleaning primarily to limit their liability should the worker fall when washing windows, to give a common example. Also in an effort to limit workers' compensation claims, a few companies do not send women to a case that involves transferring or lifting heavy men. Such self-regulation, however, can be trumped by recipient preferences. As one owner says, if the recipient requests 'a female under five feet tall … the family [would] have to help lift' (C17). Similarly, when discussing who was 'responsible' for health and safety, most owners say they merely make 'recommendations;' they do not say: 'you must have these things' (C1). Placing responsibility on the worker is most extreme in companies that treat workers as contractors since they rarely make safety recommendations and do not pay into workers' compensation, as is evident in the opening quote.

There is little training of workers on how to negotiate working conditions with recipients in the home. A few highly profitable companies with wealthy clients orient the workers to the particulars of each new case, but most companies say the recipient, or their family, provides training. As one owner described 'the reality is they [the family] teach, the patient teaches if they are in charge still' (C5). Most companies leave on the job training up to the individual worker and recipient. As one owner says 'if they worked in a nursing home as a CNA … then we know how much they know' (C3).

The private sector companies have not significantly decoupled particularism from insecurity, representing continuity with the householder-domestic relationship despite the existence of an intermediary. Although some variations between those treated as employees or contractors or working in live-in/live out jobs are evident, even workers who are considered employees of large firms with wealthy clientele are not protected from the problematic outcomes traditionally associated with particularism, namely employment and pay insecurity and poor working conditions. Rather than companies upgrading this work, as suggested in studies of profitable nanny placement agencies, (Hondagneu-Sotelo 2001, Lobel 2001), here we find weak enforcement of fair employment legislation. The private sector contrasts significantly with the collectivization of risk in the public sector.

Public Sector: Security with Particularism

In the public sector, State and County regulations were passed in 1997 allowing for a labour market unionism.[11] In contrast to multiple grey areas allowing private sector employers to treat workers as entrepreneurs, the new public model allocates various employer responsibilities to four different entities. Although the recipient is responsible for hiring/firing and supervision, the state is responsible for paying the worker. As a result, workers are eligible for employment benefits (workers' compensation, unemployment, disability and old age pension). The IHSS programme within the County Department of Public Social Services (DPSS) determines the number of hours and thus the amount of work available. In contrast to the private sector, however, funding levels are not sufficient to allow for live-in services, although paid family members may live-in and provide unpaid work. The non-profit organization, PASC, is deemed the employer for the purposes of collective bargaining and in addition has responsibility for the employment registry and recipients' training. This labour market unionism, coupled with 10 years of organizing, creates a closed shop where all workers benefit from wages and benefits bargained between PASC and the Long Term Care Workers' Union (LTCWU)[12] (Delp and Quan 2002).

Labour Market Unionism and Employment Security

> If for some reason the worker and recipient don't connect, [the worker] will go back [to the PASC registry] (P8).

> Our registry operates on the fact that we have the opportunity of 7 million worksites, just because there are 7 million seniors that live in Los Angeles (U2).

The needs of many younger adults with physical disabilities are ongoing but intermittent, thus public sector workers seek security through multiple jobs, like in the private sector. The average number of hours authorized for a recipient is 81 a month, and thus on average, a worker has approximately 20 hours of work a week with any given recipient. As one disability advocate says 'some people don't need a lot of help … somebody wants somebody for an hour in the morning and an hour at night' (D5). Similarly, one respondent describes his own personal support as '7 days a week, scattered hours' (P5). As a social worker says many workers have a second job 'because they can't live off of only one [job] 2–3 hours or 4 hours a day' (IS10).

11 See Assembly Bill 1682, Chapter 90, Sec. 9, 14132.95 (d), (State of California 1999). Chapter 3.45 (Los Angeles County Code 1997).

12 The LTCWU unites locals of the Service Employees International Union (SEIU) and the American Federation of State, County, and Municipal Employees (AFSCME) in California into one big home care workers' union.

The key difference from the private sector is that public sector workers have access to non-profit and union-run registries that include worker protections. The collective agreement provides some security to workers on the PASC registry. There is a registry advisory committee with joint PASC and union membership. The collective agreement also includes a procedure for resolution of complaints about the registry (P1). And there is no evidence that workers were penalized by PASC for turning down a recipient, as the opening quote suggests. The workers also gain access to other personal assistance jobs through a 'sophisticated' version of the hiring hall (U2). The union registry serves both the IHSS population and middle and upper class people that do not quality for IHSS. The union actively recruits recipients to the registry through various presentations so union workers can contact them and solicit work. Recipients can also call the union registry to find workers (U1). The recipient is still the employer for purposes of hiring, firing and supervision but if a recipient fires a worker, the worker may remain on the union registry (U2). Through unionization, therefore, the workers gain a means to guard against arbitrary and unfair decisions to limit their access to recipients, common in the private sector, and gain access to a larger pool of recipients.

The union also supports workers who want to build the skills necessary to take a range of recipients, in sharp contrast to the private sector. The union established a Home Care Workers' Training Center (HWTC) in 1999 as a non-profit entity. The HWTC offers courses on nutrition, caring for terminally ill people and those with Alzheimer's. Training is listed on the registry and thus might give the worker 'a little more credibility as to when people were looking who to hire and to not hire' (D5). English as a second language classes also widen the range of personal support cases for many immigrant workers. The new unionism also provides workers the means to gain wage security.

Social Movement Unionism: Toward Wage Security

> For years the home care workers have made minimum wage and been invisible but they're an important part of the economy. Mainly females, caregivers are saving the state of California a ton of money by keeping people out of institutions and providing a good benefit to the community and to long term care in our state ... For awhile and I think in most budgets the people who are perceived as able to least respond to a take away or to improve their life are targeted with budget cuts. If you've got a cut, go after seniors, people with disabilitics, home care ... but we're like: 'no this is not the group!' So we do a lot of that education and we show up at the Capitol with the people we represent because home care workers are invisible no more (U4).

Social movement unionism, based on coalitions and collective public action, helps public sector workers achieve wage security and recognition of this predominately women of colour workforce. On 1 April 2007 the wage for personal support workers in Los Angeles County was raised to \$9.00/hr, up from \$8.10 in 2005, while the minimum wage was $7.50/hr. Public workers' wages are now on par with those in several private companies and above some of them (Table 12.1). Workers who are authorized 80 hours a month for two consecutive months have health insurance for $1.00/month. Workers can combine hours from several different recipients to make up the 80 hours, thus benefits are not based on a relationship with a single employer.

Alliances of disability and senior organizations, and unions have defeated threatened funding cuts. Importantly, union strategies are modified to consider quality of services for recipients. For instance, the collective agreement between PASC and SEIU includes a no strike clause. Instead the union pressures the government funders. In the 2004 California budget, for example, the Governor threatened to eliminate the PASC, cut wages back to the minimum wage, and cut the State contribution to funding of services provided by parents and spouses (U3). Public displays of solidarity between recipients and workers were strong enough to reverse all of the proposed cuts that year (U3; D3). At the same time, pressure from the coalition must be ongoing. As one disability advocate says: 'government funding is never secure' (D4). Similarly, a union staffer says, 'the moment there is no pressure, they think it's fine to cut it' (U1).

The recipient is responsible for ensuring labour standards related to wages and hours. Disability, government and union representatives all note incidents of unpaid overtime. As one social worker says 'because they build a bond sometimes they are willing to go the extra mile and spend more time' (IS8). Disability advocates argue that the problem lies in insufficient hours. The union seeks to address the lack of funding for certain services, such as accompanying recipients to doctor's appointments and transportation costs (U3). The union also seeks to enforce fair working conditions.

Community Unionism: Toward Secure Working Conditions

> We focus on the workers whether it's our educational centre, whether it's training, we focus on that so that we can put the shield around providers knowing that this is what the provider understands his or her job to be when they go in there, so that they can say no (U2).

> There's always going to be a conflict between both sides. I mean, you can have all the rules in the world to try to prevent it; nevertheless it's still going to occur ... The most we can do is educate our communities as to what they should and should not do (D4).

The union provides both on-the-job training and broader education and leadership development. Key health and safety issues raised by public sector informants parallel those in the private sector, namely lifting and transferring, slips and falls, sexual harassment and stress. Preventing accidents and ensuring health and safety is the recipient's responsibility in keeping with their responsibility for supervision (IS1). During their visits the IHSS workers assess the environment in terms of safety for recipients but working conditions for the worker are 'left to the recipient' (IA1). PASC is not responsible for accidents or hazards either. Preventing injuries and health risk largely depends on worker and recipient training. The HWTC offers on-the-job training, including courses on safety. More broadly, the union offers political education emphasizing empowering the workers on the job, so they know what is safe and what their job entails. Disability, DPSS and union representatives all note the potential for exploitation in the recipient-worker relationship. As one union staffer rhetorically asks, 'if they're having a big party and the house gets trashed in the process, is it your responsibility to clean up after everybody or is it just to provide care to that one individual?' (U1). The union thus seeks to be a 'shield' to protect workers in negotiations with individual recipients (U2).

One possibility for workers to gain employment security stems from building a direct and respectful relationship with multiple recipient-employers. The chance that workers can do so is enhanced by the establishment of PASC since it is mandated to provide training to recipients. PASC training to recipients includes information on how to find, interview, hire and fire workers; how to be clear about what services they needed; and the various labour laws the recipients are required by law to follow (P5). The ILCs have long provided similar support to recipients who want it on how to be a 'good employer' (D4). Recipient training could provide security for workers if it incorporated workers' rights. As one PASC representative says 'we try to get them to understand that they're the boss ... but your worker also has rights. They're human beings. You cannot abuse them. You cannot overwork them. You cannot cheat on their time sheets' (P6). Such training helps recipients to hire the worker right for them and avoid conflicts that could break up the relationship later. However, recipient training is voluntary and it could be more widespread. Multi-faceted training could help workers and recipients negotiate secure working conditions as the second opening quote suggests.

Conclusion

My comparative analysis of the organization of personal support services in Los Angeles offers a theoretical framework for analysing the conditions under which particularistic employment relations result in insecurity for workers. Derived from extending key insights from scholarship on paid domestic work and comparative analysis of interviews with those who organize public and private personal support services, the framework includes the social location of recipients and workers, the organization of employment, and the organization of resistance. I argue that the tight coupling of a particularistic organization of employment with insecurity documented in studies of the direct householder-domestic relationship may begin to unravel in situations that include less asymmetrical social locations, but that more equality in the social locations of workers and recipients is not a sufficient cause of security. The analysis demonstrates that a new organization of resistance in the public sector is a key factor ushering in workers' security.

The social location of personal support workers is similar to that found in paid domestic work – overwhelmingly women of colour – but it does include more US citizens and, in the public sector, more men. It is the disability location of the recipients that is highly distinctive in this type of in-home work but its impact is not straightforward. In personal support, age related and other bodily vulnerabilities due to disability influence recipients' desires and needs for particularism in choosing the workers, and this need/desire can take racialized forms. However, when disability intersects with poverty and racial disadvantages, as it does in the public sector, recipients may be less able to act on racialized ideals. These findings suggest that asymmetrical social locations between workers and recipients are not a sufficient cause of insecurity.

Social location combines with the organization of employment to shape the impact of particularism on workers. The effort of private sector companies to match on preferences, as well as priorities, indicates recognition of particularism desired or required by recipients. Like studies of domestic work that include intermediaries, I found that organizations often reinforce, perhaps even construct, recipients' racial preferences (Bakan and Stasiulis 1995, Hondagneu-Sotelo 2001, Lobel 2001). In contrast to both the contract labour and informal/formal work studied by these scholars, the intermediaries in the LA private market are more similar to temporary agencies, who seek to *maintain* their position as the intermediary for the long term (Vosko 2000), so that they balance recipient preferences against their ability to continuously supply workers in a way that maximizes their profit levels. As a result, I find variation in companies' responses to recipient racial preferences: some reinforce, others challenge, but most are complicit with them, depending on the local labour market. The non-profit intermediaries in the public sector, by contrast, do not share an interest in maintaining a presence in the employment relationship, but do support recipients' right to hire a worker based on particularistic criteria. As a result, non-profit actors neither reinforce nor challenge recipients' racial preferences but are complicit with a racialized labour market for personal support work. However, like the recipients, their motivation lies primarily in creating good relationships and they have no ability to stratify workers through wage levels. In other words, their complicity has ideological but little material effect on workers, negative or positive.

My comparative analysis shows that a three-pronged organization of resistance can decouple particularistic employment relations from insecurity. In the public sector, the re-regulation of employment provides workers the means to achieve employment security through a labour market unionism, rather than job security with an individual recipient. Secondly, through a social movement unionism based on alliances with recipients, workers have achieved more wage security in a context of funding cuts. Thirdly, a community unionism focused on politicization of workers and recipients has the potential to challenge insecure working conditions. Together labour market, social movement and community unionism challenge the negative effects of racialized particularism in that they limit the potential for workers to be excluded from the work, or paid less and treated worse within it. In contrast, the lack of any collective resistance in the private sector results in continuity with the householder-domestic relationship in the tight coupling of particularism and insecurity.

This chapter focuses on the material consequences of particularistic and racialized employment relations in terms of security in employment, wages and working conditions in one occupation, in one region. Tackling the ideological consequences of racialized employment relations, however, would require a deeper and broader community unionism that includes an anti-racist education and politicization agenda (Leah 1999, Cranford et al. 2005). Furthermore, extending the LA public sector gains to private sector personal support and especially to the more informal, direct householder-domestic relationship will be difficult given the lack of a straightforward entity with whom to bargain. A much more extensive movement for socialized personal support is required to extend and strengthen the gains of the public sector documented here. Finally, extending the unionism of the LA public sector to other geographic areas will also be difficult. The significant time and resource commitment that the union devoted came in large part out of the lack of other options given the very low union density in Los Angeles. In other settings where labour still has reasonable densities, unions may not be pushed to organize for such an extensive re-regulation. The lack of a serious labour crisis and better funded public personal supports may also mean that labour does not have sufficient allies in disability communities to push through or sustain a labour market unionism. By examining this negative case of success, however, we are able to specify the key determinants of precarious personal support and to underscore that particularism is not necessarily one of them. The finding that particularism in hiring for recipients can cohere with security for workers can provide conceptual lessons relevant for other cases.

Chapter 13
Global Care Chains: Transnational Migrant Care Workers

Judy Fudge[1]

> It is perhaps in the global care chain that we can see most clearly the ways and institutions though which unequal resources are distributed globally. (Hassim 2008: 397)

The Feminization of Migration

Feminist scholars have argued that gender inequalities are constitutive of contemporary patterns of intensified globalization, and that gender differences in migration flows often reflect the way in which gender divisions of labour are incorporated into uneven economic development processes (Hassim 2008 above, Herrera 2008: 94). The connection between migrant care work, globalization, and the privatization of social reproduction has been variously designated the new domestic world order (Hondagneu-Sotelo 2002), the new international division of reproductive labour (Parreñas 2002), or the transnational economy of domestic labour (Young 2003).

On the demand side, the feminization of migration is fuelled by the increase in women's labour force participation, falling fertility rates, increasing life expectancy, changes in family structure, shortage of public care, and the increasing marketization of care in the North. On the supply side, economic trends such as growing inequalities between high- and low-income countries, and insecurity, vulnerability, and instability due to economic crises combine with gender-related factors such as abuse, family conflict, and discrimination to increase the numbers of women who migrate in order to obtain paid work (Benería 2008). Remittances are key for the survival of household, community, and country in a number of developing countries as exporting workers is one means by which governments cope with unemployment and foreign debt. Migrant women have become crucial agents in 'global survival circuits' (Sassen 2002).

'Historically and across a diverse range of countries, both developed and developing, women from disadvantaged racial and ethnic groups have tended to

1 Lansdowne Professor and Chair, Faculty of Law, University of Victoria. I would like to thank the SSHRC for funding the research upon which this paper is based. This paper was initially published in 28 (1) *International Journal of Comparative Labour Law and Industrial Relations* 63–70 (2012).

provide care services to meet the needs of more powerful social groups, while their own care needs have been downplayed and neglected' (Razavi 2007: 2). Nowhere is this process of racialization and subordination more evident than when it comes to the globalization of care and social reproduction (Parreñas 2005b). Many of the women who leave the South to work in the North are temporary migrant workers who do not enjoy either the right to become permanent residents in their host country or the right to circulate freely in the labour market. 'Given the basic gender division of labor in destination countries, women migrants are often restricted to traditionally "female" occupations – such as domestic work, care work, nursing, work in the domestic services, and sex work – that are frequently unstable jobs marked by low wages, the absence of social services, and poor working conditions' (Antonpoulos 2008: 38).

Global Care Chains

The term 'global care chain' was first used by Arlie Hochschild to refer to a series of personal links between people across the globe based on the paid and unpaid work of caring (Hochschild 2000).[2] Global care chains are networks of transnational dimension that are formed for the purpose of maintaining daily life; these networks are comprised of households that transfer their caregiving tasks from one to another on the basis of power axes (Orozco 2009). The concept of global care chain helps to illuminate the broader social processes that create the transnational transfer of domestic labour and assist in the conceptualization of the distributive features of this transfer. These processes embody major social divisions and inequalities such as race, class, and gender. The concept also captures household internationalization strategies and it can integrate non-material factors, such as identity formation. Moreover, the concept can be used to go beyond simple push (poverty and unemployment) and pull (employment opportunities and improved wages) explanations of migration since the literature on global care chains emphasizes the macro context of trade and uneven development (Yeates 2005b: 5). These global care chains, which not only link countries of the North and South but also contiguous countries in the South, are created in the confluence of two related phenomena – structural adjustment policies and neo-liberal reforms.

Elaborating on the concept of global care chains, Nicola Yeates emphasizes the complexity of care services, 'encompassing as they do services as diverse as domestic cleaning, family care, health care, sexual care, educational care and religious/spiritual care, provided in a wide range of settings such as the home,

2 Stewart (2011) uses the concept of global care chain together with a feminist relational framework of care to illustrate how gender is crucial to understanding global inequality while global inequality simultaneously undermines women's equality. See also Yeates (2009).

hospitals, hospices, churches, schools and brothels and in a wider range of contexts such as individualized private settings and institutionalized state and non-state settings' (Yeates 2005b: 8). Research on global care chains has focused on the 'nanny trade', which involves international transfers of care labour produced in individualized, household contexts. However, Yeates argues for the need to broaden the focus of global care chains to include migrant care workers of different skill and occupational levels (2005b: 11). Such a broadening is important because it helps to capture how rich countries drain skilled care workers from developing countries (Hassim 2008: 397). Moreover, since the skill and occupational level of migrant workers is highly correlated with a range of employment and settlement related rights to which they are entitled and can effectively exercise in receiving countries, a broader approach to global care chains helps to illustrate the variegated nature, and unequal operation of, citizenship regimes (Fudge and MacPhail 2009, Stasiulis and Bakan 2005).

Public Policy and Law

Female migration not only has implications for policies designed to reconcile paid employment and care responsibilities in both host and home countries, it has contradictory impacts. The employment of migrant women to perform care work in the receiving countries of the North is an individual and privatized solution to the broader problem of combining paid work with unpaid care work. Since this solution is only an option for families who can afford it, lower-income families are left in the lurch. In fact, as Lourdes Benería points out 'the employment of migrant women from the South might contribute to a vicious circle in the host country, in which private solutions delay collective efforts to search for appropriate public policies' (2008: 11) Moreover, 'in home countries, the need to balance family and [labor] market work shifts from the women who migrate to the individuals who assume their roles in the family' (Benería 2008: 11). Rhacel Salazar Parreñas has demonstrated, in the case of the Philippines, how the export of women's labour results in a 'depletion of care resources' that detrimentally affects their ability to provide care for the families that they have left behind (Parreñas 2005b: 15). Since it is mostly women who assume the family roles of migrant women, there is a growing need for reconciliation policies in the South (Benería 2008: 11). While women's decisions to migrate can increase their financial autonomy and increase their financial contribution to their household through remittances, their absorption into the care markets of the North reinforces the gendered nature of care. Thus, not only do global care chains illustrate the ways in which unequal resources are distributed globally (Hassim 2008: 397), they also reveal the gendered nature of this inequality.

Individualized and marketized solutions to the care crisis in the global North reinforce inequalities between states in the North and South, amongst women, and between men and women. There is there a need for public policies that provide for public and collective, and not private and individual, solutions for reconciling the competing demands of paid and unpaid work in the North and South. There is also a need for policies that provide decent work for both domestic and migrant workers around the globe.

The International Labour Organization has responded to this need. At the 100th session of the International Labour Conference, in June 2011, the ILO adopted Convention No. 189 and supplementing Recommendation No. 201 regulating the terms and conditions of work for domestic workers (Albin and Mantouvalou 2012). The adoption of these legal instruments was an important landmark both for the ILO, which recognized that care work in the household is work like any other, and for domestic workers, whose participation in the paid labour market and specific working conditions were recognized. Significantly, the Convention also recognizes that domestic workers are often migrants and is designed to address their migration status. It provides that migrant domestic workers recruited in another country should be given a written offer of employment or contract containing the terms of the offer, which is enforceable in the country of destination. The Convention also emphasizes that migrant domestic workers be entitled to keep their travel and identity documents. Crucially, it also imposes an obligation on member states to regulate private employment agencies, which are key actors in global care chains (Fudge 2011b). The key question is whether receiving countries will ratify the Convention.

'The problem of work family balance is', as Shireen Hassim notes, 'at least to some extent negotiated between states rather than only between individuals within a household or between households and the state' (2008: 397). Nation states use immigration law to police their boundaries and restrict the rights of non-citizens. While developed nations are eager to attract highly skilled care workers, the vast majority of care work, associated as it is with women's work, is regarded as low or unskilled. Thus, many care workers are temporary migrants, who will be expelled once their work is done.

As international care markets rapidly commercialize and integrate, transnational service providers and agencies seek to take advantage of the liberalization in service provision (Stewart 2007). While Mode IV of the General Agreement on Trade and Services, which relates to the temporary migration of individual service providers, potentially facilitates these processes, developed countries resist Mode IV, and limit it to business-related services or highly skilled service providers (Stewart 2007). Richer countries of the North prefer bilateral agreements to multilateral agreements to govern the migration of care workers. In a world in which women's caring labour is devalued, the ILO's approach of providing equal rights for migrant workers does little to recognize, legitimate, and value care work.[3] Moreover, since a migrant worker's entitlement to remain

3 Two ILO Conventions specifically address migrant workers, Convention 97 (C97), *Migration for Employment (Revised)*, 1949 and Convention 143 (C143), *Migrant Workers (Supplementary Provisions)* (1975).

in the receiving country depends upon maintaining an employment relationship with a specific employer, too often employment-related rights are more symbolic than real (Fudge and MacPhail 2009, Ruhs and Martin 2008). Thus, Ann Stewart concludes that 'the interaction between restrictive immigration and labour laws can make unskilled women carers, in particular, highly vulnerable and create complex power relationships, not only in more formal employment contexts but also with employers who may be recipients of care services in domestic environments' (Stewart 2007: 374).

Conclusion

It is not possible to consider gender equality in a comprehensive manner without considering global redistribution (Hassim 2008, Stewart 2007). Commodifying care work may solve the care crisis in the North at the expense of creating a care crisis in the South. Moreover, gender equality also requires consideration of the politics of choice (Lewis and Guillari 2005: 96). Policies that enhance individual choice need to attend to the broader structures of employment and social provisioning. Women in the North and the South should be free to choose the balance between employment and domestic life that is good for them (Bubsy 2011).[4] But policy discourse has barely begun to register ideas about men's greater involvement in domestic life. The problem is that so long as men can choose not to care, women will have no choice but to do so. The choices of individual women are shaped by the opportunities open to them and the cultural norms that prevail. Thus, it is important to increase the incentives for men to take on a greater share of unpaid labour and to challenge cultural norms that associate women with certain kinds of domestic labour if women are to be given a real choice about how they spend their time. Men and women must be encouraged 'to identify with each other across gender boundaries by pursuing greater equality of experience, through developing norms that require both men and women to contribute financially to their children and to care for them' (Himmelweit 2002: 247).[5] The benefit of widening the numbers of people who contribute time to caring is that it would not only reduce the individual costs of those who care, by extending the experience of caring throughout the members of a society, it may be that society would be more willing to contribute institutionally and financially to the costs of care (Himmelweit 2002: 247).

4 For a discussion of a 'right to care' see Busby (2011).

5 Referring to the South, Benería (2008: 16) claims, 'the new agenda of gender equity needs to emphasize men's equal share in the reproductive activities taking place within households'.

Chapter 14

Organizing Through State Transitions and Global Institutions: Crafting Domestic Labour Policy in South Africa

Jennifer N. Fish

South Africa's transition to democracy led to major changes in state policies concerning domestic care labour. While social and labour policies emerged as defining features of the 'new nation', domestic workers' collective organization and transnational activism played a central role in establishing some of the world's most progressive protections 'on paper'. For nearly 50 years of apartheid, the South African state institutionalized the role of black women[1] as domestic workers in private households through migration and work 'pass laws' that created large and inexpensive domestic labour pools to serve the white minority (Walker 1991, Wells 1993). In this context, the laws protecting domestic workers' rights that have been introduced under South Africa's post-1994 governments are particularly striking.

In 2000, activists established the South African Domestic Service and Allied Workers Union (SADSAWU) under the guiding slogan, 'Women Won't Be Free Until Domestic Workers are Free'. By holding government accountable to its own gender rights priorities, the organization achieved substantial policy changes that mandate working conditions, maternity protections, unemployment insurance, fair dispute resolution, the right to organize, minimum wages, and skills development for domestic workers. These policy changes had various impacts at multiple scales – from the household to the nation-state to international institutions.

In 2011, the International Labour Organization, an agency of the United Nations (UN), proposed Convention 189, the first international law that recognized domestic workers as employees and established global standards for care work. UN delegates lauded South Africa for its comprehensive inclusion of domestic workers in national labour policy. Leaders of SADSAWU also had prominent roles in ILO committees concerning 'Decent Work for Domestic Workers' and the global movement that organized to develop Convention 189. From its emergence as a new democracy to its role in international standard setting, the South African

1 I use the term 'black women' here to include both the black and 'coloured' racialized groups that maintain distinct identities in South Africa.

case provides an opportunity to observe how national domestic work policies have 'gone global'.

The role of domestic worker organizations in shaping South Africa's national domestic labour policies frames the analytic lens of this chapter. Building upon 12 years of continued scholar-activist research on domestic labour in South Africa, along with three years of ethnographic research on the crafting of international policies on care labour at the International Labour Organization,[2] this chapter moves from a brief overview of domestic service in South Africa during apartheid to analysis of how domestic workers informed labour policy changes after 1994. Building upon the prominent national transition and its impact on domestic work, I move to an analysis of South Africa's involvement in the movement to globalize standards for care labour. Each section emphasizes the collective contributions of labour activists.

Framing Domestic Work as Interactive Mutuality

Domestic labour complicates traditional assumptions about the divisions between public and private spheres that have traditionally devalued feminized household space while valourizing the masculine public sphere.[3] Feminist political theorists contest this dichotomy by positing an *interactive mutuality* of spheres that emphasizes the interconnections between the public and the private realms. Ling Ling (2002) argues 'What pertains within the individual/household/nation contributes to the community/state/world, just as what happens in the world/state/community affects us as a nation/household/individual' (174). As institutionalized care labour around the world demonstrates, this framework allows us to examine paid domestic work across scales, from the micro-level of household relations to the community, nation, and transnational levels. The concept of interactive mutuality is particularly useful for understanding paid household labour in post-apartheid South Africa – where everyday employment practices within private

2 Research findings in this chapter emerged from one year of field research with domestic worker organizations, employers, NGOs, and government policy makers in Cape Town, South Africa from 2000–01. The most comprehensive account of these findings is available in (Fish 2006). Since this initial research, I have collected data in South Africa each year over the past 12 years, by working closely with the national domestic workers union. These more recent findings inform this chapter, as well as data collected over the past three years with the International Domestic Workers Network during the annual conferences of the International Labour Organization in Geneva. I am thankful to the Social Law Project at the University of the Western Cape, the South African Domestic Service and Allied Workers Union, the International Domestic Workers Network, the International Union of Food Workers, and the WIEGO research policy institute for supporting and informing this research.

3 For analyses of this public/private division, see Pateman (1988), Enloe (1989) and Oakley (1974).

households have not changed as much as state policies concerning domestic labour. In many instances, state policies advocating a more democratic approach to the employment of domestic labour have reinforced race, class and gender divisions of power within the household (Fish 2006, Britton 2005). Through the lens of interactive mutuality, the household may be analysed as a political space where continuities and fissions in relation to global standards, national policies, and everyday practices come into clearer focus. In this regard, domestic workers' statements that 'democracy stops at my front door' illustrate how everyday social relations embedded in asymmetries of power are far more difficult to change than state policies and ideologies – even in South Africa where human rights were the focus of government policies early in the transition to democracy.

As a result of the power relations during nearly 50 years of apartheid governance, high levels of unemployment and lingering educational gaps, domestic work remains one of the top sectors of work for black women, 18 years after the democratic transition.[4] Often characterized as the 'last bastion of apartheid',[5] domestic labour symbolizes a critical disjuncture between the public emphasis on gender rights and everyday experiences of blatant power differentials between those who employ household workers and those who perform such labour. In South Africa, in addition to the inherent class-based divisions embedded in the history of colonial servitude, the sector remains distinctly racialized and feminized, which creates additional obstacles for domestic workers as they struggle to realize their rights. In a national context of 42 per cent unemployment,[6] marginalization of domestic workers persists despite new social and labour policies. Through the lens of domestic work, we see the obstacles that threaten efforts to strengthen democratic human rights in South Africa since 1994.

Although the daily lives of women employed in this sector continue to be structured by ongoing and severe inequalities, this icon of black women's labour under apartheid is also shifting as a result of women's activism and collective organization. Domestic workers continue to resist marginalization by their collective organization in unions, and more recently, their role in international policy formation. By drawing upon their own union and its alignment with

4 While Statistics South Africa 2000 October Household Survey reported two other slightly larger occupational categories for women, the number of women in official reports is severely under-reported because the employment context is the private household. Department of Labour officials in this research repeatedly referred to domestic labour as the 'largest sector of working women' in South Africa. Furthermore, disaggregation of the data by racial categories illustrates that domestic work remains the largest sector of labour for black women in South Africa.

5 This excerpt was repeated by several participants in this study, with interview data narrative data from 2001 capturing this description of domestic labour among participants who were domestic workers, employers of domestic workers, parliamentarians and non-governmental organization leaders.

6 These most recent estimates are drawn from the 2010 national South African Survey (Statistics South Africa 2010).

national gender rights initiatives and international networks, domestic workers have realized substantive policy victories, even as the economic climate reinforces social inequality. These policy victories demonstrate the rich landscape of domestic labour within South Africa – where women's collective and transnational activism confronts lingering symbols of apartheid's injustices. Domestic worker organizations are a vital conduit in expressing the link between the nation/household/individual and the community/state/world. In the South African case, women's activism has led to laudable state policies that create rights and protections for over one million women (Statistics South Africa 2010) employed in private households throughout the country.

Manifesting Apartheid through Domestic Labour

The prevalence of domestic labour in contemporary South African society stems from the apartheid ideology of 'separateness' through social relations of servitude in private households. Deborah Gaitskell et al. (1984) analysed how servitude situated black women's labour as a 'product of the complex operation of class, race and gender divisions over time' (107). Domestic labour served as a powerful agent of socialization, where black women worked within the private spaces of the elite minority, with clear social divisions maintained through a system of servitude that prescribed social norms about who cleans up after whom. Jacklyn Cock (1989) depicted the relationship between 'maids and madams' as a site of intimate racial socialization which served to reinforce the social practices central to apartheid rule:

> The role of the domestic worker is important in socialisation in the dominant ideological order. Often it is the only significant interracial contact whites experience, and they experience this relationship in extremely asymmetrical terms. Many white South African children learn the attitudes of racial domination from domestic relationships with servants and 'nannies'. The converse is also equally true in that blacks presumably learn the attitudes of submission (or at least the semblance thereof) that apartheid requires, and also the resentment it generates through some experience of domestic service. (8–9).

As Cock suggests, these intimate social interactions within the private household are integrally connected to governing public ideologies, which reproduced strict systems of race, class, and gender inequality.

Domestic work required that women migrate, leaving their own homes to provide services in white residential spaces of privilege in South African society. Under apartheid, domestic workers most often assumed 'live-in' positions, a particular form of entrapment that created serious challenges to workers' autonomy, privacy and ability to organize collectively. These characteristics of paid domestic labour created a duality in domestic workers' lives – as they negotiated the day-to-day realities of their employers' private homes, while maintaining emotional, financial and psychological relationships with their families and communities of origin. These bifurcated experiences heightened the privileged positions and power of employers, while reinforcing the geographic divides that dominated the apartheid system.

The South African experience mirrors domestic labour situations worldwide, where the household space reifies larger systems of race, class and gender oppression. The placement of black, economically disadvantaged, often migrant women in marginalized labour defines the institution in many national contexts (Romero 1992, Heyzer and Wee 1994, Chin 1998, Chang 2000, Gamburd 2000, Perrañas 2001a, Hondagneu-Sotelo 2001, Bannerjee 2004, Armenta 2009, Haskins 2012).

The social relations of domestic work exemplify *intersectionality*. They complicate women's experiences of gender oppression according to race and class.[7] In South Africa, black, economically marginalized women remain extremely marginalized as a result of what Patricia Hill Collins (1990) described as a 'matrix of domination'. Women positioned as employers are often able to draw on race and class privilege in ways that dilute their experiences of gender oppression.[8] Through the practice of paid household labour, we see how privileged women also participate in gender oppression by reinforcing the devalued nature of domestic work in the private sphere, which ultimately reinforces the social and economic privilege of men in the public arena.

This interactive mutuality came into focus in distinct yet overlapping ways under South Africa's apartheid regime. The past two decades of the national democratization project in South Africa have challenged and partially disrupted the systems of race, class, and gender oppression. The household has come under review in the formal policy realm. At the same time, day-to-day relations of domestic labour in the private sphere have not changed much. For example, most households fall short of legal requirements to pay minimum wages, provide formal work contracts and register domestic workers for social security programmes (Fish 2006). The resistance to formalizing employment relations in the private sphere suggests that domestic work remains a powerful arena for resisting change that allows employers to retain social power.

Throughout the apartheid and new democratic periods, the collective organization of domestic workers has mediated between the public and private spheres. Domestic worker unions focused on making private injustices in the household sphere central to public conversations about structural inequality. Within the new democratic state, the focus on 'gender rights as human rights'

7 For further explanation of intersectionality and its connection to domestic labour, see Guillaumin 1995, Young and Dickerson 1994, Collins 1990 and Cock 1983.

8 Throughout this chapter, I refer to employers as women. While I recognize that men also employ domestic workers, my work focuses specifically on the power relations among women in the private household labour context.

created a space for domestic worker unions and allied organizations to point out lingering aspects of 'apartheid' embedded in domestic work. By drawing upon a history of collective activism, domestic worker unions have challenged the post-94 state to 'bring democracy home' to this 'last bastion of apartheid'. The tangible products of these efforts are policy changes that offer social and labour protections to domestic workers. These policies acknowledge the central role of domestic workers in contemporary South African society; introduce formal protections into this feminized sector of the informal economy; and recognize the economic contributions of women employed in private households.

Domestic Labour and Collective Organization

Throughout the apartheid era, domestic workers' unions emphasized the injustices of the labour system that relegated black women to marginalized domestic work.[9] Although the government banned working class, predominantly black unions for much of the apartheid era, the labour movement served as a key site of resistance and collective action. The Federation of South African Trade Unions (FOSATU) and the Congress of South African Trade Unions (COSATU) supported the unionization of domestic workers, helping to form the South African Domestic Workers' Union (SADWU) in 1986. Under apartheid's heightened police enforcement, SADWU provided a space to organize workers, align women's interests and advocate for basic employment rights within the private household. The union fostered ties between domestic workers and the broader anti-apartheid struggle for social and economic justice and the elimination of racialized governance.[10]

Non-union collective efforts also provided spaces where workers met on a regular basis to share their common struggles. The Domestic Workers Association of Cape Town, for example, offered educational services for workers' children, while serving as an advocacy organization for women employed in domestic work. Through such local organizations, other nongovernmental and women's rights organizations, such as The Black Sash, invested in the protection of domestic workers. Through these organizational collaborations, women with social power under apartheid served as advocates for domestic workers' rights, while they often employed domestic workers in their own homes. These examples of domestic workers' organizations during apartheid illustrate how the asymmetric power relations between women, reified through the institution of paid household labour, stand in sharp contradistinction to the broader ideology of social equality central to the anti-apartheid struggle. In this regard, women's activism around the

9 For an extensive historical review of domestic work unionization, see Gordon 1985.

10 I am grateful to Eunice Tholakele Dhladhla, Myrtle Witbooi, Hester Stephens and Maggie Shongwe for their detailed depiction of this complex history of union organization over the past 35 years.

rights of domestic workers in their private households repeatedly confronted the overarching race, class, and gender inequalities in apartheid society.

Domestic Worker Organization and Democratization

In the context of South Africa's post-1994 democratic transition, civil society organizations aligned with the domestic workers' union to prioritize gender rights. Although the unequal relations between women persisted in private households, organizational alliances represented a means to work across social divides. The collective action of domestic worker unions and gender rights-centred NGOs illustrated the potential for civil society organizations to serve as powerful agents of change by holding individuals, households and communities accountable for achieving democratic human rights.

Despite persistent barriers to the collective mobilization of domestic workers, the efforts to create protections for this sector within new social policies contributed to the emergence of new civil society organizations. Asymmetrical power relations and persistent socio-economic inequalities will gradually lose their power as individual workers align with a broader movement for gender rights and the protection of women workers. The South African case illustrates how working through unions and NGO networks has been beneficial for domestic workers. Given the substantial barriers to social change within this 'last bastion of apartheid', aligning domestic worker organizations with other gender rights organizations facilitated gradual shifts in employment practices.

Over the past 18 years, women's political engagement surrounding domestic work in South Africa has resulted in tangible policy changes. In the global context, South Africa has the most comprehensive national legislation concerning the inclusion of domestic workers in social and labour policies. These policies have come into existence as a direct result of the activism of domestic worker unions and allied organizations within South Africa. Although the new government demonstrated a willingness to integrate the sector within emerging labour policies, the legislation that finally came into existence reflects the input of civil society organizations, in partnership with domestic worker unions. The processes that realized these policy changes in South Africa illustrate the significance of opportunities for women to organize across social divides. To explore the impact of collective action within this particular sector, let us next turn to a case study examining how domestic worker union activism and alignment with gender rights organizations led to the establishment of social security protections for domestic workers.

Building a Domestic Workers Movement

The limited democracy in South Africa's private households motivated a gender rights movement built upon the notion that 'Women Won't Be Free Until Domestic

Workers are Free'. By working with and through the Gender Machinery[11] structures of the democratic government, SADSAWU ensured that domestic workers were included in unemployment insurance for the first time.[12] A closer examination of the role of women's organization in changing domestic labour policy in South Africa offers lessons that may be relevant for changing care labour globally.

In April 2000, SASAWU emerged from the South African Domestic Workers' Union (SADWU) that had disbanded in 1996, just as the Labour Relations Act legalized domestic worker unionization.[13] The gender priorities embedded in post-1994 nation-building provided a powerful platform to launch SADSAWU. In its earliest incarnation, the leaders of SADSAWU emphasized that the social and economic conditions of domestic work had not improved despite the promises of the 'New South Africa'. As SADSAWU's National President, Hester Stephens, conveyed: 'It is our interest now in the union to build this union because we are quite aware that the struggle is still continuing, whatever is the new South Africa, nothing has changed' (Nyman 1997).

Over the past 10 years, SADSAWU has sought to build a national union of domestic workers in accordance with the principles of democracy and gender rights. In this regard, the domestic worker organization provided a space to break down the pervasive divides between the public and private spheres by demanding that household labour be included in formal public policies.

The national leadership of SADSAWU is supported by the Western Cape office of the national Congress of South African Trade Unions (COSATU), confirming the regional office's commitment to including domestic workers in the labour rights movement. According to leaders in both organizations, COSATU's national offices do not offer the same support to SADSAWU because they question the 'viability' of domestic worker unions. This cleavage between national and regional offices signifies gender power imbalances in the national union, particularly since domestic work is one of the top two forms of employment for black women in South Africa. The relationship between SADSAWU and COSATU at the national level parallels the disjuncture between the South African government's commitment to gender rights and the ongoing institutionalization of domestic labour as devalued 'women's work'.

Notwithstanding these organizational challenges, the first year after its launch, SADSAWU opened six regional offices and enrolled approximately 11,000

11 In its original inception, South Africa's Gender Machinery consisted of three governmental offices with monitoring, lobbying and advocacy functions. The Commission for Gender Equality served as the central monitory agency within the government gender structure.

12 By 'first time', I am referring to the first time since the establishment of the apartheid governance. Domestic workers were not included in unemployment insurance throughout the apartheid era from 1948–94. This 2001 victory marked a critical movement toward the formal recognition of this sector.

13 For a more extensive description of this organizational collapse, see Nyman 1997.

members.[14] Although the number of members is impressive, it pales in comparison to Department of Labour estimates that approximately one million women were employed in domestic service at the time.[15] Given these numbers, the primary organizational goal for SADSAWU during its first year was membership recruitment. The union faced the challenge of overcoming social dynamics maintained within private households where employers were suspicious about workers' union affiliation and domestic workers' empowerment. Domestic workers stated repeatedly that union membership created a serious threat to their employment, making it difficult for them to attend meetings and participate in the union. One respondent described how her employer reacted to her SADSAWU t-shirt by saying, 'Never, never, never wear this t-shirt in my house again!'

These barriers to individual membership concerned the union leadership for two reasons. First, without a central employer where union dues could be easily collected, the union's financial viability was questionable. Second, SADSAWU's main focus on policy changes that would include domestic workers in labour and social security legislation could not be achieved without a large membership base. In addition, with the exception of one member, SADSAWU's entire leadership, National Office Bearers, also worked in domestic labour. The leadership consisted of volunteers who worked full-time in private households.

National recruitment efforts also faced barriers to finding new members and providing information about the advantages of union membership without jeopardizing domestic workers' employment and safety. In their efforts to reach workers in isolated private households, the leaders of SADSAWU emphasized the individual benefits of membership.

> Yes, it [unionisation] is part of the struggle, and to make other workers aware of it, that I can talk to them about the union, because I find the union like a security for myself, you know, if I got a problem, I can go there. So I also want them to be part of that union.
>
> (Domestic worker interview, Gugulethu, March 2001)

Although union membership fosters agency, in the recruitment process, leaders focused on its individual benefits including guaranteed protection from unfair dismissal, the assurance of basic working conditions, and access to dispute

14 These data were acquired through a review of SADSAWU's organizational membership database. This estimate is based on union records as of 2001. Without national data on the exact number of women employed in this sector, the ratio of union membership cannot be precise, however local estimates suggest that SADSAWU's membership remains at approximately 1 to 4 per cent of the total number of domestic workers in South Africa – illustrating the ongoing work of collective mobilization.

15 This is according to interviews with three Department of Labour officials who consulted national records in 2001 and 2010, as well as general estimates reported The Cape Times newspaper from 2001–10.

resolution systems. Once domestic workers joined the national union, they could engage in collective action and push for policy changes for the sector. By working within new democratic governance structure, they also acquired direct access to a broader gender rights movement in South Africa.

Policy Change through Organizational Alignments

In interviews for this study, union leaders, SADSAWU members, parliamentary and non-governmental organizational leaders repeatedly noted that the alignment of the national domestic workers' union with other gender and human rights organizations provided the strongest platform to address the lingering injustices within the sector. Participants also suggested that this alignment provided a powerful network to advocate for the inclusion of domestic workers within emerging national policies. One year after its inception, SADSAWU established an organizational alliance that positioned domestic workers centrally within South Africa's gender rights movement. The alliance promoted a public discourse that challenged the inherent contradictions of excluding domestic workers from the promises of democracy. This social policy reform process will be explored next, to elucidate one of the most successful strategies for ensuring the inclusion of domestic workers within South Africa's democratic dispensation.

Attaining Social Security Rights

In 2001, SADSAWU's first major policy initiative involved securing domestic workers' access to a national Unemployment Insurance Fund (UIF) intended to provide a critical safety net for workers during periods of unemployment. The UIF has been widely viewed as one of the most important social security initiatives within the new democracy, particularly because of the estimated 42 per cent unemployment rate in South Africa. Yet, Department of Labour leaders were sceptical about including domestic workers in the UIF because of concerns about ensuring compliance by employers and the resulting criticism if their efforts to enforce compliance were not successful.[16] Assuring employers' compliance with the UIF would also require formalizing the private household as a public work space. Government officials felt that monitoring the registration of domestic workers would potentially infringe upon the privacy of the household, which is guaranteed within the South African national constitution. The national domestic workers union requested an official response to the status of domestic workers' inclusion in the UIF during formal reviews of the proposed bill in 1997 and 2000. At both junctures, officials responded that they needed an additional 18 months

16 For detailed accounts of this extensive investigation process, see the following South African government reports: the 1991 Manpower Commission Report on Domestic Workers, the 1993 Limbrick Report and the 1996 Task Team Report on Domestic Workers and the UIF.

to investigate the administrative implications of including domestic workers in the bill. In March of 2001, the Department of Labour presented a final draft of the Unemployment Insurance Fund (UIF) Bill [B3-2001] to the Labour Portfolio Committee that specifically *excluded* domestic workers from unemployment insurance coverage and requested another 18 months to investigate the administrative challenges involved with enrolling domestic workers in the UIF.

Rather than passively accepting this delay, SADSAWU joined a coalition organized by the governmental Commission on Gender Equality, an umbrella body for five nongovernmental, faith-based and union organizations and the national Parliamentary Office, which monitored the gendered impacts of legislation. Under the Gender Monitoring and Advocacy Coalition for the Unemployment Insurance Fund (GMAC-UIF) that coordinated public input from civil society organizations, the coalition presented a unified critique of the non-democratic and unconstitutional nature of domestic workers' proposed exclusion from the UIF. The coalition was the first collective organizational initiative since the 1994 transition to democracy to take on domestic labour as a central gender priority.

As a governmental monitoring body and human rights task force, the Commission on Gender Equality (CGE), led the organizational networking. The role of the CGE has been articulated as:

> The CGE exists because South Africans, when writing their Constitution, insisted that such an institution be established. But it is also there to ensure that gender issues are visible and integrated in the day-to-day policy and practice of state and non-state institutions. Until gender equality is a way of life in South Africa, the mandate of the Commission on Gender Equality remains.[17]

The CGE works within government structures to a certain degree, yet its primary mandate is as a monitoring body, holding the state and private institutions accountable for achieving gender equality. The CGE is a central mechanism for achieving the gender rights priorities of the new government. The CGE's work on the UIF campaign, in collaboration with SADSAWU and other powerful NGOs, illustrated a vision of human rights-focused democracy and a space where organizations collaborated across divides to demand rights for domestic workers on the grounds that their rights were central concerns in the first stages of nation building.

To strengthen participation in the parliamentary committees reviewing draft policy documents,[18] the civil society coalition worked to enhance the impacts

17 This statement draws upon an internal organizational document of the Commission on Gender Equality, 2001.

18 In the South African Parliamentary legislative process, policy drafts are initially written by the relevant government Department. The Portfolio Committee (composed of Members of Parliament) then reviews and critiques the bill, holds public hearings to gather input from civil society and eventually approves the final legislative document along with the National President and the relevant Minister.

of individual submissions by establishing a collective platform that called for the enactment of gender justice through the assurance of social security rights for domestic workers. Members of the GMAC-UIF aligned with SADSAWU presented 11 submissions advocating for domestic workers' protection. Each presentation clearly demonstrated the unconstitutional and discriminatory nature of the exclusion of domestic workers from unemployment insurance benefits. Furthermore, each submission challenged the contradictory nature of the government's social security philosophy – to protect the poorest of the poor – while excluding the 'most vulnerable' workers from unemployment insurance benefits.

According to parliamentarians interviewed for this research, SADSAWU's opening statements during the UIF hearings made a central contribution to the reform of the legislation by putting a 'face' on the policy and demanding public accountability. SADSAWU General Secretary Myrtle Witbooi challenged parliamentarians to acknowledge the multiple contributions that domestic workers make to the nation:

> We ask you to think seriously about domestic workers. You know ever since this slavery started in this country, domestic workers were there. We have been doing the work for all of you, yet when it comes to laws, there is just no way it can be extended to domestic workers … We find it most problematic that the bill seeks to include the poor while overlooking the poorest of the poor, the domestic worker … We feel the unemployment insurance is discriminating against us as women. … We see women that are working for 20 years. We see them walking in the streets because there is no unemployment benefits for them. There is no pension fund for them. … I am asking you this morning, listen with your heart to the domestic worker … think of your mothers because many of you were raised by domestic workers working for you while you are here now. … I am asking you this morning, please consider the domestic workers … if it were not for them in your houses, you would not have been here today, if it were not for domestic workers working for the people of Parliament there would be no Parliament today. If it were not for the domestic workers working for the factory boss, there would be no factory today because they need us to run their houses while they are building the economy of the country (Witbooi 2001).[19]

In this statement, we see the national union leadership calling for a moral accountability that is specific to the South African context. By drawing upon the history of the liberation struggle, Witbooi exposed the sharp divide between political periods and between the social positions of government decision makers and the domestic workers who 'continue to live under apartheid'. SADSAWU statements emphasized that the majority of government leaders had suffered under or fought against apartheid and used this observation to heighten their moral

19 Myrtle Witbooi, SADSAWU General Secretary; Parliamentary Public Submission in Cape Town Legislative Chambers, March 2001.

obligation to establish policies to protect those who continue to suffer under the lingering socio-economic impacts of apartheid – namely domestic workers. Denying domestic workers rights therefore became the equivalent to 'saying no to your mother'. Witbooi's call to recognize domestic workers as central to the functioning of the national government and economy links the private paid labour of women in households with the public realm. In this sense, social constructions of gender and the role of feminized labour became effective tools to advocate for policy change, particularly as the new democratic state emerged.

Throughout a full day of public hearings, each member organization of the GMAC-UIF utilized this argument to call government policy makers to task for domestic workers from critical social security benefits. The unified voice of civil society played a large role in the eventual policy outcome. Less than one week after the public submissions, the government announced that the Unemployment Insurance Fund would be extended to cover domestic workers, acknowledging that they composed the largest sector of working women in the country. Many NGO leaders and political analysts interviewed for this study suggested that pressure from civil society, and specifically the GMAC-UIF public submissions, caused this change in the national government's stance. Behind the scenes, each of the collaborating organizations was convinced to align with SADSAWU's bold public appeal, resulting in the presentation of a compelling collective voice.

Union leaders considered the unemployment insurance policy important for domestic workers because it could provide a sustainable income for women who faced unforeseen work severance, unfair dismissals, and needs for maternity leave. Women's marginalized positions in informal employment made the ability to secure resources during periods of unemployment critical for their own and their families' livelihoods. Submissions from the GMAC-UIF coalition described unemployment insurance as a central component of the new democracy's overarching commitment to equitable access to social security, rather than an isolated labour policy. Sharing this vantage point, civil society organizations presented a unified ethical stance regarding social security policy in the new South Africa. This collective voice strengthened SADSAWU's representation of domestic workers as the 'face of the UIF'. The moral authority of this representation was reinforced by the consistent arguments presented by leading human rights organizations that had fought to end apartheid.

The UIF process also established a new framework for the inclusion of domestic workers' organizations in policy formation. Through SADSAWU, domestic workers gained a pivotal space to network with other NGOs representing their cause, while representing the voices of the women affected by policy decisions. SADSAWU's presence as an equal party in the coalition informed NGOs about the practical implications of policies. In a personal interview, Fatima Seedat, Director of the GMAC-UIF, described her perceptions of the success of this innovative collaboration. She said that the coalition allowed her to develop a heightened awareness of the daily realities of domestic workers in ways she had formerly not considered, even in her work as a gender specialist. Within the broader framework of gender rights, other leaders in the GMAC-UIF process stated that their work with SADSAWU forced them to ask continually, 'Why are we here?'. Thus, South Africa's Gender Machinery constructed a successful platform for women to mobilize across race and class boundaries through coalitions of civil society organizations. The coalition made the private employment relations of domestic work public through a collective call on moral, social, and legal grounds to include domestic workers in the emerging gender rights frameworks. The resulting public policies capture the interactive mutuality of the household and public spheres. The household was considered in government deliberations regarding the social contract between governments and citizens.

As an emerging union building its membership base, SADSAWU also benefited extensively from its involvement with GMAC-UIF. By aligning with larger organizations that had lengthy track records as human rights advocates and lobbyists, and large resource bases, SADSAWU's positions gained prominence and authority. The alignment of domestic workers with many of the most powerful representatives of civil society forced government to take the sector seriously. SADSAWU leaders embraced the GMAC-UIF model, linking it directly with the successful policy reform. At an ideological level, the alignment of the domestic worker union with gender organizations and national NGOs strengthened the calls for consideration of care labour in the reproduction of society, which ultimately led to tangible policy reform. These priorities are now evident in the global movement to recognize and set enforceable employment standards for care labour.

Interactions among local, national and international spheres also emerged when South African civil society organizations took up discourses regarding gender rights and protections that were part of global initiatives. The UIF reform process garnered strength from repeated references to existing international conventions on women's rights. In particular, members of the GMAC-UIF utilized the resolutions of the Conference on the Elimination of All Forms of Discrimination against Women (CEDAW) as a tool to hold the South African state accountable for its gender rights platform. By drawing from international conventions, such as CEDAW, civil society members highlighted the state's obligation to the global community, emphasizing the contradictions between international law and state practice. References to international documents illuminated the gender discrimination inherent in the proposed exclusion of domestic workers from social security legislation. As members of GMAC-UIF pointed out, this policy contradicted South Africa's commitments to the international community. This inconsistency resonated in the new South African state that was committed to the moral and humanitarian dimensions of democracy.

In the case of the UIF policy change, international conventions substantially strengthened the ability of GMAC-UIF organizations to make claims at the national level. Because state institutions hold the greatest power to change employment standards for domestic work, they cannot be ignored or discounted. However, state accountability is enhanced when it is demanded from international organizations putting pressure 'from above', as well as from civil society organizations putting pressure 'from below'.

The Black Sash, an anti-apartheid women's organization of long-standing that is involved in domestic worker rights, built its submission around the international standards enunciated in CEDAW. Their submission captures the interrelations between civil society, state and international spheres:

> There has been a clear trend in recent years amongst international jurisdictions to bring casual workers and workers in the informal sectors within the ambit of more formal employment legislation. This trend has been brought about in recognition of the principle established under international law that to exclude them amounts to unfair discrimination. We submit that the exclusion of domestic workers from the UIF benefits is in clear contradiction of international law, is at odds with accepted international practice and for all of these reasons, as well as the reasons outlined above, is unfair discrimination (Seria 2001).

Members of the GMAC-UIF participated in a broader international women's movement in two ways. First, drawing upon CEDAW reinforced South Africa's role in formal institutions of global governance and its commitment to gender rights within the international community. At a second level, GMAC- UIF members strengthened informal networks of civil society organizations by utilizing alliances and strategic relations with global organizations to enhance their ability to hold the South African state accountable to its local population and international standards.

While the labour performed by domestic workers may remain in the private household, it is not isolated from the public spheres at the national and global levels. As workers in private households are connected to national and international movements for gender rights, their power in individual work sites increases. The collective action of the GMAC-UIF coalition contributed to a gradual shift in the social norms that govern domestic labour. When civil society organizations aligned to demand the inclusion of domestic workers in unemployment insurance, individual workers' rights are strengthened. Through the mobilization of domestic worker unions, we see that civil society organizations have the potential to align the private and public spheres of democratization.

Domestic workers themselves also participated in an imagined international civil society through their enrolment in SADSAWU. This membership, which connects their work in private households to national public dialogues are then taken up at a global level through institutions such as the United Nations and international gender rights organizations. In these ways, civil society organizations serve as a means to globalize the household as a political space where the need for labour protections transcends national contexts.

The Voice of Domestic Labour in State Structures

SADSAWU capitalized on new avenues for participation in the crafting of public policies just as South Africa's emerging democratic governance provided rich opportunities to push for domestic worker rights. Following the adoption of the revised UIF bill, the Department of Labour invited leaders of SADSAWU to join an advisory task group focused on the bill's implementation. Standards for representation of domestic workers in relevant government structures were also established in accord with a SADSAWU motto that demands, 'nothing for us, without us'.

The UIF has had tangible benefits for domestic workers. To date, 100,000 domestic workers have enrolled in the unemployment insurance programme in South Africa, and 70,000 have received benefits.[20] Furthermore, the advocacy resulted in additional policies for domestic workers, including a minimum wage requirement and recent consideration of a pension fund. Union leaders and NGO allies suggested that these additional policies stemmed directly from the success of the collective organizational strategy of the GMAC-UIF.

Domestic Labour within the Presidential Working Group

The inclusion of domestic workers in the UIF established an obligation to integrate the voices of domestic workers in relevant government gender structures. In 2006, President Thabo Mbeki invited leaders of SADSAWU to serve on the 'Working Group on Women' initiative established by his office. This initiative entailed 'promoting and monitoring the implementation of government's policies on the empowerment of women' as a measure of 'advancing gender equality in the second decade' of the nation-building process. To emphasize the role of gender in national governance, the President's Office invited delegates from women's organizations throughout South Africa to participate. During this process, the working group drew from international gender rights discourse, emphasizing 'social cohesion' and women's contribution to a 'second economy'. International initiatives such as CEDAW and the Beijing Platform of Action guided the work of evaluating gender progress within the South African state.

From 53 national organizations represented in the Working Group on Women, President Mbeki selected SADSAWU to serve on a Coordinating Committee of 12 members charged with advising the President. Organizations were chosen for the committee on the basis of presentations outlining the gender concerns of each organization's constituents. SADSAWU leadership told President Mbeki that 'we are here to represent the women that clean your houses'. Once again, we see the moral, emotional and gender appeals underpinning demands for recognition of the women who reproduce the daily lives of South Africans, particularly, its politicians.

20 These figures are drawn from the most recent enrolment rates captured by the Department of Labour, 2011.

This strategy was extremely effective because it brings the private household into the public arena, while drawing upon a demand to redress the injustices of the apartheid era. In the South African case, the realities of women's representation in domestic work make its inclusion in all government deliberations regarding gender rights that much more important.

With the coalition of national union and civil society organizations, and its role to assist with crafting the social security framework in the new democracy, domestic workers became even more difficult to overlook in the government's proposed the gender rights framework. SADSAWU's participation in the Presidential Working Group exemplifies how women's organizations can link severely marginalized workers with state processes established to promote the advancement of gender rights. The inclusion of domestic workers within the Presidential Working Group on Women positioned the national union in a direct line of communication with the nation's president and executive staff. Along with the UIF policy victory, SADSAWU's involvement in the working group reduced the distance between private households and state governance. When domestic workers sit at the executive government table to discuss gender priorities, the public and private realms meet in ways that disrupt power relations. Even though the terms of such meetings are inscribed by formalities and embedded power asymmetries, these conversations symbolize a gradual shift in ideology, as well as the practical attainment of rights. Although the presidential leadership has changed, domestic workers' inclusion in policy formation, and the centrality of the union's alignment with allied organizations, has moved to the global level, where South Africa played a leading role in establishing the first international standards for domestic work through the International Labour Organization. The emergence of policy protections at the international level has parallels with the 2001 Decent Work for Domestic Workers convention campaign. As this chapter describes next, human rights advocates, global unions, policy makers, research institutes, and domestic worker organizations from around the world utilized the United Nations policy formation process as a space to build an international movement for global care labour.

South Africa as a Model of International Domestic Care Policy

In 2006, the first global domestic worker network formed in Amsterdam to begin a transnational movement to advocate for 'respect and rights' for the world's care labourers. In 2008, the International Labour Organization – a special agency of the United Nations and the largest institution focused on workers' rights and fair labour standards – announced that a 'Decent Work for Domestic Workers' agenda item would be on the agenda of the 2010 and 2011 International Labour Conferences. The tripartite dialogues among governments, unions and employers would determine whether an international convention[21] setting standards for domestic labour across the world was possible. Unlike other international convention discussions, many civil society organizations participated in the gathering largely because of coalitions between international domestic worker organizations and their allies. It was much like the GMAC-UIF process, but at an international level.

After the formation of the International Domestic Workers Network (IDWN) following the 2006 Amsterdam conference, a research-policy organization and a global union partnered to serve as the umbrella body for the coordination of domestic workers' participation in the Decent Work for Domestic Workers campaign during the 2010 and 2011 International Labour Conferences. With the support of Women in the Informal Economy: Globalizing and Organizing (WIEGO) and the International Union of Food, Agricultural, Hotel, Restaurant, Catering, Tobacco and Allied Workers Associations (IUF), the IDWN that represented domestic workers around the world utilized the United Nations as a space to advocate for the international recognition and protection of domestic workers. Much like the GMAC-UIF process, the coordination of domestic worker organizations fostered unified messages, strategic engagement with government decision-makers, and a heightened accountability to make the ILO rhetoric of 'fair globalization' and 'decent work' tangible by setting standards for the 'poorest of the poor' in the global economy.

The WIEGO-IUF structure provided solidarity as well as material support for domestic workers to gather, learn about international policy making, establish organizational priorities, and create a 'Platform of Demands'. The IDWN network met with the Director General of the ILO, Juan Somavia, to present its demands and advocate for a convention that would create meaningful employment standards for domestic workers. Through this coordinated network, domestic workers' voices also 'got to the floor' of the tripartite deliberations. At every juncture available to NGO participants, the IDWN presented statements about the lived experiences of domestic workers, their persistent exploitation, the impact of lack of standards, and the importance of a convention in the growing care and migrant labour economy.[22] The strategic alignment resulted in a consistent and frequent message about the

21 An international Convention sets global standards of practice through the UN system. In this case, Convention 189 refers to the International Labour Organization's two-year discussion of the proposed set of standards on 'Decent Work for Domestic Workers'. Possible international conventions and accompanying recommendations are discussed during a two-year process within the annual International Labour Conference meetings, comprised of delegates from 183 governments, employers and labour representatives. For fuller discussions of the legal dimensions of Convention 189, see Blackett 2011.

22 Most global unions and international organizations are considered NGOs in the ILO structure. Therefore, their access to the ILC discussions is limited to observer status. This means that observer delegates may take part in conversations among the worker groups on particular sub-committees. All formal tripartite discussions and voting procedures, however, limit verbal participation to government representatives from the 183 member states and one representative from both the employer and worker groups.

ILO's obligation to introduce employment standards for the 'most vulnerable' women within the global labour force.

The umbrella network that brought domestic workers together created spaces for workers' substantive involvement in the formal deliberations regarding the proposed new convention. Since its inception in 1919, no International Labour Conference has seen an equivalent level of participation by the workers who would be most directly affected by its policies. And, much like the presence of domestic workers within the UIF deliberations, members of the IDWN brought a 'human face', representing the 'most vulnerable' workers. In opening statements during the first International Labour Conference in 2010, Vicky Kanyoka, representing Kenya and the African region of the IDWN stated, 'We are the "oil in the wheels" – it is our work in households which enables others to go out and be economically active. And yet our huge economic and social contribution has not until now been acknowledged' (Kanyoka 2010). Over the course of two conferences, IDWN members presented 12 formal public statements that consistently wove individual experiences with the realities of the growing global care economy. The statements were infused with a moral accountability made possible only by the presence and participation of domestic workers in the international policy-making process.

In the tripartite dialogues among governments, unions and employers, South Africa took a central role as a model for domestic labour policies. Along with Brazil, South Africa had implemented the most substantive policies for the inclusion of domestic workers in national labour and social protections. Because of the national legislation mandating unemployment insurance, minimum wages, basic employment conditions, opportunities for skills development, and maternity leave for domestic workers, advocates of the Domestic Worker Convention continually referenced the successes of South Africa's national policies. At the second conference in 2011, the Chair of the ILO Workers Group, Sir Leroy Trotman, stated that 'the International Labor Conference builds on South Africa and Brazil, and we look forward to future dialogue' (Trotman 2011). As the ILO tripartite conversations repeatedly suggested, policy implementation at the national level became a benchmark for assessing the feasibility of an international convention. Although UN conventions set in place global standards, their success requires that national governments ratify the conventions and assure that their own policies fall in line with the international instruments. South Africa heightened its influence on the ILO conversations because of the content of its policies and its demonstrated capacity to institute a legal framework for domestic workers.

Two key dimensions of South Africa's national legal framework emerged as important aspects of the ILO convention. First, the Domestic Work Convention established the need for minimum wages for women employed in private households. Opponents of the convention suggested that the minimum wage would reduce the employment of domestic workers. To refute this case, advocates referred to the South African experience where employment of domestic workers *increased* steadily after the introduction of a minimum wage. Virgil Seafield, South African government representative to the ILO, argued that with the introduction of national minimum wage standards, 'People did not buy larger washing machines and brooms' (Seafield 2011) to compensate for their inability to hire domestic workers. Rather, there is increased reliance on household labour due to growing care needs in South Africa.

The South African experience also emphasizes the integration of national systems to support domestic labour policies. With standards for unfair dismissal, minimum wages and basic conditions of employment in the international convention, opponents continually questioned the feasibility of its implementation. South Africa's established Centre for Conflict and Dispute Arbitration (CCDA) provides an exemplary institutional forum that reconciles the legal requirements for domestic labour with daily practices in private households. The CCDA has the capacity to address the specificities of domestic work and informal employment. It was invaluable for challenging the notion that policy implementation would require substantial resources to assure compliance. The CCDA served as one of the only institutions that had the capacity to ensure accountability, enforcement and reconciliation.

In addition to South Africa's national models that became important reference points for the ILO deliberations, the national union's General Secretary, Myrtle Witbooi, also served as President of the International Domestic Workers Network. During the International Labour Conferences, the executive committee of the labour group for the Decent Work for Domestic Workers Convention selected Ms. Witbooi to participate in strategic planning sessions, where she had direct access to the central decision makers within the ILO. Much like the GMAC-UIF case, domestic worker leaders' capacities to gain a place at the negotiating table and integrate the voices of domestic workers themselves demonstrate their influence on the process, as well as its outcomes.

On 16 June 2011, International Labour Conference delegates nearly unanimously voted to adopt Convention 189 on Decent Work for Domestic Workers. This landslide victory marked a turning point in the ILO. For the first time, the participation of workers themselves through the IDWN shaped ILO policy. The IDWN established a collective and powerful voice while contributing to the development of the convention, paving the way for involvement in future policy deliberations.

Through the ILO process, employment in private households formed the foundation for a global dialogue on domestic labour. South Africa also emerged as a pivotal national case of effective policy formation that solidified the interconnections among the private, national and global aspects of household care labour. This first international convention for domestic workers provides tangible measures to assess the impact of the coalition involving NGOs and allied organizations with domestic worker unions on domestic labour policies at the national and global levels. As these examples of collective activism suggest, policy formation and state transitions provide fertile spaces to integrate employment in private households into national and international dialogues that focused previously on public workplaces. As the Decent Work for Domestic Workers Convention is ratified, the next task will be to explore the extent to which global and national policies alter everyday relations in private households.

Discussion and Future Implications

Through an in-depth analysis of domestic labour in South Africa, this chapter explored a sector that presents tough obstacles to the full realization of gender rights. By examining the inclusion of domestic work within a broader gender rights initiative instituted as part of a newly democratic nation, South Africa demonstrates how social policies may bring the private sphere into public discourse. Domestic worker organizations became the conduit for publicizing the injustices often associated with employment in private households. In the post-apartheid state, the public forums and state consultations used to form the new democracy provided viable platforms to integrate the interests of domestic workers into the national project to ensure gender rights.

Domestic workers' agency at a collective level has been most evident in the case of the national union, SADSAWU. Since its 2000 launch, the organization played a pivotal role in the development of state policies on domestic labour. Notably, gender rights organizations took up the causes of domestic workers, advocating for the union motto, 'women won't be free until domestic workers are free'. The victory in the case of the unemployment insurance fund illustrates how the collective mobilization of South African organizations – particularly those with a vested history in the struggle to end apartheid – held the state accountable for protecting the rights of domestic workers.

Largely because of its national legislation about domestic workers' access to social security programmes and employment standards, South Africa played a central role in the deliberations about the world's first international convention on domestic work. The IDWN mirrored the process set in place with the GMAC-UIF, whereby domestic workers and allied organizations interjected critical voices into the deliberations. In the post-94 transition to democracy in South Africa, the structure-agency dialectic evident in domestic workers activism illustrates how civil society organizations monitored South Africa's emerging policies to ensure that they speak to the population's needs. In the current national and global contexts, the situations of domestic workers illustrate how social policies must be evaluated continuously to assure that they reflect women's everyday realities-particularly those of women whose lives are structured by the 'triple oppression' of race, class and gender inequalities (Cock 1989) and the systemic disadvantages of forced migration.

While this chapter has focused on effective policy intervention by unions and civil society organizations in South Africa, these examples must also be critiqued. From a theoretical perspective, the power relations embedded in the formation of state policies on domestic labour must be interrogated. Shireen Ally (2009) suggests that the state itself participated in the construction of women's 'vulnerability' via policies that served to marginalize and reify prevailing perceptions about women employed in private households. Ally contends that the national policies built on notions of domestic workers' 'vulnerability' as the 'poorest of the poor' in South African society reproduce a level of dependency developed under apartheid. As Ally's critique illustrates, the relationships between domestic workers and the state that undergird policy must be evaluated to look at the role these protections play in promoting particular notions of gender, the state's relation to women, and asymmetries of power embedded within the whole notion of policy *protections*.

Drawing from Ally's critique, the constructions of 'poor', 'vulnerable' and 'unprotected' women in the narratives of domestic worker leaders and affiliated organizations had an emotional appeal for government leaders by asking them to 'think of their mothers' when developing policies for 'poor and vulnerable domestic workers'. Ally's framework illustrates how emotional testimonials that 'put a human face' on domestic labour simultaneously reproduce unbalanced systems of power and privilege. They reinforce a dialectic of need and dependency between the 'most vulnerable' (women) and the (male) state protector. This analytic framework interrogates the process of policy formation, as well as its intended function within a wider context of unequal social and political power relations.

From an applied perspective, analysis of the relationships between policy and social realities in South Africa reveals several contradictions. Social inequalities due to power asymmetries among women, forced migration, and the perpetuation of racialized female servitude present pervasive barriers to domestic workers' efforts to organize. At the level of organizations, women have collaborated to ensure that domestic labour is a central gender rights concern, however, in the private household, the persistent relations of inequality between 'maids and madams' challenge this solidarity. As Britton (2005) asserts, the private sphere remains the most serious obstacle to realizing the public victories of democracy. The private nature of domestic labour affords those with power an opportunity to 'police' the extent to which the public discourse of gender rights infiltrates the private sphere, where social relations continue to be structured by a long history of servitude. In private households, employers retain enough social power to maintain systems of power and dominance.

Critics often dispute the effectiveness of social policies on domestic labour in South Africa because of incomplete compliance, monitoring, and implementation. Although South Africa's national policies for domestic workers are models for international standards, unfortunately, few households actually comply with them. Work contracts, registration of domestic workers in the UIF, and minimum wages are not standard practice. For the past 10 years, domestic workers and employers have repeatedly assessed South Africa's domestic labour policies as 'only on paper'. As one domestic worker shared, 'We've got *lovely* policies in this country, but in my work, they mean nothing'. The widely recognized gap between policy and practice suggests that implementation remains the greatest barrier to realizing the democratization of household labour in South Africa. Even though domestic work is one of the largest sources of employment for women, aligning everyday practices with state policies remains central to ensuring rights are in place.

The acceptability of noncompliance with domestic labour policies in South Africa reflects a wider disjuncture between governance and popular perceptions about the effectiveness of labour policies in realizing the centrality of human rights to democracy. Wavering confidence in South Africa's national government in the second decade of democracy contributes to the high levels of passivity in implementing its policies, particularly in the private home where notions of individual power and autonomy prevail. Since the 2001 GMAC-UIF campaign, I noticed that the conditions of domestic labour have at times been used to measure South Africa's gender progress. As one union leader noted, 'Women's rights mean little for this country unless domestic workers' lives improve'. This observation illustrates notions of interactive mutuality. What happens at the level of the state impacts the community and household, sometimes through resistance rather than compliance.

The South African case is therefore a complex example of three interconnected elements: 1) the establishment of a comprehensive policy on domestic work as a central component of a national gender rights agenda in the emergent democratic state; 2) the continuing challenges of assuring compliance with domestic labour policy; and 3) the impact of partnerships between civil society organizations and domestic worker unions on reconciling the divide between public governance and private households.

I suggest that South Africa's domestic work policies must be evaluated as part of a longer-term national transition. Over the past 10 years, the development of policies on care labour in the private household has placed representatives from civil society organizations and domestic worker unions within government structures and deliberations. The example offers a formative model, which has since been reproduced within the international policy arena during deliberations at the ILO. Furthermore, domestic workers and national governments are not monolithic entities. Social actors play pivotal roles as representatives of these systems, as we see in the case of Myrtle Witbooi's prominence as both the General Secretary of SADSAWU and the President of the IDWN. Government systems in South Africa are complicated by the limited availability of resources for implementation procedures, the challenges of aligning initiatives in one economic sector across national structures of governance, and competing political agendas. Given these factors, I contend that the South African case continues to serve as a model because of the national attention it focuses on domestic and care labour policies and the policy-making processes within the newly democratic state that allow for the legitimate, active and continued participation of domestic workers in civil society.

Taking all of these factors into consideration, statements from South Africa from within the International Labour Conference deliberations on domestic work identified two central tenets of the national framework that are applicable internationally. First, South Africa repeatedly stated that domestic work must not be viewed as an 'adjunct' to the workforce. The role of paid household labour in the reproduction of the global economy emerged as a pivotal point, reinforced by the centrality of domestic work in the South African economy. Second, Myrtle Witbooi claimed that through the realization of protective labour policies in South Africa, 'domestic workers became workers', eligible for the same protections as workers in any other sector. In her closing statement at the Domestic Work Convention in 2011, Witbooi asserted that in South Africa, 'We are committed to establishing laws that assure that domestic workers have the *same rights as all other workers*. With these laws in place, we are able to give our best to our employers, as we claim our basic human rights' (Witbooi 2011). This statement, backed by the South African government submissions, simultaneously reinforced the mandate to move away from 'special categories of workers' and recognize the role that care labour plays in domestic as well as international economies.

Within the ILO deliberations, the South African government interjected one of the few government statements on the importance of assuring an international policy that would be meaningful for domestic workers. As the national government spokesperson stated, 'This seminal event for the ILO must be as significant for domestic workers'. Pointing to the danger of implementing rhetoric without feasible application, the South African government called for an international document that would 'go beyond just using gender sensitive language and make a real difference for domestic workers' (Seafield 2011). In this statement, the South African government recognized its own need to assure the alignment of policy and practice, while advocating for international standards that could create meaningful changes in the daily work lives of domestic workers. Myrtle Witbooi called on her government to move beyond implementation of policy at the national level to influence the global adoption of international standards for domestic workers. As she appealed at the 2010 plenary session, 'So, if South Africa can do it, I am sure the world can follow and our appeal is to our government to assist us in convincing other governments that to grant domestic workers a convention with strong recommendations will only lead to better working conditions for all' (Witbooi 2010).

With the adoption of Convention 189 in June, 2011, Manuela Tomei, ILO representative for the Decent Work for Domestic Workers agenda item stated that 'this is just the beginning of a longer battle' (Fish 2012). Now that governments and international institutions are beginning to recognize the value of domestic work, their involvement in the care labour chain should shift from policy protections alone to the provision of public resources to subsidize this critical contribution to the reproduction of societies. As these policies are implemented, the established strengths of civil society organizations will facilitate this shift from protection to social investment in care labour.

Bibliography

Abramovitz, M., 1996 [1983]. *Regulating the Lives of Women: The Social Functions of Public Welfare.* Revised ed. Boston: South End Press.

ACAS, 2009. *Report of an Inquiry into the circumstances surrounding the Lindsey Oil Refinery Dispute*, s.l.: s.n.

Advisory Committee on Health Human Resources, Health Canada, 2002. *Our Health, Our Future: Creating Quality Workplaces for Canadian Nurses.* [Online] Available at: http://www.hc-sc.gc.ca.

Ahearn, L.M., 2001. Language and agency. *Annual Review of Anthropology*, 30, 109–137.

Albin, E. and Mantouvalou, V., 2012. The ILO Convention on Domestic Workers: From the shadows to the light. *Industrial Law Journal*, 41(1), 67–78.

Alexander, M.J. and Mohanty, C.T., 1996. *Feminist Genealogies, Colonial Legacies, Democratic Futures.* New York: Routledge.

Alfers, L., 2011. *Occupational Health and Safety & Domestic Work, A synthesis of research findings from Brazil and Tanzania (WIEGO Social Protection Program, Women in Informal Employment Globalizing and Organizing).* [Online] Available at: http://wiego.org/sites/wiego.org/files/resources/files/OHS_DW_Eng_2012.pdf [Accessed 6 June 2013].

Allam, R., 2001. *Real Life Monster?* Cairo: Al-Ahram Weekly, 8–14 November 2001, Issue No. 559.

Ally, S., 2009. *From Servants to Workers: South African Domestic Workers and the Democratic State.* Cornell: Cornell University Press.

Amnesty International, 2008. *Egypt continues to deport Eritrean asylum-seekers.* [Online] Available at: http://www.amnesty.org/en/news-and-updates/news/egypt-must-stop-flights-to-torture-in-eritrea-20080613 [Accessed 23 January 2009].

Anderson, B., 1993. *Britain's Secret Slaves: Investigation into the Plight of Overseas Domestic Workers in the United Kingdom.* London: Anti-Slavery International.

Anderson, B., 1997. Servants and slaves: Europe's domestic workers. *Race and Class*, 39(1), 37–49.

Anderson, B., 2000. *Doing the Dirty Work? The Global Politics of Domestic Work.* London: Zed Books.

Anderson, B., 2001. Just another job? Paying for domestic work. *Gender and Development*, 9(1), 25–33.

Anderson, B., 2006. *A very private business: Migration and domestic work.* [Online] Available at: http://www.compax.ox.ac.uk\aboout\publications/wp-06-28.shtml [Accessed 23 February 2010].

Anderson, B., 2007. A very private business: Exploring the demand for migrant workers. *European Journal of Women's Studies*, 14(3), 247–264.

Anderson, B., 2010. Mobilising migrants making citizens: Migrant domestic workers as political agents. *Ethnic and Racial Studies*, 33(1), 60–74.

Anderson, B., 2013. *Us and Them? The Dangerous Politics of Immigration Control.* Oxford: Oxford University Press.

Anderson, B. and Ruhs, M., 2010. *A Need for Migrant Labour?* Oxford: Oxford University Press.

Anderson, B., Ruhs, M., Rogaly, B. and Spencer, S., 2006. *Fair Enough? Central and East European Migrants in Low-Wage Employment in the UK.* London: Joseph Rowntree Foundation.

Anti-Slavery International, 2006. *Trafficking in Women Forced Labour and Domestic Work in the Context of the Middle East and Gulf Region, Working Paper, German Federal Ministry for Economic Cooperation and Development.* [Online] Available at: http://www.antislavery.org/includes/documents/cm_docs/2009/t/traffic_women_forced_labour_domestic_2006.pdf [Accessed 8 July 2013].

Antonpoulos, R., 2008. *The Unpaid Care Work-Paid Work Connection (Working Paper No. 541)*, New York: The Levy Economics Institute of Bard College.

Arat-Koç, S. and INTERCEDE, 2001. *Caregivers Break the Silence: A Participatory Action Research on the Abuse and Violence, Including the Impact of Family Separation Experienced by Women in the Live-in Caregiver Program.* Toronto: INTERCEDE.

Armenta, A., 2009. Creating community: Latina nannies in a West Los Angeles Park. *Qualitative Sociology*, 32(3), 279–292.

Armstrong, P., 1994. Caring and womens work. *Health and Canadian Society*, 2(1), 109–118.

Armstrong, P., Amaratunga, C. and Bernier, J., 2001. *Exposing Privatization. Women and Health Care Reform.* Toronto: Garamond.

Armstrong, P. and Armstrong, H., 1996. *Wasting Away: The Undermining of Canadian Health Care.* Toronto: Oxford University Press.

Aronson, J. and Neysmith, M., 2001. Manufacturing social exclusion in the home care market. *Canadian Public Policy*, 27(2), 151–165.

Aronson, J. and Neysmith, S., 1996. You're not just in there to do the work: Depersonalizing policies and the exploitation of home care workers labor. *Gender and Society*, 10(1), 59–77.

ASTAT-Ufficio Statistico Provincia Autonoma di Bolzano, 2012. *Popolazione Straniera residente nel 2011.* [Online] Available at: http://www.provinz.bz.it/astat/de/bevoelkerung/487.asp?Auslaender_action=300&Auslaender_image_id=248608 [Accessed 23 March 2013].

Augé, M., 1992. *Non-lieux: Introduction à un anthropologie de la surmodernité.* Paris: Éditions du Seuil.

Babin, A., 2006. *Domestic Workers.* Geneva: International Labour Organization.

Bakan, A. and Stasiulis, D., 1995. Making the match: Domestic placement agencies and the racialization of women's household work. *Signs*, 29(2), 303–335.

Bakan, A. and Stasiulis, D., eds., 1997. *Not One of the Family: Foreign Domestic Workers in Canada.* Toronto: University of Toronto Press.

Bakker, I., 2007. Social reproduction and the constitution of a gendered political economy. *New Political Economy*, 12(4), 541–556.

Baldassar, L., Wilding, R. and Baldock, C. 2007. *Families Caring Across Borders: Migration, Ageing and Transnational Caregiving.* Houndmills, UK and New York: Palgrave Macmillan.

Baldwin-Edwards, M., 2005. *Migration in the Middle East and Mediterranean (Policy Analysis and Research Programme of the Global Comission on International Migration).* [Online] Available at: http://www.gcim.org [Accessed 8 April 2012].

Balibar, E., 2004. *We the People of Europe?* Princeton: Princeton University Press.

Bannarjee, S., 2004. *Men, Women, and Domestics: Articulating Middle-class Identity in Colonial Bengal.* New York: Oxford University Press.

Barber, P. Gardiner, 1995. Invisible labour, transnational lives: Gendered work and new social fields in Coastal Philippines. *Culture*, 37(2), 181–194.

Barber, P. Gardiner, 2008a. Cell phones, complicity and class politics in the Philippine labour diaspora. *Focaal: European Journal of Anthropology*, 51, 28–42.

Barber, P. Gardiner, 2008b. The ideal immigrant? Gendered class subjects in Philippine-Canada migration. *Third World Quarterly*, 29(7), 1265–1285.

Barber, P. Gardiner, 2010. Women's work unbound: Philippine development and global restructuring, in *Gender and Global Restructuring Sightings, Sites and Resistances, 2nd Edition*, edited by M. Marchand and A. Sisson Runyan,. London and New York: Routledge, 143–162.

Bardsley, F., 2008. *Aunt Ordered Out of UK.* s.l.: Oxford Mail, 10 December.

Bar-Giora, M., 2007. *Service for the Elderly in Israel.* Jerusalem: The Department of International Relations, Ministry of Social Affairs.

Barnes, A., 1993. White mistresses and African-American domestic workers: Ideals for change. *Anthropological Quarterly*, 66(1), 22–36.

Benería, L., 2008. The crisis of care, international migration, and public policy. *Feminist Economics*, 14(3), 1–21.

Berlant, L., 1997. *The Queen of America Goes to Washington City: Essays on Sex and Citizenship.* Durham: Duke University Press.

Berlant, L., 2008. *The Female Complaint: The Unfinished Business of Sentimentality in American Culture.* Durham: Duke University Press.

Berlant, L., 2011. *Cruel Optimism.* Durham: Duke University Press.

Bernèche, F. et al., 2002. *Ville de Montréal et synthèse des arrondissements: Portrait des populations immingrante et non immigrante. Projet du Centre*

Interuniversitaire Immigration et métropoles. [Online] Available at: http://www2.ville.montreal.qc.ca/diversite/portrait.htm.

Bilge, S., 2008. Between gender and cultural equality, in *Recasting the Social in Citizenship*, edited by E. Isin. Toronto: University of Toronto Press, 100–133.

Bilge, S., 2010. Beyond subordination vs. resistance: An intersectional approach to the agency of veiled Muslim women. *Journal of Intercultural Studies*, 31(1), 9–28.

Binford, L., 2003. Migrant remittances and (under)development in Mexico. *Critique of Anthropology*, 23(3), 305–336.

Blackett, E., ed., 2011. Regulating decent work for domestic workers [Special Issue]. *Canadian Journal of Women and the Law*, 23(1), 1–46.

Blair, S. L. and Lichter, D.T., 1991. Measuring the divisions of household labor: Gender segregation of housework among American couples. *Family Issues*, 12(1), 91–113.

Blau, F. and Ehrenberg, R., 1997. *Gender and Family Issues in the Workplace.* New York: Russell Sage Foundation.

Bledstein, B., 2001. Introduction: Storytellers to the middle class, in *Middling Sorts: Explorations in the History of the American Middle Class*, edited by B. Bledstein and R. Johnston. New York: Routledge, 1–25.

Blofield, M., 2012. *Care Work and Class: Domestic Workers' Struggle for Equal Rights in Latin America.* University Park: Pennsylvania State University Press.

Boddington, E., 1983. *Domestic Service: Changing Relations of Class Domination 1841–1948.* Cape Town: Social Science, University of Cape Town.

Boddington, E., 1984. *Domestic Service in Cape Town 1891–1946: An Analysis of Census Reports.* Bellville, South Africa: University of the Western Cape.

Boileau, J., 2002. Les oubliés du 1er mai: 8000 salariées de l'Etat presque sans droits. *Le Devoir*, 1 May, 1–10.

Bonner, C., 2010. *Domestic Workers Around the World: Organising for Employment [Online WIEGO].* [Online] Available at: http://www.dwrp.org.za/images/stories/DWRP_Research/chris_bonner.pdf [Accessed 23 May 2013].

Bordogna, P.F. and Tognetti, M., eds., 2012. *Welfare transnazionale. La frontiera esterna delle politiche sociali.* Ediesse: Roma.

Boris, E. and Klein, J., 2008. Labor on the home front: Unionizing home-based care workers. *New Labor Forum*, 17(2), 32–41.

Boris, E. and Klein, J., 2012. *Caring for America: Home Health Workers in the Shadow of the Welfare State.* New York: Oxford University Press.

Brace, L., 2004. *The Politics of Property: Labour, Freedom and Belonging.* Edinburgh: Edinburgh University Press.

Branovsky, Y., 2009. Holocaust survivors say foreign children's deportation painful reminder. *Ynetnews.com*, 14 October.

Britton, H., 2005. *From Resistance to Governance: Women in South African Parliament.* Urbana: University of Illinois Press.

Brodkin, K., 1998. *How Jews Became White Folks and What That Says About Race in America.* New Brunswick, NJ: Rutgers University Press.

Brown, K. and Reynolds, A., 1994. New laws for domestic workers. *Agenda*, 76–80.

Brown, M.K. et al., 2003. *White-Washing Race: The Myth of a Color Blind Society.* Berkeley: University of California Press.

Brown, T.M., 2011. *Raising Brooklyn: Nannies, Childcare, and Caribbeans Creating Community.* New York: New York University Press.

Budlender, D., 1986. *Domestic Workers.* Cape Town: Community Agency for Social Enquiry.

Burawoy, M., 1991. Reconstructing social theories, in *Ethnography Unbound: Power and Resistance in the Modern Metropolis*, edited by M. Burawoy. Berkeley: University of California Press, 8–27.

Búriková, Z., 2006. The embarrassment of co-presence: Au pairs and their rooms. *Home Cultures*, 3(2), 99–122.

Busby, N., 2011. *A Right to Care? Unpaid Care Work in European Employment Law.* Oxford: Oxford University Press.

Butler, J., 1997. *The Psychic Life of Power: Theories of Subjection.* Stanford: Stanford University Press.

C189: Conventional Wisdom. 2012. [Film] Directed by J. N. Fish, R. Crockett, R. Ormiston. Norfolk: Sisi Sojourner Productions.

Cabinet Office, 2007. *Security in a Global Hub: Establishing the UK's New Border Arrangements.* London: HMSO.

CACC (Canadian Association For Community Care), 1995. *Health Promotion and the Home Support Worker.* Ottawa: CACC.

Caillé, A., 2000. *Anthropologie du don: Le tiers paradigme.* Paris: Desclée de Brouwer.

CAMO (Comité de Ladaptation de la Main D'Œuvre), 2001. *Profil des travailleurs salariés immigrants et membres des communautés culturelles (Québec, Région Métropolitain de Récensement de Montréal et le Communauté urbaine de Montréal).* [Online] Available at: http://www.camo-pi.qc.ca.

Cancian, F.M. and Olikder, S.J., 1999. *Caring and Gender.* London: Sage.

Caponio, T., 2008. (Im)migration research in Italy. An European comparative perspective. *The Sociological Quarterly*, 49(3), 445–464.

Caponio, T., 2009. *Multiculturalism from Below: Italian Cities Compared.* [Online] Available at: www.unescochair-iuav.it [Accessed 01 April 2010].

Caponio, T., Nielsen, A. and Mateos, N.R., 2000. The policy mirror mechanism: The case of Turin. *Papers: Revista de Sociología*, 60, 67–83.

Castagnone, E., Eve, M., Petrillo, E. and Piperno, F., 2007. *Madri Migrant. Le migrazioni di cura dalla Romania e dall'Ucraina in Italia: percorsi ed impatto sui paesi di origine, [Migrant Mothers. The care migration from Romania and Ukraina to Italy: trajectories and impacts on the countries of origin].* Roma: CESPI.

Castel, R., 1995. *Métamorphoses de la question sociale: Une chronique du salariat.* Paris: Fayard.

Castles, S. and Miller, M., 1998. *The Age of Migration.* Basingstoke: Macmillan.

Cellier, I., 1995. Le bénévolat à travers la littérature. Un objet détude à redéfinir. *Anthropologie et sociétés,* 19(1–2), 175–190.

Central Bureau of Statistics, 2009. Tel Aviv: The State of Isreal.

Chaney, E.M. and Garcia Castro, M., eds, 1989. *Muchachas No More, Household Workers in Latin American and the Caribbean.* Philadelphia: Temple University Press.

Chang, G., 2000. *Disposable Domestics: Immigrant Women Workers in the Global Economy.* Cambridge: South End Press.

Chang, K.A. and Ling, L., 2000. Globalization and its intimate other, Filipina domestic workers in Hong Kong, in *Gender and Global Restructuring, Sightings, Sites and Resistances*, edited by M. Marchand and A. Sisson Runyan. New York: Routledge, 27–43.

Chaplin, D., 1978. Domestic service and industrialization. *Comparative Studies in Sociology*, 1, 97–127.

Chell-Robinson, V., 2000. Female migrants in Italy: Coping in a country of new immigration, in *Gender and Migration in Southern Europe: Women on the Move*, edited by G. Lazaridis and F. Anthias. Oxford: Berg, 103–123.

Cheng, S.A., 2003. Rethinking the globalization of domestic service: Foreign domestics, state control and the politics of identity in Taiwan. *Gender and Society*, 17(2), 166–186.

Chin, C.B.N., 1998. *In Service and Servitude: Foreign Female Domestic Workers and the Malaysian 'Modernity' Project.* New York: Columbia University Press.

Chock, P.P., 1994. Remaking and unmaking 'citizen' in policy-making talk about immigration. *PoLAR*, 17(2), 45–46.

Choy, C.C., 2003. *Empire of Care: Nursing and Migration in Filipino American History.* Quezon City: Ateneo de Manila University Press.

Clarke, D., 1974. *Domestic Workers in Rhodesia: The Economics of Masters and Servants.* Gwelo: Mambo Press.

Cobble, D., 1991. Organizing the post-industrial workforce: Lessons from the history of waitress unionism. *Industrial and Labor Relations Review*, 44(3), 419–436.

Cock, J., 1980. *Maids & Madams: A Study in the Politics of Exploitation.* Johannesburg: Raven Press.

Cock, J., 1988. Trapped workers: The case of domestic servants in South Africa, in *Patriarchy and Class: African Women in the Home and the Workforce*, edited by J. Parpart and S. Stichter. Boulder and London: Westview Press, 205–219.

Cock, J., 1989. *Maids & Madams: Domestic Workers under Apartheid.* London: The Women's Press Limited.

Cock, J., 1990. Guilt, fear and other difficulties in researching domestic relations, in *Truth be in the Field*, edited by P. Hugo. Pretoria: University of South Africa.

Cock, J., 1993. *Women and War in South Africa.* Cleveland: The Pilgrim Press.

Coe, C., 2008. The structuring of feeling in Ghanaian transnational families. *City and Society*, 20(2), 222–250.

Cognet, M., 2002. Les femmes, les services et le don. *Cahiers de recherche sociologique, Université du Québec à Montréal*, 37, 51–77.

Cognet, M., 2003. Politiques d'immigration canadiennes et femmes d'ailleurs dans les emplois dans le secteur des soins et des services à domicile, in *Transformations sociales, Genre et santé. Perspectives critiques et comparatives*, edited by F. Saillant and M. Boulianne. Sainte-Foy, Québec: Presses de l'Université Laval and l'Harmattan, 183–205.

Cognet, M. and Fortin, S., 2003. Le poids du genre et de l'ethnicité dans la division du travail en santé. *Lien social et politiques*, 49, 155–172.

Cognet, M. and Raigneau, L., 2002. Le genre et l'ethnicité: les critères voilés de la délégation des actes en santé. *Cahiers du Groupe de Recherche Ethnicité et Société, Centre d'études éthniques des universités montréalaises, Université de Montréal*, 3(1), 25–38.

Cole, J. and Booth, S., 2006. Domestic work, family life, and immigration in Sicily. *Journal of Modern Italian Studies*, 11(1), 22–36.

Colen, S., 1995. 'Like a mother to them': Stratified reproduction and West Indian childcare workers and employers in New York, in *Conceiving the New World Order: The Global Politics of Reproduction*, edited by F.D. Ginsburg and R. Rapp. Berkeley and Los Angeles: University of California Press, 78–102.

Collins, P.H., 1990. *Black Feminist Thought: Knowledge, Consciousness and the Politics of Empowerment.* New York and London: Routledge.

Collins, P.H., 1991. Learning from the outsider within, in *Beyond Methodology: Feminist Scholarship as Lived Research*, edited by M.M. Fonow and J.A. Cook. Bloomington: Indiana University Press, 35–59.

Colombo, A., 2007. 'They call me a housekeeper, but I do everything'. Who are domestic workers in Italy and what do they do? *Journal of Modern Italian Studies*, 12(2), 207–237.

Colombo, A., 2009. *La sanatoria per le badanti e le colf del 2009: fallimento o esaurimento di un modello?* [Online] Available at: www.fieri.it [Accessed 29 November 2009].

Colombo, A. and Sciortino, G., 2004. Italian immigration: The origins, nature and evolution of Italy's migratory system. *Journal of Modern Italian Studies*, 9(1), 49–70.

Coltrane, S. and Galt, J., 2000. The history of men's caring evaluating precedents for fathers' family involvement, in *Care Work: Gender, Labor, and the Welfare State*, edited by M. Harrington Meyer. New York: Routledge, 15–36.

Commission on Gender Equality, 2001. Cape Town, South Africa: Commission on Gender Equality.

COMPAS (Centre on Migration, Policy and Society), 2006. *Changing status, Changing lives? The socio-economic impact of EU Enlargment on low-wage migrant workers in the UK.* Oxford: University of Oxford.

Congress of South African Trade Unions, 1997. *September Commission Report.* Johannesburg, South Africa: COSATU.

Constable, N., 2002. Filipina workers in Hong Kong homes: Household rules and relations, in *Global Woman: Nannies, Maids, and Sex Workers in the New Economy*, edited by B. Ehrenreich and A. Hochschild. New York: Henry Holt and Company, 115–141.

Constable, N., 2007. *Maid to Order in Hong Kong: Stories of Migrant Workers.* New York: Cornell University Press.

Contandriopoulous, A.P., Denis, J.-L. and Dubois, C.-A., 2000. *La place et le rôle du secteur privé dans la transformation du système de soins.* Montréal: Conseil de la santé et bien-être, Groupe de recherche interdisciplinaire en santé (GRIS), Université de Montréal.

Cooper, S., 2004. From family member to employee: Aspects of continuity and discontinuity in English domestic service 1600–2000, in *Domestic Service and the formation of Euorpean Idenity: Understanding the Globalization of Domestic Work, 16th–21st Centuries*, edited by A. Fauve. Bern: Peter Lang, 277–296.

Cornelius, W., 1989. The U.S. demand for Mexican labor, in *Mexican Migration to the United States: Origins, Consequences, and Policy Options*, edited by W. Cornelius and J. Bustamante. San Diego, CA: Center for U.S.-Mexican Studies, 25–48.

Coser, L., 1973. Servants: The obsolescence of an occupational social role. *Social Forces*, 52(1), 31–40.

Coutin, S., 2000. *Legalizing Moves: Salvadoran Immigrants' Struggle for U.S. Residency.* Ann Arbor: University of Michigan Press.

Cox, R., 2006. *The Servant Problem: Domestic Employment in a Global.* London: I.B. Tauris.

Cranford, C., 2005. From precarious workers to unionized employees and back again? The challenges of organizing personal careworkers in Toronto, in *Self-Employment Workers Organize: Law, Policy and Unions*, edited by J. Fudge, C. Cranford, E. Tucker and L. Vosko. Montreal and Kingston: McGill-Queens University Press, 96–135.

Cranford, C., Das Gupta, T., Ladd, D. and Vosko, L., 2006. Thinking through community unionism, in *Precarious Employment: Understanding Labour Market Insecurity in Canada*, edited by L. Vosko. Montreal and Kingston: McGill-Queens University Press, 353–377.

Cranford, C., Fudge, J., Tucker, E. and Vosko, L., eds, 2005. *Self-Employed Workers Organize: Law, Policy, and Unions.* Montreal and Kingston: McGill-Queens University Press.

de Filippo, E. and Pugliese, E., 2000. Le Donne nell'Immigrazione in Campania [Immigration's Women in Campania]. *Papers: Revista de Sociología*, 60, 55–66.

De Genova, N., 2002. Migrant 'illegality' and deportability in everyday. *Annual Review of Anthropology*, 31, 419–447.

De Genova, N., 2005. *Working the Boundaries: Race, Space, and 'Illegality' in Mexican Chicago.* Durham: Duke University Press.

de Jesus, M.L., 2005. *Pinay Power: Peminist Critical Theory.* New York: Routledge.

de la Luz Ibarra, M., 2002. Emotional proletarians in a global economy: Mexican immigrant women and elder care work. *Urban Anthropology and Studies of Cultural Systems and World Economic Development*, 31(3–4), 317–334.

de la Luz Ibarra, M., 2003. The tender trap: Mexican immigrant women and the ethics of elder care work. *Aztlan*, 28(2), 87–113.

de Melo, P., 1989. Feminists and domestic workers in Rio de Janerio, in *Muchachas No More: Household Workers in Latin America and the Caribbean*, edited by E. Chaney and M. Garcia Castro. Philadelphia: Temple University Press, 245–267.

De Nesi, D., 2013. *Italia ratifica Convenzione ILO lavoro dignitoso lavoratori domestici.* [Online] Available at: http://www.quotidianosicurezza.it/normativa/leggi/ratifica-convenzione-lavoratori-domestici.htm [Accessed 24 January 2013].

Degiuli, F., 2007. A job with no boundaries. Home eldercare work in Italy. *European Journal of Women's Studies*, 14(3), 193–207.

Delp, L. and Quan, K., 2002. Homecare worker organizing in California: An analysis of a successful strategy. *Labor Studies Journal*, 27(1), 1–23.

Delport, E., 1992. The legal position of domestic workers: A comparative perspective. *Comparative and International Law of Southern Africa*, 25, 181–201.

Department of Labor, South Africa, 2001. *Towards Determining Minimum Wages and Conditions of Employment for Domestic Workers*. Pretoria: Department of Labor.

Department of Labour, 1991. *Manpower Commission Report on Domestic Workers.* Pretoria, South Africa: Department of Labour, South Africa.

Department of Labour, 1993. *Limbrick Report.* Pretoria, South Africa: Department of Labour, South Africa.

Department of Labour, 1996. *Task Team Report on Domestic Workers and the UIF.* Pretoria, South Africa: Department of Labour, South Africa.

Derfner, L., 2002. They serve, suffer and still root for us. *Jerusalem Post Online*, 11 July.

Devine, F., 2004. *Class Practices: How Parents Help Their Children Get Good Jobs.* Cambridge: Cambridge University Press.

Devine, F., 2005. Middle class identities in the US, in *Rethinking Class: Cultures, Identities, and Lifestyles*, edited by F. Devine, M. Savage, J. Scott and R. Crompton. New York: Palgrave, 140–162.

Dill, B.T., 1988. Making your job good yourself: Domestic service and the construction of personal dignity, in *Women and the Politics of Empowerment*, edited by A. Bookman and S. Morgen. Philadelphia: Temple University Press, 33–52.

Divisione Servizi Civili, Ufficio di Statistica – Osservatorio Socio-economico e redazione editoriale, n.d. *Stranieri residenti a Torino.* [Online] Available at: www.comune.torino.it [Accessed 13 April 2013].

Doane, A.W. and Eduardo Bonilla-Silva, E., eds., 2003. *White Out: The Continuing Significance of Racism.* New York: Routledge.

Domestic Workers United, 2006. *Home is Where the Work Is: Inside New York's Domestic Work Industry.* [Online] Available at: http://www.datacenter.org/reports/homeiswheretheworkis.pdf [Accessed 26 October 2012].

Drori, I., 2009. *Foreign Workers in Israel, Global Perspectives.* New York: SUNY Press.

Efrat, A., 2006. *Economy of Compassion: The basic principles of employing migrant women for home-care services in Israel, during the years 2000–2004.* Master's Thesis. Tel Aviv: Tel Aviv University.

Ehrenreich, B., 1989. *Fear of Falling: The Inner Life of the Middle-Class.* New York: Pantheon Books.

Ehrenreich, B. and Russell Hochschild, A., eds., 2002. *Global Women: Nannies, Maids and Sex Workers in the New Economy.* London: Granta Books.

Elkin, F. and Handel, G., 1984. *The Child and Society, The Process of Socialization.* New York: Random House.

Elvir, M., 1997. The work at home is not recognized: Organizing domestic workers in Montreal, in *Not One of the Family: Foreign Domestic Workers in Canada*, edited by A. Bakan and D. Stasiulis. Toronto: University of Toronto Press, 147–156.

England, P., 2005. Emerging theories of care work. *Annual Review of Sociology*, 31, 381–399.

Enloe, C., 1989. *Bananas, Beaches and Bases: Making Feminist Sense of International Politics.* Berkeley: University of California Press.

Esping-Andersen, G., 1990. *The Three Worlds of Welfare Capitalism.* Cambridge: Princeton University Press.

Esping-Andersen, G., 1999. *The Social Foundations of Postindustrial Economies.* Oxford: Oxford University Press.

Essed, P., Frerks, G. and Schrijvers, J., eds., 2004. *Refugees and Transformation of Societies: Agency, Policies, Ethics and Politics.* New York: Berghahn Books.

Estey, K., 2011. Domestic workers and cooperatives: Beyond care goes beyond capitalism, A case study in Brooklyn, New York. *Working USA: The Journal of Labor and Society*, 14(3), 347–365.

Estrin, E., 2009. Efforts to stop deportation of illegal workers' kids. *Jerusalem Post Online*, 30 July.

Fargues, P., 2007. *'Introduction' in Mediterranean Migration 2006–2007 Report*, San Domenico di Fiesole: Robert Schuman Center for Advanced Studies, European University Institute.

Farsakh, L., 2005. *Palestinian Labor Migration to Israel, Labour Land and Occupation.* New York: Routledge.

Feder Kittay, E., 1999. *Love's Labor: Essays on Women, Equality, and Dependency.* New York and London: Routledge.

Federici, S., 2004. *Caliban and the Witch: Women, the Body and Primitive Accumulation.* New York: Autonomedia.

Ferrera, M., 1996. The Southern Model of welfare in social Europe. *Journal of European Social Policy*, 6(1), 17–37.

Filc, D., 2004. Post-Fordism's contradictory trends: The case of the Israeli health care system. *Journal of Social Policy*, 33(3), 417–436.

Filc, D., 2005. The health business under neo-liberalism: The Israeli case. *Critical Social Policy*, 25(2), 180–197.

Fine, J., 1998. Moving innovation from the margins to the centre, in *A New Labor Movement for a New Century*, edited by G. Mantois. New York: Monthly Review Press, 139–170.

Fischer, C.S., 2010. *Made in America: A Social History of American Culture and Character.* Chicago: University of Chicago Press.

Fish, J.N., 2006. *Domestic Democracy: At Home in South Africa.* New York: Routledge.

Flint, S., 1988. The protection of domestic workers in South Africa: A comparative study. *Industrial Law Journal*, 9, 1–15.

Fouron, G. and Glick Schiller, N., 2001. All in the family: Gender, transnational migration, and the nation-state. *Identities: Global Studies in Culture and Power*, 7, 539–582.

Frankenberg, R., 1991. *White Women, Race Matters: The Social Construction of Whiteness.* Minneapolis: University of Minnesota Press.

Frankenberg, R., 2001. The mirage of an unmarked whiteness, in *Making and Unmaking of Whiteness*, edited by B.B. Rasmussen, E. Klinenberg, I.J. Nexica and M. Wray. Durham: Duke University Press, 72–96.

Freedman, M., 2005. Migrant workers: License to exploit. *Challenge: A Magazine Covering the Israeli-Palestinian Conflict*, May/June, Issue 91.

Friedman, R., 2009. Yishai: We are not an asylum state. *Jerusalem Post Online*, 15 October.

Friedmann-Sanchez, G. and Griffin, J.M., 2011. Defining the boundaries between unpaid labor and caregiving: Review of the social and health sciences literature. *Journal of Human Development and Capabilities*, 12(4), 211–234.

Friesen, J., 2011. *The Philippines now Canada's top source country for immigrants – Globe and Mail.* [Online] Available at: http://www.theglobeandmail.com/news/national/the-philippines-now-canadas-top-source-of-immigrants/article573133/> [Accessed 18 March 2011].

Frye Jacobson, M., 1998. *Whiteness of a Different Color: European Immigrants and the Alchemy of Race.* Cambridge: Harvard University Press.

Fudge, J., 1997. Little victories and big defeats: The rise and fall of collective bargaining rights for domestic workers in Ontario, in *Not One of the Family: Foreign Domestic Workers in Canada*, edited by A. Bakan and D. Stasiulis. Toronto: University of Toronto Press, 119–146.

Fudge, J., 2005. Deemed to be entreprenuers: Rural router mail couriers and Canada post, in *Self-Employed Workers' Organize: Law, Policy and Union*, edited by C. Cranford, J. Fudge, E. Tucker and L. Vosko. Montreal and Kingston: McGill-Queens University Press, 56–95.

Fudge, J., 2011a. Gender, equality and capabilities, in *The Role of Labour Standards in Sustainable Development: Theory in Practice*, edited by T. Novitz and D. Managan. London: Oxford University Press and The British Academy.

Fudge, J., 2011b. Global care chains, employment agencies and the conundrum of jurisdiction: decent work for domestic workers in Canada. *Canadian Journal of Women and The Law*, 23(1), 235–264.

Fudge, J. and MacPhail, F., 2009. The Temporary Foreign Worker Program in Canada: Low-skilled workers as an extreme form of flexible labour. *Comparative Labour Law and Policy Journal*, 31(1), 5–46.

Gaitskell, D., Kimble, J., Maconachie, M. and Unterhalter, E., 1984. Class, race and gender: Domestic workers in South Africa. *Review of African Political Economy*, 27, 86–108.

Gallotti, M., 2009. *The Gender Dimension of Domestic Work in Western Europe (International Labour Office, Geneva).* [Online] Available at: http://www.ilo.org/wcmsp5/groups/public/ed_protect/protrav/migrant/documents/publication/wcms_178149.pdf [Accessed 10 May 2013].

Gamburd, M.G., 2000. *The Kitchen Spoon's Handle: Transnationalism and Sri Lanka's Migrant Housemaids.* London: Cornell University Press.

Giddens, A., 1984. *The Constitution of Society: An Outline of the Theory of Structuration.* Cambridge: Polity Press.

Giles, W., 1993. Clean jobs, dirty jobs: ethnicity, social reproduction and gendered identity. *Culture*, XIII(2), 37–44.

Giles, W. and Arat-Koc, S. eds., 1994. *Maid in the Market: Women's Paid Domestic Labour.* Halifax: Fernwood Publishing.

Glickman, A., 2011. *Migrant workers won't lose visa for pregnancy.* [Online] Available at: http://www.ynetnews.com/articles/0,7340,L-4056341,00.html [Accessed 14 April 2011].

GMA News (Pinoy Abroad), 2008. *Government Won't Lift OFW deployment ban in Lebanon, Jordan.* [Online] Available at: http://www.gmanews.tv/story/125091/Govt-wont-lift-OFW-deployment-ban-in-Lebanon-Jordan [Accessed 9 November 2008].

Godbout, J., 1995. Les bonnes raisons de donner. *Anthropologie et sociétés*, 19 (1–2), 45–57.

Godbout, J. and Caillé, A., 2000 [1992]. *L'esprit du don.* Montreal: Boréal.

Godelier, M., 1996. *L'énigme du don.* Paris: Flammarion.

Goffman, E., 1959. *The Presentation of Self in Everyday Life.* Garden City, New York: Doubleday Anchor Books.

Goffman, E., 1961. Role distance, in *Encounters: Two Studies in the Sociology of Interaction*, edited by R. McGinnis. Indianapolis: Bobbs-Merrill, 85–132.

Goldring, L., 2001. The gender and geography of citizenship in Mexico-U.S. transnational spaces. *Identities: Global Studies in Culture and Power*, 7(4), 501–537.

Goodwin, J., 1984. They want to be called 'madam', in *Cry Amandla! South African Women and the Question of Power.* New York and London: Africana Publishing Company.

Gordon, J. and Lenhardt, R.A., 2007. Citizenship talk: Bridging the gap between immigration and race perspectives. *Immigration and Nationality Law Review*, 28, 525–552.

Gordon, J. and Lenhardt, R., 2008. Rethinking work and citizenship. *UCLA Law Review*, 55, 1161–1238.

Gordon, S., 1981. *DWEP – How it Grows: a Kind of History.* Johannesburg: Domestic Workers' and Employers' Project.

Gordon, S., 1985. *A Talent for Tomorrow: Life Stories of South African Servants.* Johannesburg: Raven Press.

Gouvernement du Québec, 1994. *Les services à domicile de première ligne, cadre de référence.* Ministère de la santé et des services sociaux: Québec.

Grossett, M., 1994. *Your Domestic Worker and the Law.* Pretoria: Southern Book Publishers.

Grossman, J., 2009. Domestic workers and knowledge in everyday life, in *Learning/Work: Turning Work and Lifelong Learning Inside Out*, edited by Cooper, L. and Walters, S. Pretoria, South Africa: Human Sciences Research Council.

Guevarra, A.R., 2009. *Marketing Dreams, Manufacturing Heroes: The Transnational Labor Brokering of Filipinos Workers.* New Jersey: Rutgers University Press.

Guillaumin, C., 1995. *Racism, Sexism, Power and Ideology.* London: Routledge.

Haaretz, 2009a. Children as hostages. *Haaretz Online*, 15 October.

Haaretz, 2009b. Yishai: Migrant workers will bring diseases to Israel. *Haaretz Online*, 31 October.

Halle, D., 1984. *America's Working Man: Work, Home, and Politics Among Blue-Collar Property Owners.* Chicago: University of Chicago Press.

Hampshire, J., 2008. *Regulating migration risks: the emergence of riskbased border controls in the UK*, s.l.: London Migration Research Group.

Haney-Lopez, I., 2006. *White by Law: The Legal Construction of Race.* New York: NYU Press.

Hardt, M. and Negri, A., 2000. *Empire.* Cambridge, Massachusetts: Harvard University Press.

Harel, A., 2008. Website for IDF draft dodgers faces criminal probe. *Haaretz Online*, 15 September.

Harris, A.P., 1999. Race and esssentialism in feminist legal theory. *Stanford Law Review*, 42(3), 581–616.

Hartigan, J., 1999. *Racial Situations: Class Predicaments of Whiteness in Detroit.* Princeton: Princeton University Press.

Harvey, D., 2005. *A Brief History of Neoliberalism.* Oxford: Oxford University Press.

Harzig, C., 2006. Domestics of the world (unite?): Labor migration systems and personal trajectories of household workers in historical and global perspective. *Journal of American Ethnic History*, 26(5), 48–73.

Harzig, C. (ed.), Knothe, M., Matovic, M., Mageean, D. and Blaschke, M. 1997. *Peasant Maids, City Women: From the European Countryside to Urban America.* Ithaca, NY: Cornell University Press.

Haskins, V., 2012. *Matrons and Maids: Regulating Indian Domestic Service in Tucson, 1914–1934.* Tucson: University of Arizona Press.

Hassim, S., 2008. Global constraints on gender equality in care work. *Politics and Society*, 36(3), 388–402.

Hays, S., 1996. *The Cultural Contradictions of Motherhood.* New Haven: Yale University Press.

Heen, M.L., 1995. Welfare reform, child care costs, and taxes: Delivering increased work-related child care benefits to low-income families. *Yale Law and Policy Review*, 13(2), 173–217.

Herrera, G., 2008. States, work and social reproduction through the lens of migrant experience: Ecuadorian domestic workers in Madrid, in *States and Markets: The Challenges of Social Reproduction*, edited by I. Bakker and R. Silvey. Abingdon, Oxon: Routledge, 93–107.

Hertog, S. and Dashti, R., 2010. *Population, Labor Markets and National Identity. Gulf Research Meeting, University of Cambridge 7–10 July 2010.* [Online] Available at: http://grcevent.net/cambridge/index.php?page=workshop&wname=3 [Accessed 16 July 2012].

Heyzer, N., Nijeholt, G.L.A. and Weerakoon, N., eds., 1994. *The Trade in Domestic Workers: Causes, Mechanisms and Consequences of International Migration.* London: Zed Books.

Heyzer, N. and Wee, V., 1994. Domestic Workers in Transient Overseas Employment: Who Benefits, Who Profits?, in *The Trade in Domestic Workers: Causes, Mechanisms and Consequences of International Migration,* edited by N. Heyzer, G.L.A. Nijeholt and N. Weerakoon. London: Zed Books, 31–101.

Higginbotham, E. and Romero, M., 1997. *Women and Work: Exploring Race, Ethnicity, and Class.* Thousand Oaks: Sage.

Higman, B.W., 2002. *Domestic Service in Australia.* Victoria: Melbourne University Press.

Himmelweit, S., 2002. Economic theory, norms and the care gap, or: why do economists become parents?, in *Analysing Families: Morality and Rationality in Policy and Practice*, edited by A. Carling, S. Duncan and R. Edwards. London: Routledge, 231–250.

Hochschild, A.R., 1979. Emotion work, feeling rules, and social structure. *American Journal of Sociology*, 85(3), 551–575.

Hochshild, A., 1983. *The Managed Heart: Commercialization of Human Feeling.* Berkeley: University of California Press.

Hochschild, A.R., 1989. *The Second Shift*. New York: Viking.

Hochschild, A.R., 1995. The culture of politics: Traditional, postmodern, cold-modern and warm-model ideals of care. *Social Politics*, 2(3), 331–347.

Hochschild, A.R., 2000. Global care chains and emotional surplus value, in *On the Edge: Living with Global Capitalism*, edited by A. Giddens and W. Hutton. London: Jonathan Cape, 130–146.

Hochschild, A.R., 2002. Love and gold, in *Global Woman. Nannies, Maids and Sex Workers in the New Economy*, edited by B. Ehrenreich and A. Russell Hochschild. New York: Henry Holt and Company, 15–30.

Hochshild, A., 2003. *The Commercialization of Intimate Life: Notes from Home and Work*. Berkeley: University of California Press.

Home Office, 2007. *Enforcing the Rules: A Strategy to Ensure and Enforce Compliance with our Immigration Laws*. London: HMSO.

Hondagneu-Sotelo, P., 2001. *Domestica: Immigrant Workers Cleaning and Caring in the Shadows of Affluence*. Berkeley, California: University of California Press.

Hondagneu-Sotelo, P., 2002. Blowups and other unhappy endings, in *Global Woman: Nannies, Maids and Sex Workers in the New Economy*, edited by B. Ehrenreich and A. Hochschild. New York: Henry Holt, 55–69.

Hondagneu-Sotelo, P. and Avila, E., 1997. I'm here, but I'm there: The meanings of Latina transnational motherhood. *Gender and Society*, October, 11(5), 548–571.

Honig, B., 2001. *Democracy and the Foreigner*. Princeton: Princeton University Press.

Hornstein, J., 2005. *A Nation of Realtors: A Cultural History of the Twentieth-Century American Middle Class*. Durham: Duke University Press.

Hotline for Migrant Workers, 2009. *Migrant Workers*. [Online] Available at: http://www.hotline.org.il/english/about_migrants.htm [Accessed 15 December 2009].

House of Lords, 2008. *The Economic Impact of Immigration*. London: The Stationery Office Limited.

Hrdy, S.B., 2002. *Mother Nature: Maternal Instincts and How They Shape the Human Species*. New York: Ballantine Books.

Huda, S., 2006. *Report of the Special Rapporteur on the Human Rights Aspects of the Victims of Trafficking in Persons, Especially Women and Children, Mission To Lebanon (7 to 16 September 2005)*. [Online] Available at: http://www.arabhumanrights.org/publications/countries/lebanon/rapporteurs/e-cn4-2006-add3-06e.pdf [Accessed 20 April 2014].

Hujo, K. and Piper, N. 2007. South–South Migration: Challenges for development and social policy. *Development*, 50(4), 19–25. [Online] Available at: http://www.refworld.org/pdfid/48abd53dd.pdf [Accessed 19 May 2012].

Human Rights Watch, 2000. *Unfair Advantage: Workers' Freedom on Association in the United States under International Human Rights Standards*. [Online]

Available at: http://www.hrw.org/reports/pdfs/u/us/uslbr008.pdf [Accessed 10 September 2001].

Human Rights Watch, 2001. *Hidden in the Home: Abuse of Domestic Workers with Special Visas in the United States.* [Online] Available at: : http://www.hrw.org/reports/2001/usadom/usadom0501.pdf [Accessed 12 September 2001].

Human Rights Watch, 2007. *Exported and Exposed Abuses against Sri Lankan Domestic Workers in Saudi Arabia, Kuwait, Lebanon, and the United Arab Emirates.* [Online] Available at: http://www.hrw.org/en/node/10592/section/2 [Accessed 24 October 2010].

Human Rights Watch, 2008. *'As If I Am Not Human': Abuses against Asian Domestic Workers in Saudi Arabia.* [Online] Available at: http://www.hrw.org/reports/2008/saudiarabia0708/ [Accessed 24 October 2010].

Human Rights Watch, 2008a. *Annex: Deaths of Migrant Domestic Workers in Lebanon.* [Online] Available at: http://www.hrw.org/pub/2008/women/Lebanon.MDW.Annex.082608.pdf [Accessed 20 September 2010].

Human Rights Watch, 2010. *Slow reform: Protection of migrant domestic workers in Asia and the Middle East.* [Online] Available at: http://www.hrw.org/sites/default/files/reports/wrd0410webwcover_0.pdf [Accessed 5 June 2013].

IDI (Immigration Directorates Instructions), 2004. *Au Pair Placements (Chapter 4 Section 1).* London: UK Border Agency, Home Office.

Ignacio, E., 2005. *Building Diaspora: Community Formation on the Internet.* Brunswick, NJ: Rutgers University Press.

Ignatiev, N., 1995. *How the Irish Became White.* New York: Routledge.

Ilcan, S. and Basok, T., 2004. Community government: Voluntary agencies, social justice and the responsibilization of citizens. *Citizenship Studies*, 8(2), 129–144.

Illouz, E., 2007. *Cold Intimacies: The Making of Emotional Capitalism.* Oxford: Polity Press.

ILO (International Labour Organization), 2010. *Decent Work for Domestic Workers, Report IV(1) for the International Labour Conference, 99th Session.* [Online] Available at: http://www.ilo.org/wcmsp5/groups/public/@ed_norm/@relconf/documents/meetingdocument/wcms_104700.pdf [Accessed 12 June 2013].

ILO (International Labour Organization), 2013a. *Domestic Workers across the World: Global and Regional Statistics and the Extent of Local Protection.* [Online] Available at: http://www.ilo.org/wcmsp5/groups/public/---dgreports/---dcomm/---publ/documents/publication/wcms_173363.pdf [Accessed 11 January 2013].

ILO (International Labour Organization), 2013b. *ILO and Cooperatives (Online COOP News no. 1).* [Online] Available at: http://www.ilo.org/wcmsp5/groups/public/---ed_emp/---emp_ent/---coop/documents/publication/wcms_213244.pdf [Accessed 6 June 2013].

IRIN, 2006. *Emirats Arabes Unis: Domestic workers face abusive employers.* [Online] Available at: http://www.irinnews.org/report.aspx?reportid=27089 [Accessed 6 June 2013].

IRIN, 2009. *Israel: New report highlights exploitation of migrant workers.* [Online] Available at: http://www.irinnews.org/report/86808/israel-new-report-highlights-exploitation-of-migrant-workers [Accessed 20 December 2009].

Israel Government Portal, 2009. *Guide for Migrant Workers.* [Online] Available at: http://www.gov.il/FirstGov/TopNavEng/EngSituations/ESMigrantWorkersGuide/ESMWGMaternity/ [Accessed 15 December 2009].

Istituto Nazionale della Previdenza Sociale, INPS, 2008. [Online] Available at: http://www.inps.it/webidentity/banchedatistatistiche/domestici/index.jsp [Accessed 31 January 2013].

Italian Parliament, 2000. *Legge quadro per la realizzazione del sistema integrato di interventi e servizi sociali (Bill 328/2000, November 8, 2000).* [Online] Available at: http://www.parlamento.it/parlam/leggi/003281.htm [Accessed 23 March 2013].

Italian Parliament, 2002. *Modifica alla normativa in materia di immigrazione e di asilo (Law 189, art. 33, July 30th, 2002).* [Online] Available at: http://www.camera.it/parlam/leggi/02189l.htm [Accessed 23 March 2013].

Italian Parliament, 2004. *Disposizioni per la formazione del bilancio annuale e pluriennale dello Stato-Legge Finanziaria 2005 (Law 311, December 30th, 2004).* [Online] Available at: http://www.camera.it/parlam/leggi/04311l.htm [Accessed 23 March 2013].

James, A., Grant, D. and Cranford, C., 2000. Moving up, but how far? African American women and economic restructuring in Los Angeles. *Sociological Perspectives*, 43(3), 399–420.

Jellyfish (Meduzot). 2007. [Film] Directed by Shira Geffen, Etgar Keret. s.l.: s.n.

Jenson, J. and Sineau, M., 2001. *Who Cares? Women's Work, Childcare and Welfare State Redesign.* Toronto: University of Toronto Press.

Jerusalem Post, 2009. Barak: We are obligated to keep migrant workers' children in Israel. *Jerusalem Post*, 19 October.

Johnson, K., 2009. The intersection of race and class in U.S. immigration law and enforcement. *Law and Contemporary Problems*, 72(1), 1–36.

Johnston, P., 1994. *Success While Others Fail: Social Movement Unionism and the Public Workplace.* Ithaca: ILR Press.

Joseph, S., 1999. Theories and dynamics of gender, self and identity in Arab families, in *Intimate Selving in Arab Families*, edited by S. Joseph. Syracuse: Syracuse University Press, 1–17.

Jureidini, R., 2002. *Women Migrant Domestic Workers in Lebanon, International Migration Papers, No 48*, Geneva: International Labour Organization (ILO).

Jureidini, R., 2003. The failure of state protection: Household guest workers in Lebanon [L'échec de la protection de l'Etat: les domestiques étrangers au Liban]. *European Review of International Migration [Revue Européenne des Migrations Internationales]*, 19(3), 95–127.

Jureidini, R., 2004. Women migrant domestic workers in Lebanon, in *Gender and Migration in Arab States: The Case of Domestic Workers*, edited by S. Esim and M. Smith. Beirut: International Labour Organization, Regional Office for the Arab States.

Jureidini, R., 2005. Middle East guestworkers, in *Immigration and Asylum: From 1900 to the Present*, edited by M. Gibney and R. Hansen. Oxford: ABC-CLIO, 402–408.

Jureidini, R., 2009. In the shadows of family life: Towards a history of domestic service in Lebanon. *Journal of Middle East Women's Studies*, 5(3), 74–101.

Jureidini, R., 2009. Sexuality and the servant: An exploration of Arab images of the sexuality of domestic maids in the household, in *Sexuality in the Arab World*, edited by S. Khalaf and J. Gagnon. London: Saqi Press, 130–151.

Jureidini, R., 2010. Trafficking and contract migrant workers in the Middle East. *International Migration*, 48(4), 142–163.

Jureidini, R., 2011. State and non-State actors during the conflict in Lebanon, July–August 2006, in *The Migration-Displacement Nexus: Concepts, Cases and Responses*, edited by K. Koser and S. Martin. New York: Berghahan Books, 197–215.

Jureidini, R. and Moukarbel, N., 2004. Female Sri Lankan domestic labour in Lebanon: Contractual, slavery-like practices and conditions. *Journal of Ethnic and Migration Studies*, 30(4), 581–607.

Kabataang Montreal, n.d. *Blog.* [Online] Available at: http://kabataangmontreal.blogspot.com [Accessed 17 September 2008].

Kalayaan Centre, n.d. *Filipino groups to tackle community's barriers to settlement and integration at a historic national research conference.* [Online] Available at: http://kalayaancentre.net/pwcofbc/?p=190#more-190 [Accessed 1 September 2008].

Kalman, M., 2009. Israel's illegal immigrants – and their children. *TIME Online Edition*, 21 October.

Kanyoka, V., 2010. *Plenary Session.* Geneva, Switzerland, International Labour Conference of the International Labour Organization, June 2–18.

Kaplan, A., 1998. Manifest domesticity. *American Literature*, 70(3), 581–606.

Kaplan, E., 1987. 'I don't do no windows': Competition between domestic worker and the housewife, in *Competition: A Feminist Taboo?* edited by V. Miner and H.E. Longino. New York: Feminist Press at The City University of New York, 92–105.

Katz Rothman, B., 1989. *Recreating Motherhood: Ideology and Technology in a Patriarchal Society.* New York: Norton.

Katzman, D., 1981. *Seven Days a Week: Women and Domestic Service in Industrializing America.* Urbana: University of Illinois Press.

Kav LaOved; Migrant Forum Asia, 2009. *Report on Migrant caregivers in Israel: Problems and Recommendations.* [Online] Available at: http://www.bayefsky.com/general/cmw_dod_mdw_mfa_2009.pdf [Accessed 20 December 2009].

Kefalas, M., 2003. *Money, Morals, and Manners: The Culture of the French and American Upper-Middle Class.* Chicago: University of Chicago Press.

Kehler, J., 2000. Women will not be free until domestic workers are free! *Rights Now*, 10–11.

Kelly, P.F., 2006. *Filipinos in Canada: Economic Dimensions of Immigration and Settlement (Working Paper 48)*, Toronto: Joint Centre of Excellence for Research on Immigration and Settlement (CERIS).

Kelly, P.F., Astorga-Garica, M., Esguerra, E.F. and the Community Alliance for Social Justice, 2009. *Explaining the Deprofessionalized Filipino: Why Filipino Immigrants get Low-Paying Jobs in Toronto (Working Paper 75)*, Toronto: Joint Centre of Excellence for Research on Immigration and Settlement (CERIS).

Kemp, A., 2007. Managing migration, reprioritizing national citizenship: Undocumented migrant workers' children and policy reforms in Israel. *Theoretical Inquiries in Law*, 8(2), 663–691.

Kemp, A. and Raijman, R., 2003. Christian Zionists in the Holy Land: Evangelical churches, labour migrants and the Jewish state. *Identities: Global Studies in Culture and Power*, 10(3), 295–318.

Kemp, A. and Raijman, R., 2004. Tel Aviv is not foreign to you: Urban incorporation policy on labor migrants in Israel. *The International Migration Review*, 38(1), 26–51.

Khalaf, S., 2002. *Civil and Uncivil Violence in Lebanon.* New York: Columbia University Press.

Kimmel, M., 1996. *Manhood in America: A Cultural History.* New York: Free Press.

King, R. and Zontini, E., 2000. The role of gender in the South European Immigration Model. *Papers: Revista de Sociología*, 60, 35–52.

Kofman, E., Sales, R. and Phizacklea, A., 2000. *Gender and International Migration in Europe.* London: Routledge.

Kofman, E., and Raghuram, P. 2006. Gender and global labour migrations: Incorporating skilled workers. *Antipode*, 38(2), 282–303.

Kofman, and Raghuram, P. 2010. The implications of migration for gender and care regimes in the south, in *South-South Migrations: Implications for Social Policy and Development*, edited by Hugo, K. and Piper, N. New York: Palgrave Macmillan, 46–83.

Korac, M., 2003. The lack of integration policy and experiences of integration: A case study of refugees in Rome. *Journal of Refugee Studies*, 16(4), 398–421.

Korac, M., 2005. The role of bridging social networks in refugee settlement: A case of Italy and the Netherlands, in *Homeland Wanted: Interdisciplinary Perspective on Refugee Resettlement in the West*, edited by P. Waxman and V. Colic-Peisker. New York: Nova Science Publishers Inc, 87–107.

Korac, M., 2009. *Remaking Home: Reconstructing Life, Place and Identity.* Oxford: Berghahn Books.

Kraft, D., 2009. Native-born children of foreign workers pose demographic problem. *Jewish Telegraphic Agency, jewishexponent.com*, 24 September.

KUDHEIHA, 2011. *Organizing Domestic Workers in Kenya: A Success Story and a Call to Action (KUDHEIHA Workers Union].* [Online] Available at: http://

www.solidaritycenter.org/Files/kenya_kudheiha_dwguide2012.pdf [Accessed 15 May 2013].

Kumar, P. and Schenk, C., 2006. Union renewal and organizational change: A review of the literature, in *Paths to Union Renewal: Canadian Experiences*, edited by P. Kumar and C. Schenk. Toronto: Broadview Press, 29–60.

Kunz, R., 2008. Remittances are beautiful?: Gender implications of the new global remittances trench. *Third World Quarterly*, 29(7), 1389–1409.

Kuznesolf, E., 1989. A history of domestic service in Spanish America, 1492–1980, in *Muchachas No More, Household Workers in Latin American and the Caribbean,* edited by E.M. Chaney, M.G. Castro and M.L. Smith. Philadelphia: Temple University Press, 17–35.

Laforest, S. and Amzallag, M., 2000. *Subcontracting by CLSCs in Home Care Service Delivery. Bienviellir/Vitalaging, Montreal, CLSC René Cassin.* [Online] Available at: http://www.geronto.org/Vitalaging/February2000/subcon.htm.

Lamont, M., 1992. *Money, Morals, and Manners: The Culture of the French and American Upper-Middle Class.* Chicago: University of Chicago Press.

Lamont, M., 2000. *The Dignity of Working Men: Morality and the Boundaries of Race, Class, and Immigration.* New York: Russell Sage Foundation.

Lan, P., 2004. Jealous madams, anxious mothers: Triangular relationships in the employment of migrant domestic workers. *Taiwanese Sociology*, 8, 43–97.

Lan, P.C., 2006. *Global Cindarellas: Migrant Domestics and Newly Rich Employers in Taiwan.* Durham: Duke University Press.

Law, S.A., 1983. Women, work, welfare and the preservation of patriarchy. *University Pennsylvania Law Review*, 131(6), 1249–1339.

Layne, L., ed., 1999. *Transformative Motherhood: On Giving and Getting in a Consumer Culture.* New York: New York University Press.

Lazar, E., 2000. *'Ain't I a Citizen?': A Study of Consciousness, Resistance and Identity in the Domestic Service Sector in Post-Apartheid South Africa.* Kingston, Political Studies, Queen's University.

Le Espiritu, Y., 2003. *Home Bound: Filipino American Lives across Cultures, Communities, and Countries.* Berkeley: University of California Press.

Leah, R., 1999. Do you call me 'sister'?: Women of colour and the Canadian Labour Movement, in *Scratching the Surface: Canadian Anti-racist Feminist Thought*, edited by E. Dua and A. Robertson. Toronto: Women's Press, 97–126.

Leibelt, C., 2008. On sentimental Orientalists, Christian Zionists, and working class cosmopolitans. *Critical Asian Studies*, 40(4), 567–585.

Lejtenyi, P., 2003. *Gang Politics – Montreal Mirror 18(41).* [Online] Available at: http://www.montrealmirror.com/ARCHIVES/2003/032703/cover_news.html [Accessed 17 September 2008].

Leon, M., 1989. Domestic labor and domestic service in Colombia, in *Muchachas No More, Household Workers in Latin American and the Caribbean,* edited by E.M. Chaney, M.G. Castro and M.L. Smith. Philadelphia: Temple University Press, 323–349.

LeRoux, T., 1995. *'We Have Families Too'. Live-in Domestics Talk about their Lives.* Pretoria: Co-operative Research Programme on Marriage and Family Life, Human Sciences Research Council.

Lévesque, G., 2002. *Satisfaction, utilité, utilisation et amélioration de la pratique des infirmières auxliaires dans le réseau de la santé au québec. Résultats dun sondage réalisé en août et septembre 2001 auprès des infirmières auxiliaires.* Montreal: Ordre des infirmières et infirmiers du Québec.

Levine, M., 2009. *Impossible peace: Israel/Palestine since 1989.* London: Zed Books.

Levitt, P., 1998. Social remittances: Migration driven local-level forms of cultural diffusion. *The International Migration Review*, 32(4), 926–948.

Levitt, P. and Glick Schiller, N., 2004. Conceptualizing simultaneity: A transnational social field perspective on society. *International Migration Review*, 38(3), 1002–1039.

Lewis, J. and Guillari, S., 2005. The adult worker model family, gender equality and care: The search for new policy principles and problems of a capabilities approach. *Economy and Society*, 34(1), 76–104.

Li, T.M., 2009. To make live or let die? Rural dispossession and the protection of surplus populations. *Antipode*, 41(6), 1208–1235.

Liebenberg, S., 1995. *The Constitution of South Africa from a Gender Perspective.* Claremont: Community Law Centre.

Liechty, M., 2003. *Suitably Modern: Making Middle-Class Culture in a New Consumer Society.* Princeton: Princeton University Press.

Linebaugh, P. and Rediker, M., 2000. *The Many-Headed Hydra: Sailors, Slaves, Commoners, and the Hidden History of the Revolutionary Atlantic.* London: Verso.

Ling, L., 2002. *Postcolonial International Relations: Conquest and Desire between Asia and the West.* London: Palgrave.

Lipstiz, G., 2006. *The Possessive Investment in Whiteness: How White People Profit from Identity Politics.* Philadelphia: Temple University Press.

Lobel, O., 2001. Class and care: The roles of private intermediaries in the in-home care industry in the United States and Israel. *Harvard Women's Law Journal*, 24(Spring), 89–137.

Long, N., 2001. *Development Sociology: Actor Perspective.* London and New York: Routledge.

Longva, A., 1997. *Walls Built on Sand: Migration, Exclusion and Society in Kuwait.* Boulder, CO: Westview Press.

Los Angeles County Code, 1997. *Chapter 3.45, Board Order No. 48, Ordinance No. 97–0053*, s.l.: s.n.

Lowe, L., 1996. *Immigrant Acts: on Asian American Cultural Politics.* Durham: Duke University Press.

Lutz, H., 2004. Life in the Twilight Zone: Migration, transnationality and gender in the private household. *Journal of Contemporary European Studies*, 12(1), 48–55.

Lutz, H., ed., 2008a. *Migration and Domestic Work: A European Perspective on a Global Theme.* Aldershot: Ashgate.

Lutz, H., 2008b. When home becomes a workplace: Domestic work as an ordinary job in Germany? in *Migration and Domestic Work: A European Perspective on a Global Theme*, edited by H. Lutz. Aldershot: Ashgate, 43–62.

Lutz, H., 2011. *The New Maids: Transnational Women and the Care Economy.* London: Zed Books.

Luxton, M., 2011. *Changing Families, New Understandings.* Ottawa, ON: Vanier Institute of the Family.

MacDonald, C., 1998. Manufacturing motherhood: The shadow work of nannies and au pairs. *Qualitative Sociology*, 21(1), 25–53.

Mackintosh, M., 1981. Gender and economics: The sexual division of labour and the subordination of women, in *Of Marriage and the Market: Women's Subordination Internationally and its Lessons*, edited by K. Young, C. Wolkowitz and R. McCullagh. London: Routledge, 3–17.

Macklin, A., 1994. On the inside looking in: Foreign domestic workers in Canada, in *Maid in the Market: Women's Paid Domestic Labour*, edited by W. Giles and S. Arat-Koc. Halifax: Fernwood Publishing, 13–38.

Mahon, R. and Robinson, K., eds, 2011. *Feminist Ethics and Social Policy: Towards a New Global Political Economy of Care*. Vancouver: University of British Columbia Press.

Mahon, R., Anttonen, A., Bergqvist, C., Brennan, D. and Hobson, B. 2012. Convergent care regimes? Childcare arrangements in Australia, Canada, Finland and Sweden. *Journal of European Social Policy*, 22(4), 419–431.

Mainardi, P., 1993. The politics of housework, in *Feminist Frameworks: Alternative Theoretical Accounts of the Relation Between Women and Men*, edited by A. Jaggar and P. S. Rothenberg. New York: McGraw Hill.

Makosana, I.Z., 1989. *IZWI: The Working Conditions of African Domestic Workers in Cape Town in the 1980s.* Cape Town: MA Thesis, Sociology, University of Cape Town.

Malos, E., 1980. *The Politics of Housework.* London: Allison and Busby.

Marchand, M.H. and Runyan, A.S., 2000. *Gender and Global Restructuring: Sightings, Sites and Resistances.* London: Routledge.

Mar, P., 2005. Unsettling potentialities: Topographies of hope in transnational migration. *Journal of Intercultural Studies*, 26(4), 361–378.

Mateos, N.R., 2000. Inmigración femenina en el sur de Europa: Presentación. *Papers: Revista de Sociología*, 60, 13–34.

Mattingly, D.J., 1999. Job Search, social networks and local labor market dynamics: The case of paid household work in San Diego, California. *Urban Geography*, 20(1), 46–74.

Mattingly, D.J., 2001. The home and the world: Domestic service and international networks of caring labour. *Annals of the Association of American Geographers*, 91(2), 370–386.

Mauss, M., 1960[1925]. Essai sur le don: Forme et raison de l'échange dans les sociétés archaïques, in *Marcel Mauss, Sociologie et anthropologie.* Paris: Presses universitaires de France, 145–279 .

McCall, L., 2005. The complexity of intersectionality. *Signs*, 30(3), 1771–1800.

McKay, B., 2011. The politics of mirrored metaphors: Flor Contemplacion and the maid. *Positions*, 19(2), 463–498.

Meagher, G., 2000. A struggle for recognition: Work life reform in the domestic services industry. *Economic and Industrial Democracy*, 21, 9–37.

Meer, S., ed., 1998. *Women Speak: Reflections on our Struggles 1982–1997.* Cape Town: Kwela Books.

Meintel, D., Cognet, M. and Lenoir-Achdjian, A., 1999. *Pratiques professionnelles et relations interethniques dans le travail des auxiliaires familiaux.* Montreal: Publications du Centre de recherche et de formation du CLSC Côte-des-Neiges, No. 4.

Mendez, J.B., 1998. Of mops and maids: Contradictions and continuities in bureaucratized domestic work. *Social Problems*, 45, 114–135.

Messner, M., 1996. Studying up on sex. *Sociology of Sport Journal*, 13(3), 221–237.

Michel, S., 1999. *Children's Interests/Mothers' Rights.* New Haven: Yale University Press.

Michel, S. and Peng, I. 2012. All in the family? Migrants, nationhood, and care regimes in Asia and North America. *Journal of European Social Policy*, 22(4), 406–418.

Michelman, C., 1975. *The Black Sash of South Africa: A Case of Liberalism.* Cape Town: Oxford University Press.

Mies, M., 1986. *Patriarchy and Accumulation on a World Scale: Women in the International Division of Labour.* London: Zed Books.

Mies, M., 1994. 'Gender' and global capitalism, in *Capitalism and Development*, edited by L. Skair. London: Routledge, 107–122.

Migrant Rights Centre Ireland (MRCI), 2012. *Working Paper: Who Cares? The Experience of Migrant Workers in Ireland.* [Online] Available at: http://www.mrci.i.e./wp-content/uploads/2012/12/Who-Cares-The-experience-of-Migrant-Care-Workers-in-Ireland-Nov-2012.pdf [Accessed 2 June 2012].

Migration Advisory Committee, 2008. *Skilled, Shortage, Sensible: The Recommended Shortage Occupation Lists for the UK and Scotland,* London: Central Office of Information.

Milkman, R., ed., 2000. *Organizing Immigrants: The Challenge for Unions in Contemporary California.* Berkeley: University of California Press.

Milkman, R., Reese, E. and Roth, B., 1998. The macrosociology of paid domestic labor. *Work and Occupations*, 25(4), 483–510.

Ministero del Lavoro e delle Politiche Sociali (Circolare 19 aprile 2010, n. 14), 2010. *Oggetto: D.P.C.M. dell'1.4.2010 concernente Programmazione transitoria dei flussi d'ingresso dei lavoratori extracomunitari stagionali e di altre categorie nel territorio dello Stato italiano per l'anno 2010.* [Online] Available at: http://

www.professionisti24.ilsole24ore.com/art/Professionisti24/Lavoro/2010/04/ML_cir_14_2010.pdf [Accessed 24 February 2013].

Ministero del Lavoro, della Salute e delle Politiche Sociali, 2010. *Programmazione transitoria dei flussi d'ingresso dei lavoratori extracomunitari stagionali e di altre categorie nel territorio dello stato italiano per l'anno 2010 (Law no. 2699).* [Online] Available at: http://interno.gov.it/mininterno/export/sites/default/it/assets/files/19/0805_Decreto_stagionali_2010.pdf [Accessed 24 February 2013].

Mohanty, C.T., 1991. Under western eyes: Feminist scholarship and colonial discourses, in *Third World Women and the Politics of Feminism*, edited by C.T. Mohanty, L. Torres and A. Russo. Bloomington: Indiana University Press, 51–80.

Mohanty, C.T., Russo, A. and Torres, L., eds., 1991. *Third World Women and the Politics of Feminism.* Bloomington: Indiana University Press.

Montgomery, H., 2001. Imposing rights? A case study of child prostitution in Thailand, in *Culture and Rights: Anthropological Perspectives*, edited by J.K. Cowan, D. Marie-Bénédicte and R.A. Wilson. Cambridge: Cambridge University Press. 80–101.

Moreno-Fontes Chammartin, G., 2005. *Domestic Workers: Little Protection for the Underpaid.* [Online] Available at: http://www.migrationinformation.org/Feature/display.cfm?ID=300 [Accessed 14 June 2008].

Morris, J., 1993. *Independent Lives? Community Care and Disabled People.* London: Macmillan Press Ltd.

Moulier Boutang, Y., 1997. *De l'esclavage au salariat. Economie historique.* Paris: Presses Universitaires de France.

Mujeres Unidas y Activas and the Day Labor Program Women's Collective of La Raza Centro Legal, 2007. *Behind Closed Doors: Working Conditions of California Household Workers.* [Online] Available at: http://www.mujeresunidas.net/media/MUA_rpt.pdf [Accessed 2 September 2007].

MWC Committee, 2007. *Consideration of Reports Submitted by States Parties Under Article 74 of the Convention. Concluding observations of the Committee on the Protection of the Rights of All Migrant Workers and Members of Their Families, Egypt.* Geneva: United Nations.

Nakano Glenn, E., 1986. *Issei, Nisei, War Bride: Three Generations of Japanese American Women in Domestic Service.* Philadelphia: Temple University Press.

Nakano Glenn, E., 1992. From servitude to service work: Historical continuities in the racial division of paid reproductive labor. *Signs*, 18(1), 1–43.

Nakano Glenn, E., 2010. *Forced to Care, Coercions and Caregiving in America.* Cambridge: Harvard University Press.

Naples, N., 1998. *Community Activism and Feminist Politics: Organizing Across Race, Class and Gender.* New York: Routledge.

Naples, N. and Desai, M., eds., 2002. *Women's Activism and Globalization: Linking Local Struggles and Transnational Politics.* New York: Routledge.

Nash, J. and Fernandez-Kelly, M.P., eds, 1983. *Women, Men and the International Division of Labor.* Albany: SUNY Press.

National Alliance of Philippine Women in Canada, 2007. *Submission to the Parliamentary Standing Committee on Citizenship and Immigration.* Vancouver, British Columbia, Making the Filipino Community Count in B.C. Conference (9–11 February).

National Collective Labour Contract – Contratto Collettivo Nazionale di Lavoro Colf e Badanti (CCNL), 2013. [Online] Available at: http://www.inps.it/News/LavoratoriDomestici/CCNL%20Ebilcoba.pdf [Accessed 24 February 2013].

Nelson, M.K., 2010. *Parenting Out of Control, Anxious Parents in Uncertain Times.* New York: New York University Press.

Newman, K., 1988. *Falling from Grace: Downward Mobility in the Age of Affluence.* Berkeley: University of California Press.

Neysmith, S., 1996. Les soins à domicile et le travail des femmes: la force de l'habitude. *Lien social et politiques*, 36, 72–80.

Neysmith, S., ed., 2000. *Restructuring Caring Labour: Discourse, State Practice, and Everyday Life.* Toronto: Oxford University Press.

Neysmith, S.M. and Aronson, J., 1997. Working conditions in home care: Negotiating race and class boundaries in gendered work. *International Journal of Health Services*, 27(3), 479–499.

Ng, R., 2000. Restructuring gender, race, and class relations: The case of garment workers and labour adjustment, in *Restructuring Caring Labour: Discourse, State Practice, and Everyday Life*, edited by S. Neysmith. Toronto: Oxford University Press, 226–245.

Ng, R., 2002. Freedom from whom? Globalization and trade from the standpoint of garment workers. *Canadian Women's Studies*, 21/22, 74–81.

Ngai, M.M., 2004. *Impossible Subjects: Illegal Aliens and the Making of Modern America.* Princeton: Princeton University Press.

Ngqakayi, N., 1991. *Subjectivity in the 'Maid'/'Madam' Relationship and its Effects on the Occupational Child Care-Giving Functions of the Domestic Worker.* Cape Town: Clinical Psychology, University of Cape Town.

Nijeholt, G.L. à., 1994. The changing international division of labor and domestic workers: A macro overview, in *The Trade in Domestic Workers: Causes, Mechanisms and Consequences of International Migration*, edited by N. Heyzer, G.L. à. Nijeholt and N. Weerakoon. London: Zed Books, 3–29.

Noodle. 2007. [Film] Directed by Ayelet Menahemi. s.l.: s.n.

Ntombi, 1987. *Thula Baba.* Johannesburg: Ravan Press.

Nyman, R., 1996. *An Organisational Challenge – The Unionisation of Domestic Workers.* Johannesburg: National Labor and Economic Development Institute.

Nyman, R., 1997. The Death of SADWU: the Birth of a New Organisation? *South African Labor Bulletin*, 21(2).

Oakley, A., 1974. *The Sociology of Housework.* London: Martin Robertson.

Oakley, A., 1974. *Woman's Work: The Housewife, Past and Present.* New York: Pantheon Books.

OHCHR (Office of the High Commissioner for Human Rights), 2009. *Creative Solution: a unified contract to protect domestic migrant workers in Lebanon.* [Online] Available at: http://www.ohchr.org/EN/NEWSEVENTS/Pages/Unified ContractLebanon.aspx [Accessed 28 April 2010].

Onuki, H. 2011. The global migration of care labour: Filipino workers in Japan, in *Feminist Ethics and Social Policy: Towards a New Global Political Economy of Care*, edited by Mahon, R. and Robinson, K. Vancouver: University of British Columbia Press, 60–74.

Organization for Security and Co-operation in Europe (OSCE), 2010. *Unprotected Work. Invisible Exploitation Trafficking for the Purpose of Domestic Servitude.* [Online] Available at: http://www.osce.org/cthb/75804 [Accessed 15 May 2013].

Orozco, A., 2009. *Global Care Chains. Gender, Migration and Development Series (Working Paper 2)*, Santo Domingo, Dominican Republic: United Nations International Research and Training Institute for the Advancement of Women (UN-INSTRAW).

Orr, L., 1998. *Maternity Benefits: Proposed Amendments to the UIF*, Johannesburg: National Labor and Economic Development Institute.

Ortner, S., 1991. Reading America: Preliminary notes on class and culture, in *Recapturing Anthropology*, edited by R. Fox. Santa Fe, NM: SAR Press, 163–190.

Ortner, S., 1998. Identities: The hidden life of class. *Journal of Anthropological Research*, 54(1), 1–17.

Ortner, S., 2003. *New Jersey Dreaming: Capital, Culture, and the Class of '58.* Durham: Duke University Press.

Ouellette, F.-R., 1995. La part du don dans l'adoption. *Anthropologie et sociétés*, 19(1–2), 154–174.

Ozyegin, G. and Hondagneu-Sotelo, P., 2008. Conclusion: Domestic work, migration and the new gender order in contemporary Europe, in *Migration and Domestic Work: A European Perspective on a Global Theme,* edited by H. Lutz. Aldershot: Ashgate, 195–208.

Palmer, P., 1989. *Domesticity and Dirt: Housewives and Domestic Servants in the United States, 1920–1945.* Philadelphia: Temple University Press.

Panam, A., 2004. *Migrant Domestic Workers: from Burma to Thailand.* Nakonpathom, Thailand: Institute for Population and Social Research, Mahidol University.

Papadopoulos, D., Stephenson, N. and Tsianos, V., 2008. *Escape Routes: Control and Subversion in the 21st century.* London: Pluto Press.

Parreñas, R.S., 2000. Migrant Filipina domestic workers and the international division of reproductive labor. *Gender and Society*, 14(4), 560–580.

Parreñas, R.S., 2001a. *Servants of Globalization: Women, Migration and Domestic Work.* Stanford, California: Stanford University Press.

Parreñas, R.S., 2001b. Transgressing the nation-state: The partial citizenship and 'Imagined (Global) Community' of migrant Filipina domestic workers. *Signs*, 26(4), 1129–1154.

Parreñas, R.S., 2002. The care crisis in the Philippines: children and transnational families in the new global economy, in *Global Women: Nannies, Maids and Sex Workers in the New Economy*, edited by B. Ehrenreich and Hochschild A.R. London: Granta Books, 39–54.

Parreñas, R.S., 2005a. *Children of Global Migration, Transnational Families and Gendered Woes.* Stanford, California: Standford University Press.

Parreñas, R.S., 2005b. Gender inequalities in the new global economy, in *Domestic Service and the Formation of European Identity: Understanding the Globalization of Domestic Work, 16–21st Centuries*, edited by A. Fauve-Chamoux. Bern: Peter Lang, 369–379.

Parreñas, R.S., 2008a. Perpetually foreign: Filipina migrant workers in Rome, in *Migration and Domestic Work: A European Perspective on a Global Theme.* Aldershot: Ashgate, 99–112.

Parreñas, R.S., 2008b. *The Force of Domesticity, Filipina Migrants and Globalization.* New York: New York University Press.

Pateman, C., 1988. *The Sexual Contract.* Stanford: Stanford University Press.

Pessar, P.R. and Mahler, S.J., 2003. Transnational migration: Bringing gender in. *International Migration Review*, 37(3), 812–846.

Philippine Women Centre of British Columbia, 1997. *Trapped: Holding on to the Knife's Edge: Economic Violence Against Filipino Migrant/Immigrant Women,* Vancouver: The FREDA Centre for Research on Violence against Women and Children.

Philippine Women Centre of British Columbia, 2000. *Canada: The New Frontier for Mail-Order Brides*, Ottawa: Status of Women Canada.

Pilipinong Migrante sa Canada/Philippine Migrants Society of Canada, n.d. [Online] Available at: http://pmscontario.tripod.com/index.html [Accessed 1 September 2008].

Piper, N., 2007. International migration and gendered axes of stratification: Introduction, in *New Perspectives on Gender and Migration: Livelihood, Rights and Entitlements*, edited by N. Piper. New York: Routledge, 1–18.

Pojmann, W., 2006. *Immigrant Women and Feminism in Italy.* Aldershot: Ashgate.

Portes, A. and Rumbaut, R.G., 2001. *Legacies: The Story of the Immigrant Second Generation.* Berkeley and Los Angeles: University of California Press.

Portugali, J., 1993. *Implicate Relations, Society and Space in the Israeli-Palestinian Conflict.* Dordrecht: Kluwer Academic Publishers.

Pratt, G., 2004. *Working Feminism.* Philadelphia: Temple University Press.

Pratt, G., 2012. *Families Apart: Migrant Mothers and the Conflicts of Labor and Love.* Minneapolis: University of Minnesota Press.

Pratt, G. in collaboration with the Philippine Women Centre of British Columbia and the Filipino-Canadian Youth Alliance, 2001. *Waiting*, Toronto: Palakasin Conference Kit, University of Toronto.

Pratt, G. in collaboration with the Philippine Women Centre of British Columbia and the Filipino-Canadian Youth Alliance, 2006. Separation and Reunification among Filipino Families in Vancouver. *Canadian Issues*, 46–49.

Pratt, G.; Philippine Women Centre of British Columbia; Ugnayan ng Kabataang sa Canada, 2008. *Deskilling across the Generations: Reunification among Transnational Filipino Families in Vancouver (Working Paper 08–06)*, Burnaby and Vancouver: Metropolis British Columbia: Centre of Excellence for Research on Immigration and Diversity.

Preibisch, K.L., 2004. Migrant agricultural workers and processes of social inclusion in rural Canada: Encuentros and desencuentros. *Canadian Journal of Latin American and Caribbean Studies/Revue Canadienne Des Etudes Latino-americaines et Caraibes*, 29, 57–58.

Preston-Whyte, E., 1976. Race attitudes and behaviour: The case of domestic employment in White South African homes. *African Studies*, 35(2), 71–90.

Pries, L., 1999. *Migration and Transnational Social Spaces.* Aldershot: Ashgate.

Raijman, R. and Kemp, A., 2007. Labor migration, managing the ethno-national conflict, and client politics in Israel, in *Migration to Israel in Global Comparative Context*, edited by S.S. Willen. Lanham: Lexington Books, 31–50.

Rancière, J., 1991. *La nuit des prolétaires.* Paris: Fayard.

Rancière, J., 2004. Who is the subject of the rights of man? *South Atlantic Quarterly*, 103(2–3), 297–310.

Razack, S., 2002. *Race, Space, and the Law: Unmapping a White Settler Society.* Toronto: Between The Lines.

Razavi, S., 2007. *The Political and Social Economy of Care in A Development Context: Conceptual Issues, Research Questions and Policy Options. Gender and Development Program (Paper No. 3)*, Geneva: United Nations Research Institute for Social Development.

Rees, R., 1997. *'If the Union is Not There, Nothing is Caring for the Domestic Workers': the Feasibility of Advice Offices for Domestic Workers*. Johannesburg: National Labor and Economic Development Institute.

Reyneri, E., 1998. The role of the underground economy in irregular migration to Italy: Cause or effect? *Journal of Ethnic and Migration Studies*, 24(2), 313–331.

Reyneri, E., 2004. Immigrants in a segmented and often undeclared labor market. *Journal of Modern Italian Studies*, 9(1), 71–93.

Richmond, A.H., 2003. Reactive migration: Sociological perspectives on refugee movements. *Journal of Refugee Studies*, 6(1), 5–24.

Rivas, L., 2007. *Built to Last: Preventing Coalition Breakdowns.* Berkeley: Doctoral Dissertation, Sociology Department, University of California.

Roberts, D.E., 1997. Spiritual and menial housework. *Yale Journal of Law and Feminism*, 9(1), 51–80.

Robitaille, A.-M., 2004. *Moniteurs et campeurs: Ethnographie d'un camp de vacances spécialisé.* Montréal: Master's thesis, Département d'anthropologie, Université de Montréal.

Roediger, D., 1991. *The Wages of Whiteness: Race and the Making of the American Working Class.* London: Verso.

Roer-Strier, D. and Olshtain-Mann, O., 1999. To see and not be seen: Latin American illegal foreign workers in Jerusalem. *International Migration*, 37(2), 413–436.

Rollins, J., 1985. *Between Women: Domestics and their Employers.* Philadelphia: Temple University Press.

Romero, M., 1992. *Maid in the U.S.A.* New York and London: Routledge.

Romero, M., 1997. Who takes care of the maid's children? Exploring the costs of domestic service, in *Feminism and Families*, edited by H.L. Nelson. New York: Routledge, 151–169.

Romero, M., 2002. *Maid in the USA.* 2nd ed. New York: Routledge.

Romero, M., 2001. Unraveling privilege: Workers' children and the hidden costs of paid child care, *Chicago-Kent Law Review*, 76(3), 101–121.

Romero, M., 2008. Crossing the immigration and race border: A Critical Race Theory approach to immigration studies. *Contemporary Justice Review*, 11(1), 23–37.

Romero, M., 2011. *The Maid's Daughter: Living Inside and Outside the American Dream.* New York: New York University Press.

Rose, E., 1999. *A Mother's Job: The History of Day Care 1890–1960.* Oxford: Oxford University Press.

Rubio Goldsmith, P. et al., 2009. Ethno-racial profiling and state violence in a southwest barrio. *Aztlán*, 34(1), 93–123.

Ruderman, W. and Santora, M., 2012. 2 Children slain at home in city; Nanny arrested. *New York Times*, 26 October, p. A1.

Ruhs, M. and Martin, P., 2008. Numbers vs. rights: trade-offs and guest worker programs. *International Migration Review*, 42(1), 249–265.

Sabban, R., 2002. *United Arab Emirates: Migrant women in the United Arab Emirates – The case of female domestic workers.* [Online] Available at: http://www.ilo.org/wcmsp5/groups/public/---ed_emp/documents/publication/wcms_117955.pdf [Accessed 6 June 2013].

Safa, H.I., 1977. The changing composition of the female labor force in Latin American. *Latin American Perspectives*, 4(4), 126–136.

Salzinger, L., 1991. A maid by any other name: The transformation of 'dirty work' by Central American immigrants, in *Ethnography Unbound: Power and Resistance in the Modern Metropolis*, edited by M. Burawoy, et al. Berkeley: University of California Press, pp. 139–160.

Samela, M. I., 1993. *The Law and the Disadvantaged, Exploited Workers with Special Focus on South African Domestic Workers.* Johannesburg: Faculty of Law, The University of the Witwatersrand.

San Juan Jr., E., 2006. *Filipinos Everywhere: Displaced, Transported Overseas, Moving On in the Diaspora.* Quezon City: IBON Foundation.

Sarvasy, W. and Longo, P., 2004. The globalization of care: Kant's world citizenship and Filipina migrant domestic workers. *International Feminist Journal of Politics*, 6(3), 392–415.

Sassen, S., 1988. *The Mobility of Labor and Capital: A Study in International Investment and Labor Flow.* Cambridge and New York: Cambridge University Press.

Sassen, S., 1998. *Globalization and its Discontents.* New York: The New Press.

Sassen, S., 2000. Women's burden: Counter-geographies of globalization and the feminization of survival. *Journal of International Affairs*, 53(2), 503–524.

Sassen, S., 2002. Global cities and survival circuits, in *Global Woman: Nannies, Maids and Sex Workers in the New Economy*, edited by B. Ehrenreich and A. Hochschild. New York: Henry Holt, 254–274.

Sassen, S., 2002. Towards post-national and denationalized citizenship, in *Handbook of Citizenship Studies,* edited by E.F. Isin and B.S. Turner. London: Sage Publications, 277–292.

Schiller, N.G., Basch, L. and Szanton Blanc, C., 1999. From immigrant to transmigrant: Theorizing transnational migration, in *Migration and Transnational Social Spaces*, edited by L. Pries. Aldershot: Ashgate, 73–105.

Scrinzi, F., 2008. Migrations and the restructuring of the Welfare State in Italy: Change and continuity in the domestic work sector, in *Migration and Transnational Social Spaces*, edited by L. Pries. Aldershot: Ashgate, 29–42.

Seafield, V., 2011. *Statement on Behalf of South African Government.* Geneva, Switzerland, International Labour Conference of the International Labour Organization, June 1–17.

Séguin, R., 2003. General-strike threat rising in Quebec, unions warn: Ports, roads, hospitals, transit disrupted in day of protest against 'anti-labour' bills. *Globe and Mail*, 3 December, A-8.

Seidman, G., 1999. Gendered citizenship: South Africa's democratic transition and the construction of a gendered state. *Gender and Society*, 13(3), 287–307.

Semyonov, M. and Lewin Epstein, N., 1987. *Hewers of Wood and Drawers of Water Noncitizen Arabs in the Israeli Labor Market.* Ithaca, NY: ILR Press.

Semyonov, M., Raijman, R. and Yom-Tov, A., 2002. Labor market competition, perceived threat, and endorsement of economic discrimination against foreign workers in Israel. *Social Problems*, 49(3), 416–431.

Sennett, R. and Cobb, J., 1973. *The Hidden Injuries of Class.* New York: Vintage Books.

Seria, S., 2001. *Parliamentary Public Submission in Cape Town Legislative Chambers.* Cape Town: s.n.

Shapiro, M., 2013. *The Politics of Intimacy: An Ethnography of Illegalized Migrant Women and Their Undocumented Children in Tel Aviv, Israel. PhD Dissertation.* Toronto: York University.

Sharma, N., 2006. *Home Economics: Nationalism and the Making of 'Migrant Workers' in Canada.* Toronto: University of Toronto Press.

Sheldon, B.A., 1992. *Women, Men, and Time: Gender Differences in Paid Work, Household and Leisure.* New York: Greenwood Press.

Sigona, N., 2005. Locating 'The Gypsy Problem'. The Roma in Italy: Stereotyping, labelling and 'nomad camps'. *Journal of Ethnic and Migration Studies*, 31(4), 741–756.

Silvera, M., 1983. *Silenced: Caribbean Domestic Workers Talk with Makeda Silvera.* Toronto: Sister Vision Press.

Simmel, G., 1950. The Stranger, in *The Sociology of Georg Simmel,* translated and edited by K.H. Wolff. New York: The Free Press, 402–408.

Sintos Coloma, R. et al., eds., 2012. *Filipinos in Canada: Disturbing Invisibility.* Toronto: University of Toronto Press.

Skrbiš, Z., 2008. Transnational families: Theorising migration, emotions and belonging. *Journal of Intercultural Studies*, 29(3), 231–246.

Smith, D., 1999. *Writing the Social, Critique, Theory, and Investigations.* Toronto: University of Toronto Press.

Smith, P., 1999. Regulating paid household work: Class, gender, race and agendas of reform. *American University Law Review*, 48(4), 851–924.

Smith, P., 2011a. The pitfalls of home: Protecting the health and safety of paid domestics. *Canadian Journal of Women and the Law*, 20(1), 1–40.

Smith, P., 2011b. Work like any other, work like no other: Establishing decent work for domestic service workers. *Employee Rights & Employment Policy Journal*, 15(1), 157–198.

Soysal, Y., 1994. *Limits of Citizenship, Migrants and Postnational Membership in Europe.* Chicago: The University of Chicago Press.

Stasiulis, D. and Bakan, A., 1997. Negotiating citizenship: The Case of foreign domestic workers in Canada. *Feminist Review*, 57 (Autumn), 112–139.

Stasiulis, D.K. and Bakan, A.B., 2004. *Negotiating Citizenship: Migrant Women in Canada and the Global System.* New York: Palgrave Macmillan.

Stasiulis, D.K. and Bakan, A.B., 2005. *Negotiating Citizenship: Migrant Women in Canada and the Global System.* Toronto: University of Toronto Press.

State of California, 1999. *Assembly Bill 1682.* Sacramento: California Legislature.

State of California – Department of Industrial Relations, 2003. *Which IWD Order? Classifications.* [Online] Available at: http://www.dir.ca.gov/dlse/WhichIWCOrderClassifications.pdf [Accessed 5 March 2007].

Statistics Canada, 1996. *Census.* Ottawa: Government of Canada.

Statistics South Africa, 2000. *October Household Survey.* Pretoria: South African National Government.

Stenum, H., 2009. *Workers not slaves: The management of temporary Filipino au pair migraion in Denmark.* Helsinki, Finland, s.n.

Stewart, A., 2007. Who do we care about? Reflections on gender justice in a global market. *Northern Ireland Legal Quarterly*, 58(3), 358–374.

Stewart, A., 2011. *Gender, Law and Justice in a Global Market.* Cambridge: Cambridge University Press.

Steyn, M.E. and Grant, T., 2007. 'A real bag of mixed emotions': Re-entry experiences of South African exiles. *International Journal of Intercultural Relations*, 31(3), 363–389.

Stolcke, V., 1981. Women's labours: The naturalization of social inequality and women's subordination, in *Of Marriage and the Market: Women's Subordination Internationally and its Lessons*, edited by K. Young, C. Wolkowitz and R. McCullagh. London: Routledge, 159–177.

Stranges, M., 2006. *Gli immigrati nel mercato del lavoro: riflessioni, dati e prospettive.* Bolzano, Istituto Promozione Lavoratori.

Streek, F., 1974. *Domestic Servants: A Study of the Service Conditions of Domestic Servants Employed by Border Members of the Black Sash and South African Institute on Race Relations.* Cape Town: The Black Sash.

Suárez-Orozco, C., Todorova, I. and Louie, J., 2001. *The Transnationalization of Families: Immigrant Separations and Reunifications.* Miami, Florida, The American Family Therapy Academy (29 June).

Susser, I., 1991. The separation of mothers and children, in *Dual City: Restructuring New York*, edited by J. Hull Mollenkopf and M. Castells. New York: Russel Sage Foundation, 79–102.

Svašek, M., 2005. Introduction, emotions in anthropology, in *Mixed Emotions, Anthropological Studies of Feeling*, edited by M. Svašek and K. Milton. Oxford: Berg, 1–24.

Svašek, M. and Skrbiš, Z., 2007. Passions and powers: Emotions and globalization. *Identities: Global Studies in Culture and Power*, 14(3), 367–383.

Tahon, M., 1995. Le don de la mère. *Anthropologie et sociétés*, 19(1–2), 139–156.

Thornton Dill, B., 1994. *Across the Boundaries of Race and Class: An Exploration of Work and Family among Black Female Domestic Servants.* New York: Garland Publishing.

Traboulsi, F., 2007. *A History of Modern Lebanon.* London: Pluto Press.

Trafficking in Persons (TIP) Report, Office to Monitor and Combat Trafficking in Persons, U.S. State Department, 2007. *The Forms and Impact of Human Trafficking.* [Online] Available at: http://www.state.gov/g/tip/rls/tiprpt/2007/82809.htm [Accessed 15 August 2009].

Trifiletti, R., 2009. *Local social policies, family policies, models of service systems and their changes to converge or diverge in Italy after 2000.* s.l., s.n.

Tronto, J.C. 2011a. Caring about care workers: Caring solution to an issue of global justice, in *Feminist Ethics and Social Policy: Towards a New Global Political Economy of Care*, edited by Mahon, R. and Robinson, K. Vancouver: University of British Columbia Press, 162–177.

Tronto, J.C. 2011b. Privatizing neo-colonialism: Migrant domestic care workers, partial citizenship and responsibility, in *Europeanizing Care and Gender*, edited by H.M. Dahl, A.L. Kovalanien and M. Markera. New York: Palgrave Macmillan, 165–181.

Tronto, J.C. 2013. *Caring Democracy: Markets, Equality, and Justice*. New York: New York University Press.

Trotman, L., 2011. *Opening Remarks.* Geneva, Switzerland, International Labour Conference of the International Labour Organization, June 1–17.

Tucker, S., 1988. *Telling Memories Among Southern Women: Domestic Workers and Their Employers in the Segregated South.* Baton Rouge: Louisiana State Press.

Turner, J.H., 1988. *A Theory of Social Interaction.* Stanford: Stanford University Press.

Turton, D., 2003. *Conceptualising Forced Migration. RSC Working Paper No. 12.* Refugee Studies Centre: Oxford.

UN Committee on the Protection of the Rights of All Migrant Workers and Members of Their Families (CMW), 2006. *Consideration of Reports submitted by States Parties under Article 73 of the Convention: International Convention on the Protection of the Rights of All Migrant Workers and Members of Their Families: Initial Reports of States Parties due in 2004: Egypt.* [Online] Available at: http://www.refworld.org/docid/4731cfe30.html [Accessed 12 July 2013].

Ungerson, C., 1999. Personal assistants and disabled people: An examination of a hybrid form of work and care. *Work, Employment and Society*, 13(4), 583–600.

University of North Carolina School of Law Human Rights Policy Clinic, n.d. *Domestic Workers' Rights in the United States.* [Online] Available at: http://www.law.unc.edu/documents/clinicalprograms/domesticworkersreport.pdf [Accessed 26 October 2012].

Urbanbaby.com Thread, 2012a. *All you ladies who put your career and money above your children, this is what can happen ... .* [Online] Available at: http://www.urbanbaby.com/topics/55018629 [Accessed 19 November 2012].

Urbanbaby.com Thread, 2012b. *I think mexicans have a violent and bloody culture underlying a lot of other stuff.* [Online] Available at: http://www.urbanbaby.com/topics/55018579 [Accessed 3 November 2012].

Valtonen, K., 1998. Resettlement of Middle Eastern refugees in Finland: The elusiveness of integration. *Journal of Refugee Studies*, 11(1), 38–60.

Velasco, P.M., 1997. 'We can still fight back': Organizing domestic workers in Toronto, in *Not One of the Family: Foreign Domestic Workers in Canada*, edited by A. Bakan and D. Stasiulis. Toronto: University of Toronto Press, 157–164.

Vincenzi, S., 2000. Italy: a newcomer with a positive attitude. *Journal of Refugee Studies*, 13(1), 91–104.

Vlieger, A., 2011. *Domestic Workers in Saudi Arabia and the Emirates, A Socio-Legal Study on Conflicts.* New Orleans: Quid Pro Books.

Vosko, L., 2000. *Temporary Work: The Gendered Rise of a Precarious Employment Relationship.* Toronto: University of Toronto Press.

Walker, C., 1991. *Women and Resistance in South Africa.* Claremont: David Philip Publishers.

Walkowitz, D., 1999. *Working with Class: Social Workers and the Politics of Middle-Class.* Chapel Hill: University of North Carolina Press.

Warren, J. and Winddance Twine, F., 1997. White Americans, the new minority? Non-Blacks and the ever expanding boundaries of whiteness. *Journal of Black Studies*, 28(2), 200–218.

Weiler-Pollak, D., 2009a. Filipino children take center stage for Tel Aviv beauty contest. *Haaretz Online*, 6 October.

Weiler-Pollak, D., 2009b. Hundreds protest plans to deport migrant workers, kids. *Haaretz Online*, 15 October.

Weiler-Pollak, D., 2009c. Nonprofit throws weight behind kids of foreign workers facing deportation. *Haaretz Online*, 18 October.

Weiler-Pollak, D., 2009d. Netanyahu defers expulsion of children of migrant workers. *Haaretz Online*, 2 August.

Wellman, B., 1981. Applying Network Analysis to the Study of Support, in *Social Networks and Social Support*, edited by B. Gottlieb. London: SAGE Publications, 171–200.

Wells, J., 1993. *We Now Demand! The History of Women's Resistance to Pass Laws in South Africa.* Johannesburg: Witwatersrand University Press.

Whisson, M. and Weil, W., 1971. *Domestic Servants: A Microcosm of 'The Race Problem'.* Johannesburg: South African Institute of Race Relations.

White, G.M., 1990. Moral discourse and the rhetoric of emotions, in *Language and the Politics of Emotion*, edited by L. Abu-Lughod and C. Lutz. Cambridge: Cambridge University Press, 46–68.

Wichterich, C., 2000. *The Globalized Woman: Reports from a Future of Inequality.* London: Zed Books.

Wildman, S.M., 1996. *Privilege Revealed: How Invisible Preference Undermines America.* New York: New York University Press.

Williams, F. and Brennan, D., 2012. Care, markets and migration in a globalising world: Introduction to the Special Issue. *Journal of European Social Policy*, 22(4), 355–362.

Williams, F. and Gavanas, A., 2008. The intersection of childcare regimes and migration regimes: A three-country study, in *Migration and Domestic Work: A European Perspective on a Global Theme*, edited by H. Lutz. Aldershot: Ashgate, 13–28.

Williams, J., 2000. *Unbending Gender: Why Family and Work Conflict and What to Do About It.* New York: Oxford Press.

Wilton, R. and Cranford, C., 2002. Toward an understanding of the spatiality of social movements: Labor organizing at the private university in Los Angeles. *Social Problems*, 49(3), 374–394.

Witbooi, M., 2001. *Parliamentary Public Submission in Cape Town Legislative Chambers.* Cape Town: South Africa

Witbooi, M., 2010. *Plenary Session on Decent Work for Domestic Workers.* Geneva, Switzerland, International Labour Conference of the International Labour Organization, June 2–18.

Witbooi, M., 2011. *Closing Statement, Domestic Work Convention.* Geneva, Switzerland, International Labour Convention, June 1–17.

Wittenburg, V., 2008. *The New Bonded Labour? The Impact of Proposed Changes to the UK Immigration System on Migrant Domestic Workers.* London: Kalayaan and Oxfam.

Wolf, D.L., 1997. Family secrets: Transnational struggles among children of Filipino immigrants. *Sociological Perspective*, 40(3), 457–482.

Wolf, E., 1982. *Europe and the People without History.* Berkeley, CA: University of California Press.

Women in Informal Employment: Globalizing and Organizing (WIEGO), n.d. *Occupational Groups: Domestic Workers.* [Online] Available at: http://wiego.org/informaleconomy/occupationalgroups/domesticworkers [Accessed 6 June 2013].

Wrigley, J., 1995. *Other People's Children.* New York: Basic Books.

Yancey, G., 2003. *Who is White? Latinos, Asias, and the New Black/Nonblack Divide.* Boulder, CO: Lynne Rienner.

Yeates, N., 2005a. A global political economy of care. *Social Policy and Society*, 4(2), 227–234.

Yeates, N., 2005b. *Global Care Chains: A Critical Introduction, Global Migration Perspectives, No. 44*. Geneva: Global Commission on International Migration.

Yeates, N., 2009. *Globalizing Care Economies and Migrant Workers: Explorations in Global Care Chains.* Houndmills, Basingstoke: Palgrave Macmillan.

Yeoh, B., Huang, S. and Lam, T., 2005. Transnationalizing the 'Asian' family: Imaginaries, intimacies and strategic intents. *Global Networks*, 5(4), 307–315.

Young, B., 2003. Financial crises and social reproduction: Asia, Argentina and Brazil, in *Power, Production and Social Reproduction*, edited by I. Bakker and S. Gill. New York: Palgrave Macmillan, 103–123.

Young, G. and Dickerson, B., 1994. *Color, Class, and Country: Experiences of Gender.* London: Zed Books.

Zarembka, J.M., 2001. Maid to order. *Colorlines*, 26, 27–28.

Zhou, M., 2004. Are Asians becoming 'White'? *Contexts*, 3(1), 29–37.

Zimmerman, M.K., Litt, J.S. and Bose, C.E., eds., 2006. *Global Dimensions of Gender and Carework.* Stanford, CA: Stanford Social Sciences.

Zohar, H., 2009. *Subsidising the employment of migrant caregivers (e-newsletter).* Tel Aviv: Kav LaOved.

Zolberg, A., 2000. Ethnic republics? Citizenship in Israel and Japan: Introduction, in *From Migrants to Citizens: Membership in a Changing World*, edited by T. Aleinikoff and D. Kusmeyer. Washington, D.C.: Carnegie Endowment for International Peace, 383–385.

Zontini, E., 2004. Immigrant women in Barcelona: Coping with the consequences of transnational lives. *Journal of Ethnic and Migration Studies*, 30(6), 1113–1144.

Zussman, R., 1985. *Mechanics of the Middle Class: Work and Politics Among American Engineers.* Berkeley: University of California Press.

Index

Italic page numbers indicate tables.

Gender in a Global/Local World

Also published in this series

The Search for Lasting Peace
Critical Perspectives on Gender-Responsive Human Security
Edited by Rosalind Boyd
ISBN 978-1-4724-2096-1

Gender Integration in NATO Military Forces
Cross-national Analysis
Lana Obradovic
ISBN 978-1-4094-6476-1

Waging Gendered Wars
U.S. Military Women in Afghanistan and Iraq
Paige Whaley Eager
ISBN 978-1-4094-4846-4

Resisting Gendered Norms
Civil Society, the Juridical and Political Space in Cambodia
Mona Lilja
ISBN 978-1-4094-3431-3

No Place for a War Baby
The Global Politics of Children born of Wartime Sexual Violence
Donna Seto
ISBN 978-1-4094-4923-2

Body/State
Edited by Angus Cameron, Jen Dickinson and Nicola Smith
ISBN 978-1-4094-2449-9

Feminist (Im)Mobilities in Fortress(ing) North America
Rights, Citizenships, and Identities in Transnational Perspective
Edited by Anne Sisson Runyan, Amy Lind, Patricia McDermott and Marianne H. Marchand
ISBN 978-1-4094-3313-2

Reshaping Gender and Class in Rural Spaces
Edited by Barbara Pini and Belinda Leach
ISBN 978-1-4094-0291-6

Federalism, Feminism and Multilevel Governance
Edited by Melissa Haussman, Marian Sawer and Jill Vickers
ISBN 978-0-7546-7717-8

Contours of Citizenship
Women, Diversity and Practices of Citizenship
Edited by Margaret Abraham, Esther Ngan-ling Chow,
Laura Maratou-Alipranti and Evangelia Tastsoglou
ISBN 978-0-7546-7779-6

Politicization of Sexual Violence
From Abolitionism to Peacekeeping
Carol Harrington
ISBN 978-0-7546-7458-0

Development in an Insecure and Gendered World
The Relevance of the Millennium Goals
Edited by Jacqueline Leckie
ISBN 978-0-7546-7691-1

Empowering Migrant Women
Why Agency and Rights are not Enough
Leah Briones
ISBN 978-0-7546-7532-7

Gendered Struggles against Globalisation in Mexico
Teresa Healy
ISBN 978-0-7546-3701-1

Encountering the Transnational
Women, Islam and the Politics of Interpretation
Meena Sharify-Funk
ISBN 978-0-7546-7123-7

The Gender Question in Globalization
Changing Perspectives and Practices
Edited by Tine Davids and Francien van Driel
ISBN 978-0-7546-3923-7 (hbk) / ISBN 978-0-7546-7322-4 (pbk)

The Price of Gender Equality
Member States and Governance in the European Union
Anna van der Vleuten
ISBN 978-0-7546-4636-5

(En)Gendering the War on Terror
War Stories and Camouflaged Politics
Edited by Krista Hunt and Kim Rygiel
ISBN 978-0-7546-4481-1 (hbk) / ISBN 978-0-7546-7323-1 (pbk)

Women, Migration and Citizenship
Making Local, National and Transnational Connections
Edited by Evangelia Tastsoglou and Alexandra Dobrowolsky
ISBN 978-0-7546-4379-1

Transnational Ruptures
Gender and Forced Migration
Catherine Nolin
ISBN 978-0-7546-3805-6

'Innocent Women and Children'
Gender, Norms and the Protection of Civilians
R. Charli Carpenter
ISBN 978-0-7546-4745-4

Turkey's Engagement with Global Women's Human Rights
Nüket Kardam
ISBN 978-0-7546-4168-1

(Un)thinking Citizenship
Feminist Debates in Contemporary South Africa
Edited by Amanda Gouws
ISBN 978-0-7546-3878-0

Vulnerable Bodies
Gender, the UN and the Global Refugee Crisis
Erin K. Baines
ISBN 978-0-7546-3734-9

Setting the Agenda for Global Peace
Conflict and Consensus Building
Anna C. Snyder
ISBN 978-0-7546-1933-8

For Product Safety Concerns and Information please contact our EU
representative GPSR@taylorandfrancis.com
Taylor & Francis Verlag GmbH, Kaufingerstraße 24, 80331 München, Germany

www.ingramcontent.com/pod-product-compliance
Ingram Content Group UK Ltd.
Pitfield, Milton Keynes, MK11 3LW, UK
UKHW022010180926
475701UK00003B/297
9780367600471